LATIN AMERICA
2040

LATIN AMERICA 2040

Breaking Away from Complacency: An Agenda for Resurgence

$SAGE www.sagepublications.com
Los Angeles • London • New Delhi • Singapore • Washington DC

Copyright © CAF, 2010

All rights reserved. No part of this book may be reproduced or utilized in any form or by any means, electronic or mechanical, including photocopying, recording or by any information storage or retrieval system, without permission in writing from the publisher.

First published in 2010 by

SAGE Publications India Pvt Ltd
B1/I-1 Mohan Cooperative Industrial Area
Mathura Road, New Delhi 110 044, India
www.sagepub.in

SAGE Publications Inc
2455 Teller Road
Thousand Oaks, California 91320, USA

SAGE Publications Ltd
1 Oliver's Yard, 55 City Road
London EC1Y 1SP, United Kindom

SAGE Publications Asia-Pacific Pte Ltd
33 Pekin Street
#02-01 Far East Square
Singapore 048763

Published by Vivek Mehra for SAGE Publications India Pvt Ltd, typeset in 9/14 Helvetica Neue LT Std and printed at Rajkamal Electric Press, Kundli, Haryana.

Library of Congress Cataloging-in-Publication Data Available

ISBN: 978-81-321-0582-4 (HB)

The SAGE Team: Rekha Natarajan

Contents

Latin America 2040
Breaking Away from Complacency:
An Agenda for Resurgence

xv	**Foreword**
xvii	**Acknowledgements**
1	**Introduction** Harinder S. Kohli
19	**Part I.**
21	**Chapter 1. Breaking Away from Mediocrity to a Prosperous Future** Claudio M. Loser and Anil Sood
71	**Chapter 2. Latin America: Is Average Good Enough?** Homi Kharas
101	**Chapter 3. Successful Macroeconomic Performance: Launching Long-Term Reforms** Claudio M. Loser
139	**Part II.**
141	**Chapter 4. Is Latin America Becoming Less Unequal?** Nora Lustig
165	**Chapter 5. How Can Education Help Latin America Develop?** Jeffrey M. Puryear and Tamara Ortega Goodspeed
187	**Chapter 6. Innovation and Technology Development for Economic Restructuring** Vinod K. Goel
217	**Chapter 7. Infrastructure Needs for a Resurgent Latin America** Harpaul Alberto Kohli and Phil Basil

229 **Chapter 8. Greater Openness: Regional Cooperation and Trade**
Harinder S. Kohli and Claudio M. Loser

251 **Chapter 9. Democratic Governance and Political Sustainability: Towards a Prosperous Latin America**   Michael Shifter

267 **References**
279 **Index**
285 **About the Editors and Contributors**

List of figures, tables and boxes

Figures

Introduction

    1 Share of Regions/Countries in World GDP
    2 TFP, Relative Levels and Changes During 1980-2007 (%)

Chapter 1

    1 Per Capita Income: Latin America and Others, 1913-2008, US$
    2 Per Capita Income in PPP Terms (1955=100)
    3 Latin American Share in World GDP vs. Commodity Prices
    4 Latin America has Lagged Behind East Asia
    5 Percentage of Years Since 1981 with Growth Below 1 and 2%
    6 Gini Coefficient by Region (in percent), 2004
    7 Trade/GDP Ratio (adjusted for population)
    8 TFP Scores, 1980-2009, US 1980=100
    9 TFP Relative Changes from 1980-2009
    10 Quality of Education 2008
    11 Technology Readiness 2008
    12 Infrastructure 2008
    13 Ease of Doing Business 2010
    14 Informal Economy Estimate
    15 Competitiveness 2009-2010
    16 Per Capita Income—Alternative Scenarios (market ER)
    17 Latin American Share of World GDP
    18 Three-Pillar Strategy for a Prosperous Latin America
    19 Investment (% of GDP)
    20 Savings (% of GDP)
    21 Evolution of the Gini Coefficient (in %)
    22 Gini Index and Poverty Headcount of Selected Latin American and Asian Countries 2004-2007

23 Total Public Education Expenditure as % GNP, 2007
24 Public Spending per Student on Primary Educaiton ($PPP), 2007
25 Graduates in Science & Engineering (% of total graduates)
26 Quality of Infrastructure by Sector and Region
27 Total Infrastructure Investment Requirements: 2011-2040
28 Political Views in Latin America—2009

Chapter 2

1 Latin America Share of Developing Country Output, 1965-2009
2 Latin American and World Per Capita Income
3 Capital-Labor Ratios
4 Real US GDP Per Capita, 1870-2006
5 The Four Speed World
A.1 Regression Results
A.2 RER Convergence Process

Chapter 3

1 Growth of GDP in Developing Asia, Latin America and the World (annual percent)
2 Inflation
3 World Trade Projections (percentage change, annual)
4 Trade Growth in Latin America and Emerging Asia
5 Evolution of Commodity Prices (2005=100)
6 Latin American Trade Share (% of total)
7 Emerging Market Spreads and Comparison with Selected Markets
8 Recovery and Growth Support in Latin America
9 External Current Account, Fiscal Balance, Exchange Rate and Terms of Trade
10 Global Gains/Losses of Total Assets as % of GDP
11 Factors Behind Global Assets Losses 2003-2009 (% of GDP)
12 Breakdown of Assets Losses in 2008 by Country (% of GDP)
13 Asset Losses by Region (quarterly as % of GDP)

Chapter 4

1 Change in Gini Coefficient by Country: Circa 2000-2007
2 Latin America and Europe: Market Income and Disposable Income
3 Gini Coefficient by Region (in %), 2004
4 Gini Coefficient by Country (in %), 2004
5 Gini Coefficient (in %) for Latin America: 1990-2005
6 Headcount Ratio by Region (in %): 1990, 1996, 2002 and 2005 (in %)
7 Poverty among LAC Countries, 1990-2006

8 Poverty among LAC Countries, 1990-2006
9 Household Per Capita Income and its Determinants
A.1 Evolution of the Gini Coefficient for the Brazilian Distribution of Persons According to their Family Per Capita Income
A.2 Annual Growth Rate for Per Capita Income in Brazilia, by Percentile, 2001-2007
A.3 Education and Inequality among Workers in Brazil, 1995-2007
A.4 Evolution of Labor Earnings Differential among Metropolitan and Non Metropolitan Areas in Brazil, 1995-2007
A.5 Mexico: Gini Coefficient, 1984-2006
A.6 Mexico: Incidence of Extreme Poverty: 1968-2006
A.7 Mexico: Growth Incidence Curves, 2006/2000
A.8 Mexico: Skilled/Unskilled Wage Gap, 1984-2007
A.9 Mexico: Mean Log Wage of Male Workers by Education and Experience

Chapter 5

1 Total Public Education Expenditure as % of GNP, 2007
2 Public Spending per Student on Primary Education (US$PPP), 2007
3 Enrollment Rates, Latin America and the Caribbean, 1999 and 2007
4 Primary Completion (%), 2008
5 Difference in Attendance between Richest and Poorest 20% 7 to 12-year olds, 1990-2006
6 Secondary Graduation Rates, 2007
7 Students with Low Achievement in PISA Science Test, 2006
8 Third Grade Students with Low Achievement in SERCE Math Test, 2006
9 Third Grade Performance in SERCE Reading Test, 2006 (Cuba and Dominican Republic)
10 Tertiary Graduates in Science and Engineering, 2007
11 Scientific and Engineering Article Output of Emerging and Developing Countries by Region, 1998-2001
12 Patents Granted by United States Patent and Trademark Office, 2008
13 Population Aged 20-24 that has Completed Upper Secondary Education, Poorest 20% vs. Richest 20%, 2005
14 Gap between Rich and Poor Students in PISA Science Test, 2006
15A Boys' Advantage over Girls in 6th Grade Math Exam, 2006
15B Girls' Advantage over Boys in 6th Grade Reading Exam
16 Percent of Public Education Spending Going to Richest 20% and Poorest 20%, Latin America, 2006

Chapter 6

1 TFP, 2009 Relative Levels and Changes during 1980-2009—Latin America, Asia and OECD
2 TFP—Latin American Countries vs. OECD & NICs, Developing Asia
3 HDI: Levels and Changes, Selected Countries in Latin America and Asia, 1980-2007
4 Global Competitive Index, 2009
5 GCI Innovation Indes, 2009 Latin America, OECD and NICs, Asia
6 Quality of Education, 2008—Latin America, Asia, OECD
7 Tertiary Enrollment, 2008—Latin America, OECD and NICs, Asia
8 Science and Engineering Graduates, 2007
9 Technology Readiness, Selected Countries, 2008
10 Gross Expenditure on Research and Development as a % of GDP in Latin American Countries and Selected Economies
11 Expenditure on R&D (US$ billion PPP), 2007

Chapter 7

1 Total Investment Requirement Costs: 2011-2040
2 Total Investment over Time (billion $ and % GDP)
3 Investment Requirements, All Sectors: 2011-2040, Percent of GDP
4 Investment Requirements by Sector (2011-2040)
5 Aggregated Needs by Sector as Percent of GDP

Chapter 8

1 Latin American Trade Restrictiveness and Trade Share to GDP
2 Trade to GDP Ratios
3 Ratio of Trade to GDP, Actual and Adjusted for Population
4 Ratio of Exports to GDP in Real Terms (1979=100)
5 Destination of Exports: Latin America
6 Destination of Exports: Latin America without Mexico, Brazil, Venezuela
7 Destination of Exports: Mexico
8 Destination of Exports: Brazil
9 Composition of Exports: Latin America
10 Composition of Exports: Latin America (constant real prices)
11 Composition of Exports: Latin America excl. Mexico, Brazil, Venezuela
12 Composition of Exports: Latin America excl. Mexico, Brazil, Venezuela, (constant real prices)
13 Composition of Exports: Mexico
14 Composition of Exports: Mexico (constant real prices)

15 Composition of Exports: Brazil
16 Composition of Exports: Brazil (constant real prices)
17 Export Composition
18 High Technology Exports as Percent of Manufacturing Exports
19 High Technology Exports as Percent of Manufacturing Exports (Latin America)
20 High Tech Exports (as % of total exports)

Chapter 9

1 Democracy Guarantees Freedom of Political Participation Latin America 2007-2008/Totals by Country 2008
2 Most Important Problem: Crime and Unemployment Latin America 1995-2008
3 Evaluation of the Political Parties Latin America 2006-2008/Totals by Country 2008
4 Trust in Political Parties Latin America 1996-2008/Totals by Country 2008
5 Trust in Government Latin America 1996-2008/Totals by Country 2008
6 Democracy in My Country Works Better than in the Rest of Latin America 2008
7 Equality Before the Law Latin America 2002-2008/Totals by Country 2008

Tables

Chapter 1

1 Economic Indicators: Latin America and the World
2 Average Factor and GDP (PPP) Growth Rates, 1979-2009, Selected Regions
3 Latin America—A Fading Global Force
4 Knowledge Economy Index in World Regions
5 Access to Infrastructure Services, by Region
6 Growth in World Exports
7 Percentage of Exports within Region
8 Top 10 Emerging Markets by GDP
9 Latin American Export Destinations
10 Democracy Gets the Upper Hand in Most Countries
11 Key Issues at National Level

Chapter 2

1 Top Ten Emerging Economies and Share of Major Latin American Economies in Top Ten Economies' GDP, 1980-2009
2 Average Growth Rates, 1979-2009, Selected Regions
3 TFP Levels, 1980 to 2007, Selected Countries, USA 1980=1.00
4 Latin America—A Fading Global Force
5 Latin America—A Revival Scenario

Chapter 3

1 GDP Growth Projections
2 Inflation
3 World Trade Projections (percentage change, annual)
4 Workers Remittances (billions US$)
5 International Tourist Arrivals
6 Selected Countries—Stock Market and Exchange Rate Changes
7 Emerging Market Economies' External Financing
8 Foreign Direct Investment, Recipient Regions Flows and Stocks (billions US$)
9 Emerging Market Economies' External Financing
10 Total Financial Assets (as percentage of GDP)
11 Total Financial Assets (as percentage of GDP)
12 The G-20 Package: Estimated Availability of New Funds to Latin America

Chapter 4

A.1 Poverty and Extreme Poverty in Brazil, 2001-2007

Chapter 5

1 Percentage of 15 to 19-Year Olds who have Completed Primary Education, 2004
2 Percentage of 20 to 24-Year Olds who have Completed Secondary Education
A.1 PISA: Mean Score on the Mat Test (points), 2000, 2003, and 2006
A.2 PISA: Mean Score on the Reading Test (points), 2000, 2003, and 2006
A.3 PISA: Mean Score on the Science Test (points), 2000, 2003, and 2006

Chapter 6

1 Key Science, Technology and Innovation Indicators, Selected Countries
2 Knowledge Economy Index (KEI) for Selected Groups and Regions, 2009
3 Technological Specialization Index: Selected Countries, 1970-2007
4 Innovation Strategies for Selected Country Clusters

Chapter 7

1 Total Investment Needs (2011-2040)
2 Total Investment Requirements by Sector (2011-2040) (bn US$, 2009 prices)
3 Total Investment Requirements by Country, 2011-2040 (bn US$, 2009 prices)
4 Investments as Percentages of GDP 2011-2040, Base Case
A.1 Current State of Infrastructure in Latin American Countries

Chapter 8

1 World Export Volume (2000=100)

2 Share of World Exports
3 Export Growth (annual percentage average)
4 Intra-regional Trade 1980-2007 (in percent of total trade for the region unless specified)
5 GDP (PPP) Top in World 2009
6 GDP (MER) Top in World 2009
7 Average Growth in Trade in Past 10 Years (2000-2009)

Chapter 9

1 Support for Democracy

Boxes

Introduction

1 What is the Middle Income Trap, and how did some East Asian Countries Avoid it?

Chapter 1

1 Latin America in the Middle Income Trap?
2 What Makes East Asia Different from Latin America?
3 Importance of the Middle Class in Fueling Growth—GDP Per Capita, 1979=09; 1994=100

Chapter 6

1 Examples of Inclusive Innovation Potential
2 Innovation in BRIC Countries

Foreword

During the past decade, most Latin American countries demonstrated sound macroeconomic management which, accompanied by significant social initiatives and substantial microeconomic progress as well as favorable international economic conditions, generally led to sustained growth and improved social conditions throughout the region. Although these factors helped Latin America weather the global crisis which began in 2008 relatively well, it was also evident that our region continues to be very vulnerable to external shocks and very dependent on what happens in the financial and commercial markets of the world economy. This strengthens our conviction that there is no room for complacency among Latin American leaders and policy makers regarding our current economic and social situation.

Indeed, the region still needs to address important structural challenges if it is to attain truly sustainable levels of social, economic, environmental, and political development. These challenges include the enormous social disparities that continue to prevail in the region, the low levels of domestic savings and investment, the excessive concentration on exports of raw materials and other low value-added commodities, and the relative lack of competitiveness and productivity of the region's industries, compared with other regions of the world. To a great extent, these structural challenges explain why Latin America has increasingly lost relevance in the world economy during the last 40 years, especially as the Asian economies have advanced most dynamically.

For these reasons, with the encouragement of its shareholder countries, CAF launched a year-long process to develop a vision for the longer-term social and economic development of our region, as part of its 40th anniversary activities. The basic idea is for diverse groups of policy-makers, academics, business executives, civil society, etc., to reflect on a series of development related topics from a Latin American perspective. The underlying premise is that there are no intrinsic barriers to Latin America's emulation of the success of East Asian economies in the past fifty years, and of China and India more recently, and that CAF has a proactive role to play in helping the region attain its potential.

To develop such a longer-term vision for Latin America and to learn from the Asian experience, we commissioned Centennial Group International to prepare a study called **Latin America 2040: Breaking away from complacency, an agenda for resurgence**. This study represents an important first step in developing a long-term vision for the region's development, and lays the groundwork for a revision of CAF's own corporate strategy for the long run. Centennial Group International presented the study at a meeting of CAF's Board of Directors and other major stakeholders in early July of this year, where it was well received. This book is based on that study and reflects some of the comments and suggestions made at the meeting.

I believe that the study presents a compelling and yet realistic vision of what Latin America can become within the next thirty years—that is within one generation—should the national leaders, policy makers, and private businesses tackle the daunting policy and institutional reforms agenda identified by the authors. Indeed, the study exceeds my already very high expectations when we commissioned it, given the talent and experience of the 12-person team that worked on this project.

I congratulate the authors for the candid but respectful manner in which they have: traced Latin America's underperformance relative to the dynamic economies of East Asia; explained in plain language the basic reasons for the differential economic and social performance of the two regions; and suggested what Latin America must do to regain its past momentum and achieve a much needed resurgence.

I recommend the book to everyone—within and outside the region—interested in the long-term economic, social and political development of Latin America. They will find the book both thoughtful and thought provoking.

Finally, I must thank the three editors—Claudio Loser, Harinder Kohli and Anil Sood—for the exemplary job they have done in producing this book in record time.

Enrique García
President and CEO
CAF – Banco de Desarrollo de América Latina

Acknowledgements

This book originates from a report commissioned by the Corporacion Andina de Fomento (CAF) and prepared by the Centennial Group. At CAF, the work was coordinated by Luis Enrique Berrizbeitia, and executed by Jennifer Arencibia

All but two of the substantive chapters are based on background papers prepared by Centennial Group staff, associates and consultants. The authors of the papers, in alphabetic order, are: Vinod K. Goel (Centennial Group International), Homi Kharas (Brookings Institution and Centennial Group International), Harinder S. Kohli (Centennial Group International), Harpaul Alberto Kohli (Centennial Group International), Claudio M. Loser (Centennial Group Latin America), Nora Lustig (Tulane University and Center for Global Development), Tamara Ortega Godspeed (Inter-American Dialogue); Jeffrey M. Puryear (Inter-American Dialogue), and Michael Shifter (Inter- American Dialogue) and Anil Sood (Centennial Group International). Aaron Szyf, Katy Grober, Drew Arnold, and Charlotte Hess provided very valuable research support to the authors throughout the project. The report gained greatly from advice and counsel from discussants in the Seminar on the Vision for Latin America facing the year 2040 and in particular from Enrique Iglesias, Alicia Bárcena, Jose Antonio Ocampo and Carlota Perez, as well as members of the Consulting Panel of CAF. Among CAF members, Luis Miguel Castilla, subsequently with the Government of Peru, and Jeniffer Arencibia provided crucial help during the preparation of the report. Within Centennial, among others Jose Fajgenbaum provided invaluable comments and support.

Finally, we are grateful to Mr. Enrique Garcia, President, and Luis Enrique Berrizbeitia, Executive Vice-president of CAF respectively for their inspiration and encouragement provided—and insistence on intellectual integrity demanded during the preparation of this work.

    Harinder Kohli   Claudio M. Loser   Anil Sood

Introduction
Vision for Latin America 2040
Achieving a More Inclusive and Prosperous Society

Harinder S. Kohli

Region's Natural Endowments and Strengths

Latin America is arguably the most richly endowed developing region of the world. With vast areas of fertile land, plenty of sunshine, and abundant water resources, it stands in stark contrast to most developing regions including Africa, East, Central and South Asia as well as the Middle East, which are increasingly threatened by water stress and shortages. In addition, Amazonia has the largest remaining rainforests in the world, an intensely valuable natural defence against the threat of climate change. The harvest of its oceans, such as tuna and shrimp, is highly desired by people throughout the world. And, its abundance of mineral resources including oil, gas, copper, silver, and coal is also eagerly sought by both developed and developing countries, especially in fast growing Asia.

The region also enjoys a number of other crucial advantages that facilitate economic development and social progress. With over two hundred years of independence and self-governance, compared to Asia and Africa which achieved independence from colonial rule only after 1945, Latin America has had plenty of time to build on the institutions left by Europeans. A majority of people share a common history, language, culture and religion. There is widespread pride in being a Latin American. Furthermore, the countries enjoy strong historic ties and physical proximity to the world's two largest markets, North America and Europe.

Photo Credit: CAF

Throughout the twentieth century and continuing today the region has been building modern physical and institutional infrastructure at national and regional levels, to leverage these natural advantages. Since the 1960s the region has also invested in regional infrastructure such as the Pan American highway, linking Mexico in the north to Chile in the south (90 percent complete) and the regional hydro-electrical complexes in the Southern cone. It has set up numerous regional and sub-regional institutions and coordination mechanisms.

The strong natural advantages, proximity to, and close business ties with, North America and

Europe, and relatively advanced institutional and physical infrastructure had made Latin America the most prosperous developing region by a wide margin.

Until the late 1970s, the region enjoyed economic growth above the global average, and appeared to have great promise. Income levels compared to the United States rose from 12 percent in 1970 to 17.7 percent in 1981. In 1980, Latin America's per capita GDP was US$7,474 compared to US$789 for East Asia, US$1,798 for Sub Saharan Africa and US$4,708 for the Middle East and North Africa.[1] As Latin America's per capita income steadily rose, by 1980 most Latin economies joined the ranks of middle-income societies—well before Asia—and appeared to be steadily closing the remaining income gap with the developed countries.

Consequently, until the late 1970s Latin America was generally regarded as the developing region with the greatest promise, while Asia was not only the poorest region but also judged as both socially and politically fragile.

Recent Economic and Political Developments

After suffering repeated economic crises from the 1970s to the early 2000s, Latin America, along with most other regions, entered a new era of economic progress and robust growth during the past six years. This improved economic performance has generated a welcome combination of self-satisfaction and optimism in the region after almost two decades of pessimism. The following indicators illustrate the recent progress:

- Despite expected major variations between countries, the region as a whole enjoyed an average annual economic growth of 4.7 percent between 2003 and 2008, the highest growth recorded since the 1970s. With slowing population growth, this yielded a per capita income growth of 3.4 percent a year.
- Unlike previous periods of high growth, the latest episode was not accompanied by higher inflation or external imbalances. This hard won price stability should yield major benefits over the longer term through increased consumer and investor confidence, hopefully leading to higher savings and investments rates (provided that they are accompanied by improvements in business climate and deepening of financial systems).
- During these six years, good progress was achieved in another major social and economic problem plaguing the region: huge disparities in incomes and living standards. Between 2003-2008, there was a noticeable decline in absolute poverty and a reduction in inequities in many countries including the two largest economies, Brazil and Mexico.
- The region as a whole has weathered the latest global economic and financial crisis reasonably well though Mexico and some countries in Central America have been very hard hit. Unlike the OECD countries and some developing regions (such as Central and Eastern Europe), overall Latin America suffered a much more modest slowdown in economic activity. Its financial systems withstood the storm quite well. Many countries, led by Brazil, are already on their

---

[1] Using constant 2005 US$

way to recovery though some countries are still suffering the ravages of the Great Recession. All in all, the region can derive much satisfaction from its economic performance since 2003 (with Mexico being a major exception). An important factor behind this performance was the very positive global economic environment through 2007—including the expansionary monetary policies adopted by most major economies—under which the world enjoyed several years of unprecedented —and one might say unsustainable—prosperity, booming international trade and private capital flows. Higher global growth in turn contributed to record commodity prices. This favourable global economic environment in turn helped fuel Latin America's growth. At the same time, domestic policy reforms during the 1990s (which led to prudent monetary and fiscal policies, more realistic exchange rates, stronger regulation and supervision of banks) played a critical role in keeping inflation low and removing vulnerabilities.

Having finally secured macro-balances and price stability that had eluded it for so long, the region can now focus on policies and issues important for its longer-term growth and well being. This is the focus of this book.

Longer Term Performance and Comparison with East Asia

The above-noted progress in absolute terms during the past few years is both real and laudable. But, it must not obscure the fundamental longer-term trends and issues.

A review of Latin America's longer-term performance paints a much more sombre portrait. It portrays a region that has essentially been stagnant relative to the rest of the world through the 1990s and only keeping pace with others since then. It is a region that suffers the highest disparities in the world, and that is steadily losing, and may have already largely lost, its long standing position as the world's most advanced and prosperous developing region. Consider the following facts:

- In 1965, Latin America accounted for 5.6 percent of global GDP. Forty years later, in 2005, it still had only 5.7 percent (at market exchange rates). In other words, while Latin America's per capita income rose between 1965 and 2005 by 136 percent, so did it for the world as a whole, leaving the region no better in relative terms after forty years. Latin America's income level has similarly not converged with that of the United States (it was 12.9 percent that of the US in 1970 and 13.5 percent in 2009).
- In general, the ups-and-downs of Latin America's importance in the world economy have followed the cycles of commodity prices rather than reflecting sustained self-generated development.
- In 1981, Latin America accounted for 31 percent of developing country GDP. In 2009, Latin America's share of developing country GDP had dropped to only 20 percent.
- In 1981, Brazil and Mexico were each one-third larger than India or China, and Argentina had the same GDP as Indonesia, a country with almost six times the population. By 2009, Indonesia's GDP was 50 percent larger than Argentina's, and India's one-third larger than Mexico. Today, China is almost 50 percent larger than all of Latin America combined.
- Brazil and Mexico were the two largest emerging economies in 1980. Latin America had 4

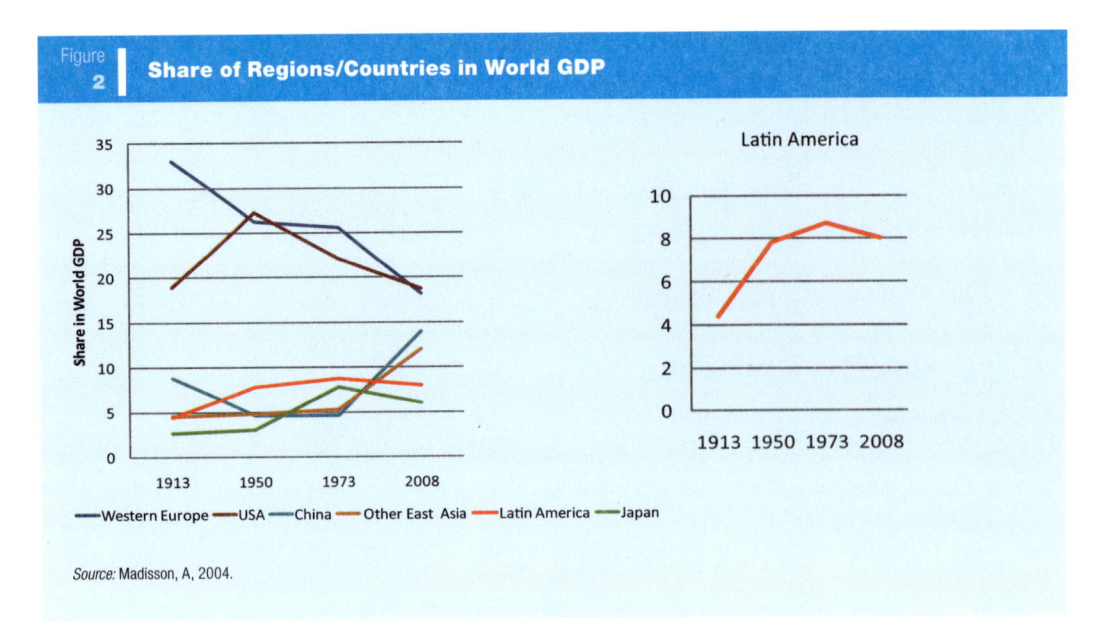

Figure 2 | Share of Regions/Countries in World GDP

Source: Madisson, A, 2004.

countries in the top ten list. Today, 7 of the top ten emerging economies are in Asia. Argentina and Venezuela have dropped off the list altogether. Now, only Brazil (#2) and Mexico (#4) are on the list.

- In contrast, successful Asian countries—the NICs, China and India—continue their unrelenting march towards converging with the developed economies. For example, in 1965 the per capita income of NICs was 10.2 percent of the US and by 2009 it had reached 47.1 percent. China has risen from 0.8 percent to 7.7 percent.
- Perhaps the single most troublesome longer-term issue is that LAC has been the most prosperous developing region for almost a hundred years, but it suffers from the highest disparities of income, even higher than in Africa. Despite the recent progress cited above, the disparities today essentially remain as large as forty years ago. These disparities are a hidden and ticking time bomb that can destroy the very social and political fabric of the region.

There are two basic messages here. First, most countries in Latin America—with the exception of Chile—have stopped converging with the United States (in the last few years Brazil has regained growth momentum but it is too soon to say whether this is a longer-term trend). Second, Latin America is gradually but steadily surrendering its leadership of the developing world to Asia.

Are Latin American Economies Mired in the Middle-Income Trap?

The inability of the Latin American economies to further close the productivity and income gap with developed countries during the past forty plus years suggests that the region has become mired in the "middle income trap" (Box 1). Their persistent subpar performance is in sharp contrast to that of most Asian economies.

> **Box 1 — What is the Middle Income Trap, and how did some East Asian Countries Avoid it?**
>
> The middle income trap refers to countries stagnating after achieving middle income status and not growing to advanced country levels. This is illustrated in the figure, which plots the income per capita of three middle income countries between 1975 and 2005. In a steadily growing country, the line would be continuously rising over time (positive growth), that is towards higher income levels. That is the experience of South Korea.
>
> But many middle income countries do not follow this pattern. Instead, they have short periods of growth offset by periods of decline. Rather than steadily moving up over time, their GDP per capita simply moves up and down. That is the middle income trap—unable to compete with low income, low wage economies in manufacturing exports and unable to compete with advanced economies in high skill innovations.

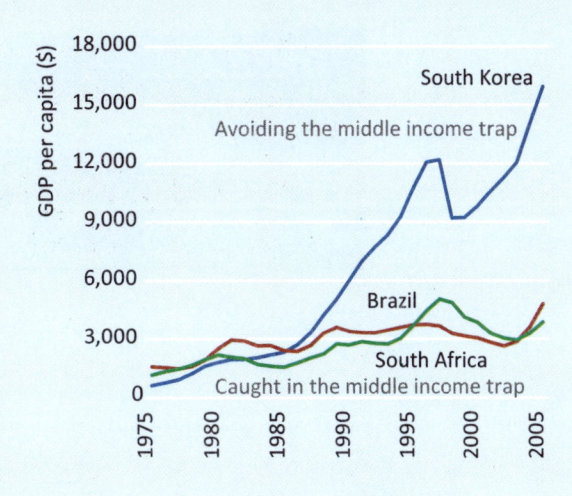

Asia's recent superior performance can be explained by many "technical" aspects, such as its much higher savings and investment rates, better human development, export orientation, better global competitiveness and cost of doing business rankings etc. However, we believe that Latin America's fundamental problems arise from deeper structural weaknesses, lack of an effective long-term development strategy, past focus on short-term issues and, above all, an ideological approach to policy.

Few countries sustain high growth for more than a generation, and even fewer continue high growth rates once they reach middle-income status. Some features differentiating growth beyond middle income from growth from low-income to middle income are clear. Growth tends to become more capital intensive and skill intensive. The domestic market expands and becomes a more important engine, especially for growth of services. Wages start to rise, most rapidly for highly skilled workers, and shortages can emerge. The traditional low-wage manufacturing for export model does not work well for middle-income countries. They seem to become trapped in a slow growth mode unless they change strategies and move up the value chain. Cost advantages in labour-intensive sectors, such as the manufactured exports that once drove growth, start to decline in comparison with lower wage poor country producers. At the same time, middle-income countries do not have the property rights, capital markets, successful venture capital, or critical mass of highly skilled people to grow through innovations as affluent countries do. Caught between these two groups, middle-income countries can become trapped without a viable high-growth strategy.

This seems to be what has happened to Latin America. In many countries, wages are too high to be globally competitive in basic manufacturing. The collapse of Latin America's garments producers after protection was withdrawn is proof of that. Yet, Latin America does not have the research and development capabilities that allow it to develop new products in advanced areas (exceptions are by now familiar: Embraer in Brazil).

Photo Credit: Ahunt

Importance of the Middle-Class in Fuelling Growth

In some middle-income countries, the domestic market can complement export markets as the economy matures and the local market becomes large. In most countries, domestic consumption typically starts to grow quickly when incomes per capita reach around US$6,000 in PPP terms. This did not happen in Latin America, perhaps because of its relatively small middle class.

Compare Brazil with South Korea, for example. Brazil's growth started to slow after 1980, when it had reached a per capita income level of US$7600 (PPP). At that time, its middle class, defined as households with incomes of between US$10 and US$100 per capita per day, was just 29 percent of the population. This made it impossible for the middle-class to drive further growth. In contrast, South Korea's income per capita reached US$7700 (PPP) in 1987. By that time, South Korea's evenly distributed growth had produced a sizeable middle class, which accounted for 53 percent of the population. The country capitalized on the demand from this large middle class to grow its service industries and create the building blocks for a knowledge economy. Today 94 percent of Korea's population is middle class.

The middle class can provide an impetus for growth in ways other than just consumption demand. For example, the middle class typically values and demands a high-quality education for their children. The causal channel is less important than the suggestion that distribution plays an important role in sustaining growth.

What Makes East Asia Different from Latin America?

Latin America's loss of its long standing position as the most prosperous and promising developing region is best illustrated by comparing its economic and social development relative to East Asia in general, and the so called NICs more specifically.

Between 1965 and 2009, the per capita income of the NICs grew at an average annual rate of 6.8

percent, while Latin America recorded a growth rate of only 3.7 percent. As a result, in terms of per capita income, the NICs—that lagged well behind Latin America in 1965 (US$1,778 vs. US$3,403)—leapfrogged over the region (US$20,308 vs. US$7,028) in 2009[2]. This illustrates how the most dynamic economies in Asia, now joined by China and India, have continued to converge with the most prosperous nations, while most Latin American economies have become mired in the middle-income trap. Other striking differences between East Asia and Latin America include:

- Political leaders in East Asia are intensely focused on economic issues and are not preoccupied with geo-political issues or ideological debates. This is in sharp contrast to Latin America.
- All successful East Asian countries, as well as China and India, have achieved major gains in total factor productivity (TFP) while Latin American countries have remained stagnant. The two largest economies (Brazil and Mexico) have even regressed somewhat (Figure 2).
- East Asian countries have much higher savings rates (51 percent vs. 23 percent of GDP) and investment rates than LAC.
- East Asia has placed much greater emphasis on human development and put a high premium on meritocracy in its education system. It has achieved, in relative terms, much higher educational standards, and graduates a significantly higher number of engineers, scientists and doctors than Latin America.
- East Asia's investment, public as well as private, in infrastructure has been much higher than in LAC, and it has deeper financial markets, particularly non-bank financial institutions.
- NICs have much more open economies than Latin America, with total trade to GDP ratios of 159 percent vs. 41.5 percent for LAC.
- The structure of production in East Asia has changed dramatically in the past forty years with the region becoming the manufacturing hub of the world, while Latin American economies remain highly dependent on commodities and agricultural products.
- Even as East Asian economies moved from low-income to middle-income and finally to upper middle-income status their income distribution and other social indicators have remained much more equitable, while Latin America continues to suffer from the highest disparities of any region in the world.
- East Asia's more equitable distribution of incomes and assets allowed it to develop a large middle class as soon as the countries achieved middle-income status and this fast growing middle class in turn gradually became an engine of innovation, entrepreneurship and domestic consumption that fuelled further economic growth. In contrast, Latin America's policies were ungeared at developing a strong middle class, but at extracting resources from there through high inflation, expropriation of financial assets and generally poor incentives for savings at an individual level.
- Intra-regional trade (over 55 percent of total trade) and investment (FDI) flows in East Asia

---

2 In constant 2009 US$

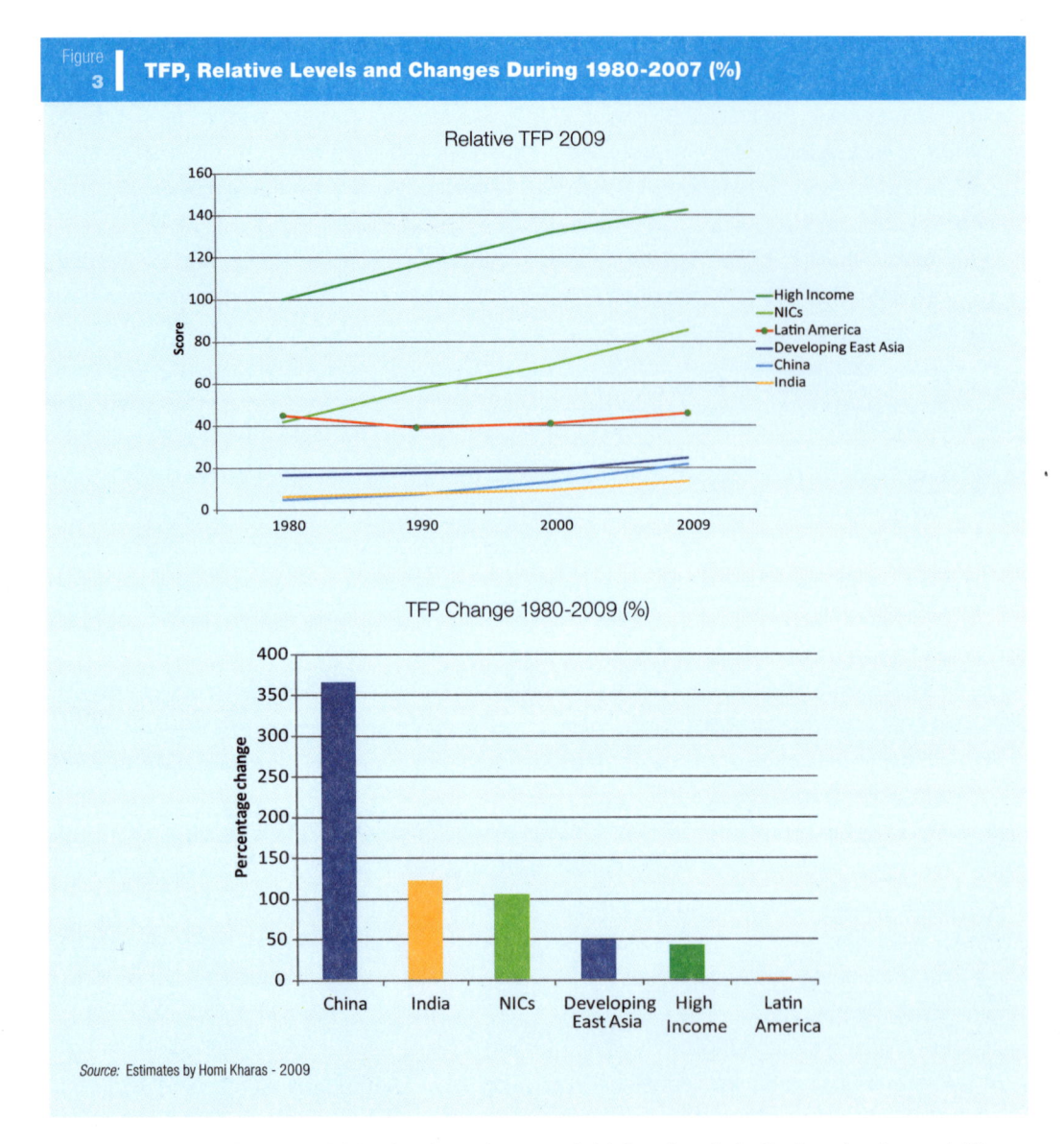

Figure 3 | TFP, Relative Levels and Changes During 1980-2007 (%)

Relative TFP 2009

TFP Change 1980-2009 (%)

Source: Estimates by Homi Kharas - 2009

approach European Union levels and are much higher than in Latin America (around 20 percent, excluding the US). Unlike the EU, these flows are market- and not policy-driven thanks to extensive production networks developed by private businesses. Latin America has few if any such production networks (except between Mexico and the US).

Latin America in 2040: Under "Business as Usual" Scenario

How would Latin America look if the trends of the recent past were to persist over the next thirty years? According to our model of the global economy, under the "business as usual" scenario, Latin

America would grow at about 4 percent a year, and less than 3 percent on a per capita basis. The region's share in world GDP would decline from about 6 percent now to 4.8 percent. Its per capita income in 2040 would be US$18,000, compared to the average global GDP per capita of US$24,000. As a result, three developing regions of the world—East Asia, the Middle East and Central and Eastern Europe—will be more prosperous, with Latin America joining Africa and parts of Asia as the laggards. Equally important, Latin America could continue to have by far the highest disparities between its citizens. Most likely, these conditions will further exacerbate the law and order situation and perhaps lead to unacceptable levels of social unrest and crime.

Chile is the only Latin American country in the sample to meet the criterion for inclusion in the "convergers" category of having a track record of at least 3.5 percent per capita income growth over the past twenty-five years, at least prior to the recent earthquake, and as recognized by its accession to the OECD.[3]

But Brazil, Mexico and other Latin American countries do not meet the criterion. What is shown in the business-as-usual scenario is what would happen if they continue down a path of relatively low TFP growth and relatively low capital investment. This scenario is presumably unacceptable to the region's political, social, business and intellectual leadership, and to its citizens at large.

Latin America in 2040: Payoffs from Reducing by Half the Growth Differential with Asia

On the other hand, what would be the economic and social outlook of the region should it manage to narrow the historic difference in its growth rate with that of Asia?

While it is not realistic to assume that Latin America can suddenly grow at the same rate as the leading economies—China and India—we have developed a scenario under which the region cuts by half its current differential with East Asia (and China and India) and lifts its growth to about 6.5 percent a year between now and 2040 (we assume that two large and two medium-sized economies would manage to escape the middle income trap and move from being non-convergers to join Chile in the convergers category).

Photo Credit: CAF

Under this scenario, the size of the region's economy by 2040 would be four times its current size. Its share of global GDP would rise to 10 percent, not including a possible impact of a secular appreciation of the currencies of the region on

---

3 It is important to point out that Mexico is also an OECD member, and has been characterized recently by a non-converging performance.

the basis of increases in productivity. This will allow the region to retain its position as one of the most prosperous developing regions (though this will still not allow the region to catch up with the NICs).

If Latin America can develop along such a "prosperous scenario", it would sharply reduce poverty within 20 years. Currently, under the World Bank's US$1.25 a day poverty threshold, the region had some (60) million poor in 2008. If the region sustains income growth at 6.5 percent, some 3 million people could be lifted out of poverty every year. Equally important, as discussed below, this higher economic growth can be achieved only by successfully tackling the current inequities. This success, combined with rising average per capita income, would bring a much greater sense of optimism and commitment to shared prosperity amongst all segments of society. It is the only way to ensure social cohesion and peace in the region.

The region's leaders and public must embrace and strive for this scenario of a more equitable and prosperous Latin America. Only then will the region continue to close the gap with OECD countries and keep pace with the successful Asian economies.

A Shared, More Ambitious Vision for the Region

Given Latin America's rich natural endowments, there is no reason why Latin America cannot do as well as East Asia. Indeed, as demonstrated by the successful Asian countries, the region's destiny is firmly dependent on its own actions. Only through its own efforts will the region prosper.

To do so, all concerned—governments, bureaucracy, the business community, academia, think tanks, media and other opinion makers as well as multilateral agencies active in the region—must adopt a focus on simultaneously achieving a much more inclusive and equitable society and much higher economic growth. The region's leaders must aim much higher, be pragmatic and focus single-mindedly on achieving this vision.

Photo Credit: CAF

Such a vision, and a commitment to realizing it, must be shared both within the countries themselves and across the region as a whole. This commonly shared vision must be accompanied by a very different mindset across the political and social landscape: abandonment of the past ideological divides and adoption of pragmatism, as has been the case in East Asia.

A main characteristic of the economic history of Latin America has been the emphasis on ideology and ideological policies, as opposed to Asia's emphasis on outcomes. In the past, policies have been formulated on the basis of economic theories under the assumption that results would follow automatically over time. Over the last quarter century two schools of thought have prevailed. According to both the standard reform-oriented Latin American model and the alternative heterodox model, if policies are right, growth will follow ultimately. In the first case the assumption is that markets will provide an adequate response to policies. The heterodox model questions the market approach of the Washington Consensus but also assumes that the alternative interventionist policies will yield growth and equity. Under both ideological camps, no significant modification of policies was considered irrespective of the results. More often than not, popular support for the policies collapsed over time because of the ideological adherence to a rigid interpretation of what would be the "right" economic model and policies even when they failed to produce expected results, mainly because of a narrow interpretation of the models.

A major lesson of the Asian success in the past fifty years is that Latin America needs to pursue a more pragmatic and non-ideological set of policies, based on strong market principles and measured government intervention, but with the understanding that the policies should be aiming at attaining commonly agreed social objectives and economic outcomes. Under this pragmatic approach, policies and the right mix of government-private sector association would be adjusted as needed to realize the outcomes sought under the shared vision (while respecting the principles of good governance, transparency, and with a good understanding of the costs of these policies).

Of equal importance, there must be a consensus on policies and objectives within the region to achieve effective complementarities between individual economies by helping integrate across the region. This is in contrast to the current practice, where polices in one country are often introduced at the expense of others rather than seeking to exploit the comparative advantages of each country for an effective integration with the rest of the world.

Realizing the Shared Vision

Given the diversity of the region and differing resource endowments, human capital, structure and efficiency of individual countries as well as vastly differing institutional capacities, it is neither prudent nor possible to lay out a detailed strategy for achieving this common vision across the entire region. That can only be done at the level of each individual country.

However, learning from the region's own experiences in the past forty years and contrasting them with East Asia, it is possible to define the broad contours of the strategy required to achieve this more ambitious vision. In our view, to realize the above vision Latin America needs to adopt a strategy that comprises three complementary pillars:
- More inclusion

- Higher productivity
- Greater competition and openness (within Latin America and towards Asia)

Importantly, actions under these three pillars will need to be underpinned by improved governance and accountability for results.

Achieving a More Inclusive Society

Latin America has recently made important strides in improving the conditions of its poor. Nonetheless, income and wealth distribution remains highly skewed. Politically and socially the current situation is unsustainable over the long term. Tackling structural inequities is therefore obviously essential from the point of view of equity. But, as demonstrated by Asia, achieving a more equitable society is equally relevant to sustaining growth over the longer term by expanding the size of the middle class and attaining greater equality of opportunities.

With significant numbers of Latin Americans not fully integrated into the mainstream economy and society (indigenous Americans, Afro-Americans and women) and with current high degrees of informality, in the past the benefits of economic growth have not reached large segments of citizens. This particularly affected those without European ethnicity and women, leading to the disillusionment of large portions of the population with the current economic policies and institutions. Only when growth is much more inclusive, will there be realistic prospects of high sustained and sustainable growth over time for Latin America, as has been achieved in Asia.

Thus, striving for a more inclusive society promises a win-win situation, and not one where there is a trade-off between growth and equity. The fundamental approach to achieving a more inclusive society will involve the removal of numerous current structural inequities by:
- Providing access to quality education and other public services including rural infrastructure,
- Breaking the current economic dominance by entrenched vested interests, and
- Ensuring jobs and finance to those who are today left at the margins of the society.

Such an approach must be clearly additional to the ongoing efforts in countries such as Brazil and Mexico that have been generally successful in reducing poverty and indigence.

Towards this goal, this book focuses on four priority areas: i) basic and secondary education; ii) infrastructure; iii) "inclusive" innovation and technological development; and iv) governance.

This list is by no means comprehensive but, in our view, includes the most critical issues requiring immediate attention by the region's political leaders and policy makers.

At the same time, Latin America must pay much more attention to the looming problems of environmental degradation, rising crime, and corruption. These issues, however, are not covered in this book.

Sharply Enhancing Productivity

The key to achieving a higher growth rate on a sustainable basis and to converging with the developed economies lies in sharply enhancing productivity and competitiveness of Latin American economies. Unfortunately, as noted above, the region has not been able to improve its total factor productivity.

Indeed, the two larger economies—Brazil and Mexico—have even regressed. This must be reversed.

Improved productivity and competitiveness would in turn help Latin America to achieve much higher economic growth than it has managed in the past forty years (or even the last five years), while loosening the historic dependence of its economic fortunes on the ups and downs in international commodity prices. This will require much more emphasis on:

- Improved human capital,
- Better business environment,
- Much higher investment rates necessary to transform the structure of production of goods and services in light of the changing global economic environment, and
- More innovation and technological development.

In our view, a better business environment is the key to unlocking the virtuous cycle of greater efficiency and competitiveness, higher business confidence, increased private investment, higher domestic savings and improved productivity. India's recent higher investments, savings and the resultant economic growth rates can be traced back to the major economic reforms undertaken starting in 1990 that significantly improved the business climate. With most of Latin America is finally enjoying macro economic stability, improvements in the business climate could add equally impressive results albeit with some time lag.

Again, without attempting to be comprehensive, this book presents suggestions in three priority areas: i) infrastructure (particularly physical connectivity and energy); ii) tertiary education, innovation and technological development; and iii) governance.

Promoting Greater Competition and Openness to Neighboring Economies, Towards Asia, and to Global Economy

The third pillar of the new strategy for the region should be the promotion of much greater competition, both in internal markets and with external sources. Given the relatively smaller share of trade in total GDP, Latin American countries must give the highest priority to enhancing domestic competition, starting with dismantling of monopolies—whether public or private—and enforcement of well-structured competition laws. In parallel, there is a need to promote and facilitate much greater openness to other countries in the region, closer links with fast-growing Asia that is emerging as the new center of gravity of the world economy, and dismantling of remaining barriers to trade and investment with the global economy as a whole.

For many decades, Latin America was characterized by an overwhelming presence of government in economic activity (as was the case in many other regions of the world), well beyond a regulatory role. The situation changed dramatically starting in the 1970s in Chile, and in subsequent decades in many countries including Argentina, Brazil, Colombia, Mexico, and Peru. Most importantly, during this period there was a major effort at privatizing many activities that were not considered as central to the role of the state or of strategic relevance. There were many different methods pursued for the sale of government assets, some of them seriously flawed. In some circumstances, public monopolies were replaced by private monopolies. Several industries continue to be dominated by one or very few companies and, frequently, the dominance in the market is accompanied by restrictions on imports of goods and services, or limitations to investment in specific areas, and thus helps consolidate the monopoly power of the companies. Improved domestic competition thus remains a work in progress in the region. While it is beyond the focus of this book to deal in depth with the specific area of domestic competition, the consolidation of the competitiveness and productivity aspects of economic policy rest in significant part on the opening of markets. A further push in the process of privatization, of improved regulations and opening of markets, as well as government sector productivity enhancements would go a long way in helping the region in attaining a more effective growth path in the future.

In parallel with measures to enhance domestic competition, Latin American economies must also pursue two avenues to improve their trade performance in support of accelerated growth: regional cooperation leading to expanded intra-regional trade; and continued diversification of export markets beyond North America and Europe and of export products beyond the dominance of commodities and fuels (except in the case of Mexico).

Latin America lags far behind Europe and Asia in regional cooperation, particularly as measured by intra-regional trade. There are three basic reasons for which the Latin America region should seriously consider significantly enhancing intra-regional trade, including through improved regional cooperation: i) to permit the economies to specialize, an important strategy to escape the middle income trap; ii) to overcome the reality that Latin America economies—with the exception of Brazil and Mexico—are small by global standards and thus do not have domestic markets large enough to permit the economies of scale needed by firms to be globally competitive; and iii) to allow local firms to take advantage of their superior knowledge and understanding of the needs of customers in the neighboring countries compared to the competitors from other continents.

Latin America must gradually reduce its dependence on the slow-growing economies of North America and Europe and develop much closer ties with the world's fastest growing region: Asia. The region also stands to make significant gains by increasing the value-added of its output and exports and, within manufacturing, to move up the technology ladder—a critical measure for getting out of the middle income trap and making progress toward high income status. Finally, dismantling of remaining barriers to trade with and investment from the global markets as a whole will be a very powerful vehicle to curb the current monopolistic power of large companies, to increase competition at all levels, and to spur innovation. This book includes specific suggestions actions in these areas.

Improved Governance: Focus on Results and Accountability

As with many developing economies, Latin America's Achilles heel is its poor governance in all its facets. Indeed, this overarching issue is the biggest hurdle to Latin America achieving a sustaining a more inclusive society and higher economic growth rate over the next thirty years.

A closer look at each and every crucial issue facing the region reveals that the most underlying problems are rooted in poor governance, and that without fundamental improvements in governance it will not be possible to tackle these issues effectively.

Most political scientists equate good governance with democratic governments. In our view, while a democratic political system is indeed highly desirable and Latin America has made marked progress in that direction, governance comprises of many facets that go well beyond the political system. The various facets of governance are intertwined with each other like pieces of a jigsaw puzzle.

Our own definition of governance comprises all facets of governance that affect economic management: role and focus of governments; importance given to economic and social development by the top political leaders and policy makers; delivery of quality and universality of basic public services (law and order, rule of law, education and health services); and focus on results and enforcement of accountability.

Specifically, Latin America must transform the following ten facets of governance in order to kick start the economies to achieve higher economic growth and make the societies much more inclusive:

- Make economic and social development the primary focus of the political leaders and policy makers, not just in words but also in reality
- Reverse the deterioration in political governance, while strengthening democratic institutions
- Make governments smarter, more focused and more credible
- Decentralize, where possible, both the authority and accountability for most public services to local bodies as close to the people as possible
- Modernize and make more effective all institutions involved in economic management
- Reform the civil service to meet the needs of modern economies and of democratic, more open and more inclusive societies
- Improve the quality, honesty and credibility of all public services including the police, judiciary, education and health services
- Actively promote and enforce competitive markets and prevent capture of state organs by big business
- Inculcate a code of self discipline and ethical behaviour within the business community
- Implement agreed policies and priorities, monitor results and enforce accountabilities at all levels of government (national, state and municipal).

Undertaking such a transformation of governance will require Latin American leaders to emulate the four characteristics that have distinguished East Asia from other developing regions:

- Sharp and primary focus of political leaders and policy makers alike on economic issues
- Ability to implement policy decisions
- Insistence on achievement of results on the ground, and
- Enforcement of accountability

These and other facets of governance are discussed in more detail in the relevant sections of the book.

Role of CAF

Advocating a More Ambitious Vision of Latin America:
CAF is in a unique position to help the region lift its sights and aim higher. It can fill a major void in the region that currently has no clear, ideologically-neutral and credible advocate for a more ambitious vision of long-term social and economic development of the region. Such a vision also must be anchored in a clear strategy on how to realize it.

CAF is well positioned to do this: it is the only multilateral institution owned exclusively by countries within the region (except for Spain); is the largest multilateral donor in its countries of operations; has a reputation for not being wedded to any particular ideology; has a well-deserved image of being a "friend" of the member countries; and its leadership has direct access to the top decision makers throughout the region.

CAF can and should help forge the needed consensus amongst top political, policy and business leaders of the region: that the current economic and social prospects are both unsustainable and unacceptable politically as well as socially; that the region needs to focus much more on higher, more inclusive and sustainable growth; and that to do so the countries must adopt different strategies and policies in addition to adopting a different mindset.

Towards that end, CAF should become a vocal and persistent advocate of this new and more ambitious vision of Latin America. CAF leadership would need to assume a leading role in this effort, starting with face-to-face meetings with the political leaders and key policy makers. A major short-term objective would be to help start a pragmatic, evidence-based and ideology-free dialogue on the region's economic performance amongst the top political leaders and decision makers in the region.

In addition, CAF could consider the following steps:
- Discussion of the proposed new vision at forthcoming meetings of the region's political leaders, policy makers and top business executives.
- Launching of a coordinated media campaign to educate general public and build a grass roost support for the proposed changes in strategy, policy and mind set.
- Creating a network of professionally led think tanks with necessary critical mass of experts and each focused on a few of the critical issues highlighted in this book. CAF supported think tanks would be regional—and not national—in their focus.
- Reporting to the heads of state at their regular Annual Summits on the progress being made by Latin American economies relative to other regions of the world as well as on any common social and economic agenda adopted by them.

Realigning CAF Operations to Above Strategy:
As a leading advocate of a new, more ambitious vision for Latin America, CAF must also align its own operations to help realize this vision. But, in doing so it must not stray away from two key reasons for its past success: remaining pragmatic and focusing its core agenda on activities in which it already has or can develop a comparative advantage.

Keeping these factors in view, CAF should carefully review its potential assistance under each of the three pillars of the proposed new strategy for the region: a) achieving a more inclusive and cohesive society; b) helping achieve and sustain higher productivity and economic competitiveness; c) and enhancing competition and openness, including through greater regional cooperation and openness to Asia.

In addition, CAF must give greater priority to environmental and climate change issues.

CAF operations already are aimed to achieve many of these adjustments. Therefore instead of starting anew, in many areas CAF will need to make only modest adjustments or put greater emphasis on some existing activities (e.g., infrastructure development and regional cooperation). But, there are also some areas that are not yet covered adequately by CAF and need to be added to the array of its core activities (articulation of a new vision for the region; addressing inequities; and promoting stronger links with Asia).

CAF should consider the following areas for particular emphasis under the above three pillars:

- *Achieving a More Inclusive Society:* Five priority activities fit well with CAF's existing strengths and should be emphasized more in its operations:
  - rural roads
  - 24/7 power supply to all
  - widespread access to the internet
  - low cost housing
  - micro-finance

In addition, CAF should consider adding two aspects of education that will involve only modest investment of CAF resources but could have a major impact on the quality of education in the region over the long term: a) training of teachers (including primary school teachers); and b) a program to systematically measure education quality at the primary, secondary and tertiary levels across countries. If the results from these activities are positive, over the longer term CAF could consider adding education to its core activities, as is currently the case with infrastructure and regional cooperation.

- *Sharply Enhancing Productivity:* Historically, this has been CAF's core area of focus, with heavy emphasis on infrastructure development.
  - The focus on infrastructure development should continue but with renewed efforts to assist the region increase overall infrastructure investment level to 4-5 percent of GDP, including through private sector participation
  - CAF's past excellent work on the region's competitiveness should be followed up with similar work at country level, and a special initiative to enhance the business environment on an urgent basis.
  - Two other new areas for CAF support should be considered to meet priority needs of the region: a) privately sponsored, funded and managed tertiary education institutions (professional colleges, universities) and vocational schools; and b) a network of technological research and development institutions and centers of excellence that also act as a bridge between the region's top universities and businesses.

- *Fostering Greater Competition, Regional Cooperation and Openness:* Fortunately, CAF is already both a leading advocate of regional cooperation in the region and a major source of financing for regional projects.
    - This traditional work should be reinforced by: a) regular analytic studies demonstrating benefits of regional cooperation; b) public advocacy of greater regional cooperation; and c) concrete support for initiatives to promote regional cooperation (e.g. above-proposed regional think tanks, networks of research and development centres.)
    - In the area of regional projects, CAF could focus more on projects that would: a) create physical connectivity between two or three countries at a time (roads, bridges, energy trade) rather than on Pan-American projects that require sustained political support and commitment from a large number of countries with different political philosophies; b) focus much more on trade logistics (border crossings, customs procedures); and c) create a network of ports and airports to facilitate trade along the Pacific within Latin America and with Asia.
    - CAF also needs to become a leading advocate of greater competition within the countries, stronger links with fast growing Asia, and of much greater openness to rest of the world and of.
    - Finally, CAF should act as an intellectual bridge between Latin America and Asia, perhaps by developing a closer institutional relationship with the Asian Development Bank.

Over time, as more and more countries put in place the above recommended reforms and the region achieves the much higher investment and domestic savings rates anticipated in this book, CAF may need to reconsider the volume of its own financial support—both to public and private sectors—to underpin and support the much higher investment levels and financial needs of the region. But, that should come after, and not before, the countries have improved their investment and savings performance through domestic policy and institutional reforms.

Latin America 2040

Part I

Chapter 1
Breaking Away from Mediocre Complacency to a Prosperous Future

Claudio M. Loser and Anil Sood

Introduction

Latin America has been one of the most prosperous regions among Emerging Economies in terms of many indicators, including per-capita income. For many years, it grew at a faster rate than the rest of the world, and GDP per capita exceeded the average for the world. It was and is a source of primary commodities and a relatively small contributor to environmental degradation (with the exception of deforestation in the Amazon) relative to other major regions of the world. It also has acquired a fairly high educational level. However, particularly in recent decades, Latin America has not managed to keep up with other Emerging Markets. The more dynamic Newly Industrialized Countries (NICs) in Asia in particular, have not only caught up with the region but are also leaving it behind. These countries have become "convergers",[1] i.e. their incomes have converged with the advanced economies. In turn, Latin American economies, with the exception of Chile, do not fall into this category and have been losing ground not only with respect to these countries but with respect to many others in the developing world. While there are many theories that attempt to explain this phenomenon, the simple fact is that Latin America's growth performance has been mediocre when compared to other regions.

Photo Credit: Aaron Szyf

Today, Latin America is an average region in the world. It had an income level in 2009 of PPP US$10,544 compared to a global average of PPP US$10,278.[2] At market exchange rates, the average income of a Latin American is a bit lower than the world average: $7,028 compared to $8,531 (in

---
1 Converging is understood as moving rapidly toward the levels of income of the advanced economies, and away from the current stagnation, characteristic of the middle-income trap
2 Using current PPP dollars.

2009).[3] The remarkable fact about Latin America is that its income level in constant dollars is estimated at 15.5 percent of that of the United States in 2009[4] which compares to 17.0 percent in 1965. In brief, Latin America is close to the global average in living standards, and it has neither converged nor diverged from the United States over a 44 year period. Latin America seems to be stuck.

The recent economic crisis hit Latin American economies (with a few exceptions like Mexico) to a somewhat milder extent than many other regions, and there are good indications that they are recovering well. Still, the weaknesses that characterize the region have become more evident, in terms of commodity dependence, volatile private financing, and serious issues of income distribution, equity and inclusion. Actions to strengthen the medium-term performance of the region are essential.

This book traces out a scenario for the global economy that suggests that Latin America's business-as-usual average performance will not be sufficient for the region to retain its global output share. It will steadily shrink, because in practice its performance in recent years has been below average.

Latin America can of course do better than it has in the past. This book presents a scenario for convergence—with growth at 6.5 percent per year (at market exchange rates). Such a growth rate could be achieved if four of the major Latin American economies join Chile and manage to achieve the same rate of catch-up TFP growth as in some other converging developing countries or if a majority of countries does moderately well. That suggests it is a feasible scenario.

But the region and its leaders need to raise their sights on economic growth and promote a vision of a vibrant, fast-growing economic region where high investment rates and rapid increases in total factor productivity are the objects of national policy. The region will need to refocus its objectives and to be pragmatic rather than ideological about it in order to re-emerge from its state of relative comfort, complacency and, in some cases, unfortunately, even sleepiness. While no two regions are equivalent, the example of East Asia, even with its own vulnerabilities, provides the most important lessons.

Historical Comparative Performance

An analysis of Latin America's past performance with a long-term perspective shows that its position within the world economy has fluctuated significantly. Over the course of a century and a half, Latin America grew at a faster rate than the world economy. Its share of world GDP doubled from 4.4 percent around the turn of the twentieth century to 8.7 percent in the 1970s; it reached a peak of 9.5 percent of world GDP by 1981, with GDP per-capita exceeding the world average by some 10 percent, during the third quarter of the century (Table 1 and Figure 1).[5] Subsequently, growth rates of overall GDP and per capita GDP lagged the rest of the world, and per capita GDP fell below the world average (Figure 2).

As can be observed, the decline in the share of Latin America in world GDP has been far from smooth, even though the rate of growth of per capita income has leveled off, compared to the most

---

3 Using 2009 constant dollars.
4 Using 2009 constant dollars
5 These numbers are subject to considerable debate and are long-term estimations of purchasing power parity (PPP), based on longer-term historical studies, like those of A. Maddison. Estimates based on values unadjusted for PPP, as most of the estimates made in this study for the last forty years may give a somewhat smaller ratio of per capita GDP for the region compared to the rest of the world.

Table 1 | Economic Indicators: Latin America and the World

	Average Annual Growth Rate				
	1870-1913	1913-1950	1950-1973	1974-1998	1999-2008
GDP					
Latin America	3.5	3.4	5.4	3.0	3.4
World	2.1	1.8	4.9	3.0	4.0
GDP per Capita					
Latin America	1.8	1.4	2.6	1.0	2.1
World	1.3	0.9	2.9	1.3	2.8
Share of Latin America in World GDP (in percent)	4.4	7.8	8.7	8.7	8.1
Ratio GDP per capita Latin America/World (in percent)	97	119	110	96	95

Source: A. Maddison, The World economy, a Millennial perspective, 2004; IMF, World Economic Outlook, 2009; and own estimates.

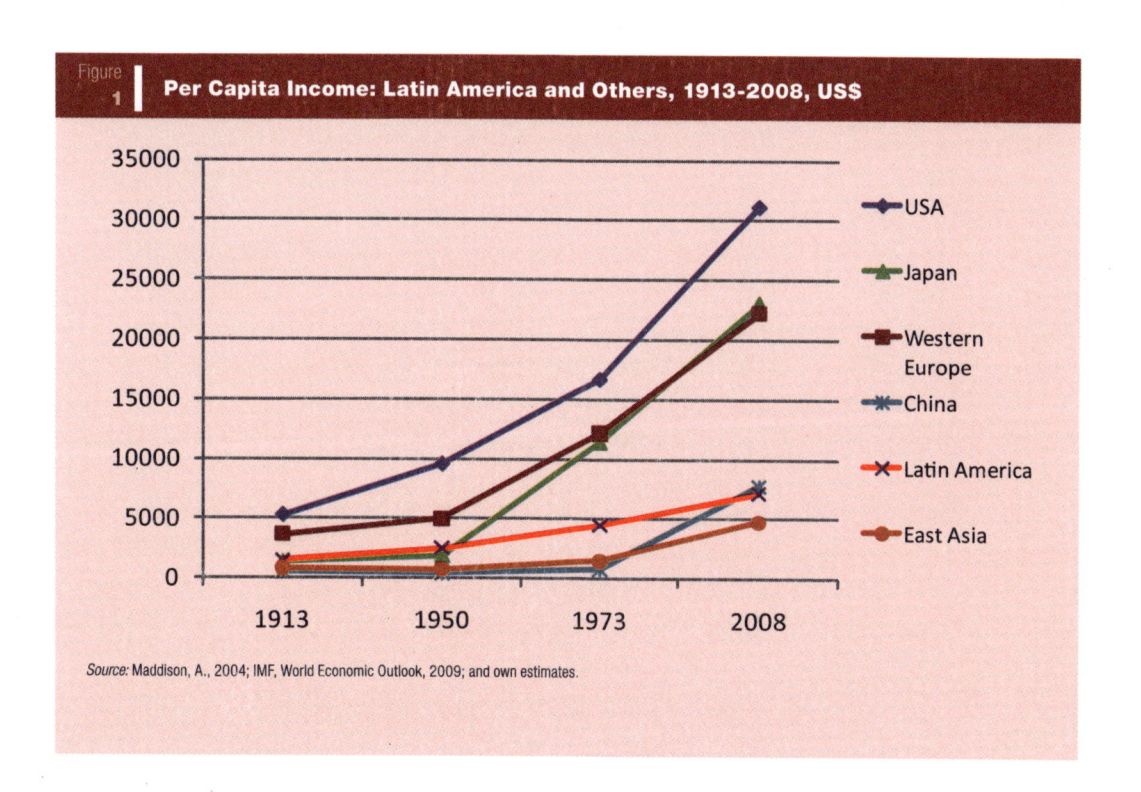

Figure 1 | Per Capita Income: Latin America and Others, 1913-2008, US$

Source: Maddison, A., 2004; IMF, World Economic Outlook, 2009; and own estimates.

Figure 2 | Per Capita Income in PPP Terms (1995=100)

Source: IMF - *World Economic Outlook*, April 2010.

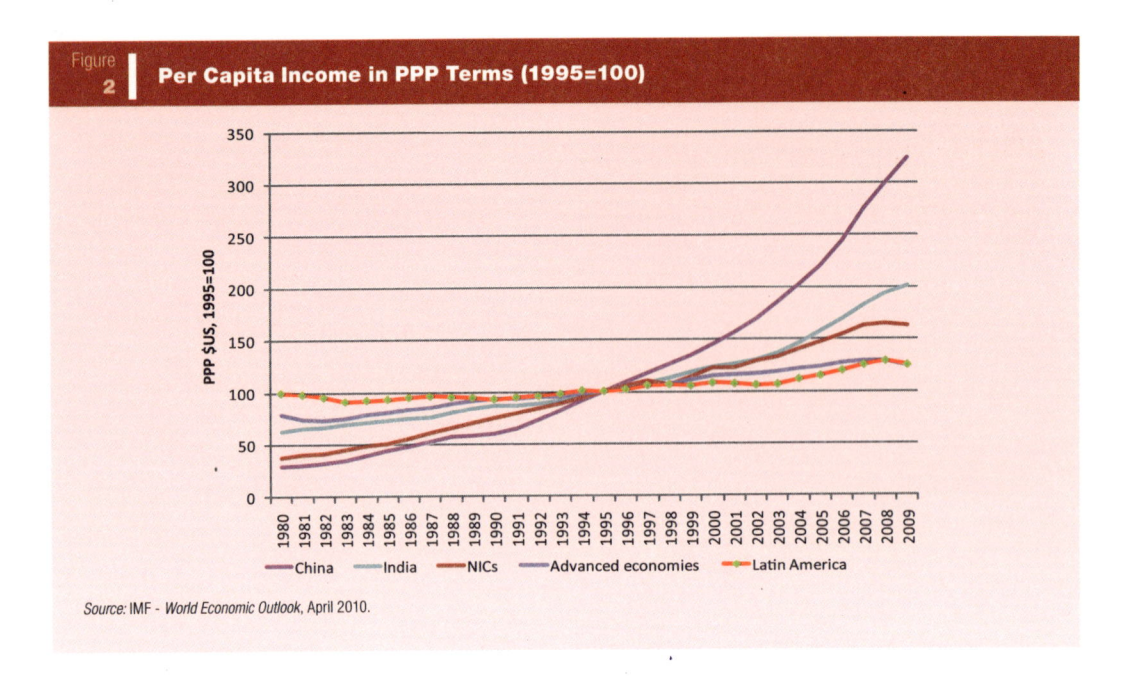

dynamic areas of the world economy. Moreover, the region's share in world GDP has fluctuated in line with commodity prices (Figure 3).[6] Large Latin American countries have also declined relative to their counterparts in Asia. This is reflected in the trajectory of per capita income for the largest Latin American countries compared to East Asia, and particularly to Japan and the NICs—a group that includes Korea, Taiwan, Hong Kong, and Singapore—as shown in Figure 4.

Volatility has been an adverse factor and is reflected in a high percentage of years of low growth in the region relative to others. This can be observed at the percentage of years since 1980 that the region's growth rates were below 1 and 2 percent respectively (Figure 5). Only more recently has the growth performance tended to improve in terms of volatility.

While growth performance has been far from stellar, many indicators for Latin America have remained relatively strong, including the Human Development Index.[7] Per capita income remains reasonably high, the region has benefitted from the major booms in commodities observed over recent decades, and many individuals in the region have been lifted from abject poverty in the last decade and a half.

Latin America's opening to international trade after years of isolation has resulted in greater capital inflows and the continent has reaped some of the benefits of a globalized world. Foreign direct investment has been attracted to the region's abundant natural resources. The region has a reasonably well-educated young and growing labor force, and it stands to benefit from a demographic dividend in

---

6 The more comprehensive index, including fuels would correspond much closer to the fluctuations in GDP share, but does not extend as far back as the non-fuel commodity index.
7 The Human Development Index was developed by the UNDP for its Human Development Reports.

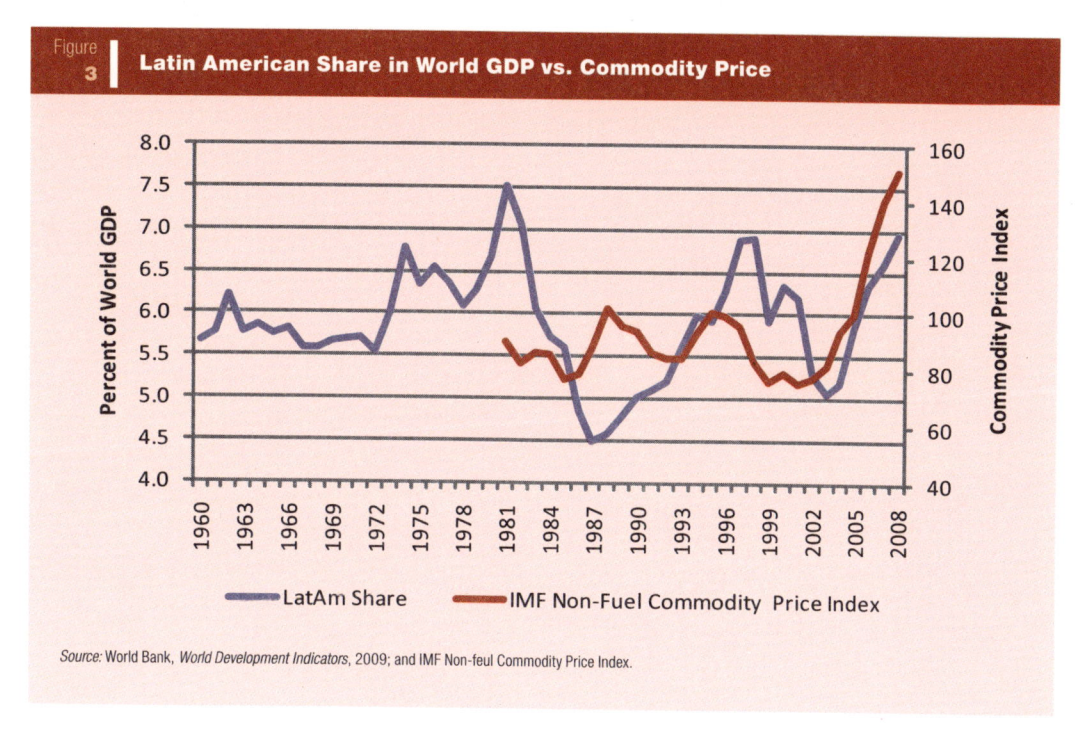

BREAKING AWAY FROM MEDIOCRITY TO A PROSPEROUS FUTURE   25

Figure 3: Latin American Share in World GDP vs. Commodity Price

Source: World Bank, *World Development Indicators*, 2009; and IMF Non-feul Commodity Price Index.

the short run. Latin America's labor force should grow by more than 1.5 percent a year over the next 15 years, with population growth at just over 1.0 percent. So, the ratio of working age population to total population is on the upswing in the next two decades, although it will change subsequently.

Poverty has been reduced after years of difficulty associated with the lost decade of the eighties, a period of adjustment and reconversion that was implemented in the 1990s with a period of macroeconomic strengthening and structural reforms. The numbers are now in line with what can be expected to be consistent with Latin America per capita income.

Now, after many years of misguided policies and poor performance, the region has much stronger fundamentals. Today, the issues of inflation, balance of payments fragility, and

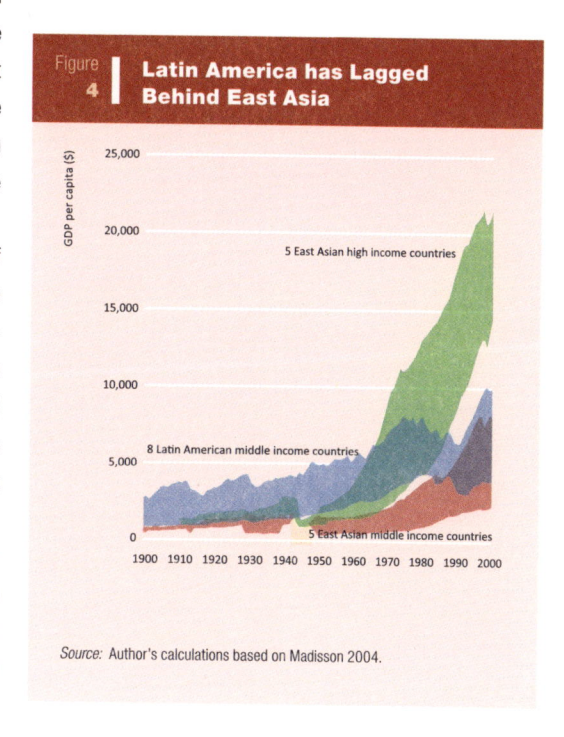

Figure 4: Latin America has Lagged Behind East Asia

Source: Author's calculations based on Madisson 2004.

Figure 5: Percentage of Years Since 1981 with Growth Below 1 and 2%

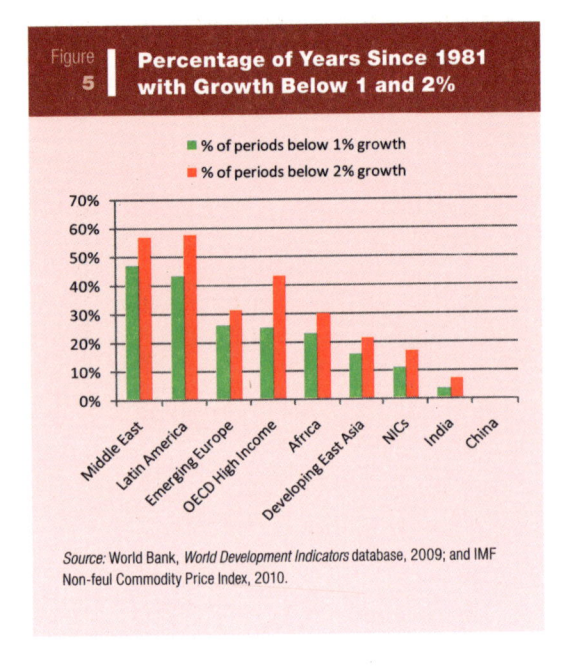

- % of periods below 1% growth
- % of periods below 2% growth

(Categories: Middle East, Latin America, Emerging Europe, OECD High Income, Africa, Developing East Asia, NICs, India, China)

Source: World Bank, *World Development Indicators* database, 2009; and IMF Non-feul Commodity Price Index, 2010.

broad fiscal imbalances seem to have been overcome, even though not everywhere and not permanently. While the recovery from the current crisis seems to be proceeding at a relatively slow pace, the region possibly suffered less than most, with a few notable exceptions, like Mexico. While this may have reflected to some extent a rebound of commodity prices, it also is accounted for by the regained strength and the relatively solid performance of a well-managed, although small, financial system.[8]

These developments have placed the region's economies in a complacent plateau, focusing on their progress with respect to other Latin American countries and not with respect to the world. But underlying these achievements, Latin America is falling behind as previously noted, and the prospects for a sustained catch up, as happened in the past, are poor without a change in strategic attitude. The current attitude will lead to a continued and continuous decline in the importance of Latin America in the world, and with increasing gaps in terms of per capita income.

While progress has been made regarding poverty, income distribution in Latin America shows the highest concentration, with correspondingly the highest Gini coefficients of any region (Figure 6). The poverty numbers suggest that the problems of distribution are between the highest income earners and the rest of the total population including the growing regional middle class, and not the poorest of the poor. The actual picture is even more marked, however, as the Gini statistics fail to capture total income, particularly the unrecorded income of the very rich. To some extent, this reflects a significant level of exclusion at the lower levels of income and high concentration at the top, with average wealth levels among the very rich well in excess of that in other areas of the world, including in the US and

---

[8] The depth and the duration of the 2008-09 global recession will remain debated amongst academics and policy makers. Many took the experience of the Great Depression as indicative of what may happen. Then, as well as in the post-World War II recession, growth exceeded its long run average during a recovery phase before returning to trend, compensating for the down period. There was little impact on permanent long-run income levels. But that period was exceptional, given the level of destruction of human and physical capital during the subsequent war. Separating the "natural" recovery from the Great Depression from the effects of World War II spending is almost impossible. The relevance of that recovery for the current crisis may well be questioned.

Notwithstanding, the post-War experience with recessions is that as the recovery gathers steam, countries grow faster than potential output. In general most analysts do not foresee a permanent impact of the current recession. As the crisis abates, growth is likely to exceed its long run average during a recovery phase before returning to trend, compensating for the down period.

The IMF has reviewed the history of financial crises and concludes that while medium term growth recovers to trend levels, output remains below trend, by an average of 10 percent. However, the IMF analysis is simply a description of what has happened compared to pre-crisis trends. This kind of analysis has a bias: the pre-crisis trend (which the IMF takes as the period covering the ten to three years prior to the crisis) may be part of a longer-term boom which in turn precipitates the crisis, and should not be counted as the long-term trend growth rate. All these caveats underline an essential point: the forward-looking figures are scenarios and not a projection or forecast.

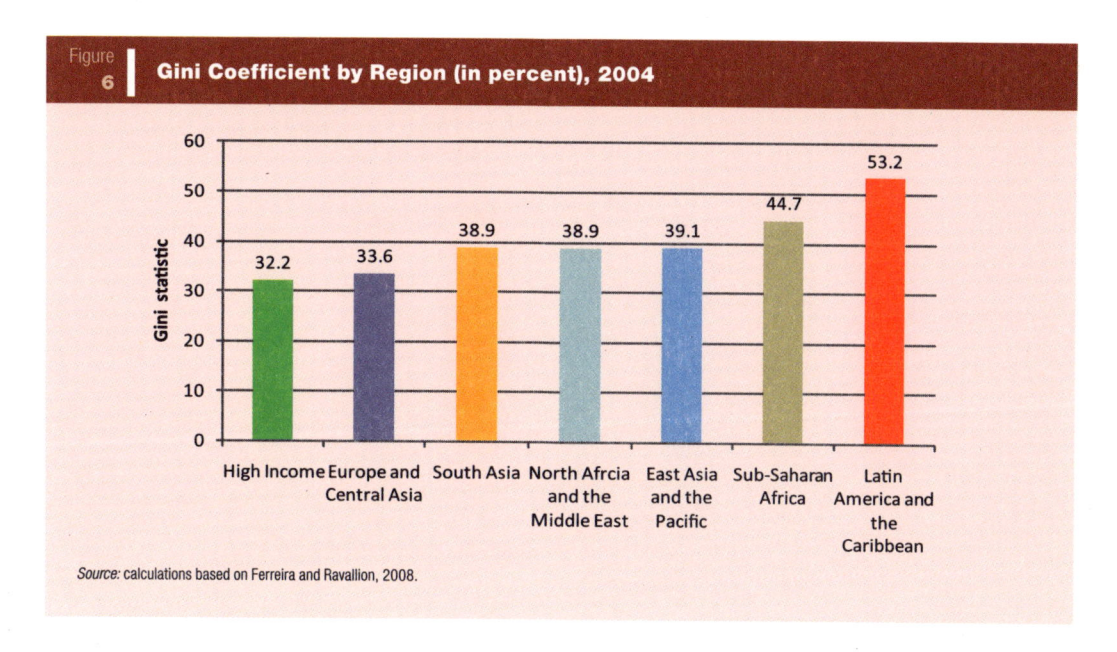

Figure 6 | Gini Coefficient by Region (in percent), 2004

Region	Gini statistic
High Income	32.2
Europe and Central Asia	33.6
South Asia	38.9
North Africa and the Middle East	38.9
East Asia and the Pacific	39.1
Sub-Saharan Africa	44.7
Latin America and the Caribbean	53.2

Source: calculations based on Ferreira and Ravallion, 2008.

Europe.[9] Moreover, serious inclusion problems remain for ethnic and cultural groups of indigenous people and afro-descendants.

Latin America's increasing openness to world trade has been a positive step toward increasing capital inflows. Gains have been concentrated in areas of traditional comparative advantage and not in new and more dynamic areas. The degree of openness, though significantly higher than in the past, is still much lower than the NICs and other countries in Asia (Figure 7).

Economic growth has accelerated in recent years but current policies seem to allow for an increase in income of no more than 3.5 percent a year. Just to preserve Latin America's share in world GDP, economic growth would have to increase to an average 5 percent a year. This cannot be achieved within the current strategic and policy framework, or with current levels of savings and investment.

Productivity and its Effect on Performance

A key underlying factor in Latin America's performance has been the region's productivity, as reflected in the measure of total factor productivity (TFP). The components of growth of Latin America, other selected regions, and the world are shown in Table 2. Latin America's GDP growth has been very similar to that of the world but the components of growth are very different. While Latin America has registered higher growth rates in both capital and labor, its performance with respect to TFP-negative growth has been much poorer.

In 1980, the region's TFP averaged around 40 percent of the US, which was high relative to other developing countries. As shown in Figure 8, TFP has remained virtually stagnant over the past three

---

9 An annual survey by Cap Gemini, a consultancy, and Merryl Lynch, now owned by Bank of America, shows that the average level of assets of high worth individuals with assets in excess of $1 million (excluding their residence, and land holdings) in Latin America, is two times higher than the average world-wide.

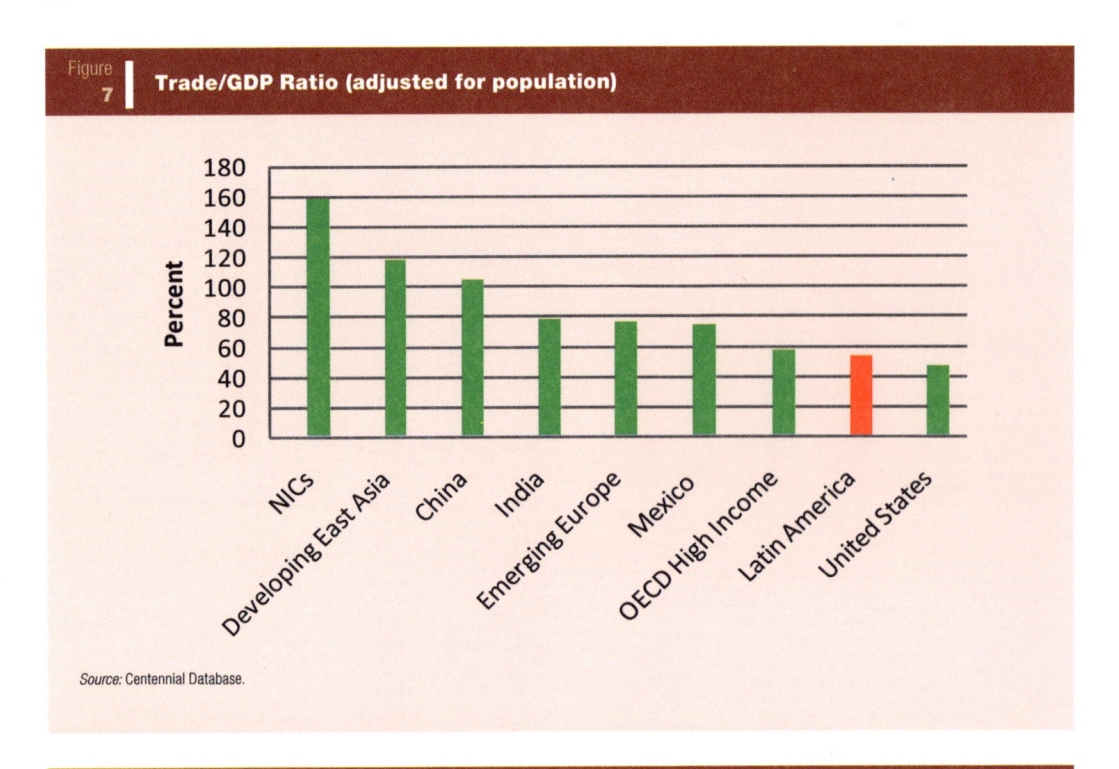

Figure 7: Trade/GDP Ratio (adjusted for population)

[Bar chart showing percentages by region:
- NICs: ~160%
- Developing East Asia: ~120%
- China: ~105%
- India: ~80%
- Emerging Europe: ~78%
- Mexico: ~75%
- OECD High Income: ~60%
- Latin America: ~55%
- United States: ~48%]

Source: Centennial Database.

Table 2: Average Factor and GDP (PPP) Growth Rates, 1979-2009, selected regions

	Capital	Labor	TFP	GDP (PPP)	GDP (MER)
Developed Countries	2.93%	0.95%	0.76%	2.45%	2.40%
Developing Asia	6.36%	1.92%	3.60%	7.08%	6.09%
Developing Middle East and North Africa	3.32%	3.53%	-0.38%	3.21%	1.82%
Sub Saharan Africa	2.56%	2.84%	0.13%	2.95%	1.64%
Latin America	**3.17%**	**2.73%**	**-0.14%**	**2.74%**	**2.77%**
World	2.34%	1.78%	0.79%	3.06%	2.78%

Source: Authors' Caluculations

decades. In 1987, South Korea's technology level was almost exactly the same as Brazil's, the technology leader in Latin America in the 1970s; Malaysia's level was at 60 percent and Thailand's at 30 percent of Brazil's. By 2009, Korea's TFP was 60 percent higher, Malaysia had almost caught up, and Thailand's was at over 55 percent. Furthermore, the rates of change in TFP of Latin American economies compared very poorly to China and India; while China's TFP more than quadrupled and India's

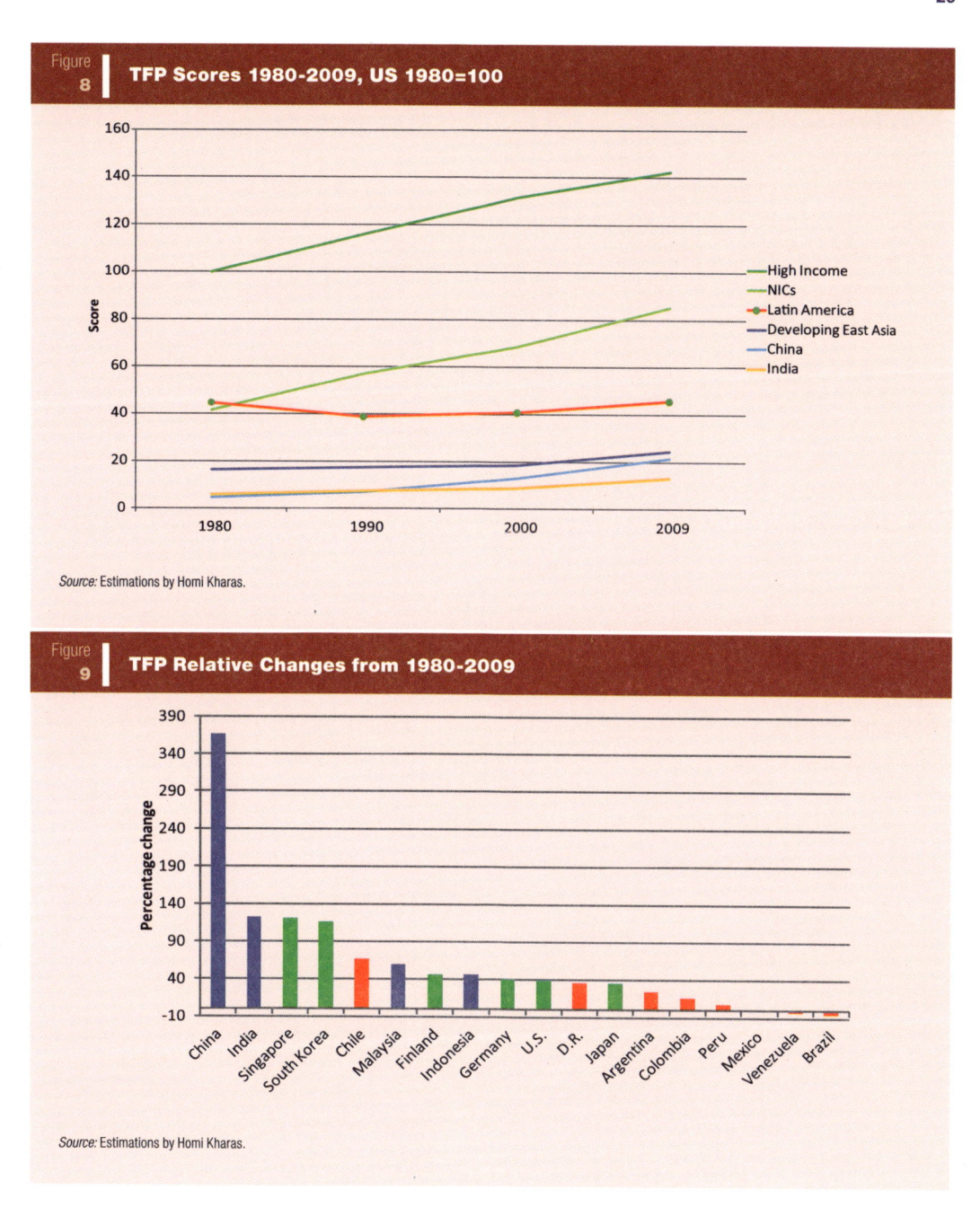

Figure 8 | TFP Scores 1980-2009, US 1980=100

- High Income
- NICs
- Latin America
- Developing East Asia
- China
- India

Source: Estimations by Homi Kharas.

Figure 9 | TFP Relative Changes from 1980-2009

(China, India, Singapore, South Korea, Chile, Malaysia, Finland, Indonesia, Germany, U.S., D.R., Japan, Argentina, Colombia, Peru, Mexico, Venezuela, Brazil)

Source: Estimations by Homi Kharas.

doubled, the TFP in the Latin America regions was virtually stagnant (Figure 9.)

The region's poor TFP performance reflects a number of factors. Most importantly, the low level of competition—domestically and through trade—has limited the incentives for higher productivity and competitiveness. This may also explain the low level of investment in the region compared with many other parts of the world. New capital in itself does not entail improved TFP. However, the technology incorporated with new higher-quality investment, and the accompanying improvement in human capital will result in higher productivity and growth. Thus, the low level of investment has resulted in a slower process of innovation.

Other aspects with direct impact on TFP include the poor overall performance with respect to the quality of education relative to international standards (Figure 10), and low technological readiness compared to other regions (Figure 11). The quality of infrastructure, reflecting the low levels of investment, compares poorly with other regions (Figure 12). Economies in the region are also hampered by the business environment, as is captured in the Ease of Doing Business indicator (Figure 13). The regulatory environment has resulted in the highest degree of informality of all regions (Figure 14). All of these factors have contributed to the poor competitiveness of the region (Figure 15).

In addition, the holdings of assets abroad, excluding direct investment by local companies, is very significant for some of the countries in the region, sometimes exceeding the level of debt and FDI of the countries themselves. These holdings had been a reaction to poor policies—only recently corrected—and detract from the growth potential of the region. Should sound macroeconomic policies persist, repatriation of these holdings could be a major source of the much needed capital and technology transformation.

A Focus on Ideology versus Outcome

A main characteristic of the economic history of Latin America has been the emphasis on ideology and ideological policies, as opposed to Asia's emphasis on outcomes. Speaking in simplistic terms, the approach to growth in many Latin American countries can be construed as "get the policies right and growth will follow". That applies particularly to macroeconomic policies and Latin America has an enviable track record of finally putting its fiscal and monetary house in order, with Chile leading the pack of those countries developing fiscally responsible rules. But the results from such an approach have not been fully reflected in higher growth. Macroeconomic stability is a necessary component. However, for this to take place, there is a need for pragmatism and to have 'rapid growth' as the objective, which also means better education, infrastructure, etc.; and government support for better technology. Chile estimates its potential output growth to have fallen to 3.9 percent. For a country at its income level, a long-term growth of 5 percent per capita should be achievable.

The attitude in Latin America stands at odds with the leadership on growth that is one of the ingredients of long-term success identified by the Growth Commission. The Commission highlights the benefits of a national purpose in pursuing rapid growth, endorsed and sustained in a consensus among political parties. In East Asia, which is recovering rapidly from the Great Recession, the past year has been one of determined efforts at structural reform and reinvention to take advantage of the changing world environment. It is that single-minded focus on growth which appears to be one secret of Asian success stories. East Asian approaches can be characterized as "set a growth target and adjust policies to make sure it happens". There is a pragmatism that serves to overcome deeply-held beliefs when the growth engine is threatened.

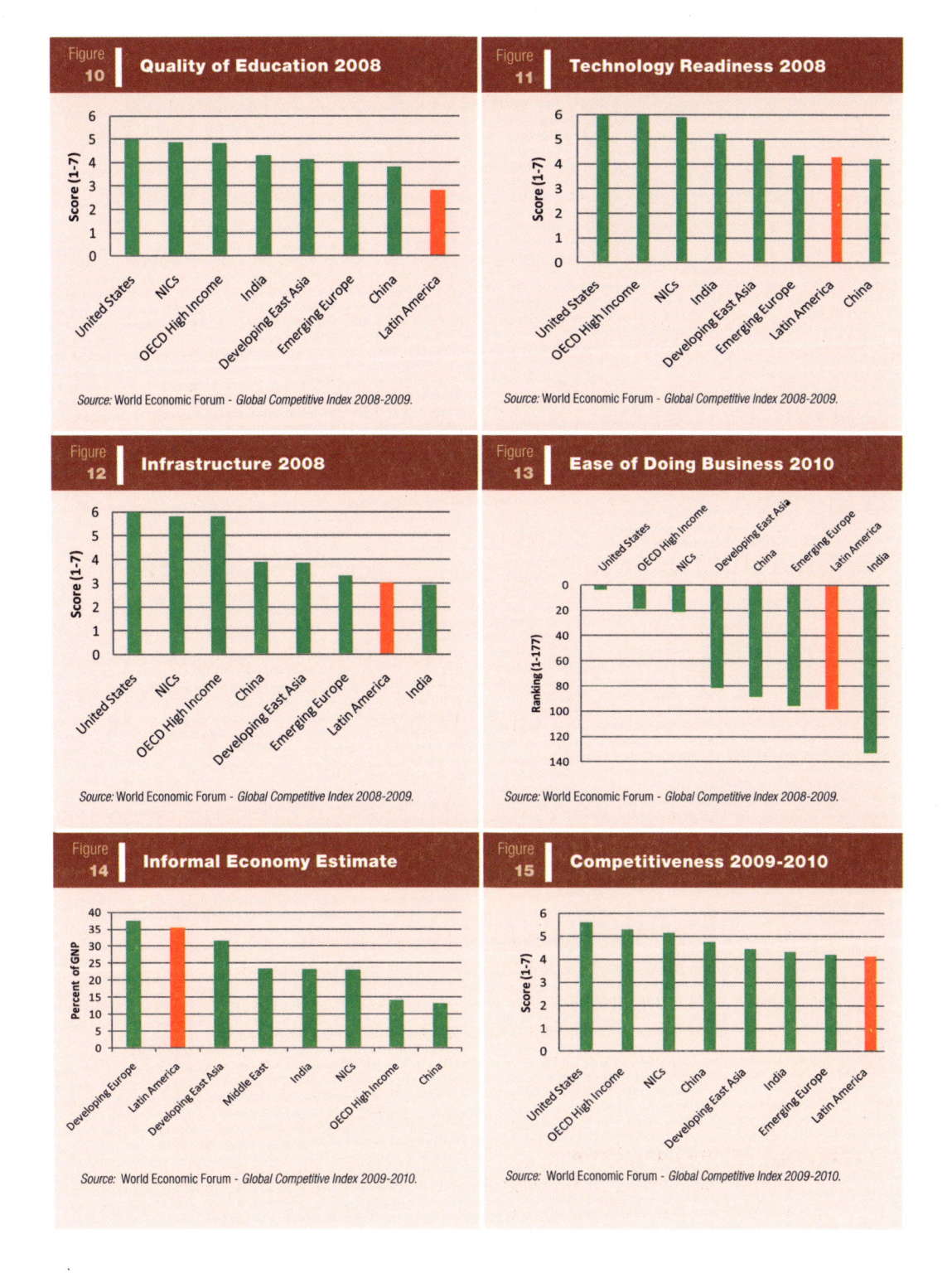

BREAKING AWAY FROM MEDIOCRITY TO A PROSPEROUS FUTURE   31

Figure 10 | Quality of Education 2008

Score (1-7): United States ~5.0, NICs ~4.9, OECD High Income ~4.8, India ~4.3, Developing East Asia ~4.2, Emerging Europe ~4.0, China ~3.8, Latin America ~2.8

Source: World Economic Forum - *Global Competitive Index 2008-2009.*

Figure 11 | Technology Readiness 2008

Score (1-7): United States ~6.0, OECD High Income ~6.0, NICs ~5.9, India ~5.2, Developing East Asia ~5.0, Emerging Europe ~4.3, Latin America ~4.2, China ~4.2

Source: World Economic Forum - *Global Competitive Index 2008-2009.*

Figure 12 | Infrastructure 2008

Score (1-7): United States ~6.0, NICs ~5.8, OECD High Income ~5.8, China ~3.9, Developing East Asia ~3.8, Emerging Europe ~3.3, Latin America ~3.0, India ~3.0

Source: World Economic Forum - *Global Competitive Index 2008-2009.*

Figure 13 | Ease of Doing Business 2010

Ranking (1-177): United States ~5, OECD High Income ~20, NICs ~20, Developing East Asia ~80, China ~90, Emerging Europe ~95, Latin America ~100, India ~133

Source: World Economic Forum - *Global Competitive Index 2008-2009.*

Figure 14 | Informal Economy Estimate

Percent of GNP: Developing Europe ~37, Latin America ~36, Developing East Asia ~31, Middle East ~24, India ~23, NICs ~23, OECD High Income ~14, China ~13

Source: World Economic Forum - *Global Competitive Index 2009-2010.*

Figure 15 | Competitiveness 2009-2010

Score (1-7): United States ~5.5, OECD High Income ~5.2, NICs ~5.1, China ~4.7, Developing East Asia ~4.4, India ~4.3, Emerging Europe ~4.2, Latin America ~4.0

Source: World Economic Forum - *Global Competitive Index 2009-2010.*

A major lesson of the East Asian success in the past fifty years is that Latin America needs to pursue a longer term and more pragmatic and non-ideological set of policies, based on market principles and measured government intervention, but with the understanding that the policies should be aiming at attaining commonly agreed sustainable social and economic outcomes. Under this pragmatic approach, policies and the mix of government-private sector association would be adjusted as needed to realize the outcomes sought under the shared vision (while respecting the principles of good governance, transparency, and with a good understanding of the costs of these policies).

Of equal importance, there must be a consensus on policies and objectives within the region toward better integrating production processes across regional economies. This is in contrast to the current practice, where policies in one country are introduced at the expense of others rather than seeking to exploit the comparative advantages of each country for an adequate integration with the rest of the world.

In summary, Latin America presents a mixed picture, but with a clear tendency toward a loss of relevance and relative importance in the world economy. Today, Latin America is becoming an increasingly left-behind continent, for good and for bad reasons:

- The region has been lagging in terms of growth, with the possible exception of Chile, Peru, and other small countries. Even Chile's growth performance is slowing.
- With the clear exception of Haiti, now even more so, and to a lesser extent Bolivia, Honduras and Nicaragua, Latin America is too prosperous for continued concessional aid, which is good in terms of poverty but not so in terms of financing.
- There are no major crises of macroeconomic management, and even those that still are present to some extent, like in Argentina, Ecuador and Venezuela, are generally more manageable and less traumatic than in the past. This is good from a fundamental growth perspective, but may reduce the incentives for reform in some of the countries as it is not seen as urgent.
- The times of easy growth have led to relatively high degrees of urbanization, moderately good levels of basic education and a limited technology gap.

However, the earlier gains are being eroded. Moreover, the region seems to be mired in the Middle Income Trap (see Box 1):

- Too rich to be globally competitive in basic manufacturing.
- Too poor to be competitive in advanced materials and innovation.

It is necessary to make fundamental policy changes, strengthen and rationalize institutions, and streamline the political process to a significant degree. The required changes are doable, but they require pragmatism and consensus on objectives and, of equal importance, significant and drastic action now.

The Prospects for the Long Term

Latin America's per capita GDP in 2009 was US$10,544 (in current PPP dollars), compared with $36,953 for the advanced economies, $13,408 for Central and Eastern Europe and $4,436 for

> **Box 1 | Latin America in the Middle Income Trap?**
>
> Few countries sustain high growth for more than a generation, and even fewer continue their high growth rates once they reach middle income status. The Commission on Growth and Development's recent review of growth in developing countries (*The Growth Report, A. Michael Spence, 2008)* identified just 13 countries that sustained growth of more than 7 percent for at least 25 years in the postwar period. They have five common characteristics: openness to the global economy in knowledge and trade; macroeconomic stability; a "future orientation", exemplified by high rates of saving and investment; a reliance on markets and market-based prices to allocate resources; and leadership committed to growth and inclusion with a reasonable capacity for administration. These success factors, deep-rooted in local institutions, are necessary, but not sufficient, for continued growth. Some countries with these characteristics grew fast, but could not sustain that growth.
>
> Even among the 13 star performers, growth has been uneven. Some East Asian middle income countries suffered severe setbacks in 1997-1998, and may not recover past rapid growth. Brazil, whose growth performance between 1950 and 1980 qualified it as a growth star, then suffered disastrous inflationary episodes and low growth in the 1980s and 1990s. Reaching incomes associated with the advanced countries is uncommon: only a few of the high-growth countries did so including the NICs. More common is for growth to slow markedly on reaching middle income. Many Latin American and Middle Eastern countries suffered the fate of falling into a slow-growth trap once they reached middle-income levels.
>
> Some features differentiating middle income from low income growth are clear. Growth tends to become more capital intensive and skill intensive. The domestic market expands and becomes a more important engine, especially for service growth. Wages start to rise, most rapidly for highly skilled workers, and shortages can emerge. The traditional low-wage manufacturing for export model does not work well for middle income countries. They seem to become trapped, unless they change strategies and move up the value chain. Cost advantages in labor-intensive sectors, such as the manufactured exports that once drove growth, start to decline in comparison with lower wage poor country producers. At the same time, middle income countries do not have the property rights, contract enforcement, capital markets, track record of successful venture capital and invention, or critical mass of highly skilled people to grow through major innovations, like affluent countries. Caught between these two groups, middle income countries can become trapped without a viable high-growth strategy.
>
> This seems to be what has happened to Latin America. In many countries, wages are too high to be globally competitive in basic manufacturing—the collapse of Latin America's garments producers after protection was withdrawn is proof of that. Yet, Latin America does not have the R&D and innovation capabilities that allow it to develop new products in advanced areas (exceptions are by now familiar:

Developing Asia. Based on this performance, Latin America is clearly a middle income region, but far behind the lowest "advanced economy" in the IMF's list—Portugal with a GDP (PPP) per capita of $21,729. Existing policies and conditions in the region have been consistent with a rate of growth well below average for the rest of the world. While growth of income per capita can be considered reasonable by many, at somewhat more than 2 percent a year, the picture is far from satisfactory when compared to the rest of the world.

This study makes projections through 2040, on the basis of a world growth model described in detail in Chapter 2. As a long-run model, the results and assumptions are stylized, and are not intended to predict the future, but to provide a context for policy formulation and reform.

Global Growth Results

The global economy fell to $57.9 trillion in 2009, measured at market exchange rates[10], dominated by the United States with $14.3 trillion, just over one-quarter of the global total. In current PPP terms, global output is almost $70 trillion. North America (24 percent), Europe (27 percent) and Asia (34 percent) dominate the world economy. Latin America's share today is about 8.5 percent.

The BRICs accounted for about 24 percent of 2009 global output in PPP terms, a post-war historical high. This is a recent phenomenon, one driven largely by China, which has expanded its global market share to almost 13 percent. Even at market exchange rates, China is set to overtake Japan as the world's second largest economy, either this year or next. Importantly, the rich countries of the world only account for 53 percent of global output now, compared to 70 percent in 1990.

By 2040, 30 years from now, the global economy may be $258 trillion in 2005 PPP dollars.[11] Such a world is very different from the one we see today. It is significantly wealthier, with per capita incomes averaging $30,000 as compared to $8,000 today. The economic center of gravity would shift to Asia, which accounts today for 34 percent of global activity, but by 2040 could account for 61 percent of global output. Three giant economies, China, India and Japan, would lead Asia's resurgence. But other large countries like Indonesia and Vietnam would also have significant economic mass. Even Thailand and Malaysia could have economies larger than France has today.

The rise of Asia would not be unprecedented. Indeed, it would bring Asia's economic share into line with its share of world population and restore the geographical balance of global economic activity to that prevailing in the 18th and early 19th centuries, before the Industrial Revolution led to the great divergence of incomes across countries.

The converse of Asia's rise would be a fall in the share of the G7 economies. Their global income share has already fallen to new post-World War II lows, and by 2040 it could be just 21 percent.

To appreciate the likelihood of this enormous change, consider the following facts. Taking out the effect of general inflation, the global economy reached $20 trillion, in terms of 2005 PPP dollars, in 1977. It took 19 years to double to $40 trillion by 1996—with 3.6 percent annual growth. Over the next 10 years, from 1996 to 2006, annual growth has been 3.7 percent. To get to $258 trillion by 2040, global growth would need to be 4.7 percent.

The reason for expecting an acceleration of global growth is that the share of rapidly growing economies has now risen to almost one-half of total output, while the share of slow growing countries has fallen. As faster growing countries also tend to have appreciating exchange rates, global output growth at market prices will accelerate simply because the fastest growing economies in the world (China and India) are also becoming ever-larger shares of global output at market exchange rates.

---

10 Using 2009 constant dollars.
11 Natural resource constraints and the effects of climate change have been ignored in this scenario. This may prove to be quite unrealistic but to take these into account would require a far more sophisticated model of global growth.

The model assumes that "advanced" country real potential output growth will slow in the next 30 years to 2.3 percent, from 2.5 percent over the last 10 years. Meanwhile the "convergers" could also slow to 8.2 percent, from the 8.4 percent over the last 10 years.

One reason that developing countries are growing faster than developed countries is that they are younger, still at an early phase in their demographic transition. Global demographic shifts are inexorably changing the distribution of global economic activity. Today's rich countries accounted for 22 percent of the world's people in 1965, but only account for 15 percent today, and their share is forecast to shrink to 13 percent of the world total by 2040. Overall, the world will add 2 billion people by 2040. But the population in today's rich countries will grow by only an estimated 100 million. Ninety-five percent of the population increase (excluding migration) will be in developing countries, mostly in Africa.

Latin America under the Business-as-Usual Scenario

How does Latin America fare under the business-as-usual scenario? Not surprisingly, the answer is average. In 2005 PPP terms, Latin America may grow by 2.2 percent per capita in the long-term, but the world will be growing faster. Latin America's income may stay at a constant ratio to advanced countries, with Mexico and Brazil possibly posting growth rates close to that of the United States, but this performance means that Latin America may slowly fade in global relevance, especially in comparison to East and South Asia. At market exchange rates, a similar pattern holds. Latin America simply grows more or less at the same pace as the United States, and falls behind the rest of the world. This is all the more disappointing as Latin America is potentially able to enjoy a demographic dividend in the coming years—its labor force will grow more rapidly than its population for the next thirty years.

Table 3 shows a trajectory of key variables for Latin America and the rest of the world under this business-as-usual scenario. The table is deliberately stylized. It shows how a business-as-usual scenario implies a growing gap between Latin America and much of the rest of the world, especially the advanced countries. The table also shows the possibilities for Latin America, exemplified by Chile. Chile is the only Latin American country in the sample to meet the criterion for inclusion in the "convergers" category of having a track record of at least 3.5 percent per capita income growth over the past twenty-five years, at least prior to the recent earthquake, and as recognized by its accession to the OECD.[12]

But Brazil, Mexico and other Latin American countries do not meet the criterion. What is shown in the business-as-usual scenario is what would happen if they continue down a path of relatively low TFP growth and relatively low capital investment. At the end of the day, the policies which will generate convergence depend on these two key variables.

Latin America Convergence Scenario and its Payoff

If a few key economies in Latin America could enter the club of "convergers" it could make a radical difference to the region's prospects. To investigate this, the model was re-run with four major Latin

---

12 It is important to point out that Mexico is also an OECD member, and has been characterized recently by a non-converging performance.

Table 3 | Latin America—A Fading Global Force

	2009	2040
Global Output (PPP)	$62.8 trillion	$258 trillion
Latin America share	8.7%	5.3%
Global Output growth (PPP) a.	3.75%	4.47%
Latin America	3.03%	2.91%
Average Income (real GDP at 2009 US$)		
World	$8,500	$30,500
Rich countries	$40,000	$85,700
Latin America	$7,000	$15,500
Mexico	$8,000	$19,400
Brazil	$9,300	$20,200
Chile	$9,500	$77,400
Rank in world (absolute GDP) size		
Brazil	10	16
Mexico	12	18
Capital-Labor ratio (per person)		
World	$32,700	$79,600
Rich countries	$146,000	$325,000
LATAM	$20,000	$42,400
TFP (US 2009=100)		
United States	100	150.3
Mexico	31.9	47.7
Brazil	29.9	44.6
Chile	37.8	91.6

a. Growth rate taken from the preceding 25 year period.
Note: All figures are in constant 2009 US$.
Source: World Bank - WDI, Brookings Institution, and author's estimates.

American countries moving into the "convergers" category, meaning they undertake the policy reforms needed to benefit from catch-up growth. The scenario is incomplete in the sense that investment rates in the selected countries would probably also increase in such a scenario, but this is not modeled. Nor is the spill-over effect onto neighboring countries which could also be substantial.

Two large and two mid-sized countries are selected as the four newly-converging Latin American economies, joining Chile in this classification. The choice is arbitrary, and implies that countries representing seventy percent of the region's economy adopt good policies. By 2040, the difference to the region is enormous. The growth acceleration to a level of 6.5 percent at market exchange rates is simply the result of faster TFP growth in the selected countries. With catch-up, selected countries could expect TFP growth of 2-3 percent per year. By 2040, the major economies would have made significant progress in terms of technology.

The convergence scenario indicates the dependence of the Latin American region on the performance of its major economies, as well as the critical issue of capitalizing on the advantages of backwardness in raising growth. Recall that the convergence scenario simply attributes to major Latin American economies the same rate of growth of technological catch-up as in the rest of the converging world. That is to say, it is an estimate of what can be considered as the potential growth for these countries. Compounded over thirty years, the impact is significant. Regional output could be three times higher by 2040, and per capita incomes could be higher by almost that much. If the region could achieve these kinds of growth rates, it would have income levels of about half of that of the US by 2040. The richer countries of the region would catch up rapidly with the United States.

Figures 16 and 17 show a comparison of different scenarios—not based on running the model of the global economy—for illustrative purposes. As compared to a GDP per capita of $13,000 in the business-as-usual scenario, the region would reach a level of over $40,000 under convergence. The region's share of the global economy in 2040 would be as higher than 10 percent under the convergence scenario versus only 4 percent under business-as-usual.

The convergence scenario presented above is far from easy to achieve. Latin America has seen many examples where fast-growing countries suddenly found themselves in a crisis, frequently self-made, and not growing at the rate they used to. Argentina over more than half a century, Mexico after

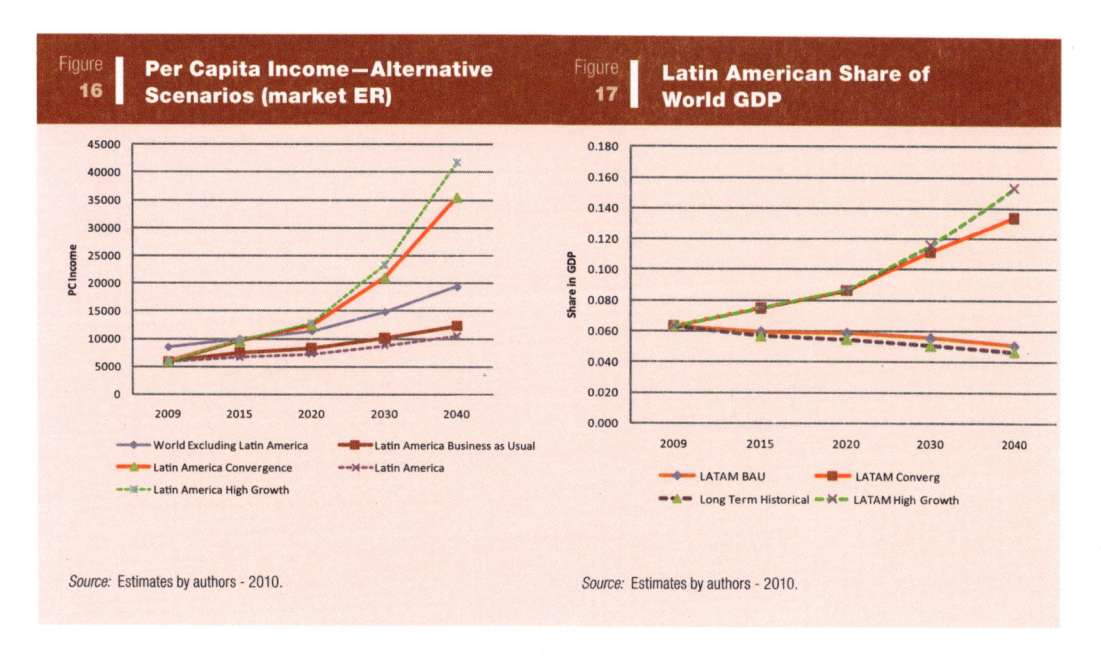

Figure 16 | Per Capita Income—Alternative Scenarios (market ER)

Source: Estimates by authors - 2010.

Figure 17 | Latin American Share of World GDP

Source: Estimates by authors - 2010.

the 1960s, Brazil more recently, and even the region's stellar performer, Chile, have seen a decline in growth.

Brazil provides a good illustration. It grew at almost 6 percent a year for almost a century. In 1965 it was a prosperous developing country with a per capita income of $1,800 (2008 dollars). It continued to grow until 1978, when it reached $5,500 per capita, with average growth of almost 9.5 percent a year. But then Brazil entered a period of relative stagnation. It did not regain its 1978 per capita income until 1995 and then only briefly in the burst of activity that followed the end of high inflation and the beginning of stabilization. It was only with the commodity boom in 2006 that Brazil again surpassed its 1978 income. But, the current global economic crisis and resultant drop in commodity prices has again blunted, though temporarily, this recent resurgence. After a century of growth, Brazil spent nearly 30 years mired in the middle income trap without further improvement in its average living standards. Although recent growth has been better, Brazil has still not demonstrated a track record of sustained fast growth that would allow it to converge rapidly with advanced economies.

Three assumptions support the convergence scenario:
1. The world is in the midst of a major restructuring—with the relative economic weight of developing countries in general and Asia in particular, set to continue becoming larger—and this restructuring can continue to proceed peacefully.
2. The current financial turmoil is being managed well, with global growth resuming and the existence of firmer principles governing the financial world. Still, there are considerable doubts about the pace of economic growth in the years ahead, with some likelihood that the average rate of potential growth for the world may decline.
3. The difficulties that many Latin American economies have had in becoming advanced are due to policy and strategy shortcomings—and are not immutable on account of natural, social, and ethnic characteristics.

IV. A Strategic Framework for Convergence:
A Shared, More Ambitious Vision for the Region

Given Latin America's rich natural endowments, there is no reason why Latin America cannot do as well as East Asia. Indeed, as demonstrated by the successful Asian countries, the region's destiny is firmly dependent on its own actions. Only through its own efforts will the region prosper. To do so, all concerned—governments, bureaucracy, the business community, academia, think tanks, media, civil society and other opinion makers as well as multilateral agencies active in the region—must adopt a laser-like focus on simultaneously achieving a much more inclusive and equitable society and much higher economic growth. The region's leaders must aim much higher, be pragmatic and focus single-mindedly on achieving this vision. Such a vision, and a sincere commitment to realizing it, must be shared both within the countries themselves and across the region as a whole. This commonly shared vision must be accompanied by a very different mindset across the political and social landscape: abandonment of the past ideological divides and adoption of pragmatism, as has been the case in

Box 2 | What Makes East Asia Different From Latin America?

Latin America's loss of its long standing position as the most prosperous and promising developing region is best illustrated by comparing its economic and social development relative to East Asia in general, and the so called NICs more specifically.

Between 1965 and 2009, the per capita income of the NICs grew at an average annual rate of 6.8 percent, while Latin America recorded a growth rate of only 3.7 percent. As a result, in terms of per capita income, the NICs—that lagged well behind Latin America in 1965 ($1,778 vs. $3,403)—leapfrogged over the region ($20,308 vs. $7,028 in 2009).[1] This illustrates how the most dynamic economies in Asia, now joined by China and India, have continued to converge with the United States, while most Latin economies have become mired in the middle-income trap. Other striking differences between East Asia and Latin America include:

- All successful East Asian countries, as well as China and India, have achieved major gains in total factor productivity (TFP) while Latin American countries have remained stagnant. The two largest economies (Brazil and Mexico) have even regressed somewhat.
- East Asian countries have much higher savings rates (51 percent vs. 23 percent of GDP) and investment rates than Latin America.
- East Asia has placed much greater emphasis on human development and put a high premium on meritocracy in its education system. It has achieved much higher educational standards and graduates a significantly higher number of engineers and scientists than Latin America, in relative terms.
- East Asia's investment, public as well as private, in infrastructure has been much higher than in Latin America, and it has deeper financial markets, particularly non-bank financial institutions.
- NICs have much more open economies than Latin America, with total trade to GDP ratios of 159 percent vs. 41.5 percent for Latin America.
- The structure of production in East Asia has changed dramatically in the past forty years with the region becoming the manufacturing hub of the world, while Latin American economies remain highly dependent on commodities and agricultural products.
- Even as East Asian economies moved from low-income to middle-income and finally to upper middle-income status their income distribution and other social indicators have remained much more equitable than Latin America, which has the highest disparities of any region in the world. East Asia's more equitable distribution of incomes and assets allowed it to develop a large middle class as soon as the countries achieved middle-income status and this fast growing middle class became an engine of innovation, entrepreneurship and domestic consumption that fuelled further economic growth (see box on page 14). In contrast, Latin America's huge income disparities led to a much slower development of its middle class at similar national per capita income levels, even though the numbers are far from small.
- In the last decade, the institutional business and investment climate has been much more favorable in East Asia, thus helping to generate the growth momentum that can be observed today. The process has been market driven, helped but not explained by the emergence of China and its strong connections with some of the more advanced countries in the region.

---

1 In constant 2009 US$

Embraer in Brazil, wine and fruits in Chile and Argentina).

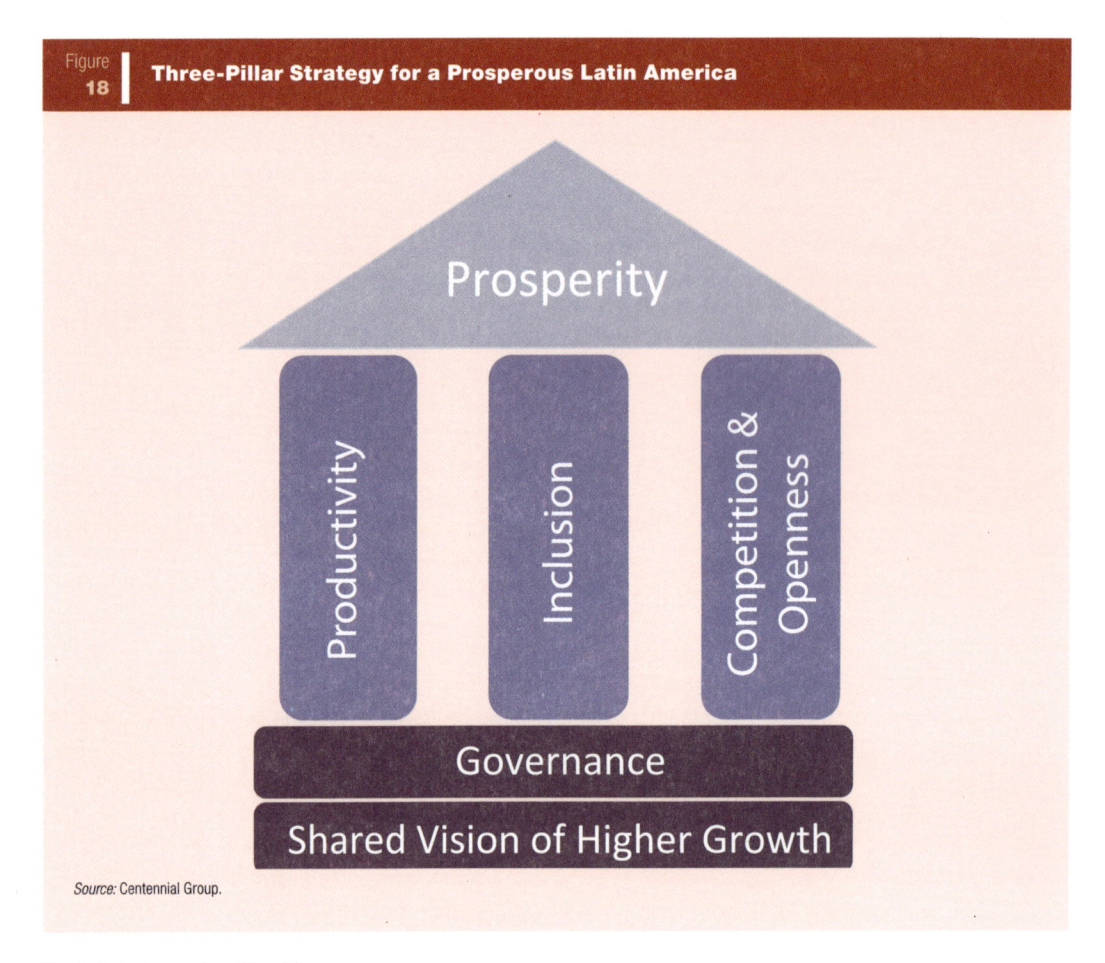

Figure 18. Three-Pillar Strategy for a Prosperous Latin America

A diagram depicting three pillars — Productivity, Inclusion, Competition & Openness — supporting a roof labeled Prosperity, with a base of Governance and Shared Vision of Higher Growth.

Source: Centennial Group.

East Asia (see also Box 2).

Given the diversity of the region and differing resource endowments, human capital, structure and efficiency of individual countries as well as vastly differing institutional capacities, it is neither prudent nor possible to lay out a detailed strategy for achieving this common vision across the entire region. That can only be done at the level of each individual country.

However, learning from the region's own experiences in the past forty years and contrasting them with East Asia, it is possible to define the broad contours of the strategy required to achieve this more ambitious vision. Latin America needs to adopt an approach that comprises three complementary pillars (Figure 18):

- More Inclusion
- Higher Productivity
- Greater Competition and Openness

Most importantly, actions under these three pillars will need to be underpinned by improved governance and accountability for results. As with many developing regions, Latin America's Achilles heel—the biggest hurdle to Latin America achieving a sustaining a more inclusive society and higher economic growth rate over the next thirty years—is its poor governance in all its facets.

Only through the pursuit of this three-pillar strategy will it be possible to visualize a prosperous Latin America.

1. More Inclusion

Latin America has recently made important strides in improving the conditions of its poor people. Nonetheless, income and wealth distribution remains highly skewed. Politically and socially, the current situation is unsustainable. Tackling structural inequities is therefore essential from the point of view of equity. But, as demonstrated by Asia, achieving a more equitable society is equally relevant to forging support for sound policies and thus sustaining growth over the longer term, including by expanding the size of the middle class.

With significant numbers of Latin Americans not fully integrated into the mainstream economy

Photo Credit: CAF

and society (indigenous people, afro-descendants and, to a large extent, women) and with current high degrees of informality, in the past the benefits of economic growth have not reached many citizens. This particularly affected those without European ethnicity, leading to the disillusionment of large proportions of the population with the current economic policies and institutions. Only significant progress toward a more inclusive society can lead to realistic prospects of sustained and sustainable growth over time for Latin America, as had been achieved in Asia.

Thus, contrary to the view that there is a trade-off between growth and equity, striving for a more inclusive society promises a win-win situation. The fundamental approach to achieving a more inclusive society will involve the removal of numerous current structural inequities, widening access to quality education and other public services including rural infrastructure, breaking the current economic dominance by entrenched vested interests, as well as ensuring jobs and finance to those who are today left at the margins of the society, toward building a large middle class. Such an approach must be clearly distinguished from, and goes well beyond, the ongoing efforts in countries such as Brazil and Mexico that have been generally successful in reducing poverty and indigence (See also Box 3 on

> **Box 3 — Importance of the Middle Class in Fueling Growth**
> **GDP Per Capita, 1979=09; 1994=100**
>
> In some middle-income countries, the domestic market can complement export markets as the economy matures and the local market becomes large. In most countries, domestic consumption typically starts to grow quickly when incomes per capita reach around $6,000 in PPP terms. This did not happen in Latin America, perhaps because of the uneven distribution of income.
>
> Compare Brazil with South Korea, for example. Brazil's growth started to slow after 1980, when it had reached a per capita income level of $7,600 (PPP). At that time, its middle class, defined as households with incomes of between $10 and $100 per capita per day, was just 29 percent of the population. This made it virtually impossible for the middle-class to drive further growth. In contrast, South Korea's income per capita reached $7,700 (PPP) in 1987. By that time, South Korea's evenly distributed growth had produced a sizeable middle class, which accounted for 53 percent of the population. The country capitalized on the demand from this large middle class to grow its service industries and create the building blocks for a knowledge economy. Today 94 percent of Korea's population is middle class.
>
> Japan also benefited from a sizeable middle class when growing from a middle income country to a rich one. In 1965, Japan's per capita income was $8,200 (PPP) and its middle class was 48 percent of the population. Japan was able to achieve per capita growth of 4.8 percent per year for the next twenty years.

the importance of the Middle Class).

2. Higher Productivity

Clearly, Latin America must strive harder to achieve a much higher economic growth than it has managed in the past forty years (and even in the last five years), while reducing the historic dependence of its economic fortunes on the ups and downs of international commodity prices. Certainly, the contribution of natural resources to the creation of wealth in the future must continue. Latin America would be ill-advised to turn its back on its natural endowment. However, as has been the case of other countries and regions with equivalent natural wealth, Latin America needs to broaden the base of its output and income, and better integrate its population to the benefits of economic growth. A more technology-intensive approach to these resources and a better integration within the region and with the world, supported by a more operationally educated and integrated labor force and a deepening of its capital base will be of the essence. Only in this way can the region break from its spotty and disappointing economic growth path.

In this context, the link between investment, total factor productivity (TFP) and growth is particularly important. Enhanced growth prospects need to be underpinned by higher TFP. Improvement in

TFP, in turn, is explained by the improvement in human capital and technological progress embodied in higher investment, supported by an environment and policies that promote higher investment.

The strategic framework to change Latin American prospects and preserve its relative importance is thus dependent on two central and interrelated issues: the quality of economic policies and the likely needed increase in investment levels in a number of specific priority areas (discussed further below). Together, these two factors would allow for the increase in total factor productivity that is essential for Latin America to preserve its relative importance. To do so, other countries in the region will need to join Chile and the club of converging economies.

In broad terms, investment in Latin America has hovered around 20 percent of GDP, more or less in line with the levels observed in the advanced economies and the Middle East, but far short of the level of around 35 percent observed in Developing Asia and the NICs (Figure 19). It should be noted that the current low levels of investment may reflect low returns from appreciated exchange rates and/or high and distorted taxes and other legislative and administrative barriers. While exchange rates may not seem overvalued from a general equilibrium balance of payments point of view, the current equilibrium may reflect existing inefficiencies, including a poor income distribution and exclusion. In fact, exchange rates may end up being more depreciated if distributional issues were not tackled in the current form, namely, through high taxes on imports. Such protectionist domestic policies tend to lead to an appreciation of the currency, although offset in some cases by taxation on exports.

In principle, a combination of adequate polices, and an associated level of investment of about 30 percent of GDP would provide for sustained growth. This level of investment would in practice entail a doubling of net investment (i.e. net of depreciation and obsolescence). The magnitude of the effort is very large, and could not be accomplished without a large increase in the ability of the government to increase its investment, and in the commitment of the private sector to the national and regional economy. Of course, these would be directly dependent on increased savings, both in the private and public sectors.

Within the broad investment magnitudes, it is clear that public finances would have to be made available in order to mobilize additional resources. While fiscal positions in Latin America have tended to strengthen, and became less dependent on foreign and domestic borrowing, public capital expenditure has not followed an equivalent behavior. Current expenditures and social programs have been given greater priority. Thus, any new growth strategy will need to consider a rebalancing of the current/capital expenditure mix. Moreover, the additional resources would have to be channeled in large part to infrastructure and other productivity-enhancing areas such as R&D, preferably with private support.

In the same context, it will be imperative for Latin America to promote savings as an essential component of increased investment. Savings rates in the region of about 20 percent of GDP compare with rates of over 30 percent in the NICs and close to 50 percent in China (Figure 20). However, studies carried out by the IDB (Haussman, Talvi and Gavin) strongly suggest that savings are dependent on economic growth, more than the other way around, at least initially. To that extent, the low level of savings registered in the region may reflect not so much an impediment to growth but a reaction to low

| Figure 19 | Investment (% of GDP) |

| Figure 20 | Savings (% of GDP) |

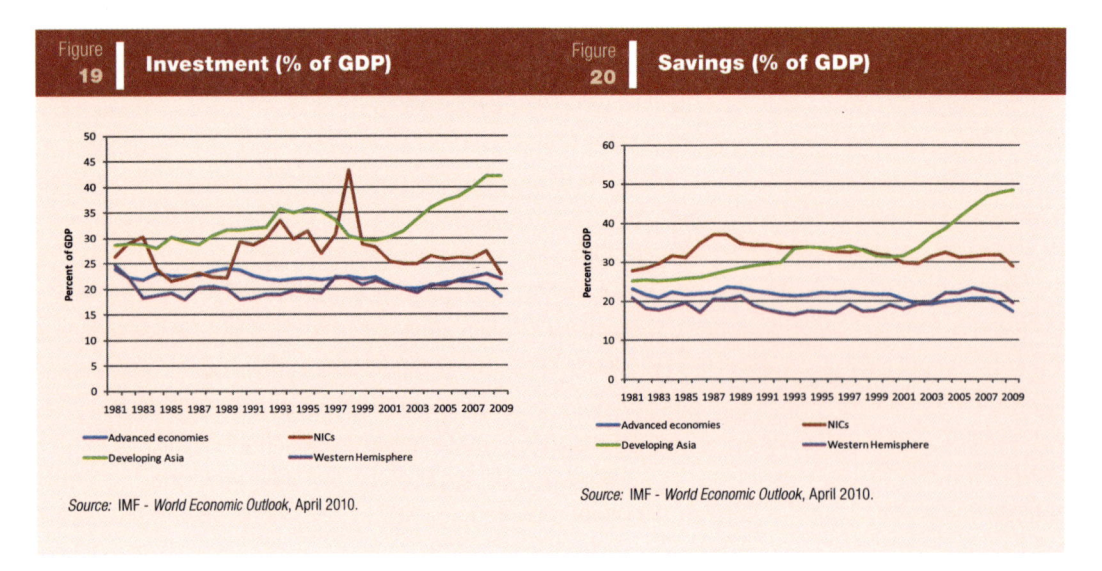

Source: IMF - *World Economic Outlook*, April 2010.

Source: IMF - *World Economic Outlook*, April 2010.

and volatile rates of growth[13], as documented by Latin America's record of numerous years of growth rates below 1 and 2 percent. In this sense, savings can be expected to pick up as conditions for growth improve over time. Of course, it will be necessary to address specific impediments to savings, in terms of the stability of the financial system, and a tax system and legal structure that creates incentives for capital flight, beyond the corporate investment observed more recently, and for investment in low-yielding but value-preserving sectors.

3. Greater Competition and Openness

The third pillar of the new strategy for the region should be promotion of much greater competition, both in internal markets and with external sources. Given the relatively smaller share of trade in total GDP, Latin American countries must give the highest priority to enhancing domestic competition, starting with the dismantling of monopolies—whether public or private—and enforcement of well-structured competition laws. In parallel, there is a need to promote and facilitate much greater openness to other countries in the region, closer links with fast-growing Asia that is emerging as the new center of gravity of the world economy, and the dismantling of remaining barriers to trade and investment with the global economy as a whole.

For many decades Latin America, like many other regions of the world, was characterized by an overwhelming presence of government in economic activity, well beyond a regulatory role. This was particularly the case in basic activities, such as: mining; metal and chemical production; agriculture; export activities; transportation; utilities; and telecommunications etc. The situation changed dramatically starting in the 1970s in Chile, and in subsequent decades in many countries including Argentina, Brazil, Colombia, Mexico and Peru. Most importantly, during this period there was a major effort at

---

13   National Accounts data may underestimate Latin America's savings ratios, as the sizeable capital flight has been made possible through under-recording of exports and over-recording of imports.

privatizing many activities that were not considered as central to the role of the state or of strategic relevance; this was accompanied by significant efforts to improve the operations of many State owned enterprises to help them compete better in a world marked by increased competition, and increasingly demanding financial markets. There were many different methods pursued for the sale of government assets, some of them seriously flawed. In some circumstances, public monopolies were replaced by private monopolies.

Under these circumstances, improved domestic competition remains a work in progress in the region. It is true that given the size of many of the economies of the region it is not justified to have a myriad of enterprises within one country. However, this applies to very specific types of activities, for example, the presence of only one or few extractive industry companies in a small country. Frequently, the dominance in the market is accompanied by restrictions on imports of goods and services, or limitations to investment in specific areas, and thus helps consolidate the monopoly power of the companies. Regional integration and the consolidation of markets may increase competition, although at times this resulted in the extension of monopoly powers to particular companies across countries in the region.

While it is beyond the focus of this book to deal with the specific area of domestic competition, the consolidation of the competitiveness and productivity aspects of economic policy rest in significant part on the opening of markets. A further push in the process of privatization, of improved regulations and opening of markets, as well as government sector productivity enhancement is important to help the region to attain a more effective growth path in the future.

In parallel with measures to enhance domestic competition, Latin American economies must also pursue two avenues to improve their trade performance in support of accelerated growth: regional cooperation leading to expanded intra-regional trade; and continued diversification of export markets beyond North America and Europe, and of export products beyond the dominance of commodities and fuels (except in the case of Mexico).

Photo Credit: CAF

Latin America lags far behind Europe and Asia in regional cooperation, particularly as measured by intra-regional trade. There are three basic reasons for which the Latin America region should seriously consider significantly enhancing intra-regional trade, including through improved regional cooperation.

First, it is important to permit the regional economies to specialize in the context of the larger regional market. The Growth Commission led by Nobel laureate Michael Spence found that a major characteristic of the economies that have successfully avoided the middle income trap and made an effective transition to becoming high income economies was their ability to become specialized in economic activities. They managed to develop a competitive advantage in the global marketplace by proactively building unique skill sets and creating economies of scale.

Second, enhanced intra-regional trade would help to overcome the reality that Latin America economies—with the exception of Brazil and Mexico—are small by global standards. Only Brazil and Mexico make the list of the world's 15 largest economies or the 10 largest emerging economies. The other economies do not have domestic markets large enough to permit the economies of scale needed by firms to be globally competitive.

Third, it would allow local firms to take advantage of their superior knowledge and understanding of the needs of customers in the neighboring countries compared to the competitors from other continents. The economies—except in the Caribbean—are linked by a contiguous land mass, a common heritage and history, similar cultures and the same language (except for Brazil and the Caribbean). It should be natural for the consumers within the region to prefer similar (though not necessarily the same) products, and companies should have a competitive advantage in forging business relations with their regional counterparts and in marketing to the consumers in other parts of the region.

Latin America must also gradually reduce its dependence on the slow-growing economies of North America and Europe and develop much closer ties with the world's fastest growing region: Asia. The good news is that there has been a sharp increase in the region's exports to Asia—albeit from a very small base; the share of China has risen from under 1 percent in 1990 to over 8 percent in 2009. With many models, including the model used in this study, predicting that Asia may account for as much as 50 percent of global GDP by 2050, increasing the region's focus on Asia should be an integral part of Latin America's long-term growth strategy.

It is important to note that the increase in exports to Asia is based mainly on raw materials, including fuels, agricultural commodities and metals—particularly the export of iron ore and copper to China. This is in line with the composition of the region's exports, which is dominated by primary commodities and fuels which account for 56 percent of total exports (75 percent if Brazil, Mexico and Venezuela are excluded). The limited exports of manufactures (mostly from Mexico and Brazil) are concentrated in the low to medium technology end. The region stands to make significant gains by increasing the value-added of its output and exports and, within manufacturing, to move up the technology ladder—also a critical measure for getting out of the middle income trap and making progress toward high income status.

Finally, dismantling of remaining barriers to trade with and investment from the global markets as a whole will be a very powerful vehicle to curb the current monopolistic power of large companies, to increase competition at all levels, and to spur innovation.

Specific Elements of the Convergence Strategy

To complement the broad contours of the three-pillar strategy described above, the region must invest in and focus on a number of specific priority areas in order to achieve the shared, more ambitious

vision of convergence:
- Promoting equity and inclusion
- Developing human capital
- Fostering technology development and innovation
- Upgrading and integrating infrastructure
- Advancing regional cooperation and trade
- Improving governance, institutions, and implementation

These six issues are discussed below and are also further elaborated in detail in their appropriate chapters in Part 2 of this book. They by no means constitute a comprehensive list, but they are the most critical issues/themes that require immediate attention by the region's political leaders and policy makers. Significant strides in these areas are essential to ensure the much needed continuous improvements in total factor productivity that can underpin sustained growth.

Two other areas, not covered at any length in this book, also need to be addressed urgently:
- Environment, including the deforestation challenge in the Amazon region and the generation of capital flows under the global cap-and-trade regime.
- Improved security and quality of life, particularly in urban centers.

A. Promoting Equity and Inclusion

Latin America is one of the most unequal regions of the world and it has been like that for decades if not centuries. The concentration of income and wealth has been striking compared to other regions of the world (see Figure 7 above). With a Gini coefficient of 0.53, Latin America is 19 percent more unequal than Sub-Saharan Africa, 37 percent more unequal than East Asia and 65 percent more unequal than developed countries. Also, some countries with Gini coefficients close to 0.60, reach levels of inequality among the highest in the world. Without an adequate correction of focus and policies, these problems will undermine the sustainability of the region's growth. The persistence of poverty and exclusion may well eliminate the great advantage of Latin America in terms of abundant natural resources, water, and generally lower levels of environmental degradation than other regions of the world.

After periods of rising inequality first in the 1980s and then in the 1990s, Latin America's concentration of income began to fall starting in 2000 (Figure 21). Two main factors account for the decline in inequality: a fall in the earnings gap of skilled/low-skilled workers and, after years of considerable neglect, an increase in government pro-poor programs, including

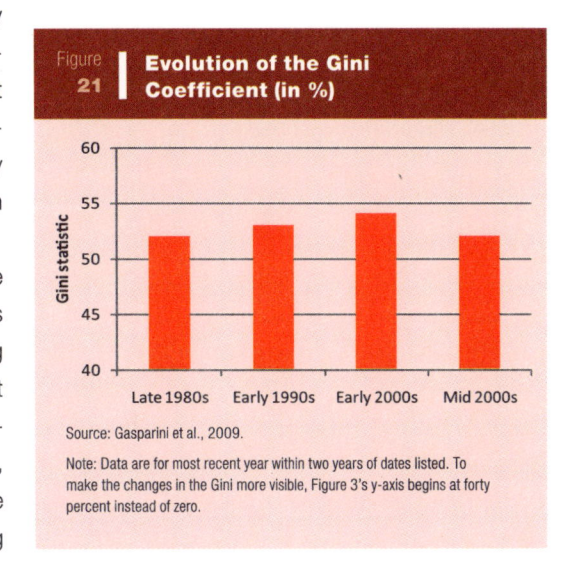

Figure 21 | Evolution of the Gini Coefficient (in %)

Source: Gasparini et al., 2009.

Note: Data are for most recent year within two years of dates listed. To make the changes in the Gini more visible, Figure 3's y-axis begins at forty percent instead of zero.

targeted transfers to the poor. The fall in earnings gap, in turn, is mainly the result of the expansion of coverage in basic education during the last couple of decades, as discussed further below.

The upgrading of skills of the poor, however, could soon face the "access-to-tertiary education" barrier—mainly due to the low quality education they receive in previous levels—and thus the decline in inequality may not continue when that barrier gets hit. In addition, despite the undeniable progress in making public policy more pro-poor, a large share of government spending is neutral or regressive in the distributive sense and the collection of personal income and wealth taxes is low. To continue on the path towards more equitable societies, making public spending more progressive and efforts to improve access to quality services—education, in particular—for the poor and the indigenous and afro-descendant populations are crucial.

While Latin America has more income inequality, the percentage of people below the extreme poverty line tends to be lower than for many of the larger Emerging Economies. (See Figure 22, which compares inequality and poverty in a number of Latin American and Asian countries.)

There is evidence that the region has been gradually moving in the "right" distributive direction. In particular, governments have been making a greater effort to correct for inequality in the distribution of opportunities, particularly as it refers to access to basic education. In addition, as mentioned above, governments have actively reduced poverty through direct transfers to the poor. However, a large share of public spending is still neutral or regressive from the distributive point of view and new measures can go in the direction of making it even more regressive. And taxes, in particular personal income taxes, are severely underutilized as a redistributive instrument in a region with a substantial number of ultra-high net worth (i.e. super rich) individuals.

As discussed earlier, while educational enrollment has become undoubtedly and significantly more equal, the same cannot be said regarding the distribution of the quality of education. If the state wants to continue strengthening the path of equalizing opportunities through education as a way to equalize the distribution of income, addressing the inequality in quality levels of basic education and finding ways to compensate for the opportunity cost so the young poor can attend tertiary education must take priority in the public policy agenda.

The dynamics of inequality in Latin America respond to its political dynamics and the power exercised by its elites. There is evidence that market liberalization might have replaced one group of predatory elites by another group who is equally predatory and which uses their newly acquired power to retain privileges and monopoly rents. An understanding of the role played by elites in Latin America in limiting growth and perpetuating inequities will be a necessary step if state action is to correct them in its budgetary interventions and in how it affects institutions and norms.

The analysis of income inequality presented above is based on household surveys which do not capture the incomes of the truly wealthy. The production and access to more accurate information to estimate income concentration and the incidence of taxes and public spending is essential to enhancing transparency, accountability, fairness and efficiency of the state.

Experience in other regions suggests alternatives which involve the development of institutions that assure genuine equity and provide incentives for innovation, investment in physical and human

BREAKING AWAY FROM MEDIOCRITY TO A PROSPEROUS FUTURE

Figure 22: Gini Index and Poverty Headcount of Selected Latin American (red) and Asian (blue) Countries 2004-2007

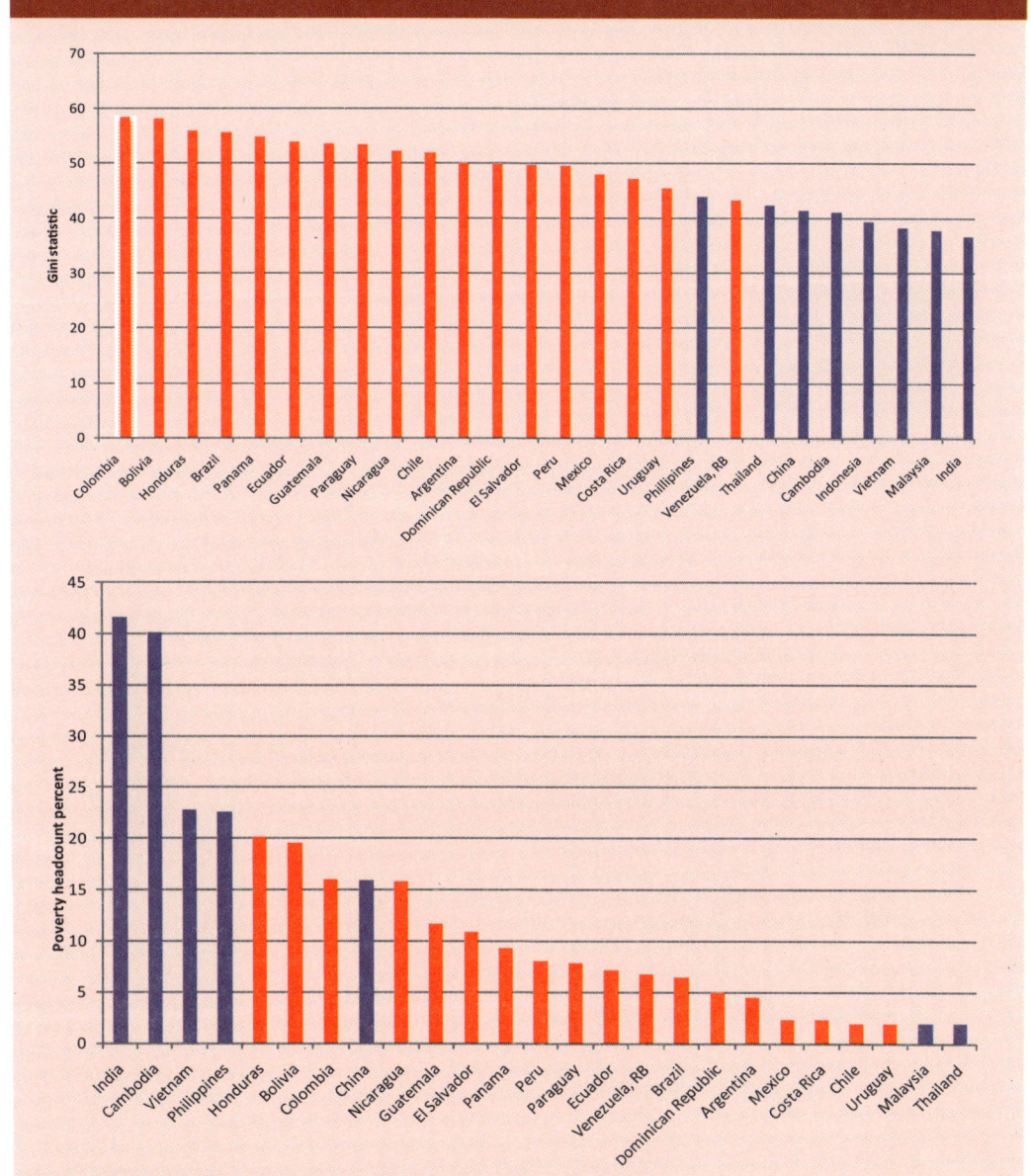

Note: The common internationally-used $1.25/ day per day, rather than the $2.50 generally used in Latin America, was chosen for this graph in order to provide a simple comparison with Asia but one must keep in mind that purchasing power is very different in the two regions.

Source: World Bank, World Development Indicators, 2009, all data from 2004-2007 depending on availability. Averaged when data is available for more than one of those years.

capital, and economic restructuring. Key areas for action include:
- Laying the institutional bases for competitive and effectively regulated markets, including in the area of labor.
- Intensifying efforts to include segments of the population left out from the process of modernization—the indigenous groups and afro-descendants in particular.

This chapter does not specifically cover spatial inequity which is tough to resolve, as illustrated by the lagging regions in the northeast of Brazil, or the mountain regions of the Andean countries. Continued decentralization with enhanced accountability to citizens, together with adequate monitoring and quality control offers a promising route to address this challenge.

B. Developing Human Capital

1. Elementary and Secondary Education

High quality education can make a significant contribution to a country's development. It boosts earnings and stimulates economic growth. It is a powerful tool for moving people out of poverty and improving the distribution of income. And it can foster democratic governance by creating an informed citizenry that can make good decisions. The region has made real progress in education. In virtually every country, governments have increased spending on education—building schools, adding teachers, raising salaries, and enrolling more children (Figure 23). These efforts have clearly expanded the quantity of education (in terms of the number of children attending school), but spending per pupil is low (Figure 24), and there is little evidence that they have improved the quality of education (measured

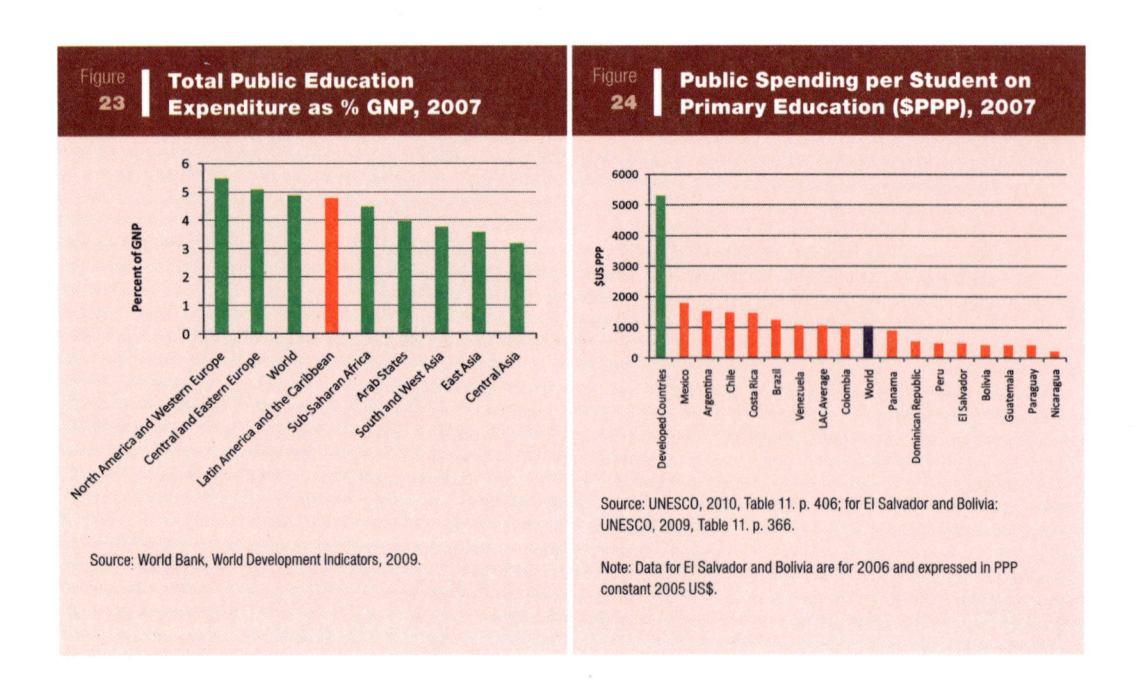

Figure 23 | Total Public Education Expenditure as % GNP, 2007

Source: World Bank, World Development Indicators, 2009.

Figure 24 | Public Spending per Student on Primary Education ($PPP), 2007

Source: UNESCO, 2010, Table 11. p. 406; for El Salvador and Bolivia: UNESCO, 2009, Table 11. p. 366.

Note: Data for El Salvador and Bolivia are for 2006 and expressed in PPP constant 2005 US$.

by scores on achievement tests). If education is to play a major role in promoting growth, equity and democracy in Latin America, governments need to move beyond their historic emphasis on expanding enrollments, to an emphasis on expanding learning.

Enrollment is much higher than the average for the world. However, the coverage of education is far from universal, with one quarter of pre-school children not having access to schooling, with only 70 percent of high school age students being enrolled, and with a high rate of attrition. And, unfortunately, Latin American schools—from pre-school to graduate school—provide low-quality education that fails to meet the needs of countries or students. Poor and minority students, mainly those enrolled in public K-12 schools, are particularly ill-served.

The Latin American countries that participate in PISA (Program for International Student Assessment) all show performance that is below what would be predicted given their countries' expenditure per student. A large share of the region's scarce resource are "lost" to inefficiencies such as high repetition rates or poor teaching, and few countries are spending enough to provide poor children with the additional attention they need. Also, wide variations in spending among countries translate into differences in the quality and equity of education that children receive. Even relatively well-off Latin American students fail to excel by world standards. In five of six countries (Chile being the exception), the richest 20 percent of Latin American students failed to outperform the poorest 20 percent of European OECD students in all three subjects (reading, math and science). While few studies track how many people speak English in any given country or their level of proficiency, existing evidence suggests that Latin American governments give English relatively low priority, and less priority than East Asian competitors.

Education is widely agreed to be one of the most powerful tools for reducing inequality. But government spending on education, despite significant growth, is making only limited headway in reducing inequality, and the region's school systems do little to reduce inequality. Poor children in Latin America tend to begin school later, repeat more grades, drop out sooner, and score lower on tests than their better-off peers—regardless of their gender, race, ethnicity, or area of residence. Differences are often greater among disadvantaged racial and ethnic groups. Indigenous children are less likely to enroll in school, and they graduate later than their peers. These gaps widen at the secondary level. Similar disparities exist between Afro-descendant children and their white counterparts.

Public spending on primary and secondary education is for the most part pro-poor or at least neutral, since most middle- and upper-class families send their children instead to private primary and secondary schools. But governments tend to overspend at the tertiary level so as to provide tuition-free higher education for all. Public spending per higher education student in Latin America is often five (or more) times public spending per primary school student in Latin America, compared with ratios of approximately 1:1 in countries like Spain or Canada. Since the vast majority of students from poor families never reach the tertiary level, the result is a massive subsidy to the middle-class.

Latin America has, however, done a relatively good job of closing the gender gap in education. Girls are as likely, and in some countries more likely, to enroll in and complete their schooling as boys. Average scores from countries participating in international exams show girls doing better than boys in reading, boys doing better than girls in math, and only sometimes in science. The big exception is indigenous girls, who remain at a disadvantage in virtually every country.

The chief obstacles to improving the region's education systems are both technical and political, and reform strategies need to address both aspects, if they are to be effective.

On the technical side, most ministries of education are weak—even incompetent—and so have limited capacity to manage a large and diverse education system. Teaching does not attract the best and brightest applicants—in part because training is inadequate, standards and prestige are low, incentives do not reward merit, and management is poor.

On the political side, government leaders are reluctant to anger powerful interest groups that benefit from the status quo—such as teachers' unions or university students—and can mobilize protests or shut down schools. The clients of public schools—mostly poor families—have almost no power in the school system. They have little information on how schools are doing, few mechanisms for influencing education policy or practice, and no tradition of citizen activism. Those parents with real power to influence schools, primarily middle- and upper-class, send their children to private schools. Consequently, they do not bring significant pressure to bear on governments (or on teachers unions) for improvement. The result is a system that serves the interests of teachers relatively well (providing great job security regardless of performance) but neglects the interests of parents and students (providing them with third-rate education in under-funded and poorly-managed public schools).

To redress this political imbalance, governments need to strengthen their position vis-à-vis at least some of the interest groups that have "captured" the public education system. It is important to design a carefully conceived strategy that pushes for change in a way that takes account of the political economy of addressing interests—teachers unions and university students, for example—that appear to stand in the way. A dual-prong strategy seems advisable. On the one hand, they need to reduce the inordinate power that interest groups, particularly teachers unions, wield. Doing so will be politically difficult. On the other, they need to develop a stronger, more effective demand for quality education—by parents and employers—that can provide political support for reform efforts.

Governments should make learning the central objective of their education systems, and stress policies that promote learning. They should consider the following policies:

(i) Provide all children with quality pre-school education and invest in high-quality basic education, ensuring that the poor, indigenous people, and afro-descendants are properly served.

(ii) Establish world-class learning standards in reading, math and science for all grades. Standards should be clear, measurable and high. Teacher training, textbooks, and student assessments should be keyed to them.

(iii) Develop robust and transparent evaluation systems that regularly assess the learning of all children in reading, math and science. Results should be used to inform teachers, parents, politicians and opinion leaders and to improve schools.

(iv) Recruit top graduates into teaching by setting high standards, making entry much more selective, and training intensively in classroom instruction.

(v) Restructure teacher management, strengthening the power to hire and fire, keying pay to

performance, assessing effectiveness and providing in-class support. Work intensively with teachers to make sure they become effective instructors, granting tenure only to the best and removing poor performers from the classroom.
(vi) Make proficiency in English a fundamental goal of the education system. Governments should make a strong effort to provide the poor with basic writing and speaking skills in English, beginning in primary school.

2. Tertiary Education

While educational issues are critical at the elementary and secondary school levels, tertiary education is also showing strains. Latin America has high levels of Tertiary Education participation, and enrollment levels have improved markedly over the last ten years but are still half the average for high-income countries and well below rates in more successful economies, like the United States and Korea. Moreover, most Latin American university students do not complete their studies. Forty percent of Argentine university students drop out in the first year, and only a quarter of those admitted go on to graduate. Only a third of those admitted in Chile and half of those admitted in Colombia graduate. The situation is similar in Mexico, where only 30 percent of those that enter in any given year graduate. This has serious implications for education finance. Taxpayers are supporting a small cadre of (largely middle-class) college students who seldom complete their degrees, with funds that might help large numbers of poor students who are failing to complete secondary school.

The issues of quality and fields of study at the tertiary level also merit attention. Hard data on quality is scarce at this level. Two of the region's largest public universities, the National Autonomous University (UNAM) in Mexico and the University of Buenos Aires in Argentina, have traditionally refused to seek national accreditation or submit to external evaluation. Brazil is an interesting exception, having evaluated university graduates, under various systems, since 1995.

The limited evidence that exists suggests that the region's universities are not globally competitive. In a 2008 ranking of the world's 200 top universities, no Latin American University ranked in the top 100, and only three (National Autonomous University of Mexico, University of Sao Paulo and University of Buenos Aires) were included—at ranks 150, 196 and 197. In a similar 2008 ranking of the world's top 500 universities conducted by the Shanghai Jiao Tong University, no Latin American university ranked in the top 100, and only three (University of Sao Paulo in Brazil, Universidad de Buenos Aires and Universidad Nacional Autónoma in Mexico) ranked in the top 200. In total, only 10 Latin American universities made the top 500 (six of them from Brazil). By comparison: South Korea had eight universities in the top 500; China (excluding Hong Kong and Taiwan), eighteen; Taiwan, seven; Hong Kong, five; South Africa, three; and India, two.

With respect to fields of study, the region's universities produce very few science or engineering graduates. The bulk of university graduates are in social science, law, or business. In most countries, less than a quarter receive science or engineering degrees. By contrast, nearly 40 percent of all Korean university graduates, and nearly 30 percent of all Irish and Finnish graduates are trained in science or engineering. In Latin America, only Mexico has similar rates (Figure 25). Not surprisingly, when business executives in 117 countries were asked to rank the availability of scientists and engineers in their country, no Latin American country scored in the top 50, and only five scored above the mean (Argentina, Costa Rica, Chile and Venezuela).

The modification of these disappointing patterns will require considerable action with a major shift in the roles of government and the private sector, including foreign direct investment (FDI). The government should be a facilitator, balancing international knowledge and financial resources, to deal with social returns which are highest. While reform efforts will need to be pushed vigorously in the area of education, Latin America finds itself in a privileged position in terms of resources. With education expenditure being relatively high as a proportion of GDP, and growth in population declining, the public sector will be able to reorient expenditure in order to improve education, at least at the elementary and secondary levels. Tertiary education (and related research) may require additional resources. Governments should focus their efforts on the following:

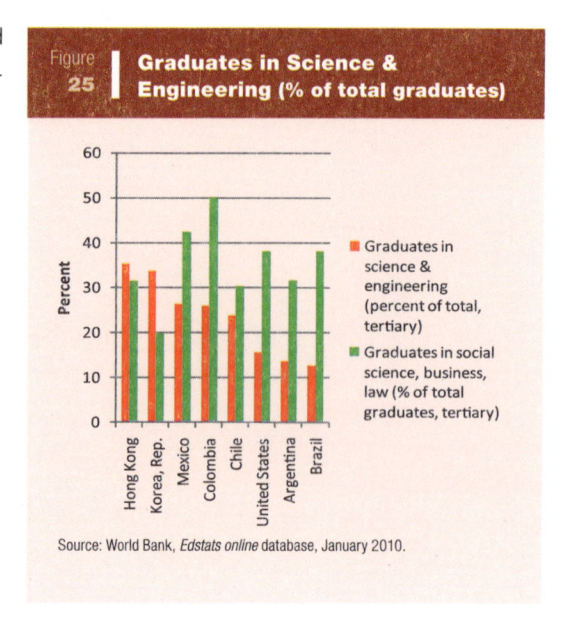

1. Conditioning funding for universities on meeting specific performance objectives. Emphasis should be placed on improving quality, strengthening science and technology, and promoting equity. Rather than channeling all public funds directly to universities, governments should experiment with providing some part of funding directly to students (principally from poor families).
2. Requiring public universities to charge tuition to those who can afford to pay. Charges should be on a sliding scale, depending principally on socioeconomic background.

However, in order to convert Latin America into a source of technological excellence, actions will be required to combine the efforts of private and public education, as well as corporate support and direct involvement.

C. Fostering Technology Development and Innovation

Innovation today is widely recognized as a major source of competitiveness and economic growth for all countries—advanced and emerging economies alike. Innovation has a critical role in creating jobs, generating incomes and in improving living standards of a society. Innovation can also be a powerful tool in broader social development including in moving people out of poverty and improving the distribution of income. "Inclusive innovation" targeted at the population at the bottom of the pyramid is gaining importance as a means of making the benefits of innovation available to all citizens. Over the

Figure 25 | **Graduates in Science & Engineering (% of total graduates)**

Source: World Bank, *Edstats online* database, January 2010.

long term, the main drivers of global economic growth include technological advance in rich countries and catch-up technology adoption in a group of fast-growing convergers (such as Chile, Republic of Korea, China and India), which are shifting resources from low to higher productivity activities. Almost half of the difference in growth performance between Mexico and the Republic of Korea over 40 years is attributable to technology-related improvement (TFP); more rapid gains in TFP growth can unleash a major source of economic growth.

TFP and, particularly, TFP growth in Latin America are low compared with many parts of the world and of course the United States and Europe. According to the World Economic Forum's Global Competitiveness Report (2008-2009), the only country in the region which features among the most competitive economies in the world is Chile (ranked 28th in the Global Competitiveness Index- GCI).

As shown in Table 4, in the Knowledge Economy, Innovation, and ICT Index, Latin America is lagging behind regions like East Asia and Pacific, and Europe and Central Asia. Furthermore, Latin America's scores are lower than the average of all countries.

Consistent with these indicators, and as discussed earlier, the region produces a limited number of scientists and advanced degree recipients, which constrains the region's technological development. While it entails too strict a standard of comparison, OECD countries produce one new PhD per 5,000 people, while in Brazil the ratio is 1 per 70,000; in Chile, 1 per 140,000; and in Colombia 1 per 700,000. Brazil produces around 7,000 PhDs per year and scores the highest in domestically formed PhDs in the region, even when adjusted by population, (accounting for more than 70 percent of total Latin American PhDs according to RICYT's estimates). Without more qualified advanced degree recipients, the ability of countries to use and generate knowledge, adapt and use technology is limited.

Table 4: Knowledge Economy Index in World Regions

Country	KEI 2009	KEI 1995	Innovation 2009	Innovation 1995	ICT 2009	ICT 1995
Latin America	5.21	5.51	5.8	6.12	5.27	6.32
High Income	8.23	8.35	9.02	9.14	8.42	8.62
Europe and Central Asia	6.45	6.25	6.99	6.9	6.46	7.02
East Asia and the Pacific	6.41	6.96	8.49	8.9	6.64	7.76
All Regions	5.95	6.35	8.11	8.2	6.22	7.52
Middle East and North Africa	5.47	5.84	7.57	7.49	5.71	7
Africa	2.71	3.37	4.31	4.57	2.45	4.89
South Asia	2.58	3.06	3.29	3.04	2.45	4.28

Source: World Bank, KEI and KI Indexes, KAM 2009.

Latin America's scientific output is also low compared to other regions, both in terms of scientific and engineering articles and patents granted.

Latin America has performed poorly in terms of its National Innovation System (NIS) consisting of the institutions, laws, regulations and procedures that affect how knowledge is acquired, created, disseminated and applied in the economy. Governments from time to time have been taking steps for promoting science, technology and innovation (STI). But most countries lack a coherent policy and related tools to implement such a policy and the actual results on the ground remain well below desired levels. Although there are exceptions, generally, the public sector dominates in most aspects of STI activities, R&D institutions are not up-to-date, innovation support institutions are mostly ineffective, use of technology and innovation by industry is low, and the workforce lacks requisite skills to generate and use technology. Also, the STI policies in the region have not paid enough attention to the structural transformation of the public R&D Institutions. The collaboration between innovation actors is either non-existent or weak.

In the global context, Latin America is still a marginal player in R&D, accounting for less than 2 percent of world R&D expenditure, well below its share of some 7 percent in world GDP, and this gap is persistent. The average R&D intensity in the region was 0.6 percent of GDP in 2006 as opposed to 2.7 percent in the USA, 3.0 percent in Japan, and 2.3 percent in OECD. Brazil, Mexico, Chile and Argentina account for almost 90 percent of total expenditure in the region. The Republic of Korea by itself spends 50 percent more on R&D than the entire Latin America region. Moreover, there is no clear trend as to the distribution of expenditure between the private and public sectors, and the private sector has a much lower participation than in advanced economies. Today, in most nations of the region, knowledge created in the R&D laboratories tends to stay in the lab, rather than being converted into licenses, patents, products, processes and services. There are problems at both the supply and demand side. On the supply side, universities and public R&D institutions which account for almost 70 percent of R&D have not created mechanisms to identify market/user needs; instead they focus mostly on the publishable mainstream science. There has not been much demand for local R&D from the industry. Government initiatives to address this imbalance have not been successful either.

The region needs to develop an integrated STI system that is driven by excellence to improve its place in the global technology ladder, as several East Asian countries (such as Japan and Korea) have done over the past half century, and as Chile, Brazil and Mexico within the region, as well as China and India are doing today. The region needs a technology and innovation system that is driven by the private sector, highly productive, globally competitive, and capable of meeting the needs of its globalizing economy. This will require an increase in R&D investments from 0.6 percent to almost 2 percent of GDP in the long run—to be invested by both the public sector and the private sector—pursuing frontier, strategic and inclusive innovation, enhancing marketable R&D, and creating a foundation to diffuse and encourage the absorption of existing and newly-created technologies. Countries in the region need to be pragmatic while designing STI policies and programs; they must give high priority to cooperation and collaboration with their regional neighbors.

To translate a technology and innovation agenda into concrete actions, Latin America will require a major shift in the roles of the government and the private sector. Governments should normally be a facilitator with intelligent regulations, proper oversight, financing, enhancing private sector participation with proper policies, tax and other incentives. They should focus on public goods where social returns are highest. A large presence of the domestic private sector and FDI will ensure expansion, higher quality output and relevance where public sector initiatives have been inefficient, insufficient and unreliable. The region has much to learn from Argentina, Chile, Brazil and Mexico in the region; as well as China, India, and South Korea; and from the US, with an STI system that excels globally.

STI strategies specific to individual countries will need to be based on the scientific and technological level of the country and the technological needs of its economy and business climate.

The key recommendations that are common across the region in the area of technology and innovation are:

(i) *Repositioned Public Sector.* Redirect the role of the Public Sector to focus on production of public goods, and facilitate innovation by the private sector, through legislation, finance and other incentives.

(ii) *Regional Cooperation.* Enhance cooperation and collaboration in and outside the region to benefit from existing STI facilities in countries with better systems. This will help achieve easier, faster results and benefits at a lower cost.

(iii) *Inclusive Innovation.* Pursue frontier as well as "inclusive innovation" with the dual purposes of global competitiveness and inclusive growth to benefit all people. Encouraging R&D Institutions and universities to focus on the needs of poor people and improving the ability of informal firms to absorb knowledge, can lower costs and create income-earning opportunities for poor people.

(iv) *Innovation Infrastructure.* Upgrade basic innovation infrastructure such as metrology standards, testing and quality (MSTQ) system, intellectual property rights (IPR), training, and skills upgrading, to enhance innovation and technology commercialization and diffusion, and to contribute to enterprise competitiveness.

(v) *Public Support for R&D and Technology Absorption.* Provide public finance for basic research, applied research, technology diffusion, and skills upgrading, thus increasing productivity by diffusing knowledge produced at the local and regional academic and R&D institutions, and knowledge available globally.

(vi) *Centers of Excellence.* Create "Centers of Excellence" in certain countries (with regional mandates as much as possible). This could include increased efforts in producing more economically relevant public goods, such as pre-competitive research, and socially-relevant innovations, such as access to clean water, urban congestion, urban transport, clean energy technologies, renewable energy, public health, and technologies for sustainable livelihoods.

D. Upgrading and Integrating Infrastructure[14]

---

14 Based upon findings in Scandizzo, Stefania and Pablo Sanguinetti, 2009

Empirical evidence has shown that the level of infrastructure is a key determinant of long-term economic growth in Latin America, as elsewhere, and that an increase in the stock of infrastructure would have significant effects on the region's growth rate. Improving the stock of infrastructure, both in terms of quantity and of quality, is a priority for Latin American countries. Important infrastructure bottlenecks are increasingly apparent, creating obstacles to trade and economic growth. Problems associated with congestion and poorly maintained infrastructure threaten the region's competitiveness and have contributed to constraining Latin America's participation in world trade and FDI. The quality of life is also affected directly by improvements in the provision of basic services and infrastructure.

With respect to access to basic infrastructure services, Latin America has made important advances, but such advances have been slow and uneven across countries and income groups. In the case of sanitation, for example, Bolivia is well below the regional average, with only 46 percent of the population with access to improved sanitation (Table 5).

Most countries in the region rank consistently in the bottom half of the ranking with respect to overall infrastructure quality, with the average Latin American country ranking well below East Asia, as shown earlier in Figure 12.

Latin America's poor infrastructure is even more evident if one considers individual sectors, as the region consistently scores behind all regions except South Saharan Africa (SSA). Moreover, in the case of railroads, Latin America scores even worse than SSA. Only in the case of electricity does Latin America score comparably to Asia (Figure 26).

Latin America's long-term infrastructure requirements thus remain substantial despite the recent global economic slowdown. Based on the model used in this study and assuming business as usual, the 21 Latin American countries covered in this study would need to invest $7.8 trillion (2009 prices)

Table 5. Access to Infrastructure Services, by Region

Region	Improved Sanitation Facilities (% of population with access) 1990	2006	Improved Water Source (% of population with access) 1990	2006	Mainline and Mobile Phone Subscribers (per 100 people) 1990	2008	Electrification Rate (% of households with access to electricity) 1990	2008
Latin America	67.9	78.3	83.9	91.4	6.0	98.8	70.0	92.7
Europe & Central Asia	88.3	88.7	90.3	95.0	12.3	135.5		100.0
Middle East & North Africa	66.7	74.5	88.8	87.7	3.3	74.3	61.0	93.6
East Asia & Pacific	48.1	65.6	68.3	87.4	0.8	174.6	56.0	90.3

Source: International Emergy Agency (IEA) 2007.

BREAKING AWAY FROM MEDIOCRITY TO A PROSPEROUS FUTURE   59

Figure 26. Quality of Infrastructure by Sector and Region
1-7 scale, with 1=underdeveloped and 7=world's best

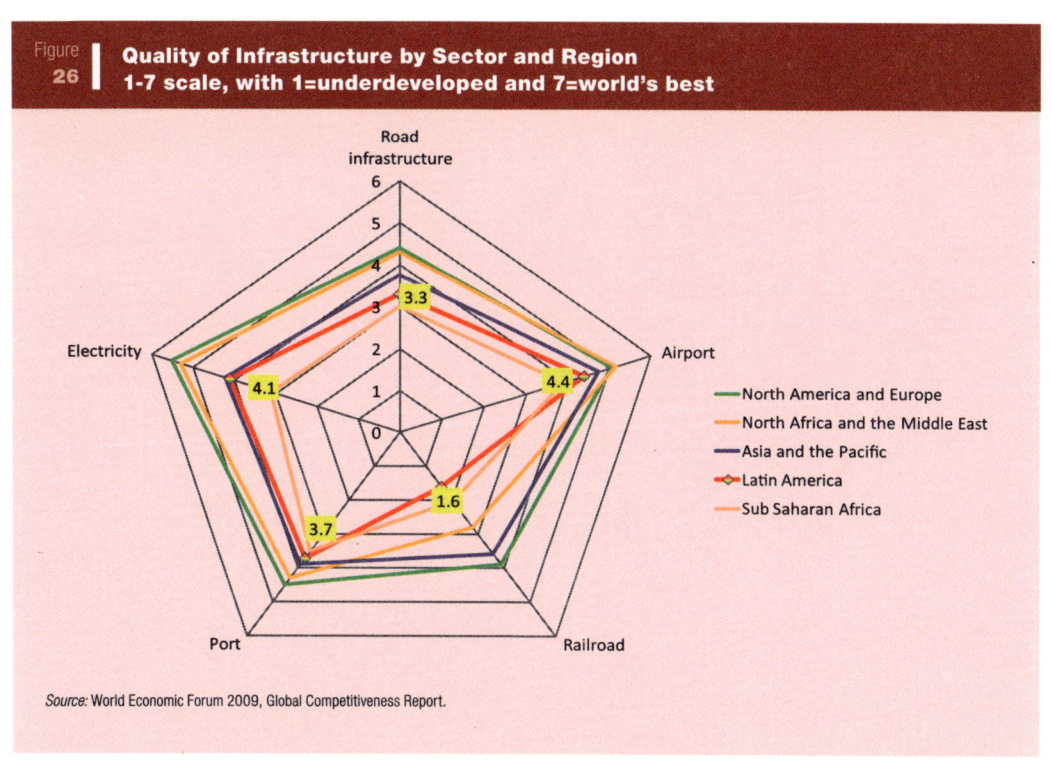

- North America and Europe
- North Africa and the Middle East
- Asia and the Pacific
- Latin America
- Sub Saharan Africa

Road infrastructure: 3.3
Airport: 4.4
Railroad: 1.6
Port: 3.7
Electricity: 4.1

Source: World Economic Forum 2009, Global Competitiveness Report.

Figure 27. Total Infrastructure Investment Requirements: 2011–2040

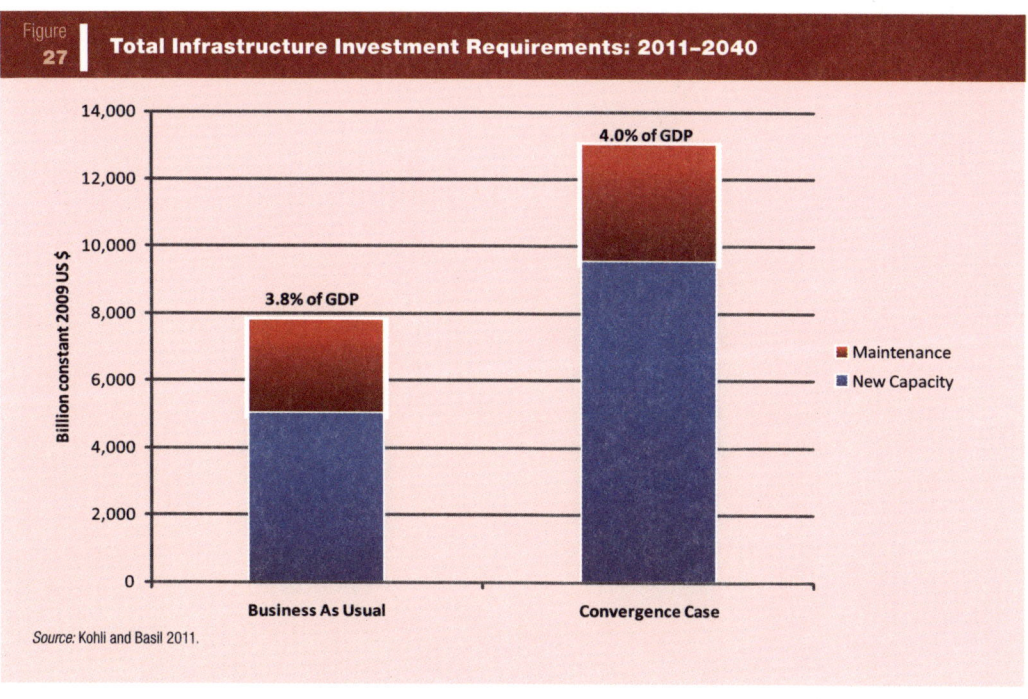

Billion constant 2009 US $

- Business As Usual: 3.8% of GDP
- Convergence Case: 4.0% of GDP

Legend:
- Maintenance
- New Capacity

Source: Kohli and Basil 2011.

during the next thirty years (2011–2040). This comprises about $5.1 trillion for new capacity and about $2.7 trillion for maintenance (Figure 27). Under the revival/convergence scenario, these needs would rise dramatically, by over two-thirds, to over $13 trillion, with about $9.6 trillion for new capacity and $3.4 trillion for maintenance. In fact, by 2040, the convergent scenario's yearly investment needs would be over double those of the business as usual case.

Although the aggregate requirements are staggering, as a percentage of GDP, these needs are significantly lower than for other countries, particularly in Asia. Latin America must invest 4 percent of GDP into infrastructure in the next 30 years for the convergent case. Although, for the most part, these requirements may mandate a doubling of current levels, they are lower than the over 6 percent of GDP demands of Asia's infrastructure over the next decade.

Sectorally, power requires the largest share (about 72 percent of total requirements in the convergent case); roads are a distant second (about 11 percent); and the third-largest needs exist in ports (about 9 percent), almost all (87 percent of the costs) for new capacity.

An examination of the state of infrastructure in Latin America underlines not only the need for greater investment, but the importance of improved management. The magnitude of the infrastructure investment requirements suggests that a strong public-private partnership should be developed, both for financing and on efficiency grounds. Moreover, these efforts need to have a strong regional perspective, with the help of international and regional institutions.

An institutional framework based on a combination of appropriate incentives for private participation, independent and effective regulation, and proper planning and coordination are thus essential. Chile, Peru and Mexico are far advanced in these areas and provide good examples for the region to follow. Governments in the region face the challenge of increasing infrastructure financing, and creating the necessary conditions to promote and retain quality investment in the sector. In particular, governments play a fundamental role in providing good institutions, and must dedicate themselves to establishing the necessary juridical and regulatory framework to promote credibility and security in the sector.

In the near term, the main focus of policy should be to:
- Further increase investment levels to overcome current bottlenecks. The region needs to invest an average of about 4 percent of GDP (including maintenance and rehabilitation) to support economic growth of 6-7 percent a year;
- Adopt programs to eliminate electricity and other shortages and accelerate completion of rural electrification and national highways programs;
- Strengthen institutional capacity, including to implement existing policies;
- Simplify and delegate government decision-making;
- Monitor results and enforce accountability.

The longer term effort should be driven by the following reforms:
- Increase the role of the private sector;
- Make markets more competitive—with stronger and independent regulatory bodies;
- Plan and design infrastructure with a long-term (30 to 50 year) perspective.

E. Advancing Regional Cooperation and Trade

Over the last thirty years, trade and capital flows to and from emerging market economies have increased at a very rapid pace. Without question, their economic and trade growth have constituted the most dynamic aspect of international cooperation and globalization in recent years. In the same period, Latin America made considerable progress in liberalizing and integrating into the world economy, possibly the most noticeable structural advance achieved in the last two decades. The impact of liberalization has been significant—albeit with a lag—and Latin America's increasing openness to world trade has resulted in considerable gains relative to its situation 25-30 years ago. The ratio of trade to GDP in actual prices increased dramatically between 1984-2009 from around 18 percent to 47 percent. However, even as Latin America has opened up considerably, it remains behind world and OECD averages (64 percent and 52 percent respectively). Its population-adjusted ratio of trade to GDP of under 60 percent compares with close to 160 percent for the NICs, over 100 percent for China and developing Asia and around 80 percent for India.

The story of Latin American exports is similar. Latin America's exports have grown but those of the NICs have grown more rapidly. While Latin America has maintained its share of world exports of 5-6 percent, the NICs have more than doubled their share, and developing Asia has more than tripled it, from under 5 percent to over 16 percent (Table 6).

Table 6 | Growth in World Exports

Region	Average Annual Export Growth (%) (1980-2009)	Share of World Exports (%) 1980	Share of World Exports (%) 2009
Developing Asia	10.1	4.7	16.3
NICs	9.8	3.1	7.5
Latin America	6.0	5.6	5.8

Source: International Monetary Fund, Direction of Trade database, 2010.

1. Intra-Regional Trade and Regional Cooperation

Trade integration has been a major objective among different emerging regions. Moreover, these efforts were further enhanced by the stellar progress of the EU over the last half a century. Asia has been able to integrate effectively without a complex institutional framework equivalent to that of the EU. Rather, the process has occurred in response to the liberalization efforts of many of its members, and particularly

Photo Credit: CAF

Table 7: Percentage of Exports within Region

Region	1980	2009
European Union	61.6	67.2
Developing Asia with Advanced Asia	55.8	74.8
Developing Asia	24.1	47.3
Latin America	21.0	21.2

Source: International Monetary Fund, Direction of Trade database, 2010.

China and India. However, this has not been the case in Latin America, notwithstanding official efforts that have extended for well over a century.

Trade flows reflect the process of regional cooperation and integration within each developing area and with other emerging economies. All areas, with the exception of Latin America, have shown a significant increase in intra-regional trade. The degree of regional integration in Asia is particularly impressive at every level, explaining two thirds of total trade for the region, and about half for the emerging economies including China.

In the Americas, the degree of regional trade including the North American countries has increased, but after reaching 40 percent, it declined and remains at about one third of total trade. However, after some years of growth, intra-Latin American trade, at some 20 percent of the total, is at about the same level as in 1980. This suggests that there has been only limited success in developing a process of integration in new activities in spite of the major efforts to establish trade agreements within the region, including trade blocks like Mercosur, the Andean Group, and the Central American Common Market, which have sought to provide the opportunity to integrate these economies (Table 7).

There are three basic reasons for which the Latin America region should seriously consider significantly enhancing intra-regional trade, including through improved regional cooperation:

a) Need for Economies to Specialize

The Growth Commission led by Nobel laureate Michael Spence found that a major characteristic of the economies that have successfully avoided the middle income trap and made an effective transition to becoming high income economies was their ability to become specialized in economic activities. Such specialization involves investments in activities with greater value-added by shifting resources—labor and capital—from labor intensive activities whose viability is dependent on low wages (and hence lower per capita income) into economic activities that have higher innovation and technology content, allowing greater returns to both capital and labor; the resulting higher wage levels in turn raise people's living standards and boost the country's per capital income.

A closer look at higher income countries (developed and NICs) reveals that, except for a few large economies, most high wage economies have achieved at least some degree of specialization in the global marketplace. Given our earlier conclusion that many—though by no means all—Latin American economies have been mired in the middle income trap, it appears logical that an important step in Latin American countries' ability to escape this trap would be their success in moving towards such specialization on a global scale so as to raise their productivity. To successfully achieve such specialization, firms need ready access to markets that are large enough to yield economies of scale at the national or regional level before they can compete in the global marketplace. Unfortunately, doing so at the national level is not possible In Latin America except in Brazil and Mexico.

b) Small Size of Most Latin Economies

Only two Latin American countries rank amongst the top 15 economies in the world: Brazil at number 9 and Mexico at number 11 in PPP terms, and at number 8 and 14, respectively, in terms of market exchange rates. In 2009, again only Brazil and Mexico made the list of the top 10 emerging markets economies (Table 8). All CAF member countries combined were equivalent to only 60 percent of the GDP of China alone. Only two economies—Brazil and Mexico—had more than 1 percent of global GDP. And, in PPP terms their combined GDP was slightly less than that of India and less than half of China.

So what is the basic conclusion from this information? While most Latin American economies belong to the upper middle-income group, they are relatively small in absolute size—with the exception of Brazil and Mexico. Therefore, local firms operating exclusively in their home country markets would find it extremely difficult to achieve economies of scale and thus face a significant challenge in

Table 8. Top 10 Emerging Markets by GDP

2000 GDP (billion US$)		2009 GDP (billion US$)	
China	1,198	China	4,909
Brazil	644	Brazil	1,574
Mexico	329	India	1,236
Korea	533	Russia	1,229
India	462	Mexico	875
Taiwan	326	Korea	833
Argentina	284	Turkey	615
Turkey	266	Indonesia	539
Russia	260	Poland	430
Saudi Arabia	189	Taiwan	379

Source: World Bank, World Development Indicators, 2009, all data from 2004-2007 depending on availability.

becoming globally competitive and creating high paying jobs. Closer regional cooperation in the hemisphere that facilitates much greater regional trade and investment flows that significantly expand the "home" markets can go a long way in helping the region aspire to create global players.

c) Unexploited Potential within the Region

The low trade between the Latin American economies (at 21 percent in 2009) is partly due to the past focus of both the region's governments and private business on the US and European markets. But, it also appears to be a natural outcome of the government policies that over the years have created barriers against trade and investment flows to neighboring countries. In addition, physical transport and logistics facilities between neighboring countries have also been a constraint.

It is critical that regional economies begin to tap the significant unexploited potential for greater trade and investment flows within the region by removing current barriers. The resulting increase in intra-regional trade and investment flows—combined with greater focus on Asia (discussed below)—would not only create newer, faster growing market opportunities but also help diversify the region's export markets and thus further reduce the current heavy reliance on exports to the US and Europe. While this process appears to be already underway, its pace can and should be significantly accelerated.

2. Trade Diversification

a) Diversifying Markets

Latin America's trade has predominantly been with the US, the region's traditional and largest trading partner, and Europe. This has begun to change, particularly over the past decade. Over the past 10 years, the sharpest growth of trade in the last decade is with China (26 percent per annum) and India (22 percent), and the slowest growth, with the US (2.2 percent) (Table 9). China's share has risen from under 1 percent in 1990 to 8.2 percent in 2009. It is worth noting that last year, China became Brazil's largest trading partner, surpassing the United States.

This sharp rise in the region's trade with developing Asia overall—and with China and India in particular—has a number of advantages: it is helping the region to diversify its trade; it is strengthening economic ties with the fastest growing region of the world; it reduces the region's dependence on the mature and slower growing markets in North America and Europe; and, through higher growth of exports, it helps boost the overall economic growth of Latin America.

Continuing to increase its focus on Asia should be an integral part of Latin America's long-term growth strategy.

b) Diversifying into Higher Value-Added Products

The composition of Latin American exports has been considerably less dynamic than the destination of exports; they continue to be dominated by primary commodities and fuels. The region's manufacturing exports are mostly concentrated at the low technology end. The proportion of high technology

Table 9: Latin America Export Destinations

Export Markets	Average Annual Growth Rate, 2000-2009 (%)	Share of Total Exports (%)
China	26.1	8.2
India	22.1	1.1
Central & Eastern Europe	13.9	0.8
Africa	13.9	1.9
Rest of World	10.5	10.5
Canada	9.9	2.4
Latin America	9.3	22
Japan	7.8	3.5
Developing Asia (w/o China, India)	7.1	1.7
European Union	7.1	13.3
United States	2.4	34.8

Source: International Monetary Fund, Direction of Trade database, 2010.

goods within manufacturing exports for the region as a whole is under 8 percent compared to 30 percent for China and 25 percent for the NICs. With Mexico and Brazil excluded, the proportion falls below that of India (5 percent).

Latin America stands to make significant gains by increasing the value-added of its output and exports and, within manufacturing, to move up the technology ladder—a critical measure for getting out of the middle income trap and making progress toward high income status.

F. Improved Governance, Institutions and Implementation

A closer look at each and every crucial issue facing the region reveals that the underlying problems in each are rooted in poor governance, and that without fundamental improvements in governance it will not be possible to tackle these issues effectively.

Most political scientists equate good governance with democratic governments. In our view, while a democratic political system is indeed highly desirable and Latin America has made marked progress in that direction, governance comprises of many facets that go well beyond the political system. The various facets of governance are intertwined with each other like pieces of a jigsaw puzzle.

As shown by a variety of reliable public opinion surveys—Latin American Barometer, Americas Barometer and others—political attitudes in the region are generally supportive of a democratic

Table 10 — Democracy Gets the Upper Hand in Most Countries

Democracy is preferable to any type of government
% of surveyed respondents who agree:

Country	1996	2001	2008	2009	Change since 2008
El Salvador	56	25	50	68	18
Honduras	42	57	44	55	11
Brazil	50	30	47	55	8
Chile	54	45	51	59	8
Guatemala	50	33	34	42	8
Panama	75	34	56	64	8
Costa Rica	80	71	67	74	7
Peru	63	62	45	52	7
Argentina	71	58	60	64	4
Bolivia	64	54	68	71	3
Uruguay	80	79	79	82	3
Venezuela	62	57	82	84	2
Mexico	53	46	43	42	-1
Nicaragua	59	43	58	55	-3
Dominican Rep.	na	na	73	67	-6
Paraguay	59	35	53	46	-7
Colombia	60	36	62	49	-13
Ecuador	52	40	56	43	-13

Source: The Economist based on Latino-barómetro 2009.

system (Table 10 and Figure 28). While there are some important reversals in the support for democracy in countries such as Colombia and Mexico, that is the model preferred by most respondents in the region. That good news is countered, however, by widespread dissatisfaction with government services, including the provision of security, justice, education, and basic infrastructure. Some of these issues are illustrated in Table 11, based on the 2009 Survey of the Latin American Barometer. Confidence in key public institutions such as political parties and justice systems is disturbingly low in a number of countries, even some with sound economic performance. For sustainable prosperity, levels of trust need to increase, which democratic governments and effective leaders can best accomplish by delivering sound services. Looking ahead, that is the primary political challenge. The pressures of globalization mean that, increasingly, pragmatism must trump ideology in policy-making throughout Latin America. That trend has significant implications for the region's long-term political landscape.

Figure 28 | Political Views in Latin America—2009

Democracy in Latin America
- Democracy is the preferred system for Latin America
- Democracy is working in our country

Effectiveness of Government
- Government works for the well-being of all
- There has been progress in reducing corruption

Democracy Helps Solve Problems

Market economy is the Best for Economic Growth

Source: Latino-barómetro 2009.

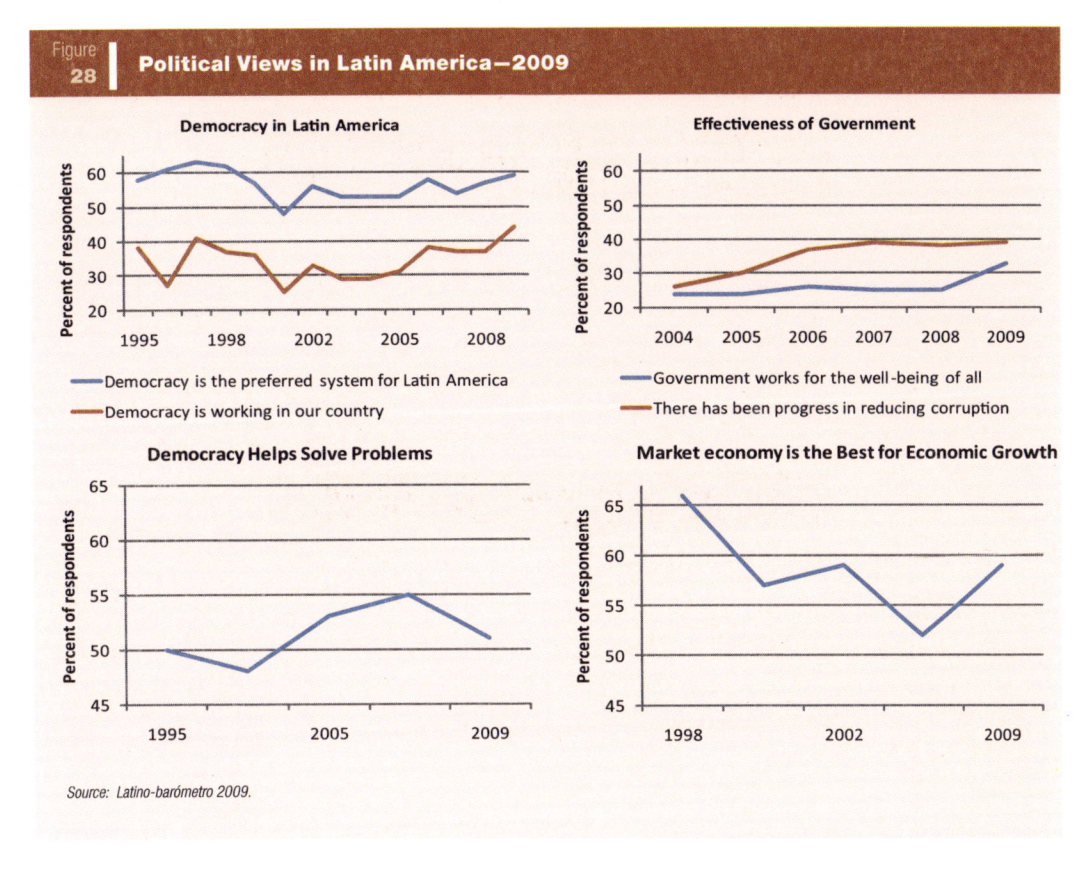

For Latin America to pursue a path towards significantly greater prosperity in coming years, it will be crucial to build more effective democratic governance throughout the region. Such a political development is not only consistent with, but essential for, the social and economic policies outlined in this book. It will be important to forge a political system based on consultation, dialogue and consensus-building. That formula has proved effective in the case of Chile, and appears to be taking hold and producing positive results in Brazil as well.

Such politics needs to be accompanied by an effective political party system characterized by competition. This is the best way to keep political leaders fully accountable, and to yield decisions that respond most effectively to citizens' demands. Alternative models can produce short-term benefits but are rarely sustainable. As globalization intensifies, the governance structures marked by an open party system will best correspond to the region's challenges and needs.

Over the coming decades, expectations are likely to continue to rise among groups that are newly incorporated into Latin America's politics. Sustainable prosperity will be difficult to achieve without being inclusive, reaching out and consulting with such key populations as indigenous and afro-descendant groups. The importance of such a political approach can be seen in the case of Peru, both in the conflicts surrounding the privatizations that took place in 2001 and the ongoing violence

Table 11. Key Issues at National Level

I. Main Problems for Latin American Countries	
Unemployment	21%
Crime and Security	19%
Economic Problems	16%
Poverty	7%
Political Issues	6%
Inflation, Violence, Corruption, Health, Education	3% each

II. Confidence in Institutions	
Church	68%
Media	49-56%
Army	45%
Government	45%
Private Sector/Banks	42-44%
Municipalities/ Police/ Congress/ Judiciary	28- 34%
Labor Unions	30%
Political Parties	21%

III. Guarantees under Democratic Regime	
Religion	79%
Gender Equality/Freedom of expression/ Professional Development	57-67%
Private Property/ Equality of Opportunity/ Environment	44-47%
Solidarity with the Poor and Social Security	33-36%
Labor Opportunities/Income Distribution	27-29%
Protection against Crime	25%

Source: Latino-barómetro 2009.

over natural resources—oil and gas—in the Amazon region. Coherent and responsive party systems, and sound political leadership, are best equipped to anticipate such problems and defuse tensions before they become destabilizing and put ambitious and worthy economic goals at risk.

Another key dimension of effective democratic governance in Latin America involves striking the right balance between national authority and local control. Decentralization is well underway throughout the region. There have been considerable advances. But it is also important to ensure a greater measure of financial autonomy in Latin American cities, while at the same time guarding against anti-democratic practices at the local level. There is no single recipe that applies in all Latin American countries, but decentralization combined with accountability to the local population is a critical area for policy experimentation and reform.

Civil service reform should be of the highest priority to contribute to more effective implementation and necessary continuity of long-term policies that can help produce sustained prosperity in Latin America. The Chilean experience particularly shows the importance of having a low turnover of key administration officials such as finance ministers. The high turnover in many countries is a major obstacle to economic progress. This is essentially a political challenge that will involve incentives and rewards for long-term public service and measures to discourage key appointments being made for short-term political advantage.

In the end, the outcome of any long-term formulation of policies will depend not only on the political environment but also on the ability to implement policies. In addition to the lack of a shared vision, a major difference between Latin America and the successful growth cases of the past has been the lack of adequate implementing structures (formal and informal). The region will have to undergo a transformation to: create a more competent and motivated civil service, geared to the challenges of the next quarter century; engage in a non-adversarial approach to public-private relations, in a cooperative environment; improve the competitive environment of the region; inculcate a stronger code of ethics for the civil service and the private sector, particularly in regards to the conduct of business with the government; ensure effective formulation of priorities and monitoring of results; and promote accountability with a clear system of rewards and punishment for the political system of government.

Of equivalent importance, there is a need for a transformation of the institutional set-up. While Latin America tends to have a sophisticated and generally comprehensive legislative structure, it has a judiciary that does not operate effectively, and is subject to considerable political pressure. Accordingly, the implementation of existing rules and regulations fall short of the requirements of a modern society. The prevalence of form over substance in the judicial process makes it even more complicated than would be expected under the current circumstances. Aside from the serious flaws in many judicial systems, and the urgent need for reform, there is an equally compelling case to be made for major governmental action on police reform. This has been a relatively neglected area of public policy, but the gap between the gravity of the problem (which, experts claim, shows no sign of abating in coming years) and the capacity of police forces to respond adequately, is growing. Rampant crime and insecurity will continue to limit growth and prosperity in a number of Latin American countries, including Brazil and Mexico. Corruption and lack of professionalism besets police forces throughout the region, and any long-term strategy for significant progress will have to tackle this problem seriously. Otherwise, the potential for huge strides forward will be jeopardized.

If Latin America is to experience significantly enhanced growth and development in the coming decades it will be critical to build a partnership—in effect, a governance model—that involves a lean, efficient government, a socially conscious, responsible, and modern private sector, and a vibrant and pragmatic civil society. In addition to the political aspects of governance, our own definition of governance comprises of all facets of governance that affect economic management: role and focus of governments; importance given to economic and social development by the top political leaders and policy makers; delivery of quality and universality of basic public services (law and order, rule of law, education and health services); and focus on results and enforcement of accountability.

Latin America should strive to emulate the four characteristics that have distinguished East Asia from other developing regions:

- Sharp and primary focus of political leaders and policy makers alike on economic issues;
- Ability to implement policy decisions;
- Insistence on achievement of results on the ground; and
- Enforcement of accountability.

This can only be accomplished if the region would undertake the required transformation of governance. Specifically, Latin America must transform the following ten facets of governance in order to kick start the economies to achieve higher economic growth and make the societies much more inclusive:

- Make economic and social development the primary focus of the political leaders and policy makers, not just in words but also in reality;
- Reverse the deterioration in political governance, while strengthening democratic institutions
- Make governments smarter, more focused and more credible;
- Decentralize, where possible, both the authority and accountability for most public services to local bodies as close to the people as possible;
- Modernize and make more effective all institutions involved in economic management;
- Reform the civil service to meet the needs of modern economies and of democratic, more open and more inclusive societies;
- Improve the quality, honesty and responsiveness of all public services including the police, judiciary, education and health services;
- Actively promote and enforce competitive markets, break down the dominance of entrenched vested interests, and prevent capture of state organs by big business;
- Inculcate a code of self discipline and ethical behavior within the business community; and
- Implement agreed policies and priorities, monitor results and enforce accountabilities at all levels of government (national, state and municipal).

Chapter 2
Latin America: Is Average Good Enough?

Homi Kharas

Introduction

Latin America is an average region in the world. It had an income level in 2009 of US$9,580 (PPP) compared to a global average of US$9,475 (PPP).[1] At market exchange rates, the average income of Latin America is a bit lower than the world average: US$5,900 compared to US$9,475.[2] But the remarkable fact about Latin America is that its income level in constant dollars is estimated at 13.5 percent of that of the United States in 2009 compared to 12.9 percent in 1965. In brief, Latin America is close to the global average in living standards, and has neither converged nor diverged from the United States over the last 44 years.

This chapter describes why Latin America should be so average. After all, the period of the last forty years or so has been one where the world has seen considerable divergence in income levels between countries[3], as well as considerable convergence of some countries, mostly in Asia, towards US living standards. So the world has not been an average place. Why then is Latin America seemingly stuck?

It was not always so. In the 1970s, Latin America appeared to have great promise. Income levels compared to the United States rose from 12 percent in 1970 to 17.7 percent in 1981, but that decade long growth spurt could not be sustained and the region fell back. Latin American countries saw a succession of crises: foreign debt crises, currency crises, banking crises, hyperinflation crises, even security crises in countries like Colombia. Coupled with periodic commodity booms and busts, the region rarely enjoyed a period of sustained prosperity. Each advance was offset by an equivalent set-back. While output and price volatility declined in the United States (the Great Moderation called by Federal Reserve Board Governor Bernanke on the basis of scholarly work done by Blanchard and Simon),[4] the opposite was happening in Latin America. Between 1961 and 2002, Latin America enjoyed 18 years when per capita income growth was over 2 percent and 23 years when it was below this level. There were 12 different years when Latin America as a region had negative income growth, about one every three years.

---

1   Using the new 2005 PPP estimates. Using current PPP dollars, Its income level is US$10,544 compared to a global average of US$10,278.
2   Measured in 2007 US dollars adjusted for changes in exchange rates. Many GDP units in this chapter differ from the rest of the book. Market exchange rate units differ from both real (constant) and current (nominal) GDP measures and are defined in the Annex.
3   Pritchett, Lant, 1997. "Divergence, Big Time," Journal of Economic Perspectives, American Economic Association, vol. 11(3), pages 3-17, Summer.
4   Blanchard, Olivier, and John Simon (2001). "The Long and Large Decline in U.S. Output Volatility," Brookings Papers on Economic Activity, 1, pp. 135-64.

Given these set-backs it is perhaps encouraging that Latin America managed to retain its global market share in output. But it may find that even this solace is a matter of history. More and more countries in the developing world, in Asia, Eastern Europe and even some in Africa, are growing rapidly. This chapter traces out a scenario for the global economy that suggests that business-as-usual in Latin America will not be sufficient for the region to retain its global share. It will steadily shrink.

Background Data and Historical Trends

In 1965, Latin America accounted for 5.6 percent of global GDP. Forty years later, in 2005, it accounted for 5.7 percent (at market exchange rates). In between, its share rose as high as 7.6 percent in 1981 and fell as low as 4.5 percent in 1987. In general, the ups-and-downs of Latin America's importance in the world economy follow the cycles of commodity prices rather than showing a pattern of sustained development.

Latin America has historically been one of the most prosperous emerging economy regions. In 1981, Latin America accounted for 31 percent of developing country GDP (at market exchange rates), but it has steadily lost share since then. In 2009, Latin American economies were estimated to have only 19 percent of top emerging economies' GDP (Table 1). Large Latin American countries have also declined in relative terms. In 1981, Brazil and Mexico were each one-third larger than India or China, and Argentina had the same sized GDP as Indonesia, a country with almost six times the population. By 2009, Indonesia's GDP was 50 percent larger than Argentina's, and India is one-third larger than Mexico. China, of course, is today almost 50 percent larger than all of Latin America combined.

In many ways, Latin America has surrendered its leadership of the developing world to Asia. Brazil and Mexico were the largest emerging economies in 1980, and the large Latin American countries accounted for 45 percent of the GDP of the top ten emerging economies as late as 1990. Today, 7 of the top ten emerging economies are in Asia. Argentina and Venezuela have dropped off the list, and Latin America no longer commands the attention it once did as a large potential market (Table 1).

Latin America is not discussed in the same terms as Asia as a region capable of helping the world rebound from the current crisis. The good news, of course, is that there is no sign of major crises in Latin America, as there are in Europe, Central Asia and Africa, as a consequence of the Global Recession of 2008-2010. That, in and of itself, is something to cheer. In the past, crises almost anywhere in the world were quickly transmitted to Latin America. This time, even though Latin America as a region has suffered badly, countries have been able to weather the storm using traditional macroeconomic instruments.

When one compares growth forecasts by the IMF for 2010-2014 with actual growth rates for 2003-2007, Latin America scores a negative difference of 1.1 percent. This is on par with other developing regions, including Asia, and much better than Central and Eastern Europe (-2.4 percent), the Commonwealth of Independent States (-4.0 percent), the Middle East (-1.5 percent) or even Sub-Saharan Africa (-1.2 percent). So Latin America has become more resilient than in the past.

Perhaps more significantly, only one Latin American country appears on the list of the top twenty countries with the largest projected growth slowdowns: Venezuela, whose 2010-2014 growth may be

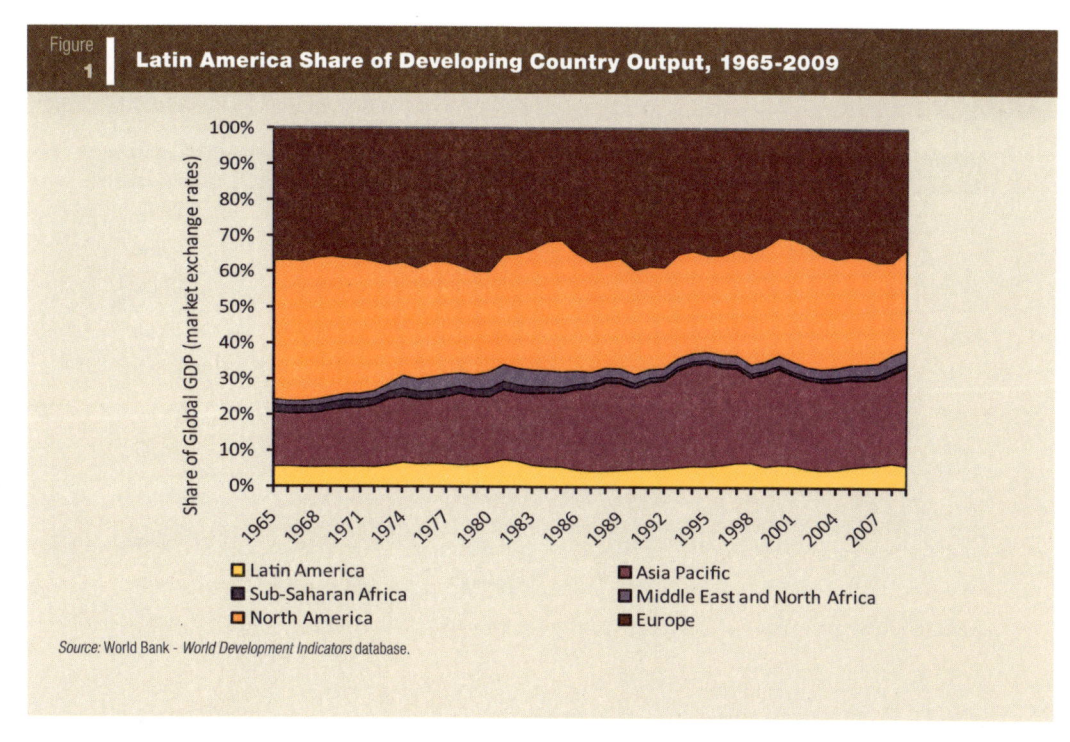

Figure 1: Latin America Share of Developing Country Output, 1965-2009

Source: World Bank - *World Development Indicators* database.

as much as 7.7 percent below the rapid (but unsustainable) growth during 2003-2007[5].

The stagnation in Latin America's share of the world economy is mirrored in the stagnation of the region's average GDP per capita level compared to that in the United States. Given the "advantages of backwardness", Latin America should have been able to converge with its large neighbor to the north. In reality, it has displayed the same swings for GDP—gaining on the United States whenever there has been a global upswing in commodity prices, but losing ground whenever commodity prices reverse themselves.

True, some countries have made some progress. Brazil's relative per capita GDP almost doubled from 7.2 percent to 14.3 percent between 1965 and 2009, but almost all of that was achieved by 1974 (14.6 percent). Even Chile, the best performing Latin American country in recent years, has a per capita income relative to the United States in 2009 (17.8 percent) that is lower than what it was in 1965 (19.6 percent).

In fact, Latin America is average, compared to the world (Figure 2). Its income per capita has risen since 1965, from approximately US$2,500 to an estimated US$5,900 in 2009 in constant terms[6], but the world average income has grown as well. Figure 2 shows that Latin America has had an average income of around three-quarters that of the world. The significant dip in the mid-1980s is the result of the debt crisis and subsequent devaluations in many Latin American countries. Conversely, earlier

---
5 Chandy, L; Gertz, G; Linn, J, 2009
6 Using Constant 2007 US$ as defined in Annex.

Table 1 | Top Ten Emerging Economies and Share of Major Latin American Economies in Top Ten Economies' GDP, 1980-2009

Ranking	1980	1990	2000	2009
1	Brazil	Brazil	China	China
2	Mexico	China	Brazil	Brazil
3	China	India	Mexico	India
4	India	Korea	Korea	Russia
5	Iran	Mexico	India	Mexico
6	South Africa	Taiwan	Taiwan	Korea
7	Indonesia	Turkey	Argentina	Turkey
8	Argentina	Argentina	Turkey	Indonesia
9	Venezuela	Iran	Russia	Poland
10	Turkey	Indonesia	Saui Arabia	Taiwan
Share of Latin America	37%	45%	33%	19%

Source: Brooking Institution and author's estimates

Figure 2 | Latin American and World Per Capita Income

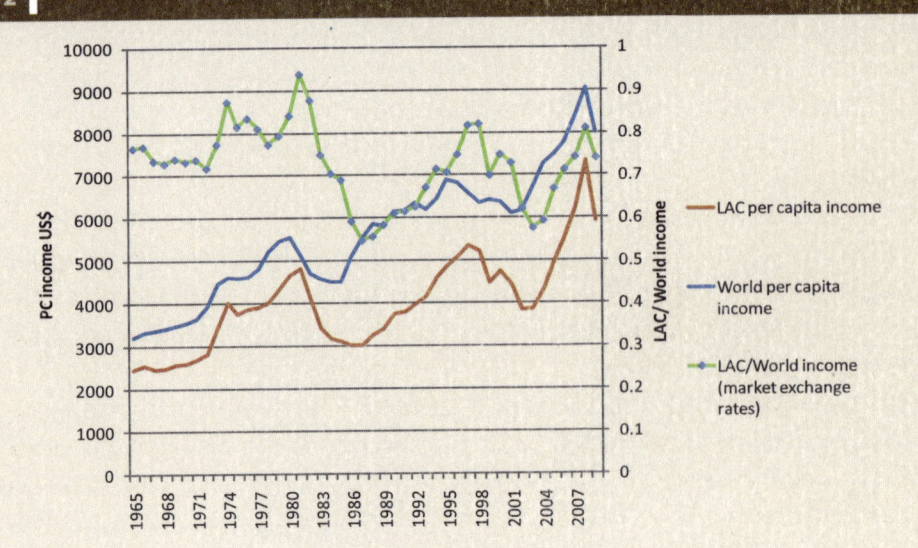

Source: World Bank - *World Development Indicators* database.

Table 2 | Average Growth Rates, 1979-2009, selected regions

	Capital	Labor	K^-L^	TFP	GDP (PPP)	GDP (MER)
Developed Countries	2.93%	0.95%	1.98%	0.76%	2.45%	2.40%
Developing Asia	6.36%	1.92%	4.44%	3.60%	7.08%	6.09%
Middle East	3.32%	3.53%	-0.21%	-0.38%	3.21%	1.82%
Sub-Saharan Africa	2.56%	2.84%	-0.28%	0.13%	2.95%	1.64%
Latin America	3.17%	2.73%	0.44%	-0.14%	2.74%	2.77%
World	2.34%	1.78%	0.56%	0.79%	3.06%	2.78%

Source: Brooking Institution and author's estimates.

peaks in Latin America's relative income correspond to peaks in oil prices. Figure 2 shows that the "lost decade" of the 1980s actually extended much further with another dip in Latin American income levels in the early part of this decade, mainly accounted for by Argentina, before the sharp recovery during the recent commodity boom.

When incomes are measured in purchasing power parity terms, the story is similar, if less dramatic. Today, Latin American income levels in PPP terms are exactly the same as those of the world as a whole. Latin America may have escaped the "Divergence, Big Time" of the post-War period, but it has not shown signs of convergence over a forty year horizon.

Sources of Growth

What has accounted for this average performance in Latin America? Table 2 shows a traditional sources of growth analysis for different regions in the world over the last thirty years. As the charts above showed, Latin America's growth in GDP, measured at market exchange rates, is very close to the world average (2.78 percent). But the sources of this growth are quite different. Latin America has had a much faster growth of labor than the world as a whole, reflecting both its high population growth rate and the growing labor force participation rate in many countries, but it has had a much lower growth rate of total factor productivity. In this, Latin America is closer to the Middle East region, another area dominated by commodity production. Both the Middle East and Latin America have negative TFP growth over thirty years, while Sub-Saharan Africa showed more growth.

The Middle East and Latin America share another characteristic. Their growth of capital is low compared to the growth rate of the labor. In fact, the change in the capital-labor ratio, given by the difference in growth rates between capital and labor, is only 0.44 percent per year in Latin America, compared to 2 percent in developed countries and 4.44 percent in developing Asia.

Table 3 | TFP levels, 1980 to 2007, selected countries, USA 1980=1.00

	1980	1990	2000	2007
United States	1.00	1.17	1.33	1.36
Chile	0.31	0.36	0.45	0.49
Argentina	0.33	0.26	0.34	0.41
Bolivia	0.15	0.13	0.14	0.15
Brazil	0.44	0.37	0.37	0.40
Colombia	0.24	0.24	0.23	0.27
Costa Rica	0.31	0.30	0.33	0.36
Dominican Republic	0.22	0.20	0.25	0.29
Ecuador	0.22	0.19	0.18	0.22
El Salvador	0.24	0.21	0.24	0.25
Guatemala	0.24	0.21	0.24	0.24
Guyana	0.08	0.06	0.10	0.11
Honduras	0.16	0.15	0.14	0.15
Jamaica	0.18	0.22	0.23	0.24
Mexico	0.44	0.39	0.42	0.43
Nicaragua	0.13	0.09	0.10	0.10
Panama	0.25	0.24	0.29	0.37
Paraguay	0.00	0.16	0.14	0.16
Peru	0.26	0.19	0.22	0.27
Trinidad and Tobago	0.55	0.37	0.43	0.67
Uruguay	0.34	0.32	0.37	0.43
Venezuela, RB	0.48	0.42	0.40	0.46

Source: Estimations by Homi Kharas

Low TFP growth and low capital-deepening per worker account for most Latin America's inability to grow rapidly and converge with developed countries.

It is the large Latin American countries, particularly Brazil, where TFP growth has lagged. In several smaller countries, including Chile, Argentina, Panama and Uruguay, TFP growth has been reasonable. Table 3 shows the levels of TFP for a number of countries, benchmarked against the United States in 1980. The United States itself has seen a 36 percent increase in TFP since 1980. Few Latin American countries have matched that growth.

In 1980, Brazil and Mexico were the technology leaders in Latin America (besides oil-rich Trinidad and Tobago). They had relatively high levels of TFP considering their incomes. Roughly speaking, two-thirds of the income gap between these countries and the United States in 1980 could be explained by differences in TFP and another one-third by differences in capital-labor ratios. By 2007, the United States was four times richer than Mexico and Brazil, and 80 percent of the gap was accounted for by technology.

Comparing Brazil to East Asian countries gives another comparison. In 1987, Brazil's technology level was about the same as that of South Korea, while Malaysia (60 percent of Brazil's level) and Thailand (30 percent) were way behind. By 2007, South Korea's technology level was 60 percent higher than that of Brazil, while Malaysia had almost caught up and Thailand was at 55 percent.

Eastern European countries had also overtaken Brazil by 2007: the Baltic nations, Hungary, Poland, Croatia and Slovakia had pulled ahead, although this may have reversed by 2010. Within Latin America, Chile has emerged as the technology leader.

Technological progress and capital investments often go hand-in-hand, although growth accounting permits a formal separation between the two. But infrastructure investments, for example, can raise the productivity of private capital and labor. Investment in new machinery is a way of capturing the latest technologies. Investment in new industries allows both capital and labor to be used more effectively. So it is not surprising, perhaps, that Latin American technological progress has been low, given its low rate of investment. Figure 3 shows the steady capital-deepening in East Asia, contrasted with relatively slow capital-deepening in Latin America, especially since the early 1980s.

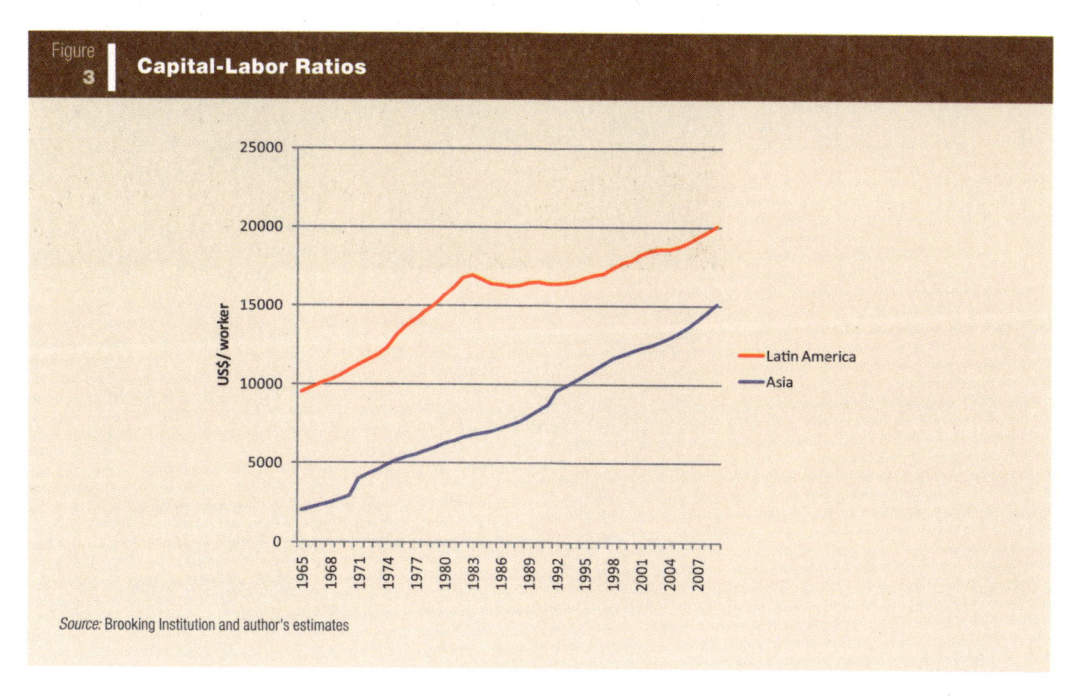

Figure 3 | Capital-Labor Ratios

Source: Brooking Institution and author's estimates

Latin America is in a "Middle Income Trap"

Few countries sustain high growth for more than a generation, and even fewer continue their high growth rates once they reach middle income status. The Commission on Growth and Development's recent review of growth in developing countries identified just 13 countries that sustained growth of more than 7 percent for at least 25 years in the postwar period.[7] They have five common characteristics: openness to the global economy in knowledge and trade; macroeconomic stability; a "future orientation", exemplified by high rates of saving and investment; a reliance on markets and market-based prices to allocate resources; and leadership committed to growth and inclusion with a reasonable capacity for administration. These success factors, deep-rooted in local institutions, are necessary, but not sufficient, for continued growth. Some countries with these characteristics grew fast, but could not sustain that growth.

Even among the 13 star performers, growth has been uneven. Some East Asian middle income countries suffered severe setbacks in 1997-1998, and may not recover past rapid growth. Brazil, whose growth performance between 1950 and 1980 qualified it as a growth star, then suffered disastrous very high inflationary episodes and low growth in the 1980s and 1990s.

Reaching incomes associated with the advanced countries is uncommon: only six of the high-growth countries did so. More common is for growth to slow markedly on reaching middle income. Many Latin American and Middle Eastern countries suffered the fate of falling into a slow-growth trap once they reached middle-income levels. The facts speak for themselves. Why this is so common, however, is less understood.

Photo Credit: CAF

Some features differentiating middle income from low income growth are clear. Growth tends to become more capital intensive and skill intensive. The domestic market expands and becomes a more important engine, especially for service growth. Wages start to rise, most rapidly for highly skilled workers, and shortages can emerge. The traditional low-wage manufacturing for export model does not work well for middle income countries. Cost advantages in labor-intensive sectors, such as

---

7   The Growth Report, A. Michael Spence (chair), The Commission on Growth and Development, 2008.

the manufactured exports that once drove growth, start to decline in comparison with lower wage poor country producers. At the same time, middle income countries do not have the property rights, contract enforcement, capital markets, track record of successful venture capital and invention, or critical mass of highly skilled people to grow through major innovations, like affluent countries. Caught between these two groups, middle income countries can become trapped, unless they change strategies and move up the value chain.

This seems to be what has happened to Latin America. In many countries, wages are too high to be globally competitive in basic manufacturing—the collapse of Latin America's garments producers after protection was withdrawn is proof of that. Yet, Latin America does not have the research and development capabilities that allow it to develop new products in advanced areas (exceptions are by now familiar: Embraer in Brazil, wine and fruits in Chile and Argentina).

In some middle income countries, the domestic market can complement export markets as the economy matures and the local market becomes large enough. In most countries, domestic consumption typically starts to grow quickly when incomes per capita reach around US$6,000 in PPP terms.[8] This did not happen in Latin America, perhaps because of the uneven distribution of income that the first phase of rapid growth generated.

Compare Brazil with South Korea and Japan, for example. Brazil's growth started to slow after 1980, when it had reached a per capita income level of US$7600 (PPP). At that time, its middle class, defined as households with incomes of between US$10 and US$100 per capita per day, was just 29 percent of the population.[9] This made it impossible for the middle-class to drive further growth, in the fashion described by Murphy, Schleifer and Vishny (1989) who argue that the middle class can pay a little extra for differentiated products, and this creates an incentive for innovation and extensive growth.

South Korea's income per capita reached US$7700 (PPP) in 1987. By that time, South Korea's evenly-distributed growth had produced a sizeable middle class, which accounted for 53 percent of the population. The country capitalized on the demand from this large middle class to grow its services industries and create the building blocks for a knowledge economy. It has continued its strong per capita growth at a 5.5 percent rate for another twenty years, in the process becoming one of the most advanced economies in the world. Today, 94 percent of Korea's population is middle class.

Japan also benefited from a sizeable middle class when growing from a middle income country to a rich country. In 1965, Japan's per capita income was US$8,200 (PPP) and its middle class was 48 percent of the population. Japan was able to achieve per capita growth of 4.8 percent per year for the next twenty years.

The middle class can provide an impetus to growth in ways other than just consumption demand. The middle class typically values, and demands, a high-quality education for their children. Hanushek (2009) documents the relatively low quality of Latin American education and ascribes the region's slow growth to that factor. The causal channel is perhaps less important than the suggestion that distribution, or more precisely inclusive growth policies, may play a role in sustaining growth in Latin America,

---

[8] Nomura International, 2009.
[9] H. Kharas et al., The Four Speed World, (forthcoming), The Brookings Institution, 2010.

if growth can be jump-started.

Note that the focus on the middle class is not the same as the traditional focus on income distribution as measured by the Gini coefficient. As Palma (2009) has shown, movements in the Gini tend to be dominated by movements in the income shares of the top and bottom deciles of the population. For middle-income countries, the middle class is found somewhere between the fifth and ninth deciles of the income distribution. Policies that improve income distribution, therefore, are not necessarily policies that expand the middle class (and vice versa).

A Global Growth Scenario under Business-as-Usual Policies[10]

To understand trends in the global middle class, a scenario for GDP growth for each country is developed and the assumption is made that the income of each household in a country grows at this rate. The details of the scenario methodology are provided in Annex 1, but broadly speaking the same techniques are used as Goldman Sachs in their pioneering scenario work, starting in 2003.[11]

Separate growth scenarios are made for 145 developed and developing countries, comprising 98 percent of global output. Taking a stylized view of the world, these countries are classified into one of four categories, each with GDP growth drivers that have different parameters—hence the model is called the Four Speed World.[12]

At the outset, it is important to emphasize that like all long-run models, the purpose is illustrative, to foster debate through presentation of a scenario rather than predict the future. Within broad analytical categories that might shape country economic performance, there will inevitably be large variations between countries, which are left unexplained, and equally large variations for any given country over time. The purpose is not to develop forecasts or projections for any country or any time period, but to indicate a scenario of the contours of the global economy over the next three decades.

The basic framework is a constant-returns-to-scale Cobb-Douglas production function with growth for each country dependent on capital accumulation, labor force growth, and technological improvements.[13] Capital accumulation is determined by investment which is assumed to remain at the average rate of the ten years, 1998-2007. Labor force growth is taken from UN population projections of the working age group of 15-64 year-olds.

What remains is the estimation of technological improvements.

Following Goldman Sachs and others, assume that the rate of technological improvement in each country has two components. First, the global technology frontier is shifting out with new advances in science, new products and new processes. Second, most countries are operating within this global frontier and can catch up rapidly. Assume that the rate at which catch-up occurs is inversely proportional to the gap between the per capita income level of the country and that of the United

---

[10] This section is based on H. Kharas "The Emerging Middle Class in Developing Countries", September 2009, background paper for the Global Development Outlook of the OECD, 2010, and on Kharas et al. (eds.) "The Four Speed World", Wolfensohn Center for Development, 2010 (forthcoming).
[11] Dreaming with BRICs: the path to 2050", Goldman Sachs.
[12] See The Four Speed World, Wolfensohn Center for Development (forthcoming) for more details.
[13] That is, $Y = AL^\alpha K^\beta$, where $\alpha + \beta = 1$, where Y is GDP, A is a parameter, L is labor, and K is capital.

States which is represented as the global leader in technology. That is, countries with very low income levels can catch up fast, while countries which have income levels closer to that of the United States will see a slower technological improvement.

The rate at which the global technology frontier moves out is taken as 1.3 percent per year. Given the historical rate of capital deepening in the United States, this parameter yields an estimate for US labor productivity growth of 1.8 percent, the average long-run rate which has been observed for the past 125 years. As Figure 4 shows, this rate has been very stable over time and can therefore be taken as a good proxy for future potential technology growth. In this sense, the model does not rely on any "new economy, information technology" assumptions and is calibrated to replicate the long-run history of global growth.

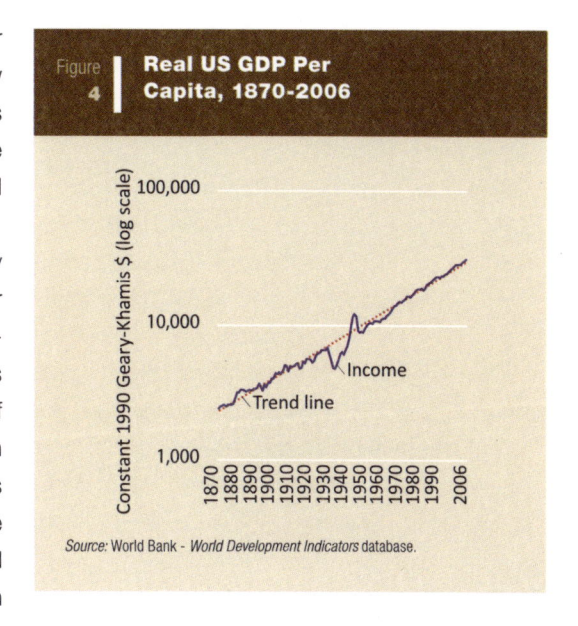

Figure 4 | Real US GDP Per Capita, 1870-2006

Source: World Bank - *World Development Indicators* database.

By assigning rapid catch-up technological progress to all countries with income levels below that of the United States, the model would tend to produce fast rates of convergence in income levels across the world. As a matter of practice, this has not occurred. Convergence has actually been limited to a small sub-set of developing countries. These countries have shifted resources into high productivity activities demanded by the world. In this way, their productivity growth has been driven by domestic structural changes that have leveraged the global economy to produce rapid technical change. It is useful to call this group of countries "convergers" because the strategies they have adopted, including an outward orientation, appear to have resulted in long-run income convergence with advanced countries.[14]

There is also a group of middle income countries which appear to have become trapped and are either not converging with the rich countries or converging very slowly. Countries in the "middle income trap" are those that appear squeezed between low wage, poor developing countries that can outcompete them in standardized manufacturing exports, and high-skilled, rich countries that grow through innovation. Countries in the middle income trap have yet to find a growth strategy that can navigate between these other competitors.[15]

Last, there are a number of poor countries which, for reasons of conflict, poor governance or adverse geography have stagnated in poverty. Paul Collier identifies a number of "low income traps"

---

[14] See Phillippe Aghion and Peter Howitt, "Appropriate Growth Policy," Schumpeter Lecture, Journal of the European Economic Association, Papers and Proceedings (2006) on why Europe converged with the US after WWII, but more recently has faced slower tfp growth.
[15] I. Gill and H. Kharas, An East Asian Renaissance, 2007, were the first economists to develop this concept of the middle income trap.

that these countries have been unable to escape.[16]

The classification of non-convergers into low and middle income groups is done based on the World Bank's classification of their Gross National Income per capita levels as of 2005. The cut-off income level is US$875.[17]

This gives a typology of four groups of countries:
- Affluent, advanced economies, with rather low rates of technological progress.
- Converging developing economies closing the income gap with the United States.
- Stalled, middle income developing economies with no convergence trends.
- Poor, low income developing economies with no convergence trends.

The classification of countries into these categories depends on (i) their income level in 2005 (our base year); and (ii) their demonstrated tendency towards convergence.

Countries that have had sustained growth of more than 3.5 percent per capita over 25 years are included in the convergence group.[18] This implies that Russia, India and China are included as convergers, but not Brazil where per capita income growth has been much more limited even since the stabilization program of the mid-1990s.

There are several surprises in the category of converger countries. Many would dispute the inclusion of Russia and the exclusion of Brazil (especially given its recent discovery of massive oil deposits and its excellent recent track record of macroeconomic management) and South Africa, for example. It is important to emphasize that the classification does not necessarily represent any judgmental views of country prospects. It results from the application of a quantitative formula to drive the classification, which is preferable to an attempt to impose subjective predispositions and beliefs about countries. What is more, it is hard to have the expertise to seriously review all 145 countries, so some quantitative, mechanical shortcut method is inevitable. Figure 5 shows how each country is classified into our Four Speed World categories. Each color represents one of the four country groupings.

Once potential growth rates are formulated, they are applied to a base year to generate a series that can be projected into the future. The base year is taken as the three-year average GDP in 2005 to 2007, all measured in PPP terms. To build global output, individual country output is simply aggregated.

To summarize the model, there are four drivers of global economic growth:
- Technological advance of the global production frontier at the rate of 1.3 percent per year.[19]
- Catch-up technology in a group of fast-growing convergers who are in the midst of a process of shifting resources from low to higher productivity activities; the speed of catch-up depends on each country's income level relative to that of the US.
- Capital accumulation, derived by assuming each country maintains its investment rate at its historical average.[20]

---

16 Paul Collier, The Bottom Billion, (New York: Oxford UP, 2007).
17 Data taken from World Develoment Indicators, on-line, accessed 2008.
18   For transition economies, the criterion is 3.5 percent per capita growth or more between 1995 and 2005.
19 This tfp rate is consistent with the US long-term labor productivity growth of 1.8 percent.
20 This assumption may be somewhat overoptimistic in the long term in the case of high-investment countries, where the ratio of investment to GDP is above 35 percent.

> Figure 5 | **The Four Speed World**

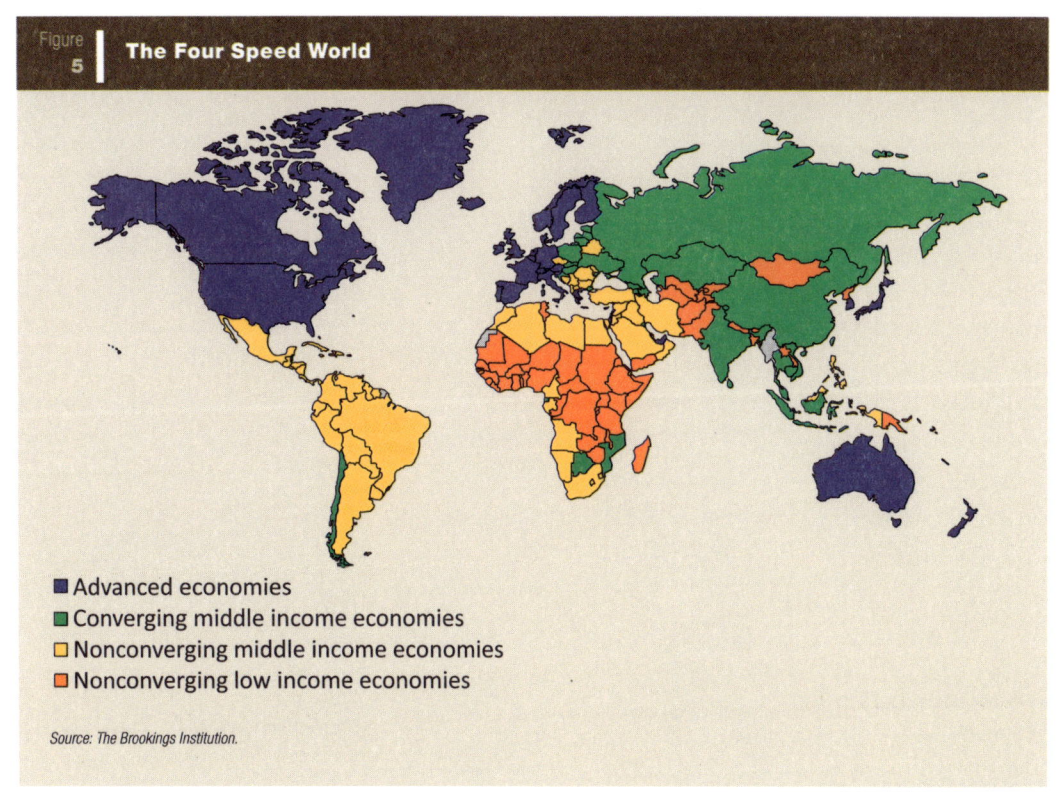

- Advanced economies
- Converging middle income economies
- Nonconverging middle income economies
- Nonconverging low income economies

Source: The Brookings Institution.

- Country specific demographic changes of the 15-64 age group, assuming constant labor force participation rates in each country.

What are the main differences between this Four Speed World model and other global models?

- Here, the sample consists of 145 countries.[21] Many countries have small GDP but large populations and the larger sample allows a better understanding of the interaction between demographic trends and economic trends. It also means trends for geographic regions and local neighborhoods, like Latin America can be computed.
- All countries are not assumed to converge with the US. Importantly, Brazil and Mexico for now are classified as being caught in the middle-income trap rather than as being part of the group of converging globalizers. That is because this is a business-as-usual scenario, rather than a forecast. In actuality, there is significant potential for Brazil and other Latin American countries to join the group of convergers and grow much faster than during their recent history (see alternative scenario).
- Parameters for capital accumulation and total factor productivity growth are based on actual data and simulations, rather than on ad hoc assumptions. For example, in their 2003 study,

---

21 Goldman Sachs first looked only at 6 developed countries and 4 BRIC countries, and then extended their analysis to a further 11 emerging economies. PWC look at 30 emerging economies.

Goldman Sachs assumed an investment rate for India of 22 percent of GDP and a growth rate of 6 percent. In actuality, India's investment rate today has risen to 36.7 percent and even in the face of the current crisis, 6 percent growth seems low.[22]

The modeling framework may appear overly deterministic and devoid of policy content, but several of the variables reflect policy choices. For example, some analysts emphasize the role of undervalued exchange rates in promoting rapid growth over long periods of time.[23] In this model, the same growth result is achieved because undervalued exchange rates lower a country's income level relative to the United States and induce more rapid technological growth. As another example, openness and other reform measures may show up in higher investment rates as businesses enter new sectors or may be captured by a demonstrated track record of convergence, boosting projected TFP growth.

Implementation effectiveness, governance and institutional development are captured by giving higher rates of technical progress to countries with demonstrated high levels of past growth which are indicative of their institutional depth. Indeed, the countries in the four tiers show a pattern of governance that reflects their performance: affluent countries do best, followed by the convergers, stalled and poor, in that order.[24] Thus, deep policymaking structures are captured in the model through higher rates of technological change and investment, even though actual policies themselves are not explicitly specified.

Global Growth Results

The global economy fell in size to US$53 trillion, measured at market exchange rates,[25] in 2009, dominated by the United States, with a US$13.6 trillion economy, just over one-quarter of the global total. In 2005 PPP terms, global output reached almost US$63 trillion. North America (24 percent), Europe (27 percent) and Asia (34 percent) dominate the world economy. Latin America's share today is about 8.7 percent in PPP terms and 6.3 percent at market exchange rates.

The BRICs accounted for about 24 percent of 2009 global output in PPP terms, a post-war historical high. This is a recent phenomenon, one driven largely by China which has expanded its global market share to almost 13 percent. Even at market exchange rates, China is set to overtake Japan as the world's second largest economy, either this year or next. Most importantly, the rich countries of the world only account for 53 percent of global output now, compared to 70 percent in 1990. This is one reason why global growth (calculated using a chain-weighted method) may actually accelerate: the share of fast growing economies is much higher than was the case twenty years ago.

By 2040, 30 years from now, the global economy may be US$250 trillion in PPP dollars.[26]

Such a world is very different from the one we see today. It is significantly wealthier, with per capita incomes averaging US$30,000 as compared to US$8,000 today. The economic center of gravity

---

22 Indeed, in their 2007 update, Goldman Sachs analysts Poddar and Yi raise their sustainable growth forecast for India to 8 percent through 2020. See Tushar Poddar and Eva Yi, "India's Rising Growth Potential," Goldman Sachs Global Economics Working Paper, No 152 (2007).
23 Surjit Bhalla, "Indian Economic Growth, 1950-2008", (October, 2008), available at: http://oxusresearch.com/downloads/CE140309.pdf.
24 Means of governance values in the Kaufmann, Kraay, Mastruzzi index. The pattern of mean values by tier is the same across all six of the KKM indicators.
25 Measured in 2007 US dollars adjusted for changes in exchange rates
26 Natural resource constraints and the effects of climate change have been ignored in this scenario. This may prove to be quite unrealistic but to take these into account would require a far more sophisticated model of global growth.

would shift to Asia, which could account for 61 percent of global output in 2040. Three giant economies, China, India and Japan, would lead Asia's resurgence. But other large countries like Indonesia and Vietnam would also have significant economic mass. Even Thailand and Malaysia could have economies larger than France has today.

The rise of Asia would not be unprecedented. Indeed, it would bring Asia's economic share into line with its population share and restore the balance of global economic activity to that in the 18th and early 19th centuries, before the Industrial Revolution led to the great divergence of incomes across countries.

The converse of Asia's rise would be a fall in the share of the G7 economies. Their global income share has already fallen to new post-World War II lows, and by 2040 it could be just over one-fifth of the world, or 21 percent.

To appreciate the likelihood of this enormous change, consider the following facts. Taking out the effect of general inflation, the global economy reached US$20 trillion, in terms of 2005 PPP dollars, in 1977. It took 19 years to double to US$40 trillion by 1996—with 3.6 percent annual growth. Over the next 10 years, from 1996 to 2006, annual growth has been 3.7 percent. To get to US$250 trillion by 2040, global growth would need to be 4.7 percent from now on.

The reason for expecting an acceleration of global growth is that the share of rapidly growing economies has now risen to almost one-half of total output, while the share of slow growing countries has fallen. The model assumes that rich country real potential output growth will slow in the next 30 years to 2.3 percent, from 2.5 percent over the last 10 years. Meanwhile the "convergers" could also slow to 8.2 percent, close to the 8.4 percent over the last 10 years.

Photo Credit: CAF

In other words, although growth is slowing in individual country groups, overall global growth (chain-weighted) will accelerate simply because of the larger share in global output from fast-growing countries. As faster growing countries also tend to have appreciating exchange rates, global output growth at market prices will accelerate simply because the fastest growing economies in the world

(China and India) are also becoming ever-larger shares of global output at market exchange rates.

One reason developing countries are growing faster than developed countries is that they are younger, still at an early phase in their demographic transition. Global demographic shifts are inexorably changing the distribution of global economic activity. Today's rich countries accounted for 22 percent of the world's people in 1965, but only account for 15 percent today, and their share is forecast to shrink to 13 percent of the world total by 2040. Overall, the world will add 2 billion people by 2040. But the population in today's rich countries will grow by only an estimated 100 million. Ninety-five percent of the population increase (excluding migration) will be in developing countries.

The Impact of the Global Economic Crisis

The fallout from the economic crisis has been quick and painful. In September 2008, the year-long tremors in the US housing market developed into a full-fledged financial crisis that quickly spread to all developed countries. When the real economies of advanced countries stalled, so did global demand, dashing hopeful talk of 'decoupling' even in rapidly growing emerging economies. In a matter of months the IMF revised downward its global growth forecast for 2009, from 3.0 percent in October 2008 to 2.2 percent in November to just 0.6 percent in January 2009, -1.3 percent in April and -1.1 percent in October. This makes 2009 the first year of global economic contraction since World War II.[27] Global output is expected to decline back to 2007 levels.

The depth and the duration of the global recession are currently being hotly debated amongst academics and policymakers. Most take the experience of the Great Depression as indicative of what may happen.[28] Then, as well as in post-War recessions, growth exceeded its long run average during a recovery phase before returning to trend, compensating for the down period. There was little impact on permanent long-run income levels. But that period was exceptional, given the level of destruction of human and physical capital during the war. Separating the "natural" recovery from the Great Depression from the effects of World War II spending is almost impossible. The relevance of that recovery for the current crisis may well be questioned.

Notwithstanding, the post-War experience with recessions is that as the recovery gathers steam, countries grow faster than potential output. While the depth and the duration of the global recession are hotly debated amongst academics and policymakers, many do not foresee a permanent impact. When the crisis does abate, growth is likely to exceed its long run average during a recovery phase before returning to trend, compensating for the down period.[29]

This premise remains controversial. The IMF has reviewed the history of financial crises and concludes that while medium term growth recovers to trend levels, output remains below trend, by an average of 10 percent.[30] However, the IMF analysis is simply a description of what has happened compared to pre-crisis trends. This kind of analysis has a systematic bias: the pre-crisis trend (which

---

27   Decline occurs in GDP at constant prices. In PPP terms, global GDP in 2009 is forecast to continue to expand, albeit very modestly.
28   For example, see Council of Economic Advisers, "Economic Projections and the Budget Outlook," (February 28, 2009), available at: www.whitehouse.gov/administration/eop/cea
29   For example, see the report of the United States Council of Economic Advisors, Economic Projections and the Budget Outlook, February 28, 2009.
30   "World Economic Outlook", IMF, September 2009 Ch. 4

the IMF takes as ten to three years prior to the crisis) may be part of a longer-term boom which in turn precipitates the crisis, and as such should not be counted as the long-term trend growth rate.

These debates underline an essential point of this chapter. The forward-looking figures are one scenario of what the world could look like, not a projection or forecast.

The Shift to Asia

The changes represented above mark a significant shift in the global economy towards Asia. For simplicity, assume each country's economic mass is concentrated in its capital city. If the world is thought of as a two-dimensional plane, with its origin at zero degrees latitude and zero degrees longitude, then one can plot the point where the center of gravity would lie, and trace the shift over time of that point.[31]

In 1965, the global economic center of gravity was somewhere in Spain. This is not surprising. The three great masses in the global economy were in Europe, the United States and Japan. All of these are in the Northern Hemisphere. The center of gravity actually lay very close to an axis connecting Washington DC and Beijing (shown in orange on the map). Over time, two drifts in global growth are apparent: a slight movement to the south and a dominant one to the east. These shifts reflect the growth in the large emerging economies of the southern hemisphere. Brazil, Mexico, and South East Asia became more prominent during this period. Even Japan and Korea are located south of the Beijing-Washington axis. Over time, in our scenario for the future, it is India, China, Indonesia, and Vietnam that keep pulling the center of economic gravity in the world to the East

Latin America under the BAU Scenario

How does Latin America fare under this business-as-usual scenario? Not surprisingly, the answer is simply average. In PPP terms, Latin America may grow by 2.2 percent per capita in the long-term, but the world will be growing faster. Latin America may stay at a constant level compared to advanced countries, with Mexico and Brazil both posting growth rates close to that of the United States, but this performance means Latin America may slowly fade compared to the rest of the world, especially East and South Asia. At market exchange rates, a similar pattern holds. Latin America simply grows more or less at the same pace as the United States, and falls behind the rest of the world. This is all the more disappointing as Latin America is potentially able to enjoy a demographic dividend in the coming years—its labor force will grow more rapidly than its population for the next thirty years.

Table 4 shows a trajectory of key variables for Latin America and the rest of the world under this business as usual scenario.

Table 4 is deliberately exaggerated. It shows how a business-as-usual scenario implies a growing gap between Latin America and much of the rest of the world, especially the advanced countries. It also shows the possibilities for Latin America, exemplified by Chile. Chile is the only Latin American

---

31   One degree of either latitude or longitude is not the same distance everywhere in the world, so an adjustment needs to be made. For this calculation, coordinates of global capital cities are projected onto a two-dimensional plane where the x- and y- coordinates are in meters, via the Global Sinusoidal (0) projection. The center of gravity is then computed and plotted and presented in terms of the standard WGS84 map. Dan Hammer, Center for Global Development, graciously provided the maps and projections.

Table 4: Latin America—A Fading Global Force

	2009	2040
Global Output (PPP)	$62.8 trillion	$258 trillion
Latin America share	8.7%	5.3%
Global Output growth (PPP) a.	3.75%	4.47%
Latin America	3.03%	2.91%
Average Income (Market Exchange Rates)		
World	$8,000	$28,500
Rich countries	$36,750	$78,600
Latin America	$5,912	$13,700
Mexico	$7,000	$17,00
Brazil	$6,250	$13,500
Chile	$7,760	$63,000
Rank in world (absolute GDP) size		
Brazil	10	16
Mexico	12	18
Capital-Labor ratio		
World	$32.7k/person	$79.6k/person
Rich countries	$146k/person	$325k/person
Latin America	$20k/person	$42.4k/person
TFP (US 2009=100)		
United States	100	150.3
Mexico	31.9	47.7
Brazil	29.9	44.6
Chile	37.8	91.6

a. Growth rate taken for the preceding 25 year period.

Note: This chart differs from that in Chapter 1 and uses 2007 US dollars adjusted for changes in exchange rates. Market exchange rate units used throughout this chapter differ from both real (constant) and current (nominal) GDP measures and are defined in the Annex.

Source: World Bank - WDI, Brookings Institution, and author's estimates.

country in our sample to meet the criterion for inclusion in the "convergers" category of having a track record of at least 3.5 percent per capita income growth over the past twenty-five years. Obviously, if a country is included as a converger, it grows very rapidly, and indeed we show Chile as converging towards the incomes of other advanced economies by 2040.

But Brazil, Mexico and other Latin American countries do not meet the criterion. What we show in the business-as-usual scenario is what would happen if they continue down a path of relatively low

TFP growth and relatively low capital investment. At the end of the day, the policies which will generate convergence depend on these two key variables.

Latin America Revival Scenario

If a few key economies in Latin America could enter the club of "convergers" it could make a radical difference to the region's prospects. To investigate this, the model was re-run with four major Latin American countries moving into the "convergers" category, meaning they undertake the policy reforms needed to benefit from catch-up growth. The scenario is incomplete in the sense that investment rates in the selected countries would probably also increase in such a scenario, but this is not modeled. Nor is the spill-over effect onto neighboring countries which could also be substantial.

Two large and two mid-sized countries are selected as the four newly converging Latin American economies, joining Chile in this classification. The choice is arbitrary, and implies that countries representing seventy percent of the region's economy adopt good policies. By 2040, the difference to the region is enormous, with output levels almost tripling. Growth accelerates to a level of 6.5 percent at market exchange rates (Table 5) as a result of faster TFP growth in the "newly converging" countries. With catch-up, selected countries could expect TFP growth of 2-3 percent per year. By 2040, the major economies would have the same technology on average as that in the United States in the 1990s.

Table 5 | Latin America—A Revival Scenario

	2040 BAU	2040 Revival
Regional Output (MER)	$10 trillion	$29 trillion
Output growth (MER)[a]	4.86%	6.57%
GDP pc (MER)	$13,675	$39,624

a. Output growth at market exchange rates includes real exchange rate changes. Growth is computed over the preceding 25 years.

Source: Author's Calculations.

The revival scenario indicates the dependence of the Latin American region on the performance of its major economies, as well as the critical issue of capitalizing on the advantages of backwardness in raising growth. Recall that the revival scenario simply attributes to major Latin American economies the same rate of growth of technological catch-up as in the rest of the converging world. That is to say, it is an estimate of what can be considered as the potential growth for these countries. Compounded over many years, the impact is significant. Regional output could be three times higher by 2040, and per capita incomes could rise by almost three times. If the region could achieve these kinds of growth rates it would have income levels of about half of that of the US by 2040. The richer countries of the region would catch-up rapidly with the US.

A Vision for Convergence

There is of course a vibrant debate as to what policies can best lead to higher TFP growth and higher rates of capital investment. Some of the key issues are taken up in other chapters: education, poverty and the middle class, the role of institutions and governance. Another policy that has become fashionable again in the current debate is the real exchange rate.[32] The debate about the relevance of these and other intervention points is sure to continue for a long time to come. But one key factor for achieving high growth is precisely to start the debate on why Latin America is not converging.

Crudely speaking, the approach to growth in many Latin American countries can be construed as "get the policies right and growth will follow". That applies particularly to macroeconomic policies and Latin America has an enviable track record of finally putting its fiscal and monetary house in order, with Chile leading the pack of those countries developing fiscally responsible rules. But the growth results from such an approach have been modest. Chile estimates its potential output growth to have fallen to 3.9 percent. For a country at its income level, a long-term growth of 5 percent per capita should be achievable. Or to take another example: during the 2009 Great Recession, many Latin American countries like Brazil were congratulating themselves on avoiding a major crisis while their Asian rivals were busy rethinking their growth strategies.

That attitude stands at odds with the leadership on growth that is one of the ingredients of long-term success identified by the Growth Commission. The Commission highlights the benefits of a national purpose in pursuing rapid growth, endorsed and sustained in a consensus among political parties. In East Asia, which is recovering rapidly from the Great Recession, the past year has been one of determined efforts at structural reform and reinvention to take advantage of the changing world environment. It is that single-minded focus on growth which appears to be one secret of Asian success stories. East Asian approaches can be characterized as "set a growth target and address structural problems while enforcing strong macroeconomic policies to make sure it happens". There is a pragmatism that serves to overcome deeply-held beliefs when the growth engine is threatened.[33]

Consider the following examples. Singapore overcame its traditional antipathy towards gambling and encouraged a new resort-casino industry once it realized it could not meet its ambitions of doubling tourist arrivals without an attraction of this sort. Malaysia has recently moved to liberalize its social policy towards local minority groups in selected service sectors. Once considered to be taboo for economic policymaking, the 2009 recession persuaded the Prime Minister that action was needed to jump-start the economy. Korea decided to break up the chaebol and move towards a knowledge economy in 2000, after reviewing prospects for the economy post-Asian crisis. In each case, the primacy of growth succeeded in overcoming thorny political obstacles that previously had been thought to be intractable.

The same cannot be said for Latin America. Each country has its own particular set of growth-inhibiting issues which are well-known internally, but where the political will and consensus to address the issue is lacking. This is partly reflected in very low rates of public investment that would signify a long-term commitment of the government to growth. Even in Chile, the policy-making process is short-term and devoid of the detailed staff work at the micro level that gives credibility to a growth strategy. Chile has an Innovation Commission that produced a National Innovation Strategy in January

---

32 "Devaluing Your Way to Prosperity", Surjit S. Bhalla, Peterson Institute, 2010 (forthcoming).
33 The East Asian experience has also been characterized by a consistent set of macroeconomic policies that created the basis for sustained growth and allowed for the implementation of serious structural reforms and social policies (particularly education).

2007, endorsed by President Bachelet. While breaking new ground in setting quantitative targets for outputs and outcomes, the Chilean program has not generated much enthusiasm among business leaders who are expected to provide most of the increase in R&D spending recommended by the Commission.

The Chilean strategy has no clear implementation plan. For example, the development of Chile as a major business processing off-shoring center is thought to require 40,000 English-speakers over the next two to three years, but no agency is tasked with providing such training. Contrast this with the Korean approach to its move to a knowledge economy which involved 83 action plans, 19 ministries, and 17 research institutes, all to be tracked by the Ministry of Finance and Economy and reported to the President by the private committee of the National Economic Advisory Council.[34]

Latin America lacks a vision of growth, a stretch target to which leaders commit themselves that can develop into a mechanism for forging public-private partnerships, for developing the details of growth strategies, for considering the adequacy of public investment and major public infrastructure projects, for reforming education, labor laws, social security and other major political hurdles. Such a vision needs to be multi-year and needs to involve all political parties and private sector stakeholders. It can be built around the premise that without such a vision the region is destined to be average—neither converging nor diverging from the United States and other advanced economies. Latin America would slowly lose the attention of the world. It would avoid the negative attention that it received in the past from crises and poverty; but it may not get the positive attention of being at the forefront of the developing world and the new emerging global economy.

Latin America can do better than average. In this chapter, there is a scenario for growth at 6.5 percent per year (at market exchange rates). Such a growth rate could be achieved if four of the major Latin American economies manage to achieve the same rate of average catch-up TFP growth as in other developing countries. That suggests it is a feasible scenario. But the region and its leaders need to raise their sights on economic growth and promote a vision of a vibrant economic region where high investment rates and rapid total factor productivity growth are the objects of national policy.

---

34   H. Kharas et al. "Chilean Growth through East Asian Eyes," Working Paper No. 31, Commission on Growth and Development, 2008.

Annex: Projections Methodology

Introduction

This chapter utilizes three units with which to measure GDP:

- "Constant 2007 $" does not represent the conventional definition of "real growth" but instead is a composite of real growth and real exchange rate appreciation. These figures are derived by deflating nominal GDP by the US GDP deflator and are just used as a convenience to make future projections in "real" terms. These can be used to compare countries' changing market power.
- "Market exchange rates" is a hybrid: It is nominal GDP assuming zero inflation but taking exchange rate movemetns into account. For years prior to 2007, this is calculated by taking current GDP and eliminating the effect of inflation but keeping exchange rate movements (accompolished by deflating by US GDP). For years after 2007, this is calculated by taking the "constant 2007 dollars" above and adding expected exchange rate movements but not inflation. As will be described, this is based on certain assumptions of nominal exchange rate movements, although if this is done through price increases in the home country, the impact on GDP is the same. For the most part, cross country comparisons use these units.
- PPP rates are market rates in 2005, converted into PPP dollars and then held constant. These are used to measure poverty and compare living standards across countries.

Projections Methodology[35]

Step 1: Historical database

The first step was to create a country-level database covering the period 1965-2007, which both forms the basis for our projections and is useful for historical comparisons.

The study begins by obtaining data on real GDP growth rates for each country from the World Bank's World Development Indicators 2007 (WDI).[36] Where there are gaps, this is supplemented with data from the IMF's World Economic Outlook, Angus Maddison's historical dataset, the IMF's

---

35 Prepared by Geoffrey Gertz
36 Accessed July 2008.

International Financial Statistics, and national sources.[37] Real GDP in constant 2007 US$ for the years 1965-2007 is calculated by taking current GDP in US$ for 2007, again from WDI and WEO, and projecting backwards using these growth rates.[38]

Data on GDP at current exchange rates is primarily sourced from WDI with missing data once again supplemented for certain countries and years as detailed in footnote 2. GDP at market exchange rates is calculated by deflating GDP at current exchange rates by US CPI obtained from the US Bureau of Labor Statistics. GDP at purchasing power parity is obtained by taking the most recent World Bank estimates of GDP at PPP (for 2005) and projecting backwards using real growth rates.[39] All of our measures of GDP are also expressed in per capita terms, using population estimates from the United Nations Population Prospects dataset (2006).[40]

The database also includes information on each country's capital stock, which is necessary for our future projections of GDP. Our data coverage varies by country based on data availability, but in each case we calculate capital stock from an initial year (the earliest year for which data is available for that particular country) up to 2005.

For each country the initial capital stock (K0) is calculated according to the following equation, following the method of Caselli and Feyrer (2007)[41]:

$$(1) \quad K_0 = \frac{I_0}{(\delta + g)}$$

where I_0 is investment in constant 2000 US$ for the initial year, as provided by WDI[42]; δ is the depreciation rate, set at 0.06 following Caselli and Feyrer and based on economic consensus; and g is the average real GDP growth rate for the ten year period following the initial year, again taken from WDI.[43]

---

37 The IMF World Economic Outlook is used as the source for all growth rates for the years 2006 and 2007, as at time of writing World Development Indicators did not yet include this data. Angus Maddison's historical dataset (Maddison Historical Statistics, World Population, GDP, and Per Capita GDP, 1-2003 AD: Last Update August 2007 (http://www.ggdc.net/maddison/); Variable: GDP in million 1990 International Geary-Khamis dollars, 1820-2003) is used for Bahrain to 1979, Germany to 1970, Kuwait to 1993, UAE to 1972, Cambodia to 1986, Bosnia 1991-93, Indonesia to 1966, Mauritius to 1979, Mozambique to 1979, Vietnam to 1984, Angola to 1984, Jamaica to 1965, Jordan to 1974, Paraguay to 1988, Saudi Arabia to 1967, Serbia 1991-92, Swaziland to 1969, Turkey to 1967, Ethiopia to 1980, Gambia to 1965, Mali to 1966, Tanzania to 1987, Uganda to 1981 and Yemen to 1990. Prior to 1990, data for Armenia, Azerbaijan, Belarus, Estonia, Georgia, Kazakhstan, Kyrgyzstan, Latvia, Lithuania, Moldova, Russia, Tajikistan, Turkmenistan, Uzbekistan, and Ukraine are combined under the heading former USSR, and data for East Germany, Albania, Bulgaria, Czech Republic, Slovak Republic, Hungary, Poland, Romania, Slovenia, Serbia & Montenegro, Croatia, and Bosnia & Herzegovina are combined under the heading Eastern Europe. These data series are constructed by summing the 1991 GDP values of the individual countries in the groupings and projecting backwards using Maddison's growth rates for Eastern European countries and former Soviet countries for the years 1965 to 1990. Cyprus data for the years 1965 to 1974 are from the IMF's International Financial Statistics. Taiwan data for the years 1965 to 2005 are from National Statistics, Republic of China (Taiwan), available online at http://eng.stat.gov.tw.
38 Accessed July 2008.
39 Global Purchasing Power Parities and Real Expenditures: 2005 International Comparison Program, World Bank, 2008.
40 The United Nations Population Prospects dataset (2006) provides estimates for every fifth year (e.g. 1965, 1970, 1975, etc). Estimates for between years are calculated using compound annual growth rates (CAGR).
41 "The Marginal Product of Capital," Francesco Caselli and James Feyrer, Quarterly Journal of Economics, May 2007.
42 Accessed July 2008.
43 Accessed July 2008. We have investment data for two-thirds of the countries from at least 1975, and for all but three (Bosnia & Herzegovina, Serbia, and Liberia) from 1992. For those countries where current US$ investment is available more than 15 years before constant 2000 US$ investment, we use the current US$ investment and convert it into constant 2000 US$ by multiplying the figure by the ratio of constant 2000 US$ GDP to current US$ GDP for the relevant year.

Given the initial capital stock, the capital stock in each subsequent year up until 2005 is calculated according to the following equation:

$$(2) \quad K_t = K_{t-1} \cdot (1-\delta) + I_{t-1}$$

The depreciation rate (δ) remains constant across time at 0.06. As with initial investment I_0, investment (I_t) is given in constant US$ and comes from WDI.[44]

Step 2: Constant GDP projections, 2010-2050

The heart of the model is constant GDP projections for the years 2008 through 2050, using a simple Cobb-Douglas function in which GDP is a function of labor (L), capital (K), and technological progress or total factor productivity growth (TFP). For each year GDP is estimated according to the following equation:

$$(3) \quad Y = TFP \cdot L^{\alpha} \cdot K^{(1-\alpha)}$$

where α equals 2/3 based on historical evidence and economic consensus. We follow an iterative process to obtain GDP projections based on estimates of labor, capital, and total factor productivity for each subsequent year.

For labor (L) projections the study again turns to the United Nations Population Prospects (2006) dataset to obtain estimates of the working age population (15-64) by country for every fifth year up to 2050. Figures for intervening years are calculated using CAGR. The size of the economically active population for each country is calculated by multiplying these figures by the labor force participation rate from WDI.[45]

The capital (K) projections build on the capital stock estimates from the historic database. As an initial step, we convert our estimated 2005 capital stock levels from constant 2000 US$ to constant 2007 US$ to ensure compatibility.[46] Capital stock projections follow a similar approach to equation (2). However, whereas previously the accumulation of new capital was based on actual investment, in our forward projections the accumulation of new capital is estimated by multiplying the previous year's GDP by the country's estimated long run investment rate i_{95-05}, equal to the average investment rate for the period 1995 to 2005.[47]

---

[44] Accessed July 2008. As with initial investment, where current US$ investment data is available more than 15 years before constant 2000 US$ investment data, we employ current US$ investment data and convert it into constant US$ using the same method.

[45] Accessed July 2008. Labour force participation rate data is available for all countries other than Serbia, Seychelles, Taiwan for which regional averages were used.

[46] We use a conversion ratio of 2005 GDP in constant 2000 US$ to 2005 GDP in constant 2007 US$.

[47] The investment rate for each year is obtained by dividing investment by GDP (both in constant prices). Data from WDI, accessed July 2008. For Serbia and Liberia, we use a shorter average investment period due to data restrictions.

(4) $\quad K_t = K_{t-1} \cdot (1-\delta) + i_{95\text{-}05} \cdot Y_{t-1}$

Total factor productivity (TFP) is the most complex calculation. The initial level of TFP for the year 2007 is calculated by re-arranging the Cobb-Douglas formula above (3), filling in actual GDP, labor, and capital figures for 2007. Future levels of TFP are then calculated according to the following equation:

(5) $\quad TFP_t = TFP_{t-1} \cdot \left[1.013 - \beta \ln \left(\dfrac{GDPpc_{i,\,t-1}}{GDPpc_{US,\,t-1}} \right) \right]$

Changes in TFP occur through two channels. As a first step, the basic rate of long-term technology growth is assumed to be 1.3 percent, based on historical data.[48] This is the starting point for all countries' changes in TFP.

As a second step, one must model changes in TFP as a process of convergence with the United States, with the assumption that as an economy grows closer to the per capita income levels of the United States, its productivity growth rate slows.[49] The speed of convergence (β) is set to 0.015 for all countries in tiers 1 and 2, based on their strong historical productivity and GDP growth rates. For all countries in tiers 3 and 4, β equals zero. This reflects the fact that these countries have struggled to produce dynamic growth and have failed to converge with United States living standards over recent years. For countries in tiers 3 and 4, the rate of TFP growth is therefore equal to 1.3 percent.

Step 3: GDP at market exchange rate projections, 2007-2050

Once constant 2007 US$ GDP projections are calculated using the Cobb-Douglas formula (3), real GDP growth rates are derived and are then used to generate future GDP projections in 2009 constant US$ by applying these real growth rates to each country's 2009 nominal GDP.
changes in exchange rates must be estimated to express the forecasts at market exchange rates.

Real exchange rates are expected to appreciate as economies grow, approaching PPP exchange rates as economies converge with US living standards, as posited by the Balassa-Samuelson effect.[50]

To project changes in the real exchange rate (RER), the relationship between the real exchange rate and relative income levels is estimated by running the following simple OLS regression for all available countries, using mean data for the years 2005 through 2007 to smooth over short-term fluctuations[51]:

---

48 Note, this is broadly in line with the Goldman Sachs paper by Wilson & Purushothaman, "Dreaming with BRICs: The Path to 2050", which assumes long run US TFP growth of 1.33%.
49 Given the process of convergence, countries that begin with living standards above the US will see their TFP growth begin below that of the US but rising towards US levels (of 1.3%) as their living standards converge.
50 For a discussion of the Balassa-Samuelson effect see: I. Kravis & R. Lipsey, "Towards an Explanation of National Price Levels", Princeton Studies in International Finance, No. 52, 1983.
51 Data from WDI, accessed January 2009. We include all countries in our regression for which there is data, excluding: countries whose population in 2007 was under 1 million; four countries who have rebased their currency regimes during the 3 year period (Sudan, Mozambique, Venezuela and Ghana); three

Figure A.1 | Regression Results

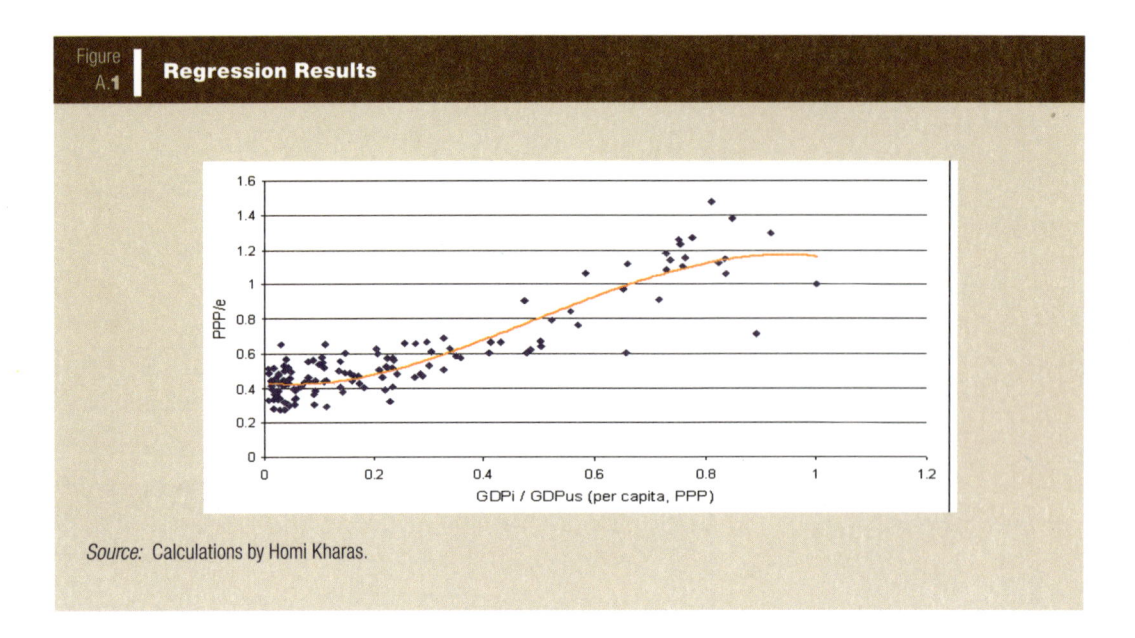

Source: Calculations by Homi Kharas.

$$(6) \quad RER^* = \frac{PPP_i}{e_i} = \alpha + \beta \left(\frac{GDPpc_i}{GDPpc_{US}}\right) + \gamma \left(\frac{GDPpc_i}{GDPpc_{US}}\right)^2 + \delta \left(\frac{GDPpc_i}{GDPpc_{US}}\right)^3 + \varepsilon_i$$

where PPPi is the PPP conversion factor for country i with respect to the US (US$=1); e_i is the exchange rate of country i with respect to the US (US$ = 1); $GDPpc_i$ is the GDP per capita (constant 2005 US dollars PPP) of country i; $GDPpc_{US}$ is the GDP per capita (constant 2005 US dollars PPP) of the US; α, β, γ and δ are coefficients and εi i is the error term for country i.

Power terms of the independent variable are included to capture the changing speed with which the real exchange rate appreciates as economies converge on US per capita income levels. Changes in the real exchange rate at different levels of convergence (or development) are expected to follow an S-shaped (logistic) curve, reflecting changes in the relative price of tradeables and non-tradeables as economies develop.[52]

The regression results bear out this relationship, as illustrated by the fitted line of the regression results (Figure A.1). The regression obtains coefficient values of 0.4317912 for α; -0.3184848 for β;

---

countries for which the currency and PPP data are at odds (El Salvador, Syria, Myanmar); and 8 countries whose average per capita income between 2005 and 2007 (constant 2005 US dollars PPP) exceeded that of the U.S. (Macao, Kuwait, Singapore, United Arab Emirates, Brunei, Norway, Qatar and Luxembourg). This leaves a total sample of 132 countries.

52 Second Among Equals: The Middle Class Kingdoms of India and China; Surjit. S. Bhalla, 2008.

3.190494 for γ; and -2.140511 for δ. The R-squared value is 0.8248, demonstrating the regression's high explanatory power.

The regression results suggest that an economy's real exchange rate, as measured by PPP/e, typically peaks at around 1.174. This is consistent both with our base year data, where a number of advanced countries are found to exceed parity with the US, and with others' estimates.[53]

For 2007, the real exchange rate is approximated by the three-year average (2005-2007) value of PPP/e. For each subsequent year changes in the real exchange rate for each country are projected using the following equation:

$$(7) \quad RER_{it} = \left[RER_{it-1} + 1.174 - RER_{it-1} \right] \cdot \left[\left(RER_t^* - RER_{t-1}^* \right) / \left(1.174 - RER_{t-1}^* \right) \right]$$

where RER_{t^*} is an estimate of the real exchange rate, as determined by the regression results, given the ratio of an economy's average per capita income to that of the US at time t.

The projected real exchange rate level, for country i and time t, is a function of the estimated level in the previous year and an incremental change predicted by the regression curve based on changes in relative incomes. The final double-bracket term estimates the closure of the "real exchange rate gap"—the difference between the real exchange rate and its estimated maximum—in response to a change in relative incomes according to the regression. This rate of closure is then applied to the gap between the estimated maximum and the estimated RER_{it} for the previous year (the first bracket term) to obtain projected values of the real exchange rate for all countries on a yearly basis.[54]

This results in estimated real exchange rate values which approach the fitted line of the regression as incomes converge with that of the US. For example, Figure A.2 traces the real exchange rate path of two outlier countries, Belize (red) and Belarus (blue), whose initial RER (as estimated by PPP/e) differs markedly from the fitted line. The markers indicate the years 2007 and 2050, illustrating how the RER deviation from the fitted line diminishes during the convergence process.

The estimated real exchange rate values are based to 2007=1 and multiplied by our growth projections in constant dollars to obtain projections at market exchange rates.

Step 4: GDP at PPP exchange rate projections, 2008-2050

In addition to market exchange rates, constant GDP projections are converted into purchasing power

---

53 ibid
54 For countries whose real exchange rate is above the regression curve's highest point in the base year, the real exchange rate is assumed to remain constant. For countries whose per capita income level exceeds that of the US in the base year, the real exchange rate is assumed to remain constant. For countries whose per capita income level overtakes that of the US over the series, the real exchange rate is assumed to remain constant from the year in which it reaches its peak. For Ghana, Mozambique, Sudan and Venezuela, adjustment is made to accommodate the rebasing of currencies. For Myanmar, Syria, Taiwan, Turkmenistan and Uzbekistan, for whom accurate e values cannot be obtained from the WDI, we use 2005 real exchange rates obtained or derived from "Global Purchasing Power Parities and Real Expenditures - International Comparison Program", World Bank, 2005. For Zimbabwe, for which no estimate of the current real exchange rate can be obtained, we assume no change in the real exchange rate over the series.

Figure A.2 | RER Convergence Process

Source: Calculations by Homi Kharas.

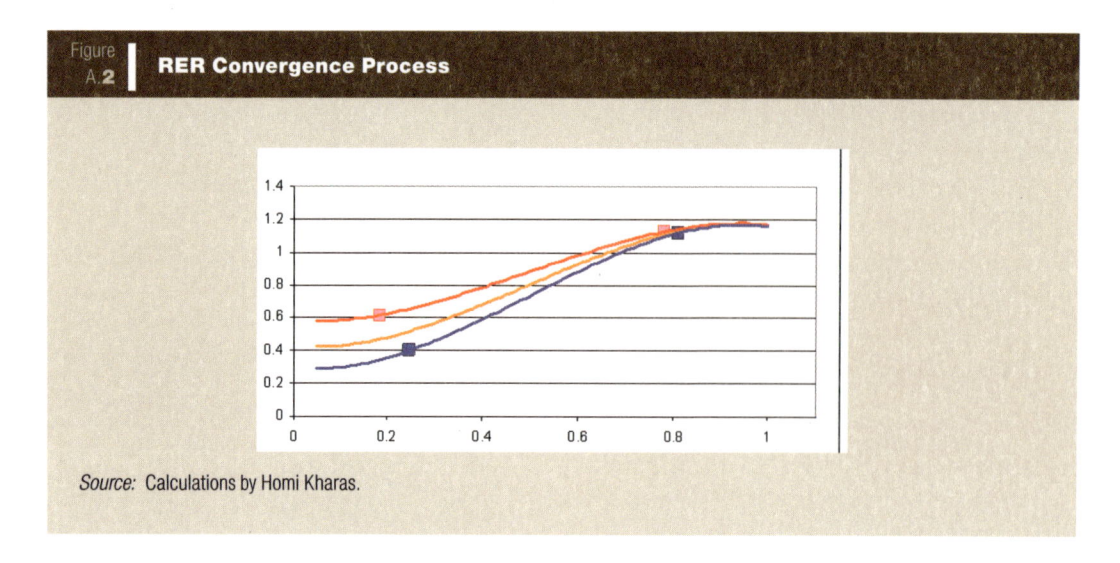

parity (PPP) terms. The approach here is the same as that used to obtain historical data in PPP terms; simply an application of the future growth rates to the 2005 levels of GDP PPP as estimated by the World Bank.

Step 5: Per capita projections, 2008-2050
As with the historical data, all three of the GDP units (constant 2007$, market exchange rates, and PPP rates) are also expressed in per capita terms. The calculations again rely on the UN Population Prospects projections of total population for each country.

Step 6: Poor, Middle, and Rich Class Projections
The next estimate realted to how the size and make-up of the global poor, middle, and rich classes will evolve between now and 2050 based on the growth projections. The global poor class is defined as those living on less than US$10 a day, the global middle class as those living on between US$10 and US$100 a day, and the global rich class as those living on more than US$100 a day, all figures in 2005$ PPP terms. To calculate the share of each country's population which belongs to each class, one requires, in addition to the existing dataset, inequality measures and current estimates of mean consumption per capita (rather than simply GDP per capita) for all countries.

This step begins by assembling a database on the share of total income accruing to each decile of the population for each country in the dataset. This data is obtained from two World Bank sources: the PovcalNet database, which contains the most up-to-date data (most frequently from 2005) for a wide-range of developing countries, and the Inequality Around the World: Globalization and Income Distribution Dataset, which contains data for both developed and developing countries (most frequently from 1998).⁵⁵ From these two sources, the most recent data available for each country in our dataset is chosen. There are a total of 14 countries which are not represented in either database, primarily countries in the Middle East and small island economies. For each of these countries, we use the average available inequality data of the country's neighbors.⁵⁶

This income share is transformed by decile data into Lorenz curves—graphs which plot the cumulative distribution of income against the cumulative population, moving from poor to rich—for each country using the World Bank's Povcal software.⁵⁷ The Povcal software produces three parameters —a, b, and c—for the generalized quadratic (GQ) Lorenz curve for any given income distribution dataset.⁵⁸ These parameters are then used in the following equation to calculate the headcount index—the share of the population below any given income level:

$$(8) \quad H_z = -\frac{1}{2m}\left[n + r(b+2z/\mu)\{(b+2z/\mu)^2 - m\}^{-1/2}\right]$$

Note:
$e = -(a + b + c + 1)$
$m = b^2 - 4a$
$n = 2be - 4c$
$r = (n^2 - 4me^2)^{1/2}$

where H_z is the headcount index for the income line z; a, b, and c are parameters of the Lorenz curve computed using the Povcal software; and μ is the mean consumption level.

To obtain current estimates of mean consumption per capita, the World Bank's 2005 International Comparison Program database is used, which provides estimates of real per capita private consumption expenditure based on national accounts data, measured in 2005 international dollars (PPP).⁵⁹ Plugging these mean consumption figures into the equation above enables a calculation of the percentage of the population living on less than US$10 a day and less than US$100 in every country. These values are multiplied by the population data to derive the number of people in the global poor,

---

55 The PovcalNet database and the Inequality Around the World: Globalization and Income Distribution Dataset can be found at http://go.worldbank.org/NT2A1XUWP0 and http://go.worldbank.org/0C52T3CLM0, respectively. Both accessed December 2008.
56 Data are missing for Bahrain, Kuwait, Libya, Oman, Saudi Arabia, Syria, and the United Arab Emirates; for these countries we use the average of Middle Eastern countries for which data are available: Algeria, Egypt, Iran, Jordan, Morocco, Tunisia, and Yemen. Data are also missing for Belize (for which we use the average of Guatemala, Honduras, and Mexico), Fiji (for which we use Papua New Guinea data), Iceland (for which we use the average of Denmark, Finland, Norway, and Sweden), Malta (for which we use the average of Cypress, Greece, and Italy), Mauritius and Seychelles (for which we use the average of Kenya, Madagascar, Malawi, Mozambique, and Tanzania), and Sudan (for which we use the average of Central African Republic, Chad, Egypt, Ethiopia, Kenya, and Uganda).
57 This software can be downloaded from http://go.worldbank.org/YMRH2NT5V0.
58 For a full explanation and discussion of these computations, see Gaurav Datt, "Computational Tools for Poverty Measurement and Analysis", FCND Discussion Paper No. 50, International Food Policy Research Institute, October 1998.
59 There are 18 countries in our database for which the ICP does not provide this data: United Arab Emirates, Belize, Algeria, Costa Rica, Dominican Republic, El Salvador, Guatemala, Guyana, Honduras, Jamaica, Libya, Nicaragua, Panama, Seychelles, Trinidad and Tobago, Turkmenistan, Haiti, Uzbekistan and Burundi. For all these countries other than Burundi, we use the ICP estimates of PPP GDP per capita (see table 8 in the methodology section of the ICP report), multiplied by the share of household consumption in GDP for each country taken from the World Development Indicators. For Burundi we do the same, except we use the 2005 GDP per capita PPP figure from the World Development Indicators as none is available in the ICP report.

middle, and rich classes in 2005.

To calculate projections of the evolving poor, middle, and rich classes, the real GDP per capita growth rate projections are simply applied to the 2005 consumption figures to obtain projected consumption per capita numbers and then the percentage of people living on less than US$10 and US$100 a day are recalculated using equation (8).[60] Note that this implicitly assumes a) that consumption grows at the same rate as GDP, i.e. the share of consumption in GDP will remain constant over time, and b) that the Lorenz curve remains constant over time, i.e. that growth is distributionally neutral. Finally, the number of poor, middle class, and rich individuals in each country is calculated using the population projections.

---

[60] We also use past real GDP pre capita growth statistics to calculate consumption per capita data back to 1991. We do not attempt to go back further than this due to data limitations from the Soviet era.

Chapter 3
Successful Macroeconomic Performance: Launching Long-Term Reforms

Claudio M. Loser

Introduction

Events in the emerging world have been far from predictable over the two years beginning in early 2008. At that time, the prospects for Emerging Economies looked promising. There were concerns about the effect of a shallow recession in the United States, but the general perception was that Asia and, to a large extent, Latin America and other regions were doing well. Most thought they had "decoupled" from the advanced economies, and wealth would grow with few restrictions. Policies had been conducive to significant improvements in fiscal and external balances, with a few exceptions, and international reserves were at record levels. Policymakers felt comfortable. Commodity prices were going up, foreign demand was strong and there was no serious worry about financing, as creditworthiness was solid. Problems were hitting only the United States and a few other developed countries.

From then on, the world financial crisis became the worst in the last fifty years, and became known as the Great Recession. There has been a rebound since then, and many of the Emerging Economies are quickly recovering from this deep recession. However, the problems are far from over as of mid-2010, as is clearly shown by the debt problems of Dubai early in the year, and the as to now not-fully-played out debt and adjustment saga in Greece and other countries of the European Union and Euro area. Some analysts considered that the intensity of the crisis was equivalent to that of the Great Depression of 1929-1933. While the financial sector suffered enormously, the comparison has clearly been an exaggeration unjustified by the facts. Particularly GDP has fallen by far less than during that period. Yet, the crisis had serious consequences for the Emerging Economies. Now, almost two years after the onset of the recession, the prospects are more upbeat but far from clear. The conditions in the financial markets have improved from the dramatic position of late 2008, even though with hesitation, and the real economy has shown a solid but far from impressive recovery in the advanced economies, although there is clearly a strong spurt of growth in the developing world. Asian and Latin American countries were able to absorb the impact of the crisis after consolidating economic performance and growth is generally recovering strongly. Nevertheless, some countries continue to face difficulties. The difficulties remain in Eastern Europe and Russia, as they were even more dependent on credit and high export prices, respectively. Moreover, while the United States has come out from the recession, unemployment is still very high, and the offsetting and timely stimulus measures applied over the last years are leaving behind a heavy burden of debt and loose monetary policy, which needs to be corrected. This is also the case for Europe and many Emerging Economies. In the end, the stimulus carried out has helped stabilize economic performance but it cannot be carried out in the long run without creating a serious debt problem, and thus undermining the global recovery.

From mid-2008 to early 2009, commodity prices declined by more than one half, and recovered subsequently, even though they have dropped in the wake of the Euro-zone crisis; demand for manufactured goods declined sharply all over the world; stock market capitalization also declined by about one half but showed a good recovery subsequently, even after the recent declines of May 2010; currencies in many emerging countries depreciated as capital flows reversed seeking a safe haven, but in many countries inflows have recovered. Governments were reasonably careful with their policies, but some private enterprises held "toxic" assets to an unexpectedly large extent, with serious effects for their own financial health as well as that of their countries and markets, which are only recovering modestly. Lenders are being particularly cautious after a period of loose credit throughout the earlier years of the decade. The loss of financial wealth that the crisis brought about has been partly reversed, but the costs were nonetheless enormous and the consequences for the economies of the world have been, unfortunately, commensurate. There are serious economic and political stumbling blocks and the recovery remains tentative and dependant on lax policies.

Photo Credit: CAF

This chapter is intended as a background piece that shows the close interaction between Latin America and the rest of the world, and the importance of pursuing strong macroeconomic policies. The latter, which had been elusive for long, seems to have become an integral part of economic policy for most of Latin America with clearly favorable results for the region, even in the context of the turmoil surrounding the world economy. The chapter reviews on a world-wide basis the origins of the crisis and how it affected the emerging market economies, mainly in Asia and Latin America. It also discusses what can be realistically expected, given that financial volatility and recessionary forces may continue to prevail even during the current recovery.

The Conditions in Asia and Latin America Prior to the Crisis

While the financial crisis began in the West, neither Emerging Asia nor Latin America had reacted in response to the international turbulence. The authorities viewed their continued growth as a clear signal of a new resiliency. Without seeking to over-generalize, described below are the broad developments that may explain the perceived resiliency[1]:

- Until very recently, Latin America was characterized by high volatility and about the lowest overall growth rate of any emerging region. However, during 2003-2008 there was an acceleration of growth, helped by the favorable conditions in the world, with sharp reductions in poverty. Growth in Asia had persisted for more than two decades, with the exception of the traumatic "Asian Crisis" period, but with a high and steady performance subsequently. Strides in terms of poverty and in quality of life have been impressive.

- Before the 1990s, Latin America had been the worst performer with regards to inflation, but now it has converged to world inflation, helped by its efforts to control both monetary and fiscal policy. Developing Asia has been less successful in reducing inflation, but in most cases had not experienced hyperinflation. Monetary policy was generally prudent, particularly after the Asian Crisis, and fiscal policies helped reduce public debt. The NICs had low inflation and generally good fiscal policies as well.

- Both regions have seen an increasing role of international trade and FDI. Latin America has reduced its trade barriers, which had been very high in the past, but to a large extent, exports and investment have focused on natural resources and commodities.[2] In Asia, with considerably more differences, there was also an emphasis on natural resources in South and South East Asia. However, a major process of incorporation of an excluded workforce in China and India, a complex process of industrialization, and a rapid integration in the productive process helped create a sophisticated and highly integrated production process.

- There was a sharp reduction in the previously high dependence on private capital flows, while international reserves rose to record levels throughout the emerging world and the debt burden was reduced. These trends have been strengthened by growing workers' remittances to Asia and Latin America.

- Many of the changes described above were the result of the efforts in the 1990s by many countries to engage in market-friendly reforms, including reforms on taxation, public finances, financial sector, trade, privatization, and labor markets. The impact of these policies was dramatic, even though certain countries went through major crises due to individual or regional circumstances (the Asian Crisis, Argentina, Brazil and Mexico come to mind).[3]

- Under these circumstances, with improved productivity, and in the case of Asia, ample markets and large supplies of initially unskilled but increasingly skilled labor, both Asia and Latin America became attractive destinations for FDI, as investors saw an opportunity to share in

---

1   Claudio Loser: The Prospects for Latin America: Risks and Opportunities with a Historical Perspective (Rev. June 2008).
2   Claudio Loser: "Cross-Border Trade and Investment among Emerging Economies: Lessons from differing experiences in Africa, Asia and Latin America", Emerging Market Forum 2008.
3   The market-friendly reforms of the 1990s have been subject to considerable controversy in political and economic circles in developing countries. For example, some poorly implemented privatizations, and the creation of protected private monopolies instead of public companies gave privatization a bad reputation, well beyond what was warranted. Most privatizations had worked well, but those few that did not, were described as emblematic of what the critics considered the wrong way.

the new regional prosperity.[4] Moreover, countries like Brazil, China, India and Mexico have become key players in the international cooperation dialogue.

Recent Evolution of the World Economic Environment

Over the last decade, Asian countries were able to emerge from the serious crisis that had brought many of them down in the late 90s. Helped by the consistent growth of China and, to an increasing extent, India, the Asian region witnessed a stellar performance. Concurrently, after a period of low economic growth, persistent crises, and high volatility that extended through the 1990s, Latin America made a very strong recovery. The crisis has hit hard and the impact on the balance of payments and on domestic activity became very serious. The adverse terms of trade effect aggravated the situation, compounded by a massive loss in financial wealth. But the economies began to recover quickly, in response to the demand support actions taken by the major countries in the system, and more recently the recovery has firmed up.

Genesis of the Great Recession

The reasons for the 2008-2009 crises are complex and linked to the financial market tensions of previous years. A period of extraordinary growth was fraught with dangers that were not anticipated by most even a year ago. For four years through the summer of 2007, the global economy boomed. Global GDP rose at an average of about 5 percent a year, the highest sustained rate since the early 1970s. About three-fourths of this growth was attributable to a broad-based surge in the emerging and developing economies. Inflation remained generally contained, even if with some upward pressures.

These developments led to the perception that the world economy was entering a new and prosperous stage and, using an abused phrase, entailed a new economic paradigm of uninterrupted strong growth. The value of financial and real assets was growing without a perceptible limit, and commodities were reaching record heights, as described in further detail below. Unfortunately, the most important factor behind these developments was not a change in paradigm. It was the emergence of growing imbalances among the main economies of the world. The US, with low rates of savings at the time, embarked on a consumption binge and a growing fiscal deficit, and experienced growing external current account deficits. These were financed by the surpluses of oil producing countries, China, Japan and, to a lesser extent, surplus countries in Europe and Latin America. These imbalances grew rapidly, but markets did not respond significantly to the mounting dangers on the horizon before 2007. However, the US dollar started to weaken in international markets and there were growing signs of impending problems. These trends were magnified by an increasingly integrated global trading and financial system which accelerated the transmission process; inadequate regulation and supervision of national financial systems and fragmentation of global regulation; and weak surveillance by the IMF and other multilateral organizations. The problems were aggravated by weak and uncoordinated policy

---

4 Corporacion Andina de Fomento: Reflexiones sobre como retomar el Crecimiento, RED 2004-Corporacion Andina de Fomento; América Latina en el comercio global, RED 2005 CAF; Camino a la Transformación Productiva en América Latina, RED 2006. CAF, Caracas, RED; Oportunidades en América Latina: Hacia una Mejor política social- RED 2007-2008 CAF.

responses to the initial signs of trouble in the financial markets.[5]

In the end, the markets and the world economy overall responded strongly to these imbalances. After experiencing a growth rate of about 5 percent a year in the period 2004-2007, growth slowed to 3 percent in 2008, and actually output declined by 0.6 percent in 2009—the first such contraction since the Second World War—although with a strong rebound in 2010. However, the modest decline numbers hide significant differences among countries and regions (Table 1). Economic growth rates in 2009 declined by two thirds among developing and Emerging Economies. Latin America experienced a GDP decline of 1.8 percent, mainly on account of Mexico and, to a lesser extent Venezuela. The worst affected regions include emerging Europe and the CIS countries, with contraction rates of 3.7 percent and 6.6 percent respectively. The advanced economies declined by more than 3 percent. Some other regions did much better, including the emerging market countries of South Asia, Africa and the Middle East, most of which avoided recession. While emerging Asia as a whole grew by some 5 percent, the NICs contracted by 1 percent. The worst hit counties were Singapore, Hong-Kong and Taiwan, but they showed a subsequent strong recovery. China and India, the largest Emerging Economies in the region grew by 8.7 percent and 5.7 percent, respectively. While surprisingly good in the current environment, these growth rates were somewhat below those registered by these countries in recent years.[6] Of course, this is shocking for all of the regions that had experienced very strong growth from 2002 onward. Under these conditions, policy makers embarked in a stimulus action that helped their economies recover. In some cases the recovery was so strong that they required some reversal of the stimulus to lead to some slowdown, as has already taken place in China in early 2010.

The global contraction has given way to renewed growth in 2010, with world GDP increasing by 4 percent, well above the projections of a few months ago. Again, however, the performance in the advanced economies is expected to be markedly different from that in the emerging market economies; and growth rates within regions are also expected to vary substantially. The major industrial economies are expected to see somewhat over two percent growth year-on-year in 2010, and to return to potential only at the end of the year. The Emerging Economies are projected to grow by over six percent, with Asia leading the way at almost 9 percent; Latin America is projected to grow 4 percent (Figure 1). There are significant caveats about these projections, particularly in light of the debt crisis in the Euro area, which will certainly entail a slowdown in growth from current (April 2010) projections. However, the bottom has clearly been reached in most countries. There are lags in the recovery process—including in the recovery of employment. This is particularly the case in the advanced economies where employers commit to new hiring only after clear signs of a rebound in activity. Thus, unemployment is expected to stabilize in mid 2010, causing continued pain. Renewed global growth will be secure only if the macroeconomic structures of a number of economies—especially the savings balances in the United States and China—emerge as significantly different from what they were in the lead up to the current crisis.

---

[5] Jack Boorman: Remarks for the South Asia Forum on the Global Economic and financial Crisis, March 2009.
[6] The Impact of the Financial Crisis on Emerging Market Economies: The Transmission Mechanism, Policy Response and Lessons-Jack Boorman, Mumbai, India, June 23, 2009.

Table 1: GDP Growth Projections

	2002-2007	2008	2009	2010	2011
World	4.4	3.0	-0.6	4.6	4.3
Advanced Economies	2.5	0.5	-3.2	2.6	2.4
US	2.6	0.4	-2.4	3.3	2.9
EU	2.4	0.9	-4.1	1.0	1.3
Japan	1.8	-1.2	-5.2	2.4	1.8
China	10.7	9.6	9.1	10.5	9.6
India	8.0	7.3	5.7	9.4	8.4
Latin America	4.1	4.3	-1.8	4.8	4.0
Argentina	5.5	6.8	0.9	3.5	3.0
Brazil	3.8	5.1	-0.2	7.1	4.2
Chile	4.5	3.7	-1.5	4.7	6.0
Colombia	5.3	2.4	0.1	2.3	4.0
Mexico	3.0	1.5	-6.5	4.5	4.4
Peru	6.3	9.8	0.9	6.3	6.0
Venezuela	5.0	4.8	-3.3	-2.6	0.4

Source: IMF, World Economic Outlook, October 2009

Inflationary Pressures

After attaining significant lows, particularly in Latin America, inflation rose in 2007 in line with commodity prices and almost reached 10 percent, with higher levels of inflation in Asia than in Latin America. Eventually, inflation declined somewhat in 2008 as price pressures receded towards the end of the year, but still remained high at 9 percent, with over 7 percent in Asia and 8 percent in Latin America. During the first part of 2008, high inflation reflected the increase in world demand. In the second half, as these trends reversed and capital flows reversed, many countries experienced major currency devaluations, precluding a decline in local prices, on account of lower commodity prices in international markets (Table 2 and Figure 2).

Inflation initially subsided but with some recovery and commodity prices picking up, inflation may rise, though it is not expected to reach the levels observed in 2007-2008. In the advanced economies, oil price increases had pushed up headline inflation, but underlying inflation pressures were contained. In fact, concerns about inflation are now evenly divided between those that are more preoccupied with deflation, in response to recent declines in commodity prices and weak world aggregate demand, and those that are more concerned about inflation in the medium-term because of the lagged effects of the expansionary macroeconomic policies.

Figure 1 | Growth of GDP in Developing Asia, Latin America and the World (Annual Percent)

Source: IMF, ECLAC, and own estimates

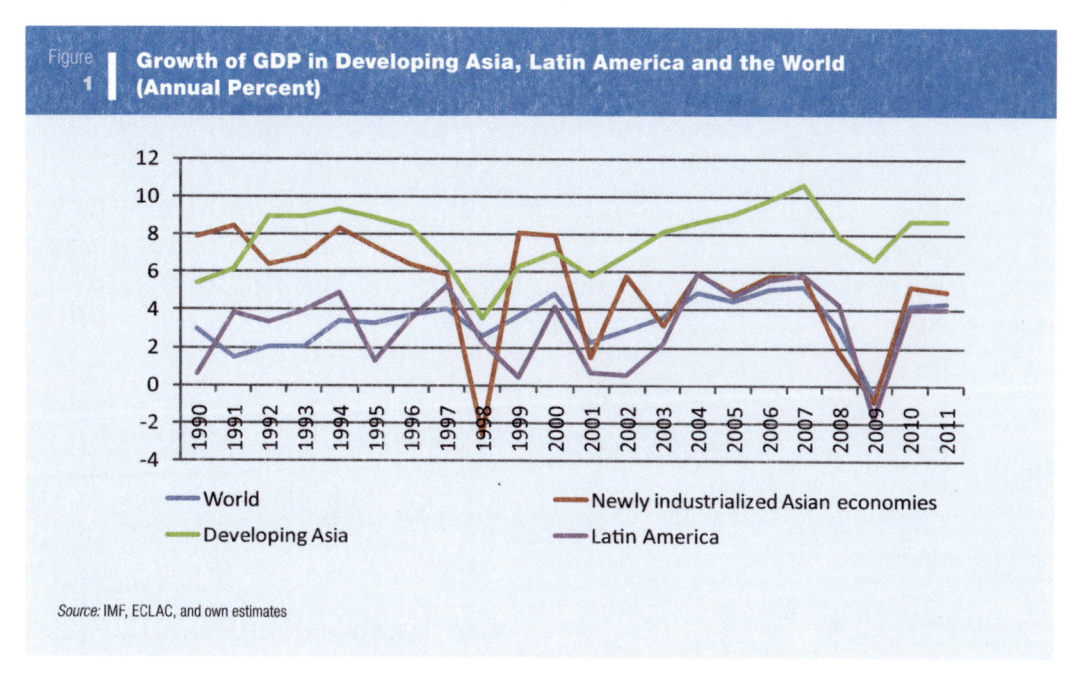

Among some of the most traumatic consequences of the crisis was the loss of valuation of financial assets worldwide, which reached well over US$50 trillion, equivalent to about one year of world GDP. The decline reflected the reduced capitalization of stock markets, loss in the value of mortgage-backed securities and other assets, and the depreciation of many currencies with respect to the US dollar. While this has been reversed in part, the impact of this financial loss continues to weigh upon the world economy. This issue is discussed in detail below.

The Liquidity Crisis

Interbank markets virtually locked up in the fourth quarter of 2008, as trust in contractual counterparties evaporated. In September, the disintermediation process that had been observed for at least a year led to the worst liquidity crisis of the last thirty years, or perhaps since the great depression of 1929. The closing of the venerable Lehman Brothers aggravated the panic in the financial markets, as doubts about the stability of the domestic and international payments system increased.[7] The cost of intermediation rose rapidly between financial organizations, together with a generalized paralysis in transactions between financial institutions.[8]

To respond to this situation, the authorities of many countries, particularly the European Union and

---

[7] Although subject to debate, part of the financial collapse may have occurred because of actions, or omissions by the authorities. A possible example is the demise of Lehman Brothers, without looking carefully at the consequences, and that many actions were seen as haphazard measures, without a systematic approach.

[8] During this period an obscure concept became instantly fashionable, the TED spread. The Ted rate is the differential between US treasury rate and LIBOR (London Interbank Offer Rate), which measures the lending costs among financial intermediaries. The TED differential, which had been below 1% for most of the last quarter century, showed significant volatility in mid-2007 and rose to a peak of 5% in October. It has fallen since then and now is back to historical levels, helped by key Central Banks.

Table 2 | Inflation

	2002-2007	2008	2009	2010	2011
World	3.7	6.0	2.4	3.7	3.0
Latin America	7.1	7.9	6.0	6.2	5.9
Argentina	12.2	8.6	6.3	10.1	9.1
Brazil	7.4	5.7	4.9	5.1	4.6
Chile	2.9	8.7	1.7	2.0	3.0
Colombia	5.7	7.0	4.2	3.5	3.7
Mexico	4.3	5.1	5.3	4.6	3.7
Peru	1.9	5.8	2.9	1.5	1.8
Venezuela	20.6	30.4	27.1	29.7	33.2
Developing Countries	6.2	9.2	5.2	6.2	4.7
Developing Asia	3.7	7.4	3.1	5.9	3.7
China	2.1	5.9	-0.7	3.1	2.4
India	4.8	8.3	10.9	13.2	5.5

Source: International Monetary Fund, World Economic Outlook Database, April 2010

Figure 2 | Inflation

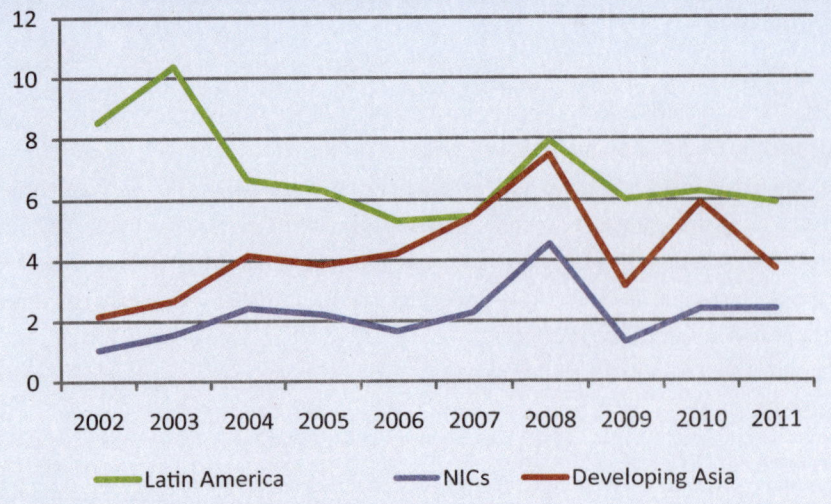

Source: International Monetary Fund, World Economic Outlook Database, April 2010

the US, adopted extraordinary measures to stabilize the markets, by providing liquidity and other financial support on a massive scale, extending deposit guarantees and adopting legislation whereby public funds are used to support problematic assets of banks. In the case of the US, it was done through the TARP program (Troubled Asset Relief Program), with further actions taken in February by the new US administration regarding a stimulus to the US economy, and recently with Congress tightening legislation covering the financial system. Similar actions were announced in other major countries, including programs of bank acquisitions in the United Kingdom and initially poorly coordinated actions within the Euro zone and in other European Union members and elsewhere. As described below in more detail, actions were also taken in Latin America and Asia.

The national rescue operations were followed by major swap transactions between the Federal Reserve of the US and a number of other central banks of industrialized economies in order to provide sufficient liquidity in response to a steady demand for US dollars. These swaps were also extended to the Central Banks of Brazil, Korea, Mexico, and Singapore, to support their currencies in the face of continued pressures in foreign exchange.

In the more recent past, core European countries, again after a hesitant beginning, have come out to the rescue of those economies in serious trouble, particularly over-indebted Greece, and to a lesser extent Portugal, Ireland, Spain and Italy. Specifically they announced the prospective mobilization of Euro 750 billion, or about US$900 billion, two thirds from the European Union itself and the rest prospective funds from the IMF. This would be the first time in thirty years that the IMF would provide support to the core economies of Europe, although it had already done so with other countries in the region. The first step has been an Euro 110 billion loan to Greece. With such high financing requirements, access to the International Financial Institutions was imperative. The IMF has already shown greater lending flexibility and can mobilize significant resources. In the past, any borrowing had to be based on what was seen as burdensome conditions. By contrast, the recent programs were supported by the IMF, in the form of assistance on the basis of fewer conditions for countries seen as generally good performers.[9]

The creation of the G-20 Summits is another noteworthy development. Until last year, many decisions had been taken at the level of the G-7/G-8, the group formed by the largest advanced economies, and Russia. The G-20 includes the G-8 and the largest Emerging Economies, such as China, India, Korea, South Africa, and in Latin America, Brazil, Mexico, and Argentina. This forum better reflects the growing importance of the emerging world and may also open the door to a more representative governance system at the international financial institutions (IFIs), and make these institutions more relevant.

The Transmission of the Crisis

The financial crisis erupted in August 2007 after the collapse of the US mortgage market and entered a tumultuous new phase in September 2008 following the collapse of Lehman. These developments shook confidence in global financial institutions and markets, and triggered a cascading series of

---

9 There have already been several loans with such conditions, including to Mexico, Colombia, and Poland.

bankruptcies, forced mergers, and public interventions in the United States and Western Europe, which eventually resulted in a drastic reshaping of the financial landscape. When the real estate bubble burst in the US and Europe, investors moved to commodities, where experts expected a continuous increase in prices. The commodity bubble peaked in mid 2008, with a subsequent collapse, through early 2009. In particular, losses were large in the case of metals and oil.

The transmission of the crisis from the United States and Europe to the rest of the world came through a number of channels. The financial institutions in most emerging market economies had not engaged in the kind of practices seen in the major industrial countries. Balance sheets were typically not exposed to toxic assets. Derivatives were employed much less frequently and were generally limited to the more traditional instruments employed to hedge against currency and other risks associated with trade. Financial institutions in the Emerging Economies either shied away from exotic instruments, or were prevented by regulation from holding or trading such instruments. But, in the end, this did not protect these countries, as they were hit by the impact on the current account through declines in export prices and aggregate demand; a decline in remittances; the withdrawal of funds by financial institutions from their subsidiaries; a sharp decline in capital inflows; and certainly the general perception that the crisis was taking over. These factors can be seen in a stylized form on the basis of Figure 3, and quantified subsequently.

Economic Activity

The impact of the crisis on economic activity—in the first instance, in the United States and Europe, and subsequently in Japan, was reflected in a decline in exports from those emerging market countries that had become the largest exporters to the industrial world. Quite rapidly, exports declined from other Emerging Economies, i.e., those whose exports consisted of raw and intermediate goods shipped to emerging market countries, particularly China, that had become key providers of final manufactured goods in the increasingly complex supply chains that came to populate world trade. This fall in exports—at a virtually unprecedented extent—created a feedback loop whereby the initial reduction in trade weakened the domestic economies of the emerging market countries, with further negative feedback on the financial sectors in those countries as the quality of domestic credit deteriorated.

Over the last quarter century, the volume of world trade had grown at an average rate of 6 percent, or about double the rate of world output. Asian exports had grown at a rate of 10 percent a year and those of Latin America and the Caribbean by some 7 percent, with a marked transformational impact. NICs, which have become highly integrated with the rest of the world, recorded an average ratio of Exports to GDP of 71 percent for the period 2002-2007. Developing Asia recorded a ratio of 55 percent, tempered by lower but growing ratios for China (31 percent) and India (12 percent), which were dominated by domestic developments. In Asia, the ratio of exports to GDP reflected increased volumes of trade, but to some extent also some real depreciation of national currencies. Latin America, which became much more open in the 1990s, registered a stable ratio of exports to GDP of 21 percent notwithstanding the impact of a strong real appreciation of the currencies, as export volumes increased. According to the IMF, world trade volumes contracted by 11 percent in 2009 after a peak

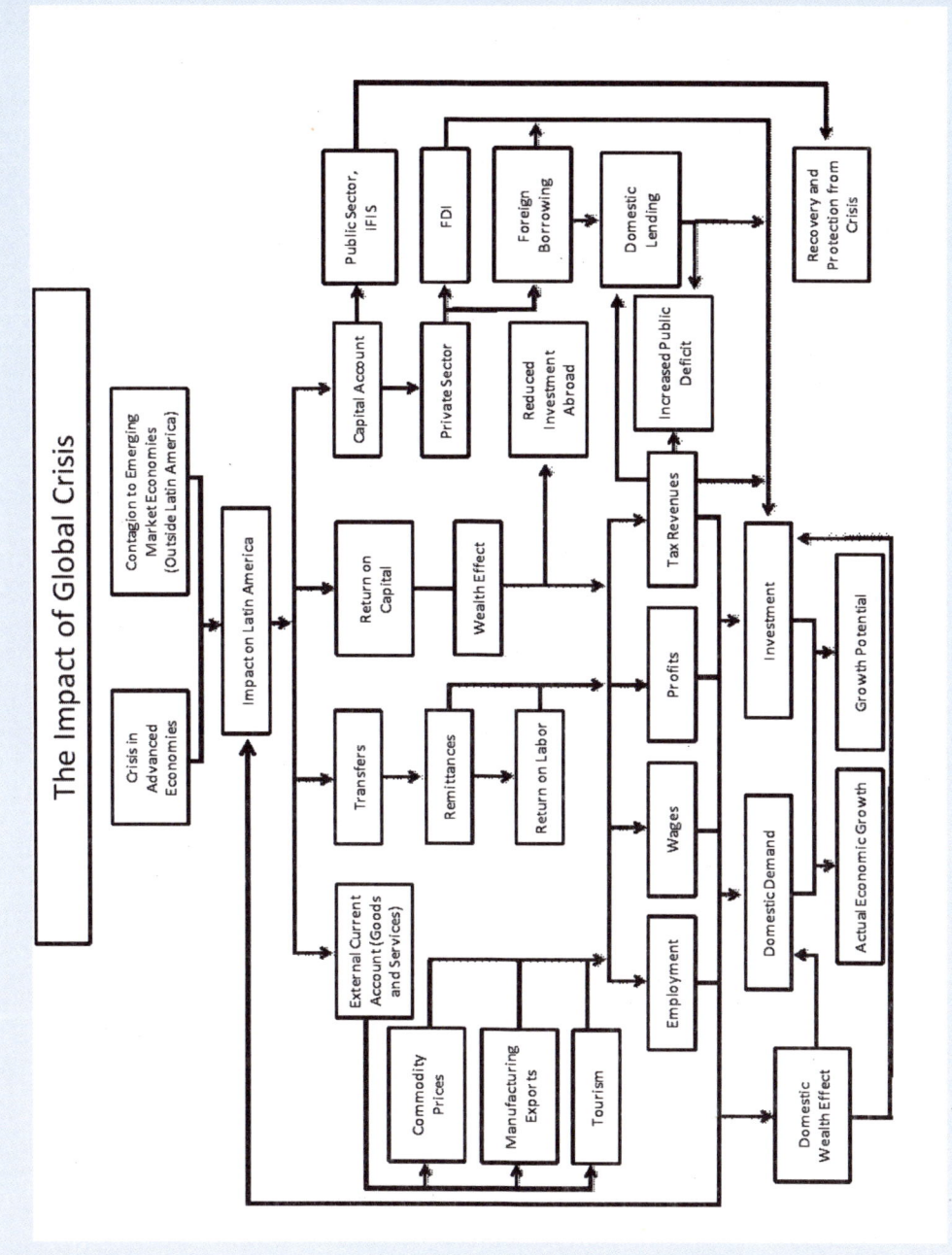

SUCCESSFUL MACROECONOMIC PERFORMANCE: LAUNCHING LONG-TERM REFORMS

Figure 3. World Trade Projections (percentage change, annual)

Source: Claudio M. Loser.

growth of 9.4 percent in 2006 (Table 3). The impact differed around the world. In this regard, Latin America experienced declines of 6 percent in exports and of 4 percent in imports in 2009.

These trends are confirmed by the monthly movements in trade on a 12-month basis. Trade actually declined sharply in Latin America, as seen in Figure 4, in line with Asia. Imports have slowed down but are now recovering. However, because of the composition of exports, half of which are commodities, the region was particularly hit by declining prices (Figure 5), thus magnifying the impact of lower export volumes, for example in Mexico. The slowdown in the US, Europe and the region, the main trading areas for Latin America, explains this contraction in exports (Figure 6).

The losses in income due to terms of trade effects are also significant, with considerably smaller effects in Asia, with a very small net balance in raw materials and intermediate goods, but with considerable differences among countries.

It would be easy to suggest that the countries that have been most open to international trade may be subject to the greatest shock on account of reduced world demand, thus justifying protectionism. However, this should be viewed in a broader light. Countries that opened more vigorously to trade grew the fastest, and benefitted more from global prosperity. It may be the case that they will experience a significant short-term loss, as is being observed in Taiwan and Korea. Most significantly, the more open traders in fact are benefitting from an increasingly flexible productive structure that allows them to adjust more efficiently than most closed economies.

Remittances

Remittances over the last fifteen years have become a major channel of prosperity. The merits of

Table 3 | World Trade Projections (percentage change, annual)

	2006	2007	2008	2009	2010
World trade volume	8.8	7.2	2.8	-10.7	7.0
Imports					
Advanced Economies	7.6	4.7	0.6	-12.0	5.4
Emerging and Developing Economies	10.9	12.7	8.5	-8.4	9.7
Latin America and Caribbean	12.9	12.4	7.0	-15.4	10.1
Exports					
Advanced Economies	8.6	6.3	1.9	-11.7	6.6
Emerging and Developing Economies	10.4	9.7	4.0	-8.2	8.3
Latin America and Caribbean	7.8	5.9	3.1	-8.3	8.6

Source: International Monetary Fund, World Economic Outlook Database, April 2010

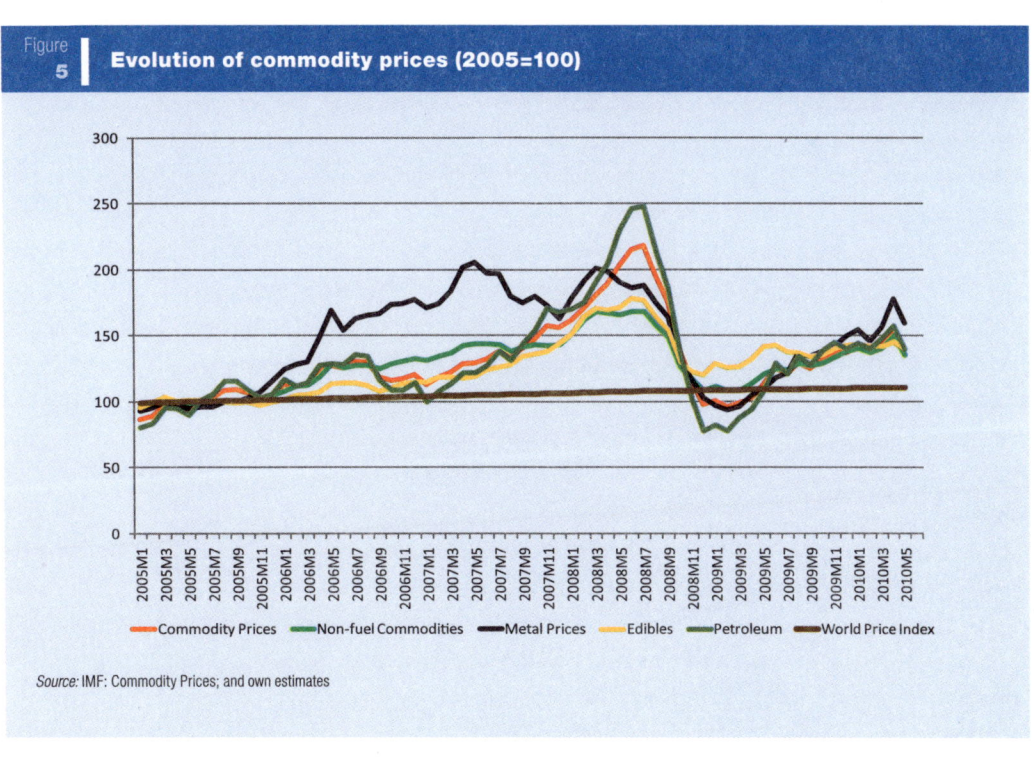

SUCCESSFUL MACROECONOMIC PERFORMANCE: LAUNCHING LONG-TERM REFORMS   113

Figure 4 | Trade Growth in Latin America and Emerging Asia

Source: International Monetary Fund, World Economic Outlook Database, April 2010

Figure 5 | Evolution of commodity prices (2005=100)

Source: IMF: Commodity Prices; and own estimates

Figure 6 | Latin American Trade Share (% of total)

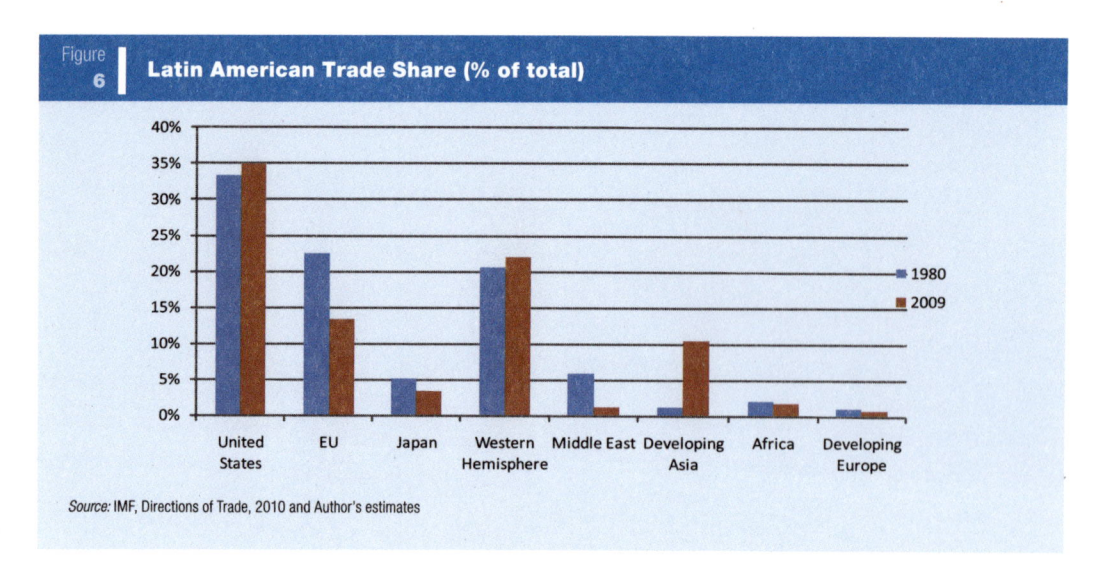

Source: IMF, Directions of Trade, 2010 and Author's estimates

increased mobility of large numbers of workers to well-paying jobs in prosperous destinations may be subject to debate. However, the impact of the consequent remittances to their home countries have helped increase prosperity and reduce poverty, particularly in Asia and Latin America- India, Mexico and the Philippines being the largest recipients of workers' remittances. Remittances to emerging markets amounted to some US$443 billion in 2008 (some 3 percent of GDP of the receiving countries), with nearly US$158 billion to Asia, and US$64 billion to Latin America. These flows were stable, and were a countercyclical force in the receiving countries (Table 4).[10] However, they are highly sensitive to economic conditions in the countries of employment. With many emigrants working in the US, Europe, and the Middle East, remittances started to fall in late 2008, for the first time in a quarter century. The outcome in 2009 was equally dire, with an estimated decline to US$414 billion, with adverse consequences for the well being of many millions of households among developing countries.

Like unemployment, remittances tend to lag the decline in economic activity—and will likely lag in the recovery. Remittances however are expected to increase in 2010-2011, depending on the recovery of the global economy. The return of workers from abroad could put additional pressure on the labor markets as those workers seek employment in already weakened economies.

Tourism

Tourism is another area of concern. Receipts from tourists are a significant source of income, particularly for Mexico, Central America and the Caribbean, and some countries in South America. Even though transportation costs are declining, tourism from the richer countries has fallen and will continue to do so. Nevertheless, there is expected to be some recovery in 2010 thanks to tourist arrivals from Emerging Economies, which are arguably the most dynamic segment of international tourism (Table 5).

---

[10] Claudio Loser, "The Macro-Economic Impact of Remittances in Latin America-Dutch Disease or Latin Cure?" G-24 Technical Papers, 2006 (See G-24 website, Technical Meetings).

Table 4 | Workers Remittances (billions US$)

	2006	2007	2008	2009	2010	2011
World	317	385	443	414	437	465
Emerging Asia	58	71	86	86	94	103
Emerging South Asia	43	54	72	75	79	83
Latin America	59	63	64	57	60	64

Source: Migration and Development Brief 12, World Bank; April 23, 2010

Table 5 | International Tourist Arrivals

% y/y	2007	2008 Q1	2008 Q2	2008 Q3	2008 Q4	2009 Q1	2009 Q2	2009 Q3	2009 Q4	2010 Q1
World	6.1	8.5	4	-0.5	-2.3	-10.4	-6.8	-2.3	1.6	7.1
Europe	4.1	6.8	2.2	-0.9	-4.2	-13.1	-7.4	-2.7	-1.9	3
Asia and Pacific	9.6	8.3	3.4	-1.9	-4.4	-7.4	-6.1	-0.5	6.4	10.2
Americas	5.2	9.6	3.4	1.7	-2.3	-7.1	-7.3	-5.7	1.4	2.6
South America	6.5	7.9	1.0	6.2	-1.5	-4.2	3	9.8	7.9	2.8

Source: UN World Tourism Organization, World Tourism Barometer April 2010

Developments in Employment[11]

In the second quarter of 2009, more than a million jobs were lost in the region according to ECLAC. The economies in the region expanded in the last quarter of the year, but the prospects for 2010 are surrounded with considerable uncertainty. In the context of a continued decline in activity, further job losses may take place together with growth in the informal sector and rising unemployment rates.

ECLAC and ILO estimated that in Latin America the average urban unemployment rate for the year would rise from 7.5 percent to about 8.5 percent, in 2009, and then decline marginally to 8.3 percent in 2010 depending on the behavior of the labor supply. In absolute numbers, this means that there are about 18 million unemployed at present in Latin America, 3 million more than in 2008. According to ECLAC, given the difficulty in finding wage employment, the working-age population is expected to engage in informal activities and in low-productivity and low-income activities as a means of subsistence. Likewise, the formal sector is expected to introduce more informal contracts to reduce labor costs, with concomitant adverse consequences in terms of job security (Figure 7 shows the trends so far in 2009).

---

11   Crisis in the labor Market ECLAC/ILO, June 2009.

Financial and Credit Markets

The impact that the crisis has had in the financial markets can be seen from different points of view, but fundamentally in terms of the valuation of companies, particularly those being quoted in stock markets; the investments by some economic agents in toxic assets; the general conditions of the banking system in the region; and problems of external financing.

The stock markets experienced a sharp fall that in 2008 exceeded that of the stock markets in the advanced countries. Initially the markets in Emerging Economies seemed insulated from the crisis, and did not decline. The fall was particularly strong from mid-2008, in contrast with what happened in the US and Europe, where the reduction began in the middle of 2007, although in the end, the cumulative decline was equivalent. For example, the S&P 500 index of the United States fell by 36 percent from June to end-2008 and the Japan Nikkei index fell by 37 percent. The stock market index in Brazil fell by 49 percent, and in Mexico, the other key Latin stock market, the valuation fell by 29 percent. Among Asian countries, the stock market valuation declined by 36 percent in Korea, 41 percent in India, and 48 percent in China (Table 6), reflecting the wide-ranging effect of the world financial crisis. Since the end of the year there has been a significant recovery, as seen in that table.

Photo Credit: CAF

Initially, it was thought that because of the characteristics of the developing financial markets, there would be no significant presence of "toxic" financial assets. Nevertheless, in many of them, including in Korea, India, China, Brazil and Mexico, some companies were invested in derivatives, particularly regarding foreign exchange risk, and, to a lesser extent, commodities. The fall in international prices and the depreciation of local currencies had an important impact on the finances of these companies and therefore, their share values suffered. This, together with uncertainty regarding the scope and extent of these derivatives, generated strong pressures on the exchange markets.

There have been significant improvements in the conditions from the trough in the fourth quarter of 2008, as reflected in Figure 7.[12] Nevertheless, the financial markets remain volatile, generating some uncertainty about the capacity of some countries in Latin America and Asia, to cover their financing needs, even though this is far less problematic than in the past. However, the perceived risk of investments had resulted in a sharp increase in risk premiums, with particularly marked increases for Argentina, Ecuador and Venezuela. In the case of these countries, the risks caused by the fall

---

12   Capital Flows to Latin America: Recent Developments, ECLAC Washington DC, June 2009.

SUCCESSFUL MACROECONOMIC PERFORMANCE: LAUNCHING LONG-TERM REFORMS

Figure 7 | Emerging Market Spreads and Comparison with Selected Markets

Collaterized Debt Security Spreads for Selected Latin American Countries and European Countries

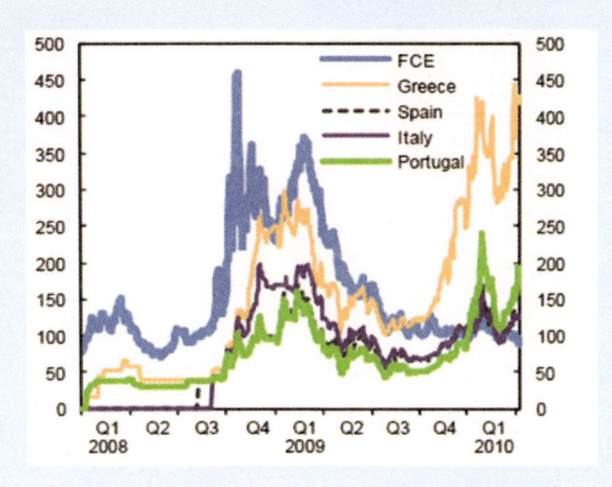

Equity Markets and Interest Rate Spreads

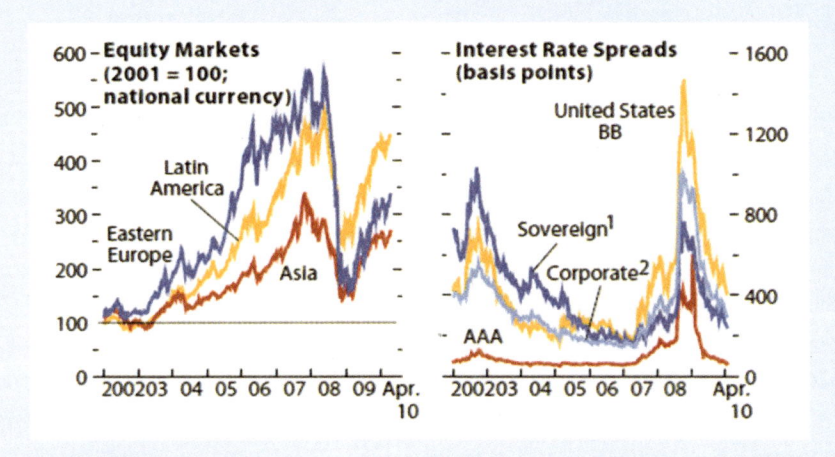

Source: IMF, World Economic Outlook, 2009.

Table 6. Selected Countries—Stock Market and Exchange Rate Changes

Country	Stock Market Changes (%) 2008	2009	2010 (through April)	Exchange Rate Changes (%) 2008	2009	2010 (through May)
Argentina	-48.9%	103.6%	7.5%	-9.5%	-8.9%	2.7%
Brazil	-41.2%	82.7%	-1.5%	-29.8%	25.2%	4.0%
Chile	-19.6%	46.9%	8.5%	-28.2%	20.3%	4.6%
Colombia	-29.3%	53.5%	7.8%	-11.4%	10.1%	-4.3%
Mexico	-24.2%	43.5%	1.8%	-25.3%	5.9%	-0.4%
Latin America	-34.6%	68.3%	1.6%	-25.0%	14.4%	1.9%
China	-65.4%	80.0%	-12.4%	6.0%	0.2%	-0.1%
Hong Kong	-46.9%	42.9%	-2.8%	4.3%	-0.1%	0.5%
India	-57.1%	90.2%	2.9%	-23.8%	6.0%	0.6%
South Korea	-40.7%	49.7%	3.5%	-34.6%	8.7%	2.8%
Japan	-30.5%	5.6%	8.8%	20.4%	-2.0%	-1.2%
Euro Area	-38.6%	24.8%	4.0%	0.0%	0.0%	0.0%
USA (NYSE)	-38.60%	17.58%		0.00%	0.00%	

Source: World Federation of Exchanges, OANDA

in international oil prices were accompanied by macroeconomic and structural policies that can be regarded as weak or deficient. Subsequently, however, the risk premiums declined, although they have not yet achieved the levels prior to mid-2008. Moreover, the corporate spreads had increased at a much slower pace than for Europe, which had been hit hard by the crisis.

Data on capital flows by IIF show a dramatic picture. Private flows to emerging market countries (net of equity investment abroad) declined from US$980 billion in 2007 to US$360 billion in 2008, and declined further to US$350 billion, with a recovery expected in 2010 to about US$400 billion, far below 2007. The withdrawal of portfolio investment was a key factor behind a decline in emerging stock markets. Increases in official flows entail only a small portion of this decline (Table 7). Within these totals, Latin America saw a decline in net private flows from US$173 billion in 2007 to US$100 billion in 2008, with a slight recovery in 2009 and subsequently. However, as is the case in general, the lower flows will only be offset in small part by the increase in official flows during the period, mainly on account of the greater availability of financing from the IMF, and a greater willingness to borrow on the other.

Table 7. Emerging Market Economies' External Financing

	2007	2008	2009	2010
Emerging Economies				
Private Flows, net	1252.2	588.2	530.8	708.6
Equity Investment, net	601.9	420.8	465.8	528.8
Private Creditors, net	650.2	167.5	65.0	179.8
Official	42.9	61.4	62.4	55.2
Resident Lending/Other	-482.6	-535.4	-211.6	-293.2
Reserves (Increase -)	-1056.7	-477.2	-549.8	-613.5
Latin America				
Private Flows, net	228.9	129.6	156.6	190.4
Equity Investment, net	134.3	89.4	114.9	123.3
Private Creditors, net	94.5	40.3	41.7	67.1
Official	6.3	14.0	23.7	14.9
Resident Lending/Other, net	-79.4	-68.8	-61.8	-49.4
Reserves (Increase -)	-127.8	-43.5	-42.4	-40.7
Developing Asia				
Private Flows, net	422.2	107.4	282.9	272.4
Equity Investment, net	240.7	158.7	231.0	243.4
Private Creditors, net	181.5	-51.3	51.9	29.0
Official	28.6	22.5	10.4	15.4
Resident Lending/Other, net	-148.7	-122.0	-65.6	-77.8
Reserves (Increase -)	-587.8	-347.8	-518.1	-454.9

Source: IIF, April 2010

Foreign Direct Investment

Foreign Direct Investment (FDI) also suffered in the short run. FDI stocks and flows grew at a very fast rate in recent years, reflecting both the emergence of new countries as origin and destination of capital flows, and rapidly evolving capital markets. This allowed for a sharp increase in available capital within the private sector, and resulted in a decline in lending by IFIs. Most interesting was the change in the composition of these flows. While total FDI directed to developed countries retained the lion's share of the total inflows (70 percent of the total), both Asia and Latin America became increasingly important, even with some volatility in the case of Latin America (Table 9).[13] Flows in the next years will remain low, as credit and financial market conditions remain weak but should come up from the crisis levels of 2009 (See Table 8).

Commercial Banks

Commercial banks in Latin America did not invest to any significant degree in "toxic" financial instruments, but were hit by the sharp contraction in external credit. These institutions, not being strongly exposed to external risks, and focusing mainly on domestic markets, are not incurring risks similar to financial institutions in the advanced countries. In Asia, where the banking system is much larger than in Latin America, banks have tended to be more invested in the troubled assets, with the possible exception of India, among the larger countries. Latin America has been helped by the relatively small size of the national financial systems and the strong supervision and prudential regulations that has followed the crises of the last ten to fifteen years.[14][15] Thus, the risks have tended to be concentrated in possible disruptions in the traditional flows related to international trade and foreign investment; and the contraction in international economic activity.

A separate issue is that the banking system is highly concentrated, and has a large presence of foreign banks. In the case of Mexico, the latter may well create pressures on the system, to the extent that US, Spanish and other foreign-owned banks may withdraw lines of credit from Mexico to preserve the health of their home operations, as detected in a recent IMF study.[16] The general contraction of the balance sheets of the major institutions and the need to rebuild their capital base has constrained the funding available to other institutions in both the industrial countries and in the emerging world. This has been the case notwithstanding the massive support injected into banking systems in the financial centers that are home to most of the major international banks.

Cross Border Flows and the Impact of the Crisis

With significant levels of assets abroad, either in the form of investments by companies or in the hands of individuals that have taken money out in response to uncertainties with regard to domestic policies, the international crisis will have an additional impact on EEs due to the reductions in returns on those investments abroad, and financing difficulties in connection with these investments. This problem did not exist when the main EEs were fundamentally on the receiving end and were not capital exporters, as is the case at present.

Table 9 provides data for the net external financial position in Asia and Latin America through 2009.

---

13 NCTAD, World Investment Report, 2006-2008. Also see: Loser, Claudio, Cross-Border Trade and Investment among Emerging Economies: Lessons from differing experiences in Africa, Asia and Latin America", Emerging Market Forum 2008.
14 The index of Financial development and Stability, developed by the Centennial Group, and presented in Emerging markets in October of 2008 show that the countries in Latin America have developed considerable institutional strength, with index levels that exceed what could be expected in light of their levels of income. In turn the development indices (reflecting the depth and structure) are below what is expected in light of the region's per capita income. This is the opposite of what was observed in the case of Asian countries, where the development indicators tend to run ahead of their relative institutional strength, with the exception of the NICs.
15 "Financial Markets in Latin America, Claudio Loser, in "Growth and Development in Emerging market Economies", Harinder Kohli, Ed. Sage Publications, 2008.
16 IMF, World Economic Outlook, Chapter 4, April 2009.

Table 8 | Foreign Direct Investment, Recipient Regions Flows and Stocks (billions US$)

	Flows					
	1980	1990	2000	2006	2007	2008
World	55.3	201.6	1411.4	1461.1	1978.8	1697.4
Developed economies	47.6	165.6	1146.2	972.8	1358.6	962.3
Developing economies	7.7	35.9	256.1	433.8	529.3	620.7
of which:						
Africa	0.4	39.8	9.7	57.1	69.2	87.6
Latin America	6.5	35.1	97.8	93.3	127.5	144.4
South, East and South-East Asia	3.9	49.8	144.8	214.5	253.8	297.6
Southeast Europe and CIS	0.0	0.0	9.0	54.5	90.9	114.4
	Stocks					
World	551.2	1942.2	5757.4	11998.8	15210.6	14909.3
Developed Economies	410.9	1412.6	3960.3	8453.9	10458.6	10212.9
Share in total	74.5	72.7	68.8	70.5	68.8	68.5
Developing economies	140.4	529.6	1736.2	3155.9	4246.7	4276.0
Share in total	25.5	27.3	30.2	26.3	27.9	28.7
of which:						
Latin America	35.1	110.5	502.5	908.6	1140.0	1181.6
Share in total	6.4	5.7	8.7	7.6	7.5	7.9
South, East and South-East Asia	49.8	311.7	1008.5	1684.3	2353.1	2212.4
Share in total	9.0	16.0	17.5	14.0	15.5	14.8
World FDI stock (real terms)1/	858.8	2387.6	7947.6	11998.8	14767.6	14447.0

1/ Adjusted by world export prices
2/ 2007 values for Asia are estimates

Source: UNCTAD, World Investment Report (2008), Centennial Database, and own estimates

Table 9 | Emerging Market Economies' External Financing

	2002	2003	2004	2005	2006	2007	2008	2009
Latin America								
Net Asset Position	-642.3	-709.3	-749.2	-792.6	-845.2	-997.6	-1005.8	-1052.5
Percentage of Total Assets	-37.2%	-31.8%	-25.8%	-21.9%	-18.5%	15.0%	-16.2%	-16.16%
FDI	-342.8	-406.3	-456.4	-528.7	-569.3	-695.4	-787.3	-852.3
Monetary Authority and Reserves	119.3	145.6	174.7	241.9	302.8	445.9	496.8	554.6
Other	-418.7	-448.6	-467.5	-505.8	-578.6	-748.1	-715.3	-754.8
Developing Asia								
Net Asset Position	1310.5	1380.4	1809.4	1629.9	2071.2	2823.2	3221.2	3526.7
Percentage of Total Assets	15.59%	15.31%	15.16%	12.24%	10.78%	9.45%	9.24%	9.24%
FDI	-21.0	-64.5	-422.2	-508.8	-610.6	-728.7	-862.2	-929.0
Monetary Authority and Reserves	914.4	1209.4	2098.8	2342.6	2771.0	3348.9	3789.4	4250.2
Other	417.1	235.5	132.8	-203.9	-89.2	202.9	293.9	205.4

Source: IMF- Int. Financial Statistics and own estimates

The net position tends to be small. The largest net (negative) position corresponds to Latin America, equivalent of 16 percent of total assets. Even under these circumstances, the financial impact can be considerable. As an example, using the numbers for developing Asia, the net creditor position is dominated by Reserves and Related Assets, mostly invested in US official securities, while the FDI position reflects a combination of large positions of assets and liabilities that may have been hit in a differential fashion by the crisis. FDI assets may have suffered from a milder shock in advanced economies, than FDI liabilities held by foreign investors in Asia.

Medium Term Prospects

While dramatic and painful, the recent deterioration of the global economic performance follows a sustained expansion built on the increasing integration of emerging and developing economies into the global economy that is unlikely to unwind. Over the last quarter century, trade, remittances and capital flows to and among emerging regions have risen significantly. Without question, their economic and trade growth have constituted the most dynamic aspect of globalization in recent years.

The current crisis slowed down the process but the recovery, even if tentative in some areas, should not take more than two to three years. The mechanisms of recovery are as complex as those of crisis transmission (Figure 8). The sources of recovery can be divided into exogenous forces, domestic efforts, and sources of financing, in particular from regional and international financial organizations where CAF would play a major role.

The external current account of Latin America deteriorated by one percent of GDP between 2007 and 2008, and recorded a deficit for the first time since 2002 (Figure 9, first panel). The current account had moved to a surplus that year, because of fiscal policies and strong depreciations, but weakened subsequently. In 2009, the deficit remained stable because of much lower imports. Tax revenue has declined on this account, with adverse effects on the fiscal outcome, but with growth in the region ahead of its main trading partners the current account deficit will widen in 2010.

In the case of Asia, because of the trade composition of developing and emerging Asia, the impact of lower export prices is minimal, although there is a significant divergence among countries. However, the impact of the recession on exports can also be estimated to be the equivalent of 2 percent of GDP, and was translated into a significant decline in imports, thus reducing the impact on the external current account, which may only weaken by 1 percent of GDP. The fiscal accounts may weaken but from a position of strength achieved through hard work over recent years (Figure 9, panel 2). To some extent, the adverse effect on the balance of payments and the public accounts will be mitigated by the strong devaluation that has been observed since mid 2008, particularly in Latin America, after the appreciation of earlier years.

External Prospects[17]

The global economy is expanding again, pulled up by the strong performance of Asian economies and stabilization or recovery elsewhere, but clouded by crises in Europe. In the advanced economies, unprecedented public intervention stabilized activity and has even fostered a return to modest growth. The rebound in commodity prices, even if interrupted at times, and supportive policies are helping many of the emerging and developing economies. Many countries in emerging Europe and the Commonwealth of Independent States have been hit particularly hard by the crisis, and developments in these economies are generally lagging those elsewhere.

The triggers for the global rebound are strong public policies across advanced and many Emerging Economies that have supported demand and all but eliminated fears of a global depression. These fears contributed to the steepest drop in global activity and trade since World War II. Central banks reacted quickly and Governments launched major fiscal stimulus programs while supporting banks with guarantees and capital injections. Together, these measures reduced uncertainty and increased

---

17 This section closely follows the World Economic Outlook, IMF, April 2010.

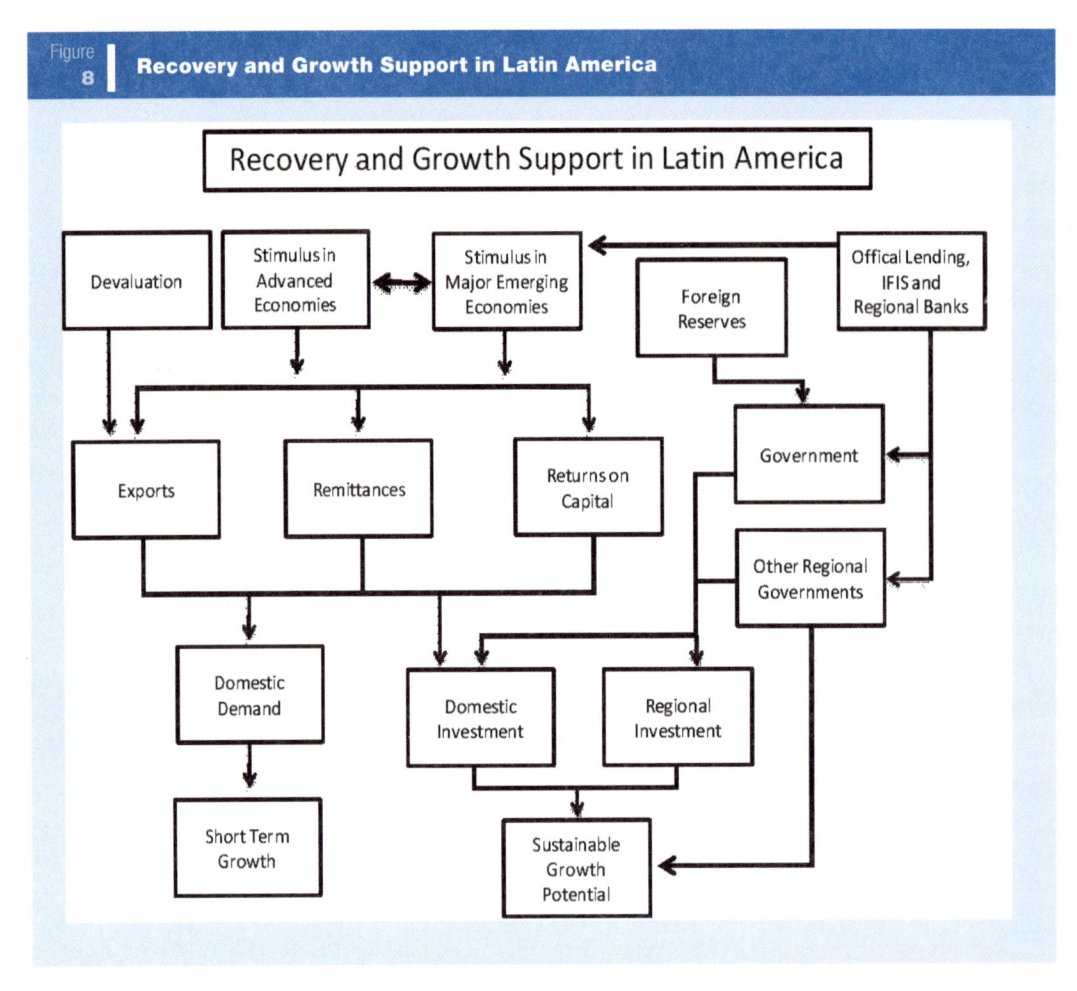

Figure 8: Recovery and Growth Support in Latin America

confidence, fostering an improvement in financial conditions, as evidenced by strong rallies across many markets and a rebound of international capital flows. However, the environment remains very challenging for lower tier borrowers. More generally, the risk of a reversal is a significant market concern, and a number of financial stress indicators remain elevated.

Looking ahead, the policy forces that are driving the current rebound will gradually lose strength, and real and financial forces, although gradually building, remain weak. Specifically, fiscal stimulus will diminish and inventory rebuilding will gradually lose its influence. Meanwhile, consumption and investment are gaining strength only slowly, as financial conditions remain tight in many economies. Thus, after contracting by about 1 percent in 2009, global activity is forecast to expand by about 3 percent in 2010, which is well below the rates achieved before the crisis.

The key policy priorities remain to restore the health of the financial sector and to maintain supportive macroeconomic policies until the recovery is on a firm footing. The premature withdrawal of stimulus seems the greater risk in the near term, but developing the medium-term macroeconomic

Figure 9 | External Current Account, Fiscal Balance, Exchange Rates and Terms of Trade

Latin America

Developing Asia

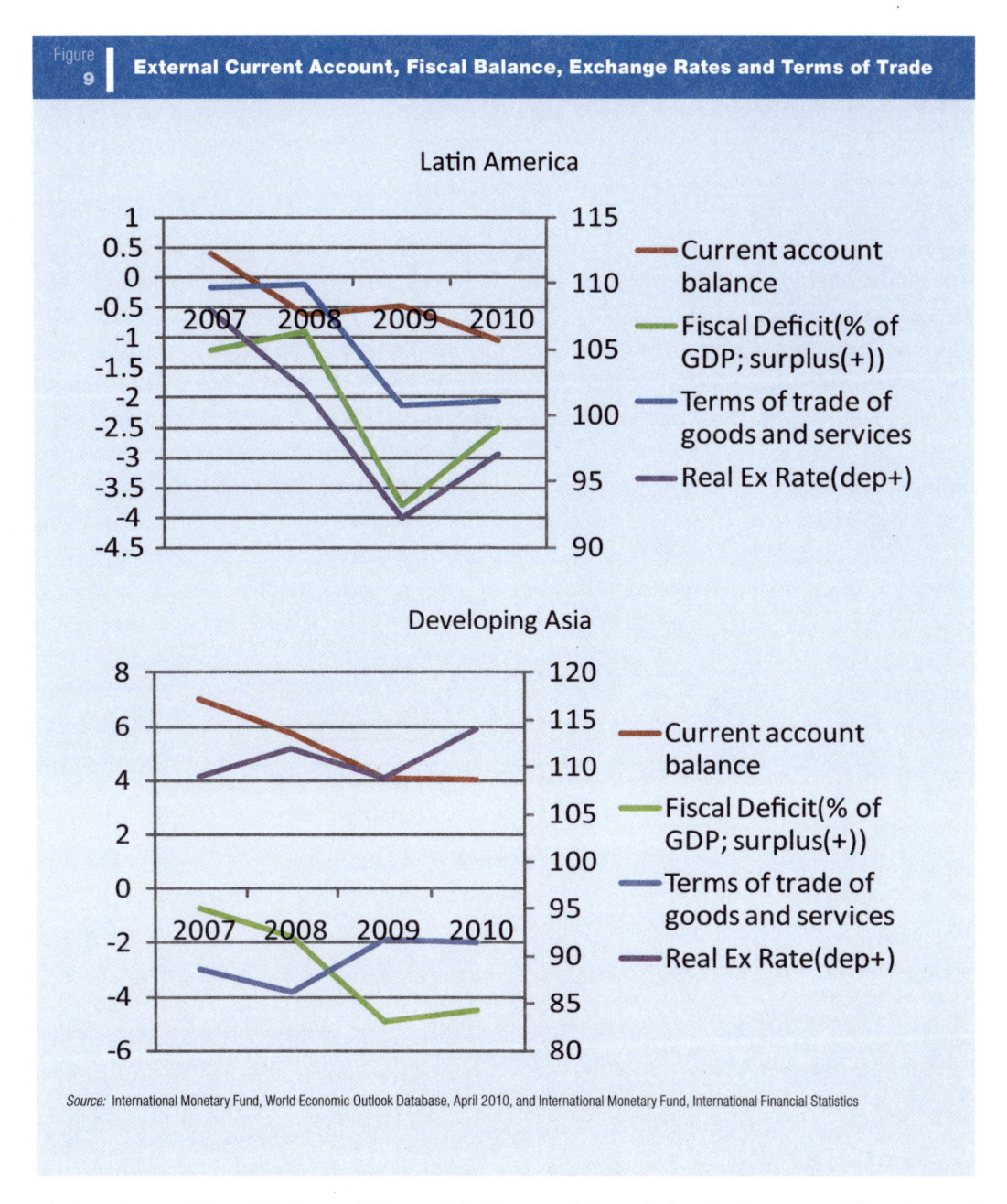

Source: International Monetary Fund, World Economic Outlook Database, April 2010, and International Monetary Fund, International Financial Statistics

strategy beyond the crisis is crucial for maintaining confidence in fiscal solvency and for price and financial stability. The challenge is to map a middle course between unwinding public interventions too early, which would jeopardize the progress made in securing financial stability and recovery, and leaving these measures in place too long,

Policy support was essential to jump-start the recovery. Monetary policy has been highly expansionary and supported by unconventional liquidity provision. Fiscal policy provided a major stimulus in response to the deep downturn. Among advanced economies, the United States is off to a better start than Europe and Japan. Among emerging and developing economies, emerging Asia is in the lead. Growth is also solidifying in key Latin American and other emerging and developing economies but continues to lag in many emerging European and various Commonwealth of Independent States countries. The recoveries in real and financial activity are mutually supportive, but access to credit remains difficult for some sectors. Money markets had stabilized until the recent turmoil in Europe created new pressures, although far less disruptive than two years ago. Corporate bond and equity markets have rebounded. In advanced economies, the tightening of bank lending standards is ending, and the credit crisis seems to be bottoming out. Even as conditions improve, and because of the legacy of the financial crisis of the recent past, financial conditions remain difficult. Especially in advanced economies, bank capital is likely to remain a constraint on growth. Consumers and small and medium-size enterprises are likely to continue to face tight limits on their borrowing. Rising public deficits and debt have contributed to a sharp increase in sovereign risk premiums, posing new risks to the recovery.

Cross border financial flows from advanced to many Emerging Economies have also rebounded strongly, as growth in this part of the world economy has rebounded much more solidly than in the past and than in advanced economies. But this recovery is fragile, as has been witnessed by the recent turmoil in financial markets and a broad-based decline in stock market valuation. Flexible exchange rates have helped mitigate the effect of a changing economic reality more focused on Asia, and with greater risks in some advanced areas of the world. But the dangers of recurring imbalances remain in place, and policies will need to be exceedingly cautious if a new mega-crisis is to be avoided.

Financial Wealth: An Estimate of the Buildup and Destruction of Wealth 2002-2009

Financial wealth over the last decade has become the clearest sign of economic advancement and well-being. The collapse of financial markets in the last two years has been a cataclysmic event. Conditions under which financial markets have been operated for a few decades are unlikely to be replicated in the next few years. The enormous generation of wealth witnessed in recent years may come back, but in the context of a much more sedate and controlled financial system, and subject to stricter rules. Even though a recovery is perceived by many analysts, the road ahead is difficult. The loss of financial wealth has been enormous, and the consequences for the economies of the world are commensurate. The loss of capital value of financial assets world-wide may have reached US$50 trillion in 2008, the equivalent of one year of world GDP. This section provides an estimation of the changes in financial wealth since 2002, and the possible causes for the changes. The study is based on a more detailed study prepared earlier this year.[18]

---

18 The basis for this paper are the calculations presented in the Global Financial Stability Report, of the International Monetary Fund, for the period 2002-07, with additional estimates specifically prepared for this paper for 2008. These do not include the complex set of financial derivatives like CDS (Credit Default Swaps) that further multiplied the size of the financial market.

Table 10 | Total Financial Assets (as percentage of GDP)

Country/Region	2002	2003	2004	2005	2006	2007	2008	2009
World	330.8	342.3	369.2	341.5	401.5	439.6	358.6	425.7
EU	418.4	405.4	457.8	433.6	541.7	580.7	488.5	580.3
United States	344.6	373	401.6	402.9	430.6	445	373.6	450.6
Japan	381.9	454.2	467.2	450.5	459.4	546.6	467.8	504.5
Emerging Asia	242.2	232.9	251.3	246.8	306.6	389.0	331.6	444.3
Emerging Latin America	105.2	129.1	144.1	148.5	155.1	182.3	141.6	216.0
Emerging Africa, Middle East, Europe	83.7	85.1	99.1	86.0	142.8	176.3	118.1	154.7

Source: IMF, Global Financial Stability Report, various issues, Centennial database, and own estimates

Available data shows that the value of financial assets more than doubled between 2002 and 2007 (125 percent), at a time that GDP grew by 70 percent, entailing an increase in the ratio of financial assets to GDP of 330 percent, to 440 percent by end-2007 (Table 10). During the period under review, the ratio of financial assets to GDP in Advanced Economies rose by 35 percent. In Developing Asia, the ratio rose by 60 percent. The rise in the ratio of Financial Assets to GDP in Latin America was an impressive 75 percent.

The pace of financial asset accumulation came to an abrupt halt and reversed in 2008, when the ratio to GDP declined by 18 percent, in response to the crisis, and 10 percent in nominal terms, notwithstanding the massive injection of liquidity by Central Banks and governments alike. When these increases in liquidity are subtracted, the loss of financial wealth at a world-wide level may amount to an astounding US$50 trillion. (Figure 10) The implications for aggregate demand, including for investment have not yet been quantified, but clearly explain the expected decline of almost 3 percent in GDP in 2009, as recently suggested by the World Bank, and beyond the estimates of -2 percent that the IMF had indicated earlier.

Figure 11 provides data on the main sources of explained changes (stock market valuation changes; exchange rate movements; changes in spreads; and movements in nonperforming loans) during the period under study. Clearly, during the period, the main source of change has been the stock market, with more limited changes in the area of debt and bank assets. Only in 2003, at a time when financial markets were recovering, and in 2008, when financial markets collapsed, were other items affected in a significant way.

The impact of the current crisis has been overwhelming in terms of the geographic coverage. All

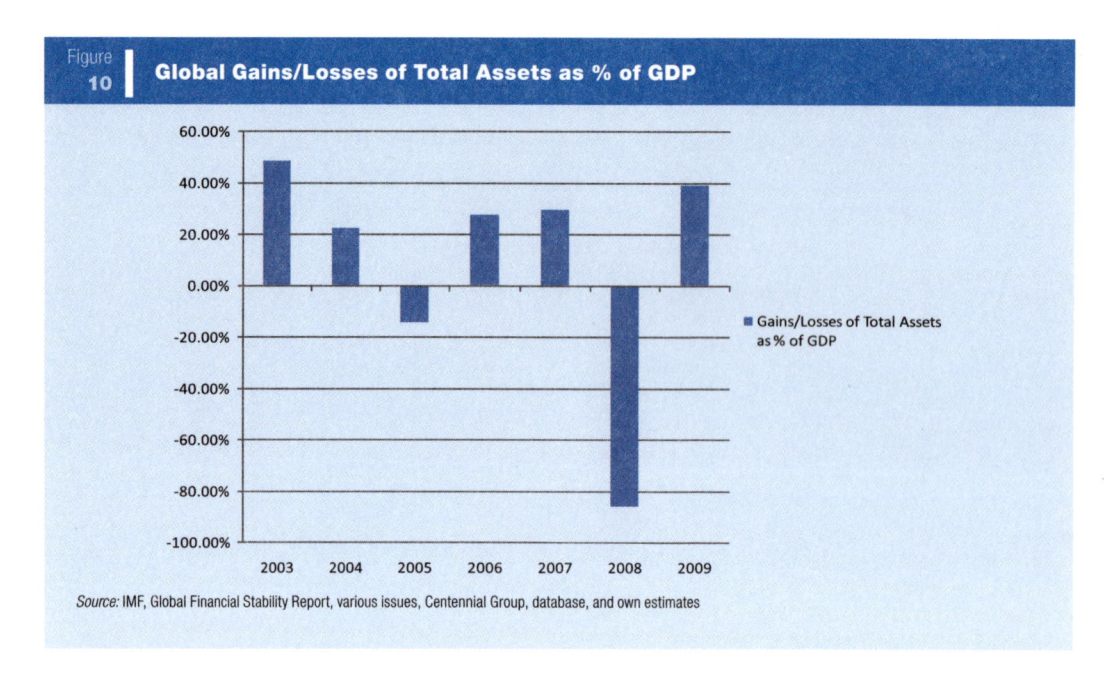

Figure 10: Global Gains/Losses of Total Assets as % of GDP

Source: IMF, Global Financial Stability Report, various issues, Centennial Group, database, and own estimates

regions of the world suffered the consequences of the crisis, showing again that the decoupling theory that had been prevalent during earlier years was misplaced. Figure 12 shows the magnitude of the fall in 2008 after years of relative tranquility, with particularly large declines in the case of Developing Asia, Latin America, and to a surprising extent in the case of the European Union. This is explained by a combination of the impact of the crisis on the stock market, the large financial system, and the effect of a depreciation of the currencies. In the case of Asia, it is explained by the stock market and the losses in the banking system, while in Latin America, the losses are explained mainly by the stock market, because of the smallest financial systems as a proportion of GDP.

The impact of a decline in stock market values by almost one half and the reduction in the values of financial assets and higher spreads on debts are having a direct effect on the performance of economies world-wide. Different estimates show wealth-elasticities of consumption to financial wealth in the order of up to .05, and of .06 in the case of housing equity for increases in wealth. However, the association seems to be stronger in the case of declines in wealth.[19] On that basis, a decline in financial wealth in the order of 20 percent could have an impact on consumption of 2 percent. In addition, the effect on investment is significant on account of the perceived reduced prospects for growth in the near future because of significant existing excess capacity. Thus, the decline in activity observed in 2009 of about 3 percent a year is consistent with the loss of wealth described here. This decline is taking place notwithstanding the significant efforts among major countries to reactivate their economies.

Notwithstanding the large governmental packages of late 2008, the financial losses continued

---

[19] Raphael Bostic Stuart Gabriel and Gary Painter, University of Southern California, and Ziman Center for Real Estate, University of California, Los Angeles, (2008).

Figure 11: Factors behind Global Assets Losses 2003-2009 (% of GDP)

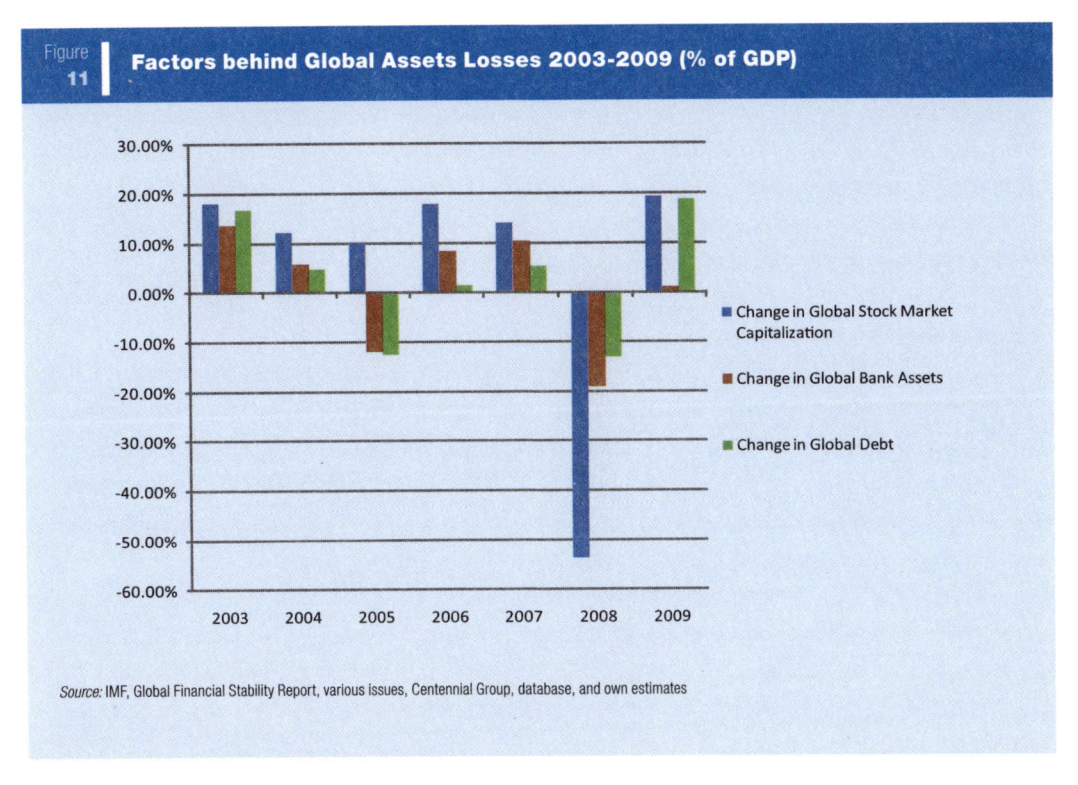

- Change in Global Stock Market Capitalization
- Change in Global Bank Assets
- Change in Global Debt

Source: IMF, Global Financial Stability Report, various issues, Centennial Group, database, and own estimates

Figure 12: Breakdown of Assets Losses in 2008 by Country (% of GDP)

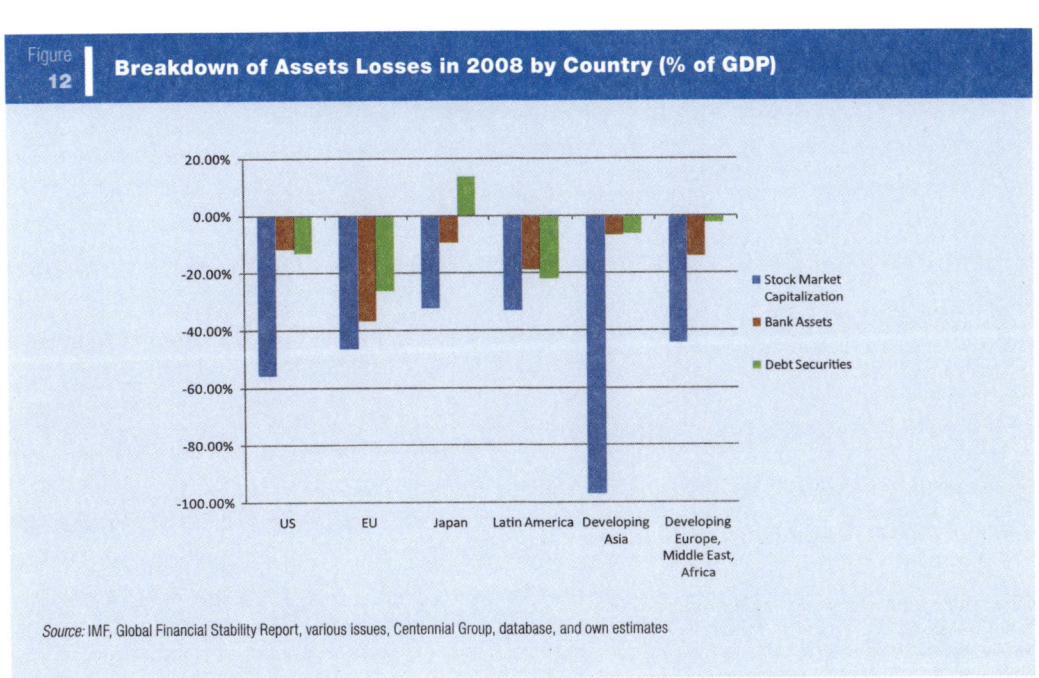

- Stock Market Capitalization
- Bank Assets
- Debt Securities

Source: IMF, Global Financial Stability Report, various issues, Centennial Group, database, and own estimates

unabated until early 2009, when commodity prices bottomed, and coordination among the main economies of the world, embodied in the G-20, started to become evident beyond statements and into practice (Figure 13). Among the various regions of the world, the one showing the greatest rebound, relative to end 2006, was Latin America, helped by reasonable macro-policies after decades of mismanagement, and the closest to its more moderate peak. Developing Asia, reflecting the strength of China and India, the emerging giants of the region, and the appreciation of their currencies vis-à-vis the US dollar, has recovered but remains further away from its maximum.

Stimulus Packages: How much can Emerging Economies afford?[20]

With widespread economic crises, authorities announced fiscal and credit packages aimed at softening the impact of lower commodity prices and reduced external demand. These measures were being taken on top of the currency devaluations in many larger countries. Questions arose about the size of these packages in Emerging Economies, and how they compared with those in the more advanced economies of the World. Moreover, were they able to afford them in a fundamental sense? Table 11 helps elucidate these questions. The table lists the stimulus packages in some Latin American and Asian countries, as well as those in the US, Germany, Japan and the UK. The numbers are adjusted to reflect multi-year programs. For example, in the case of China and the US, the program extended for two years. The table includes numbers for public debt, both total and net of international reserves, to reflect the ability of the countries to finance the increased spending.

With the exception of those announced by China and Singapore, the packages among EEs were considerably smaller than those to be implemented in the US and Japan (6 percent of GDP) and Germany (3 percent). In these countries, even with high levels of debt to GDP, their size and the depth of capital markets allows them to increase spending. In China and Singapore, a very low level of net debt and high reserves allowed for the proposed effort. In Latin America, the two countries that announced larger packages are Chile and Peru. Both countries have a very low level of net debt, and in the case of Chile, the authorities built a successful stabilization fund. All other countries announced packages amounting to about one percent of GDP, about the maximum they could afford, either because of the level of their debt (Argentina, Brazil and Mexico in Latin America, and India and Korea in Asia), or the size of their financial markets (Indonesia). And while expansionary fiscal and monetary policy had a favorable impact on demand, the higher the level of debt to GDP, the lower the prospects for a strong positive effect. It even can have a negative impact to the extent that debt is too high.

The Future Access to International Financial Organizations

Emerging markets economies only have limited room for expansion and some countries have already used it. Thus, to the extent they need more stimulus, they will have to rely on the effect of the external stimulus packages, more than on their own actions, with the possible exception of monetary policy, where margins may be greater. Still, an important additional component of recovery was the ability to

---

20 C. Loser, By the Numbers, Latin American Advisor, Inter-American Dialogue, January 2009.

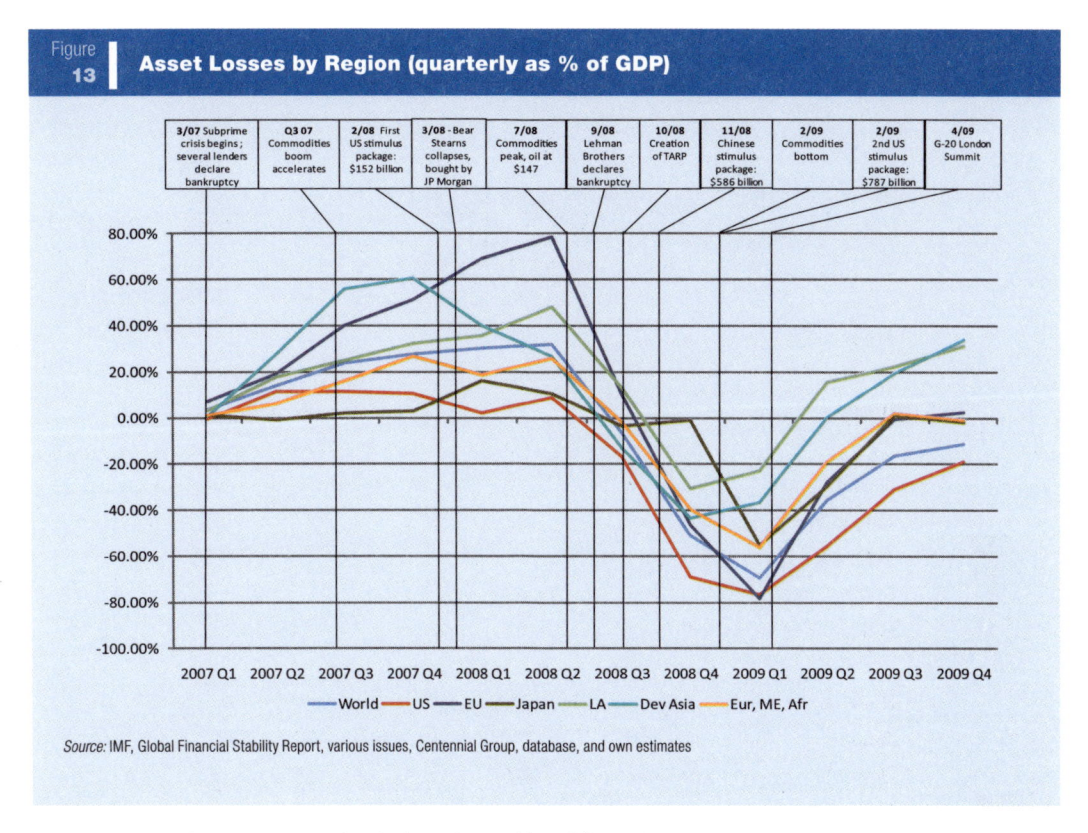

Figure 13: Asset Losses by Region (quarterly as % of GDP)

Source: IMF, Global Financial Stability Report, various issues, Centennial Group, database, and own estimates

raise funds and use reserves. Latin America, with US$500 billion in reserves as of end-2008, mostly held by Brazil, and Mexico, had the ability to withstand some pressures with respect to lower financing. Furthermore, the recent extension of credit to Mexico, Colombia and a number of smaller countries in Latin America by the IMF suggests a capacity to raise official funds that had not been taken fully into account so far.

The G-20 has shown a major commitment to a massive mobilization of resources. The approval by the US Congress of additional funds further enhances these for the region, but the money will be available over several years, and will not fully offset the loss of private flows. Table 12 provides an estimate of what the region may be able to receive. The table includes: (1) increases in the amount of SDRs, assigned proportionally on the basis of IMF quotas or shares; (2) possible new lending by the IMF and other International Financial Institutions, assuming that China, India and Saudi Arabia will not be borrowing from them; (3) trade related financing by developed countries. On this basis, Latin America and the Caribbean could have the potential to obtain US$180 billion in loans, or about 5 percent of GDP.

This is a substantial amount, but there are a number of constraining factors: the disbursements will occur over at least two years; recent estimates for debt service payments for the region are in the order of US$200 billion, of which more than half are official obligations; and private capital inflows can be expected to decline, with a significant fall in foreign direct investment. With exports declining, the

Table 11: Total Financial Assets (as percentage of GDP)

Country/Region	Announced Amount of Stimulus	Gross Public Debt	Public Debt, net of International Reserves
		(% of GDP, 2008)	
Peru	2.5	31	1
Chile	2.2	19	6
Argentina	1.2	59	46
Mexico	1.1	22	14
Brazil	1.0	57	46
China	7.1	18	-30
Singapore	3.2	92	2
Indonesia	1.3	17	5
South Korea	1.1	32	11
India	0.7	58	37
USA	5.6	38	38
Japan	5.2	153	128
Germany	2.7	67	64
Great Britain	1.1	44	41

1/ Estimated expenditure in 2009. Number in parenthesis is total package

Sources: National data; Press Releases; IMF; Eurostat, and own estimates.

financial outlook for the region is problematic, but with the additional resources, prospects are clearly brighter. The package reflects the right policy approach, with the official sector acting as a countercyclical force at a time of financial catastrophe. Within the totals, CAF can play a significant role and it has already indicated its intention to grant loans for a total of US$20 billion to help the region deal with the expected decline in private financing over the next few years.

The return of the IFIs has been difficult to accept for many of the possible clients in the region, which had made a point of breaking their previous close financial ties to the IMF, the World Bank and the Inter-American Development Bank. Argentina, Bolivia, Ecuador, Venezuela, and to a lesser extent Brazil and Colombia, had considered that their improved circumstances meant that they no longer needed the IFIs now that they had strong trade performance, robust levels of international reserves, and a much easier access to international financial markets. Both assumptions have been shattered, at least for the foreseeable future.

Table 12: The G-20 Package: Estimated Availability of New Funds to Latin America

	IMF Quotas (% of total)	SDR Allocation 1/	Additional Lending IMF 2/	Multilat. Dev. Banks 3/	Trade Related Lending 4/	Total Financing
Total World	100.0	250	500	100	250	1100
Advanced Economies	59.6	149	-	-	172	321
Emerging and NICS, Excluding LATAM	32.6	82	378	77	60	596
Latin America and Caribbean	7.8	19	123	23	18	183

1/ SDR Allocation on the basis of Existing IMF Quotas

2/ Additional Lending by IMF on the basis of existing quotas, excluding advanced economies

3/ Multilateral Development Bank lending on the basis of GDP, excluding advanced economies

4/ Trade related lending on the basis of GDP, including Advanced Economies

Sources: IMF, G-20 Declaration - April 2009, and own estimates.

With high financing requirements, access to the IFIs will be a necessity for many countries in the region. Such access, even if difficult from their point of view, will be eased by the fact that these organizations now seem willing to give greater representation to Emerging Economies, and are showing greater lending flexibility. The strength of the G-20 is a good indication of the major changes occurring in the world political economy. The G-20 includes the G-8 and China, India, Korea, South Africa, Brazil, Mexico and Argentina. This forum better reflects the growing importance of the emerging world and may also open the door to a more representative governance system at the world financial level. Over-represented countries in Europe and elsewhere will need to accept the realities of the new world and to shift part of their voting power to the "new" countries. If that occurs, the perceived stigma of the IFIs may disappear for many countries in Latin America.

The trend toward more flexible lending mechanisms by the IFIs also helps. The most controversial lending organization remains the IMF. According to its own information, the IMF has increased its lending capacity by some US$500 billion, in addition to the SDR allocation that has been agreed. The IMF had played a major role in financing Latin America in the past. However, after lending to Latin America reached about US$50 billion at the beginning of the decade, it had fallen to less than US$1 billion in late 2008. After the recent announcements of increased flexibility, Mexico has benefited from the new approach of the multilateral organizations, and particularly from the less conditional approach embodied in the Flexible Credit Line (FCL). Specifically, Mexico has been granted US$47 billion, and Colombia US$21 billion, on the basis of its track record, and with the right to draw on the credit line at any time. Disbursements are not phased nor conditioned on compliance with policy targets as in traditional IMF-supported programs. Other smaller Latin American countries further changed the trend. The IMF is now ready to deal with requests for assistance under what it defines as fast-track emergency financing procedures. There have already been several loans to other countries under these conditions, including in Europe and Asia.

The FCL is available for countries that are seen as having carried out reasonable policies and are willing to take the necessary measures to put their economics on track. Once agreement with the authorities has been reached on a lending program, the IMF Executive Board, which is kept informed of the negotiations, considers the request for a loan within up to 72 hours. This is in contrast to the six weeks to two months required under normal lending circumstances. If policy failures are significant, then the IMF would follow more traditional lending procedures. Countries that need financing most urgently in the region may be unwilling to engage in negotiations. They will, however, be attracted by the fact that the IMF will emphasize only a few basic macro economic conditions, as opposed to a wide array of issues, as had been the practice in the past.

The World Bank, in November 2008, also launched the Debt Management Facility to help developing countries prevent future debt problems. It also called on donor countries to meet their debt relief commitments. According to the World Bank, the new facility will accelerate the implementation of debt management programs in partnership with several other organizations, with the objective of strengthening debt management capacity and institutions in developing countries. This supplements the Bank's financial assistance for poor countries, but with only very few qualifying members in the region, this only has limited impact on Latin America. However countries will make increased use of World Bank resources to finance their programs of reform, as well as the public expenditure/investment programs that many of them are putting in place to deal with the current slowdown.

The Inter-American Development Bank also approved a record volume of loans in 2009 and is setting up a new fast-disbursing $6 billion liquidity facility to help Latin American and Caribbean economies. The IADB's $6 billion Liquidity Program for Growth Sustainability is available to domestic firms via commercial banks that may face temporary difficulties in accessing foreign and inter-bank credit lines as a result of the financial crisis. In addition, the IADB accelerated loans to finance projects and enhance social programs and approved a record $12 billion in 2009.

These efforts on the part of the IFIs are very significant, but they will work only to the extent that the countries themselves are willing to draw down these funds and use them effectively. Many recognize the advantages of these loans, as they are contracted on a longer term basis and with relatively low interest rates. However, some countries may choose not to use these funds on ideological grounds. They may actually harm themselves, since they may end up having to make more drastic adjustments, or declare a default on outstanding obligations with even worse consequences than availing themselves of help from the IFIs. The number of such countries is small, without major contagion to the other, more responsible countries in the region.

Lessons from the Current Financial Turmoil[21]

There are a number of important lessons in relation to the Financial Crisis of the last two years:
1. Globalization and the increase in the size of international financial markets have dramatically raised the mutual dependence of economies around the world.
2. Large financial institutions are increasingly global in their operations, which link together financial markets worldwide.
3. Financial instruments created and regulated in one country are bought and sold throughout the world.
4. Capital markets and capital flows now exceed commercial lending operations in their size and profitability as well as in their influence on the performance of overall financial markets.
5. Financial crises emerge with great regularity, but their origin and nature have been impossible to predict; increasingly such crises develop suddenly and quickly spill over beyond national boundaries, posing threats to the global system itself; their resolution exceeds the capacity and resources of individual countries and institutions.

While the financial system has evolved rapidly, its monitoring and regulation have lagged behind:
- The institutional architecture and governance of the global financial system, as well as its governance structure, does not yet reflect the massive changes that have taken place in global financial markets and in the position of the most rapidly growing economies in that system.
- The current system relies on regulation and supervision at the national level, while many major financial institutions and their instruments are global in their reach and influence.
- At the country level, there are important differences in the approach to regulation and supervision; some very profitable and dynamic parts of the system were virtually unregulated (hedge funds, private equity, derivatives, etc.).
- In some critical areas, including the analysis and oversight of capital markets and capital flows, no international body currently has a clear mandate.
- There are serious gaps in the codes and standards that guide transparency at national and global levels.
- There has been no effective "early warning system" regarding some of the risks that can develop at the global level.
- There is an asymmetry in the willingness of institutions, including the IMF, to comment candidly on the policy weaknesses and risks being taken by the key players in world financial markets.

---

21 This discussion reflects the presentation of Global Governance and Reform of the International Monetary Fund: An Update, by Jack Boorman, Advisor Emerging market forum, 2009.

Principles for Reform

- The current gaps, disparities and fragmentation in the setting and monitoring of standards, and in the regulation and supervision of different parts of the financial system, should be eliminated.
- Future responsibilities should be based on a three-tier system: national, regional and global institutions.
- The setting of standards and information reporting should be coordinated and monitored at the global level.
- While there is a need for some regulations at the global level applicable to institutions and financial instruments with global reach, these regulations should be designed to facilitate globalization. The primary responsibility for regulation and supervision should rest at the national level.
- "Early warning systems" must be developed at the national and global levels.
- Periodic discussions on the stability and vulnerabilities of national and regional financial systems, and peer review of financial systems and the sharing of experience should rest at the regional level.
- During financial crises, the primary responsibility for the requisite analysis and coordination of financial assistance would need to be centralized, possibly by the IMF but not as a sole player; in particularly acute cases, major governments and central banks could contribute.
- To ensure its legitimacy and credibility, the new global financial architecture should reflect the current economic realities and provide for a larger role for the major emerging market economies.
- The IFIs must have the tools and authority to address weaknesses in the economic and financial policies of all its members, including the largest economies and the most important financial systems in the world, and must be independent in using that authority.

Financial Sector Regulation[22]

In the light of the above developments, the world's main Economies have embarked in a serious effort to reform the financial system operations. The ongoing financial regulatory reform process—spearheaded by the G-20is aimed at addressing the inadequacies in the regulatory framework that the crisis has revealed. The process is gradually yielding recommendations at both the national level and internationally, which is generating some uncertainty for the financial sector. Proposals are most advanced in the area of strengthening bank capital. Enhancements to the Basel II capital framework—specifying higher capital requirements for banks' trading books and some securitizations—were announced in mid-2009, and are to be implemented by end-2010.

Other reform proposals (announced in December 2009) focusing on bank capital and liquidity are yet to be finalized, with the final calibration for capital requirements announced by end-2010 and

---

[22] This discussion reflects "Recent Developments in Financial Regulation Reforms" by Aditya Narain and Kornélia Krajnyák in World Economic and Financial Surveys: Regional Economic Outlook; Western Hemisphere-Taking Advantage of Tailwinds- Washington DC May 2010.

implementation by end-2012.

The proposals target:
- Improving the quality of bank capital (by increasing the share of common equity in Tier 1 capital; harmonizing the definition of Tier 2 capital internationally; and enhancing the risk coverage of the capital framework).
- Supplementing risk-based capital requirements with a leverage ratio, with details yet to be worked out.
- Dampening pro-cyclicality (by conservative adjustments to capital adequacy to reflect stressed periods; forward-looking provisioning; building up target capital buffers; and upward adjustment of capital buffers after a period of rapid credit growth). Work on the details of the proposals is ongoing.
- Addressing systemic risk and interconnectedness (through a better-calibrated asset value correlation factor in internal ratings that would imply higher capital requirements for exposures to large regulated financial firms or to unregulated leveraged entities such as hedge funds).
- Reducing the reliance on external ratings in the capital adequacy framework.
- Introducing internationally common standards of minimum high quality liquidity buffers, with the dual aim of (i) being able to meet liquidity outflows over a 30-day stress period; and (ii) matching liability and asset profiles over a 1-year horizon.

Recommendations in other areas are less advanced. The framework for macro-prudential supervision is still evolving, with a view to alleviating credit cycles and contagion risks. Discussions on issues related to systemic risk and systemically important institutions are complicated by, among other things, political and legal issues. On the agenda are extending the regulatory scope, introducing differential prudential regulations for systemically important institutions, possibly creating a systemic risk regulator, setting up a resolution framework for systemically important institutions, and rethinking regulator issues in the over-the-counter derivative and securitization market.

Of course, these proposals do not cover all areas where improvements would be needed to strengthen financial stability. Ensuring adequate supervisory responses, improving risk management and governance in the financial sector, and leveling the playing field internationally (by proper and consistent implementation of prudential standards) and across sectors (by stepping up lagging reforms in the insurance sector and securities markets) remain outstanding tasks.

Concluding remarks

Most emerging market economies, including in developing Asia and Latin America are coming out of the Great Recession, but the next twelve months will remain very difficult, particularly in light of the European crisis. The perception that they had broken the links with the larger economies has been refuted by the hard facts of the last 18 months. Financial markets of the world are closely interconnected, and the impact of the world financial collapse on Emerging Economies is a witness to this fact.

Even as Asia and Latin America diversified their investment and trading partners, the effect of the slowdown on exports, finance and investment is significant. Growth fell sharply, and the external accounts are reflecting the consequences of the fall in prices, economic activity, and in wealth, and capital flows are falling drastically.

In hindsight, poor macroeconomic and regulatory policies allowed the global economy to exceed its capacity to grow and contributed to a buildup in imbalances across asset and commodity markets. Policy and market shortcomings prevented equilibrating mechanisms from operating effectively and market stresses rose. These errors occurred mainly in Advanced but also in Emerging Economies, so that the blame cannot be easily shifted to others. However, there has been no destruction of physical and human capital, boding well for a strong recovery, possibly more cautious and sustainable, after the adjustments in the financial markets have worked through over the next year or so.

The situation is serious and the effect on output, wealth, and poverty is critical. However in Latin America and other Emerging Economies, particularly in Asia, national authorities see the situation with a greater degree of realism. The main countries of the world have reacted positively, helping restore international stability. Emerging Economies are better prepared than at any time in the last quarter century or so. Unfortunately, the shock was greater than in the past, and defenses have been effective in the short run but may not be sufficient in the medium term to protect the two regions. Each country will have to follow a difficult path, and populist and protectionist temptations will remain a major threat. These tendencies carry a high cost. Even with better defenses, the world faces a serious economic challenge. Countries are now confronted with the need to find a balance between economic stimuli on the one hand, and financial stability on the other. Such a task is not simple, and will require effort and clarity of vision.

Latin America 2040

Part II

Chapter 4
Is Latin America Becoming Less Unequal?

Nora Lustig

After a period of rising inequality in the 1990s, Latin America's concentration of income began to fall since 2000. Of the 17 countries for which comparable data is available, 12 experienced a decline at an average pace of -1.1 percent per year (Figure 1). The fall in inequality has contributed to a faster decline in poverty for a given growth rate. Inequality in Latin America is the result of state-capture on the part of predatory elites, capital market imperfections, inequality of opportunities (in particular, in terms of

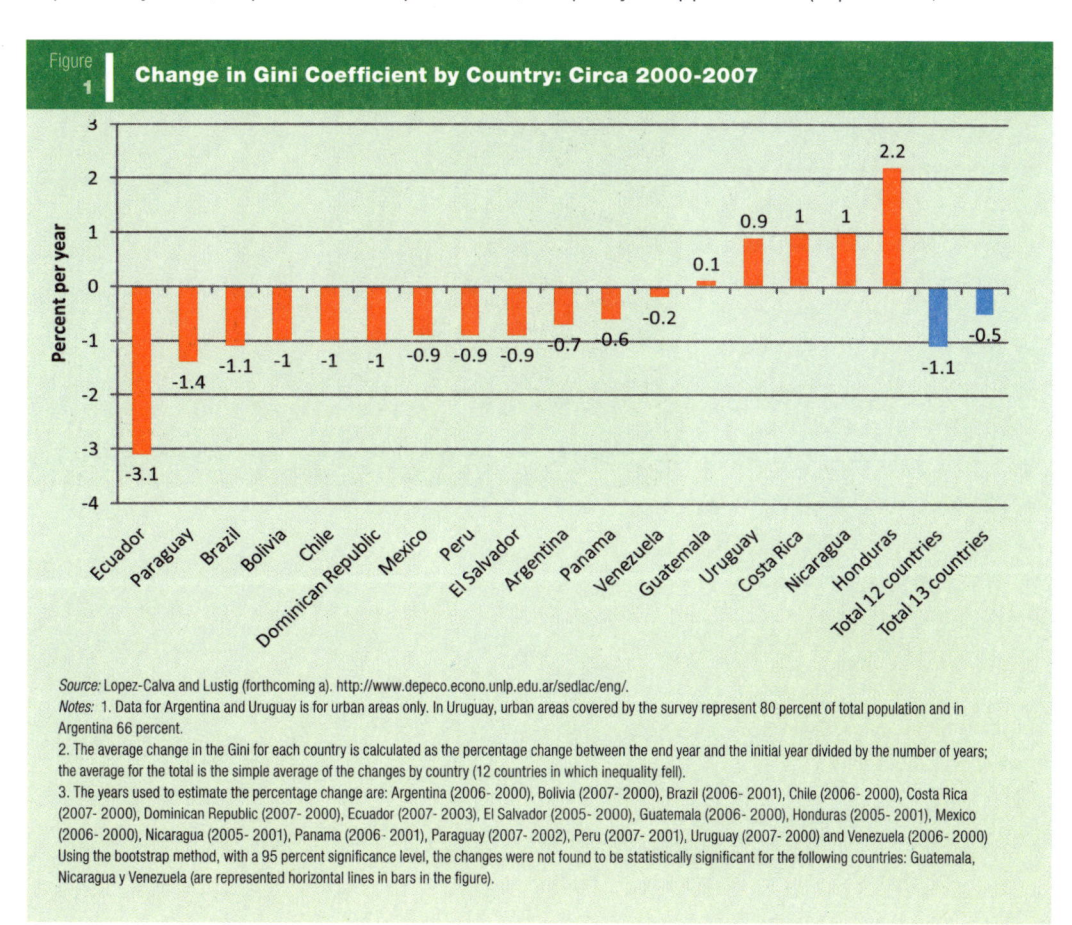

Figure 1: Change in Gini Coefficient by Country: Circa 2000-2007

Country	Percent per year
Ecuador	-3.1
Paraguay	-1.4
Brazil	-1.1
Bolivia	-1
Chile	-1
Dominican Republic	-1
Mexico	-0.9
Peru	-0.9
El Salvador	-0.9
Argentina	-0.7
Panama	-0.6
Venezuela	-0.2
Guatemala	0.1
Uruguay	0.9
Costa Rica	1
Nicaragua	1
Honduras	2.2
Total 12 countries	-1.1
Total 13 countries	-0.5

Source: Lopez-Calva and Lustig (forthcoming a). http://www.depeco.econo.unlp.edu.ar/sedlac/eng/.

Notes: 1. Data for Argentina and Uruguay is for urban areas only. In Uruguay, urban areas covered by the survey represent 80 percent of total population and in Argentina 66 percent.
2. The average change in the Gini for each country is calculated as the percentage change between the end year and the initial year divided by the number of years; the average for the total is the simple average of the changes by country (12 countries in which inequality fell).
3. The years used to estimate the percentage change are: Argentina (2006- 2000), Bolivia (2007- 2000), Brazil (2006- 2001), Chile (2006- 2000), Costa Rica (2007- 2000), Dominican Republic (2007- 2000), Ecuador (2007- 2003), El Salvador (2005- 2000), Guatemala (2006- 2000), Honduras (2005- 2001), Mexico (2006- 2000), Nicaragua (2005- 2001), Panama (2006- 2001), Paraguay (2007- 2002), Peru (2007- 2001), Uruguay (2007- 2000) and Venezuela (2006- 2000). Using the bootstrap method, with a 95 percent significance level, the changes were not found to be statistically significant for the following countries: Guatemala, Nicaragua y Venezuela (are represented horizontal lines in bars in the figure).

access to good quality education), labor market segmentation, and discrimination against women and nonwhites.[1] Hence, the observed fall in inequality is good news.

The decline in inequality has been widespread. Inequality has fallen in high inequality countries (Brazil) and low inequality—by Latin American standards, that is—countries (Argentina); fast growing countries (Chile and Peru), slow growing countries (Brazil and Mexico) and countries recovering from crisis (Argentina and Venezuela); countries with a large share of indigenous groups (Bolivia, Ecuador and Peru) and countries with a low share (Argentina); in countries governed by the left (Brazil and Chile) and in countries governed by non-leftist regimes (Mexico and Peru); in countries with a universalistic social policy (Argentina and Chile) and in countries with a traditionally exclusionary state (Bolivia and El Salvador).

This is indeed an intriguing phenomenon and it immediately begs a number of questions. Does the fall in inequality signal a break with the past? Is inequality likely to continue to decline in the future? If not, what policies should governments pursue in the coming years? In order to address these questions, we must understand the factors that lie behind the recent decline in inequality. This chapter does this by focusing on the experience of five countries: Argentina, Bolivia, Brazil, Mexico, and Peru.

The results can be summarized as follows. Two main factors account for the decline in inequality: a fall in the earnings gap of skilled/low-skilled workers and an increase in government transfers targeted to the poor. The fall in earnings gap, in turn, is mainly the result of the expansion of coverage in basic education during the last couple of decades. It is also the result of the petering out of the one-time unequalizing effect of skill-biased technical change in the 1990s associated with the opening up of trade and investment.

Photo Credit: CAF

The upgrading of skills of the poor, however, will sooner or later face the "access-to-tertiary education" barrier—mainly due to the low quality education they receive in previous levels—and thus the decline in inequality is not likely to continue when that barrier gets hit. In addition, despite the progress in making public policy more pro-poor, a large share of government spending is neutral or regressive in the distributive sense and the collection of personal income and wealth taxes is low. Figure 2 shows the distribution of market income (pre-taxes and transfers) and disposable income in selected

---

1 See, for example, de Ferranti et al., 2004; Atal, Ñopo and Winder, 2009; Barros et al., 2009; and Levy and Walton, 2009.

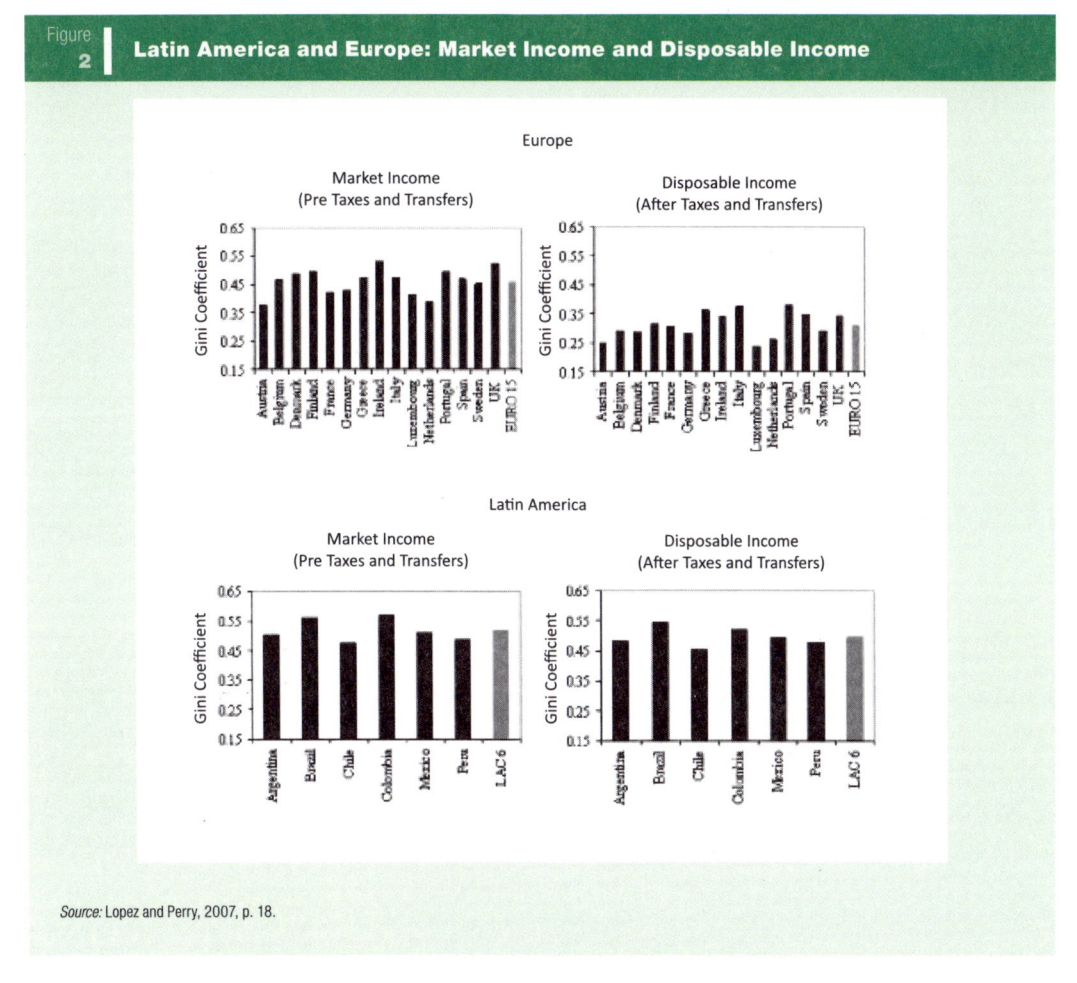

Figure 2 | Latin America and Europe: Market Income and Disposable Income

Source: Lopez and Perry, 2007, p. 18.

European and Latin American countries. What we observe is quite striking. In European countries, the Gini coefficient after taxes and transfers is on average over 10 percentage points lower than the market-determined Gini (with transfers explaining two thirds and taxes one third of the difference) while in Latin America the difference is between one or two percentage points.

Clearly, this indicates that state-sponsored programs and taxes are far less progressive (and many are still regressive, that is, unequalizing) in Latin America than in Europe. To continue on the path towards more equitable societies, making public spending more progressive and efforts to improve access to quality services—education, in particular—for the poor are crucial.

This chapter first presents a brief overview of inequality and poverty in Latin America compared to other regions of the world. This is followed by an analysis of the determinants of the fall in inequality in Argentina, Bolivia, Brazil, Mexico and Peru. Finally, it presents conclusions and policy recommendations.

Figure 3: Gini Coefficient by Region (in %), 2004

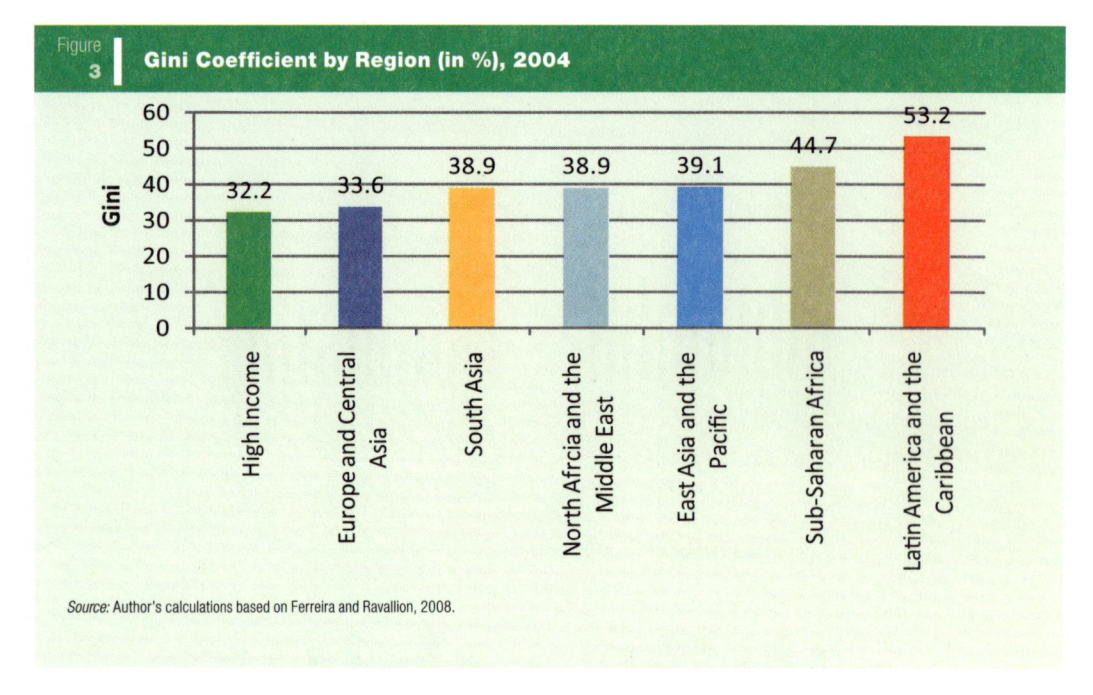

Region	Gini
High Income	32.2
Europe and Central Asia	33.6
South Asia	38.9
North Africa and the Middle East	38.9
East Asia and the Pacific	39.1
Sub-Saharan Africa	44.7
Latin America and the Caribbean	53.2

Source: Author's calculations based on Ferreira and Ravallion, 2008.

Latin America: Inequality and Poverty in Comparative Perspective

How much inequality and poverty is there in Latin America in comparison with other parts of the world? Latin America has more income inequality and less extreme poverty than other regions. With a Gini coefficient[2] of .53, Latin America is 19 percent more unequal than Sub-Saharan Africa, 37 percent more unequal than East Asia and 65 percent more unequal than developed countries (Figure 3). Also, with a Gini coefficient of close to 0.60, some of the countries reach levels of inequality among the highest in the world if individual countries are considered (Figure 4). The encouraging news is that, after a period of rising inequality in the 1990s, since 2000, the region's Gini coefficient began to decline (Figure 5). Between 2000 and 2007, of the 17 countries for which comparable data is available, 12 experienced a decline; and, with the exception of Venezuela, the decline in the Gini was found to be statistically significant[3] (see Figure 1). Taking the 12 countries together, the average Gini coefficient fell at 1.1 percent per year.

Latin America's poverty rate[4] of 24.1 percent (using the US$2.50 a day international poverty line) is lower than in other regions. In particular, East Asia and the Pacific's poverty rate (52.4 percent) is nearly double Latin America's, and poverty rates in Sub-Saharan Africa (79.9 percent) and South Asia (84.4 percent) are roughly four times higher (Figure 6). This should come as no surprise: Latin America

---

2 Named after his proponent, the Gini coefficient is a very commonly used indicator to measure inequality. The Gini coefficient is an index that can take values between zero and one (or, between zero and 100 if in percent). The closer it is to zero (one), the less (more) unequal the distribution in question. Available Ginis are usually never above .65 or below .20.
3 The declines in inequality are generally robust even if other inequality measures are used.
4 The incidence of poverty is measured with the headcount ratio equal to the number of people living below the poverty line divided by the total population. The figure is for 2005.

Figure 4 | Gini Coefficient by Country (in %), 2004

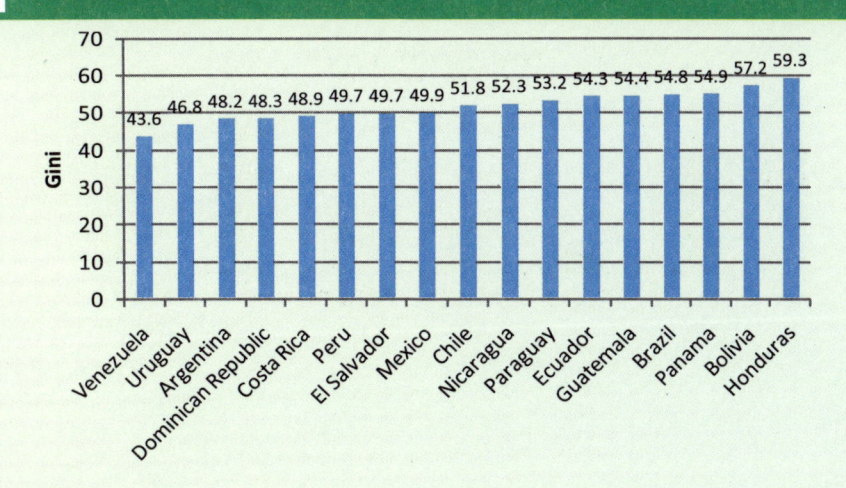

Country	Gini
Venezuela	43.6
Uruguay	46.8
Argentina	48.2
Dominican Republic	48.3
Costa Rica	48.9
Peru	49.7
El Salvador	49.7
Mexico	49.9
Chile	51.8
Nicaragua	52.3
Paraguay	53.2
Ecuador	54.3
Guatemala	54.4
Brazil	54.8
Panama	54.9
Bolivia	57.2
Honduras	59.3

Source: Author's calculations based on data from SEDLAC (July 2009).

Notes:
1. In order to make the differences in the Gini coefficients easier to compare, the vertical axis starts at 40 percent instead of zero.
2. the years used to estimate the Gini coefficient are: Argentina (2006), Bolivia (2007), Brazil (2006), Chile (2006), Costa Rica (2007), Dominican Republic (2007), Ecuador (2007), El Salvador (2005), Guatemala (2006), Honduras (2005), Mexico (2006), Nicaragua (2005), Panama (2006), Paraguay (2007), Peru (2007), Uruguay (2007) and Venezuela (2006). The difference in the average for the region with Figure 2 is due to the fact that the latter uses the Gini coefficients for (circa) 2005 and here the numbers correspond to later years.

Figure 5 | Gini Coefficient (in %), for Latin America: 1990-2005

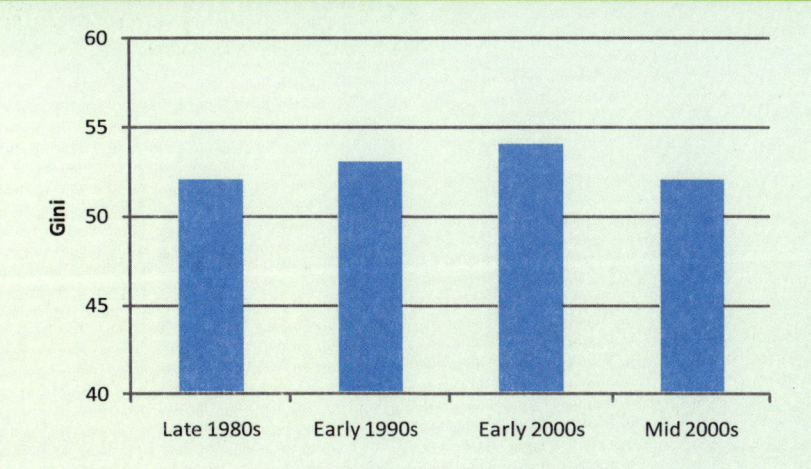

Period	Gini
Late 1980s	52
Early 1990s	53
Early 2000s	54
Mid 2000s	52

Source: Gasparini et al., 2009.

Figure 6 | **Headcount Ratio by Region (in percent): 1990, 1996, 2002 and 2005 (in percent)**

Poverty ($2.50 PPP per day)

Region	1990	1996	2002	2005
East Asia and Pacific	87.4	75	63.3	52.4
Eastern Europe and Central Asia	12.5	19	18.1	14.7
Latin America and Caribbean	27.9	29.4	27.8	24.1
Middle East and North Africa	33.7	34.9	31.8	30.9
South Asia	89.9	88.7	86.5	84.4
Sub-Saharan Africa	80.6	82.2	80.7	79.9

Source: Gasparini et al. (2009).

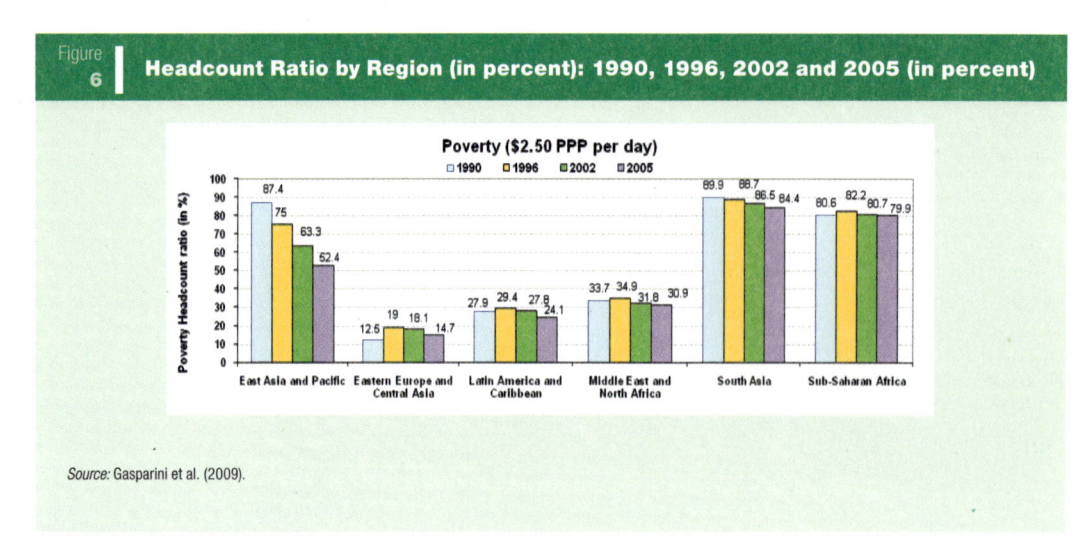

is richer than other regions. However, there are countries in the region—Honduras, for example—in which extreme poverty is as high as in the other poor countries in the world (Figure 7). In addition, although the incidence of extreme poverty[5] is relatively low in countries such as Brazil and Mexico, because of their large size, the absolute numbers are not negligible. In fact, the number of people living in extreme poverty in Brazil and Mexico (around 18 million)[6] is equivalent to the total population of eleven least developed countries.[7] The good news is that with the decline in inequality, poverty and extreme poverty have been falling faster for given growth rates than in the past.

The five countries analyzed in this chapter can be considered a "representative" sample (not in the statistical sense but in terms of their profile) of lower and upper middle-income countries in Latin America. The sample includes two of the five most unequal countries in Latin America (Bolivia and Brazil); a traditionally low-inequality country but which witnessed the largest increase in inequality of the region in the past three decades (Argentina); three of the largest (both in population and GDP) countries in the region (Argentina, Brazil and Mexico); two of the countries where innovative large-scale

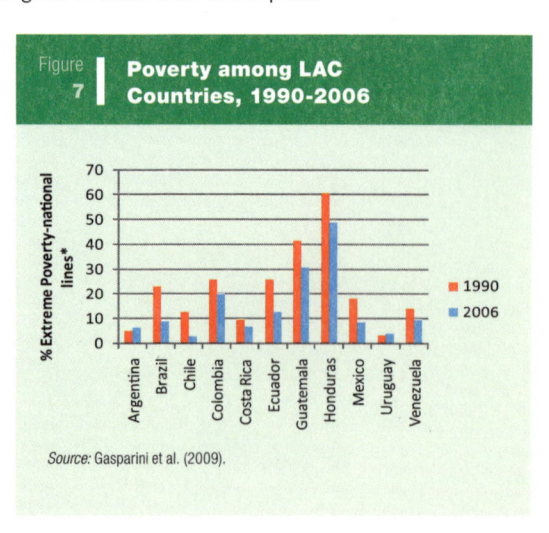

Figure 7 | **Poverty among LAC Countries, 1990-2006**

Source: Gasparini et al. (2009).

---

5 Measured with the international poverty line of US$1.25 per day in PPP.
6 These are figures corresponding to around 2004. Until 2008, poverty continued to decline in some countries. In 2009, however, poverty in Brazil and Mexico is likely to rise as a consequence of the fallout of the "great" recession in advanced countries.
7 Bhutan, Cape Verde, Comoros, the Maldives, Mauritania, Samoa, Sao Tome y Principe, Timor-Leste, Vanuatu, Eritrea and Solomon Islands.

conditional cash transfers have been implemented (Brazil and Mexico); two of the countries with a large proportion of indigenous population (Bolivia and Peru[8]); one country with a so-called universalistic social policy (Argentina), two of the countries with a dualistic social policy (Brazil and Mexico), and one with an exclusionary state (Bolivia); and, finally, two countries governed by populist or radical leftist regimes (Argentina and Bolivia), one country governed by the social democratic left (Brazil), and two countries governed by non-leftist regimes (Mexico and Peru).

All five countries experienced substantial market-oriented reforms in the 1990s (and, in the case of Mexico, since the 1980s). In particular, trade and foreign investment were liberalized, many state-owned enterprises were privatized and markets in general were deregulated. These five countries also faced significant macroeconomic crises between 1990 and 2006 and, except for Argentina, have broadly pursued prudent fiscal and monetary policies in particular since 2000. Starting in 2003, Argentina, Bolivia and Peru benefited from very favorable terms of trade as a result of the boom in commodity prices. As a result, Argentina and Peru have enjoyed high per capita growth rates between 2003 and 2006: 7.8 and 5.2 percent per year, respectively. In Bolivia, Brazil and Mexico, GDP per capita growth was modest: 2.3, 2.7 and 2.8 percent per year, respectively.[9] Furthermore, income inequality as measured by the Gini coefficient fell by 5.6 percentage points in Bolivia (2000-2006), 4 percentage points in Brazil (2001-2006), 3.7 percentage points in Mexico (2000-2006), 3.1 percentage points in Peru (2001-2006) and 2.2 percentage points in (urban) Argentina.[10]

What forces were behind these significant (both statistically and in order of magnitude) declines in inequality? What was the contribution of demographic factors (changes in the proportion of adults in the household, for example)? Were changes in the distribution of labor income important? Were they driven by changes in the distribution of personal characteristics (in particular, in the distribution of educational attainment or human capital) or changes in the returns to personal characteristics (returns to education, in particular)? How important were changes in gender and ethnic earning gaps in accounting for the decline in overall inequality? Did changes in government transfers account for a significant part of the change in inequality in non-labor and overall income inequality?

A useful way to think about the determinants of inequality is to consider the income sources and its proximate determinants at the individual and household levels. These can be broadly summarized as they appear in Figure 8.

Factors that cause the distribution of income to change can be broadly classified into four categories: (i) changes in the underlying distribution of physical and financial assets, personal characteristics (that is, the racial, ethnic, age, gender, health and educational make up of the population) and population's location (rural or urban areas, for example); (ii) changes in the returns to assets and

---

8 It is estimated that about 55 percent of the population in Bolivia and 37 percent in Peru is indigenous.
9 The GDP data is from World Development Indicators (WDI) database, World Bank, January 2009. The GDP per capita growth (annual %) was calculated based on the GDP per capita at PPP prices (constant 2005 international dollars). The income per capita calculated from the surveys is considerably lower than the GDP per capita figures. Part of this is due to the fact that GDP includes more concepts than personal income. However, surveys also underestimate average income per capita because of under-reporting of incomes at the very top of the distribution. This is a well-known problem that has plagued household surveys in Latin America since the first years in which these surveys started to be collected.
10 The declines are statistically significant at the 95 percent level of significance. According to Gasparini and Cruces (forthcoming), trends in urban Argentina are representative of changes for the country as a whole.

Figure 8 | Poverty among LAC Countries, 1990-2006

Source: Barros et al. (forthcoming).

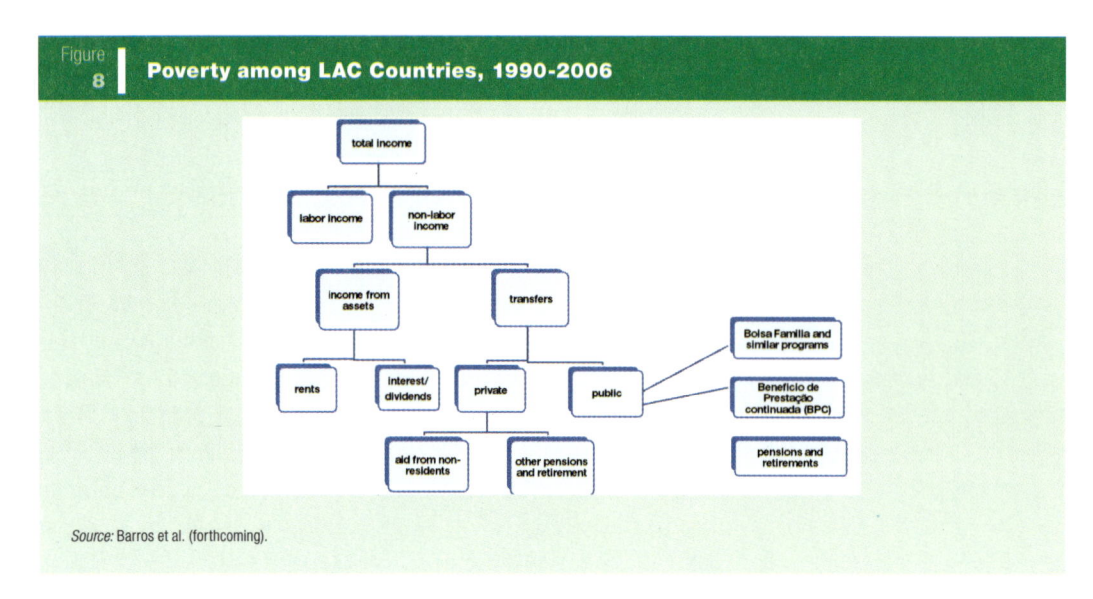

personal characteristics (in particular, the return to human capital); (iii) changes in how people use assets (for example, utilization of arable land) and participate in the labor market (for example, active/inactive, self-employment/wage labor and hours worked); (iv) changes in transfers, both private (e.g., remittances) and public (e.g., cash transfers or in-kind transfers). At the household level, changes in the distribution of income will be affected by: (i) changes in marriage/couple formation patterns (e.g., assortative matching, single parenthood); (ii) changes in consumption patterns; (iii) changes in fertility rates, and (iv) changes in life expectancy. The last two affect the dependency ratio.

State action can modify the distribution of income through two main channels: (i) directly, through fiscal or budgetary interventions (taxes and transfers) that change disposable income and purchasing power (including indirect taxes and subsidies)[11], and (ii) indirectly, through interventions that affect the determinants of market or primary income. Indirect interventions can be of two types: measures that affect economic power and access to assets and government actions that change the distribution of voice and power among different groups in society. Government actions through direct and indirect interventions can affect the level and distribution of assets, returns to those assets, and post-fiscal (after taxes and transfers) incomes. Here we focus on the role played by the expansion of basic education and public monetary transfers in accounting for the observed decline in inequality, in particular.

Total income, in turn, can be viewed as the result of the proportion of adults and the average income per adult. The latter in turn can be disaggregated into non-labor and labor income per adult. In turn, labor income per adult is the product of working adults times their average remuneration. With this approach we can bring in demographic and labor market variables into the picture (Figure 9).

The empirical approaches to identify the 'causes' of changes in inequality rely on a variety of parametric and non-parametric methods which is usually combined with circumstantial (that is,

---

[11] Fiscal interventions also include general and targeted indirect subsidies and indirect taxes that affect the purchasing power of disposable income.

Figure 9. Household Per Capita Income and its Determinants

Source: Barros et al. (forthcoming).

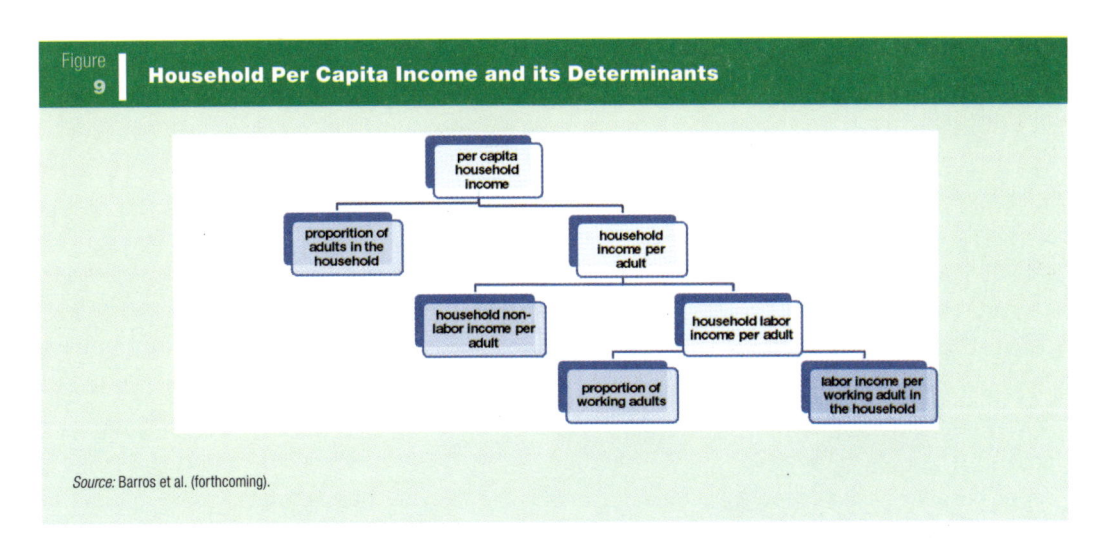

indirect) evidence and historical narratives. The application of this approach to the five selected countries suggests several recurrent patterns which are described in what follows.

First, in all five countries changes in the distribution of the dependency ratio were equalizing but the contribution of this factor to the fall in overall inequality was small (in some cases, it was negligible). Also, the equalizing contribution of demographic changes was already underway in the 1990s reflecting the reduction in fertility rates that has characterized the region in the past two or three decades. It is not a new phenomenon.

Second, in all five countries labor earnings inequality fell[12] and this change contributed significantly to the decline in overall inequality (in varying degrees depending on the country). Declines in labor earnings inequality appear to be associated with an upgrading of the labor force's education which reduced the inequality in school attainment (human capital). The educational upgrading of the labor force was due to an expansion in coverage of basic education. The significant increase in coverage in basic education, in turn, seems to be associated with conscious government efforts (including those of past administrations). Higher spending per student in basic education and an effort to make education accessible in rural areas eased supply-side constraints. In addition, the conditional cash transfer programs Bolsa Familia (Brazil) and Progresa/Oportunidades (Mexico) reduced demand-side constraints by compensating poor households for schooling costs and the opportunity cost of children's labor.[13]

For the younger generations, the gender and ethnic gaps in educational attainment have been narrowing. In an increasing number of countries, girls have higher school attainment levels than boys. As for the ethnic education gap, let's take the case of Bolivia, for example, where by some estimates indigenous groups comprise 55 percent of the population. The indigenous population has,

---

[12] In the case of Peru, the result is found for individual earnings but not at the household level indicating that assortative matching probably dampened the equalizing effect at the individual earnings level.
[13] For more details, see Barros et al (forthcoming) and Esquivel, Lustig, and Scott (forthcoming).

on average, lower levels of educational attainment than the non-indigenous individuals. In 2002, of the total indigenous population, 15.9 percent had no education and 9.6 percent had post-secondary while the numbers for the non-indigenous population were 4.3 percent and 20.9 percent respectively.[14] A closer look at educational attainment by age cohorts suggests that there has been a narrowing of the gap at the extremes. The proportion of individuals with no education among the 15 to 29 year olds is very small (below 5 percent) for both indigenous and non-indigenous. Also, for individuals under the age of 29 there is almost no ethnic gap at the highest levels of education. This is significant, schooling parity is not unachievable for the youngest age cohort at the highest level of education. When we look at average schooling attainment, the gap between indigenous and non-indigenous for under 29 year-olds is statistically insignificant. For people in school age after 1982, the gap has narrowed. This period coincides with the high rural-to-urban migration wave. The indigenous population largely improved its educational attainment by moving to urban areas.

The quantity effect of changes in the educational structure has thus been pervasively equalizing. What about the price or returns effect to education? In contrast to the 1990s, the earnings gap between skilled and low-skilled workers fell, although this was not analyzed for the case of Bolivia. In Brazil, Mexico and Peru this seems to have been driven mainly by changes in the composition of labor supply. As a result of a significant increase in coverage of basic education, low-skilled labor has become relatively scarce and therefore can command relatively higher wages. In Argentina, however, the reduction in this gap seems to be associated with other events as well: the post-2002 commodity boom, which increased total employment; the 2002 devaluation of the peso, which shifted demand in favor of sectors intensive in low-skilled labor; government mandated wage increases (including the minimum wage) and stronger labor unions. In Brazil, higher minimum wages appeared to have played a role as well. However, this was not the case in Mexico and Peru. Changes in gender wage gaps did not have a contribution to the decline in labor earnings inequality and changes in ethnic wage gaps were not specifically analyzed.

Photo Credit: Aaron Szyf

The reduction in labor earnings inequality—and of the skill premium in particular—contrasts with what occurred in the previous decades. In the 1980s and, in particular, in the 1990s returns to education rose. The evidence suggests this was caused by the opening up of the economies to

---

14   Gray Molina and Yañez (2009), Table 8

international trade and foreign investment and the concomitant skilled-biased technical change. The reduction of the returns to education in the late 1990s and first half of this decade suggests that the unequalizing impact of the skilled-biased technical change had run its course. Labor market dynamics became increasingly affected by the structural changes in the composition of labor supply by skill (years of schooling).

An interesting result in the case of Brazil was the reduction in earnings differential between metropolitan areas and smaller municipalities. This may be have been caused by changes in location of firms and in the composition of output. The link between the dynamics of inequality and the spatial and compositional characteristics of production deserves further analysis. In particular, it would be interesting to explore whether the declining returns to metropolitan areas (in relative terms, that is) is observed in other countries and how that might be linked to changes in production patterns and comparative advantage.

Third, the reduction in the inequality of non-labor income was the second major factor behind the fall in inequality, again, in varying degrees depending on the country. Non-labor income includes quite disparate income sources (Figure 8): (i) returns to physical and financial capital (interests, profits and rents), (ii) private transfers (for example, remittances) and (iii) public transfers (monetary, and in the case of Peru, some transfers in kind). The contribution of changes in returns to physical and financial capital tended to be small and unequalizing. In terms of private transfers, remittances proved to be equalizing and became even more so in the 2000s, because they closed the gap between rural and urban household per capita incomes. Remittances were particularly relevant in the case of Mexico and perhaps in the cases of Bolivia and Peru (though this was not analyzed empirically).

Fourth, within non-labor income the role of monetary public transfers (in the countries where they already existed in the period under study) acquired more prominence as an equalizing factor. A detailed analysis of the contribution of programs such as Bolsa Familia (Brazil) and Progresa/Oportunidades (Mexico) shows the remarkable redistributive power of well-targeted cash transfers to the poor in reducing inequality (and, of course, poverty). These programs are a small share of total government redistributive spending (and GDP) but go a long way in terms of redistributing income to the bottom of the distribution.

Finally, there is evidence that government spending on transfers (monetary and non-monetary) became more progressive in Argentina, Mexico and Peru in the 2000s.[15] This trend went beyond targeted cash transfers. Spending on health, education, nutrition and basic infrastructure (electricity and water and sanitation, for example) became more progressive –that is, more pro-poor.

Concluding Remarks

The above results suggest that the region has been gradually moving in the "right" redistributive direction. In particular, governments have been making a greater effort to correct for inequality in the distribution of opportunities particularly as it refers to access to basic education. In addition,

---

15 For Bolivia and Brazil such an analysis was not available.

governments have actively reduced poverty through direct transfers to the poor: making distributive outcomes, and not just opportunities, more equal. At the same time, however, the detailed analyses of government spending that exist for Argentina and Mexico and some of the new initiatives (such as Bolivia's block grants to departments) reveal that a large share of public spending is still neutral or regressive from the distributive point of view and that new measures can go in the direction of making it even more regressive. Although for reasons that will be mentioned below, I have chosen not to discuss the incidence of taxes, existing analyses reveal that taxes, in particular personal income taxes, are severely underutilized as a redistributive instrument in a region characterized by having a substantial number of ultra-high net worth (i.e. super rich) individuals.[16] A lot of work is still pending in the redistributive agenda of the state. In particular, an increasing portion of government spending should be progressive in absolute terms.

We know that the upgrading of the educational attainment of the labor force will face a tough barrier in terms of post-secondary education. While educational attainment has become undoubtedly and significantly more equal, the same cannot be said regarding the distribution of the quality of education. The poor and middle ranges of the distribution receive an education of significantly lower quality than the top ten percent, which usually attends better quality private schools.[17] This reduces the probability of poor children—even if they completed secondary education—being able to access tertiary education, because they cannot compete with the better prepared children from richer households. In addition, compensating for poor children's opportunity cost of attending the post-secondary level is more expensive. If the state wants to continue strengthening the path of equalizing opportunities through education as a way to equalize the distribution of income, addressing the inequality in quality levels of basic education and finding ways to compensate for the opportunity cost so poor children can attend tertiary education must take priority in the public policy agenda.In spite of the progress made in narrowing the ethnic and gender educational gaps, ethnic and gender discrimination in Latin America still appears to loom large. Empirical evidence shows that unexplained (econometrically, that is) earnings gaps between whites and non-whites and men and women are significant.[18] Even with lower educational attainment, Latin American men earn 10 percent more than Latin American women and the ethnic gap is much larger yet. Regarding the ethnic earning gap these results reveal, again, the prevailing inequality in terms of access to education of good quality. They also reveal that prejudice—in terms of access to certain types of jobs, for instance—may still be a major factor that needs to be tackled.

As a consequence of the global recession, GDP in Latin America has contracted or slowed down, depending on the country. This, of course, will cause poverty to rise. Based on what we know from previous crises, inequality could go either way.[19] It is too early to tell whether the impact of the crisis on poverty and inequality will be lasting. Regardless of what happens after the crisis, however, one

---

16 See Loser, 2007.
17 See Puryear and Ortega Goodspeed, 2009.
18 See the review by Atal, Ñopo and Winders, 2009, for example.
19 See Lustig, 2009.

thing is clear: the poor will suffer while the crisis lasts. Furthermore, the impact of the global recession comes on top of the negative effects that rising food prices have had on the poor since 2006.[20] The problem is that in Latin America the safety nets to help the poor cope with the impact of rising food prices and the fallout of the economic crisis are still woefully inadequate.

As argued elsewhere, governments that are serious about helping the poor should add coping with adverse shocks to their concerns.[21] This means that "…they should pursue counter-cyclical fiscal policies, putting resources aside when times are good and using them to stimulate economies when times are difficult. They should prepare pro-poor fiscal austerity programs that are ready to implement when economies decline. Finally, they should develop social safety nets that can quickly and automatically respond to those harmed when economies decline" or when other adverse shocks such as natural disasters or a pervasive increase in food prices occur. Protecting the poor from adverse systemic shocks should be as much a part any long-term strategy to help the poor as providing traditional social services or targeted cash transfers.

Before closing, there are four caveats that must be pointed out. First, although inequality fell in the vast majority of countries, it also rose in a few. Inequality increased in one of the poorest and most unequal countries: Honduras. But it also increased in two of the most equal and progressive: Costa Rica and Uruguay. This chapter does not analyze what factors lie behind the exacerbation of inequality in Honduras or the equity-reversals in Costa Rica and Uruguay.

Second, Latin America is in the midst (albeit at different stages) of its demographic transition and in the next thirty years the proportion of people above 65 years of age will rise significantly (sooner in some countries than others). An older population in terms of the demographic pyramid will eventually increase the dependency ratio of households. In terms of public policy, it will imply some major shifts. An older population pyramid will put fewer strains on the educational sector. However, it will represent increasing challenges for the health sector and social protection and social security systems more broadly. Important as these issues are for their potential impact on poverty and inequality in the future, their analysis goes beyond the scope of this book.

Third, the dynamics of inequality in Latin America respond to its political dynamics and the power exercised by its elites. There is evidence that market liberalization might have replaced one group of predatory elites by another group who is equally predatory and which uses their newly acquired power to perpetuate privileges and monopoly rents.[22] An understanding of the role played by predatory elites in Latin America in limiting growth and perpetuating inequities will be a necessary step if state action is to become truly redistributive not only in its budgetary interventions but also in how it affects institutions and norms.

Fourth, the analysis of income inequality presented above (and, for that matter, all the existing analysis) is based on household surveys; we know well that household surveys do not capture the incomes of the truly wealthy. For example, in 2006 the monthly income of the top two income-earners

---

20 For a synthesis see Lustig, 2008.
21 See Lustig (2000, 2008, 2009).
22 Levy and Walton, 2009.

recorded in the corresponding household surveys was US$14,600 for Chile and US$2,800 for Argentina. For other countries and other years the figures are equally low. This has two important implications for the analysis (and all the existing analyses from other sources too): (i) the estimates and analyses of inequality and its determinants in Latin America do not include the rich; and (ii) the available income tax incidence studies are, at best, a very rough approximation of reality and, at worst, a full-blown distortion of how much taxes the Latin American high net worth individuals pay. We know that the pre- and post-tax income concentration is highly sensitive to the tax burden in the top 1, .1 and .01 percent of the population.[23] Given this limitation, this chapter does not discuss the incidence of taxes except in passing.

This brings us to a final policy recommendation which should be given utmost priority. In order to improve the redistributive power of the state through fiscal interventions, collection and access to information will have to undergo some fundamental changes. An analysis of the 'true' concentration of income and the tax burden of wealhy individuals in Latin America will require access to tabulations based on income tax returns. In advanced countries, these tabulations are available and exist as far back as the beginning of the 20th century. In general, these tabulations report, for a large number of income brackets, the corresponding number of taxpayers, as well as their total income and tax liability. They are usually broken down by income source: capital income, wage income, business income, rents, etc. These tabulations are used both (i) to estimate the concentration of income at the top more accurately than with household survey-based data and (ii) to estimate tax burdens at the very top of the distribution. Regretfully, Latin American governments have not been forthcoming with these tabulations. Convincing governments of the importance to make income tax returns-based tabulations available to the research and policy community should be an objective of multilateral agencies.

Although the spending side of the public sector appears to be more amenable to empirical incidence analysis than the (income) tax side, the truth is that many countries lack the information to do it, or to do it right. This is another area in which multilateral agencies could make an important contribution. Convincing (and, when necessary, helping) countries to design their household surveys to capture the amount of monetary and non-monetary transfers that are received by households could provide the basic information that is needed to assess the progressiveness (or the lack of it) of government spending.

The production and access to information to estimate income concentration and the incidence of taxes and public spending more accurately should be viewed as essential to enhance transparency, accountability, fairness, and efficiency of the state.

---

23 See Atkinson and Piketty (2007, 2010); Piketty and Saez, 2006.

Appendix

Two Cases of Falling Income Inequality: Brazil and Mexico

Brazil

Brazil has one of the highest levels of income inequality in the world. At times, its Gini coefficient was equal to .63, almost a historical and worldwide maximum. After a few years with very little change, the Gini coefficient has been falling steadily since 1998. The steepest decline occurred after 2000 when Brazil's Gini coefficient declined 4.1 percentage points from 0.593 to 0.552—that is, to the tune of 1.3 percent per year[24] (Figure A.1). Extreme poverty and moderate poverty have also been falling between 2001 and 2007 in spite of the fact that average income growth during the period was modest of the order of 2.5 percent per year[25] (Table A.1).

Thus, based on the observed trends in poverty and inequality, Brazil's growth pattern could be defined as "pro-poor:" i.e., the growth of the income of the poor has been higher than the growth of the income of the rich. In fact, this is exactly the case. From 2001 to 2007, the per capita income of the poorest 10 percent grew 7 percent per year, a rate of growth nearly three times the national average (2.5 percent) while that of the richest 10 percent grew only 1.1 percent (Figure A.2). Two thirds of the decline in extreme poverty can be attributed to the reduction in inequality.

The recent decline in inequality in Brazil resulted from three main factors: i) decreasing wage differentials by educational level and reductions in the inequality in education; ii) increasing spatial and sectoral integration of labor markets, in particular among metropolitan and non-metropolitan areas; and, iii) increasing generosity of contributory and non-contributory government transfers.[26] If one decomposes the change in household income inequality, it is found that roughly half of the decline can be attributed to a reduction in labor income inequality and half to a reduction in non-labor income inequality.[27]

In contrast to the episode of falling inequality in the late 1970s, demographic factors and the role of employment was not significant in either direction. That is, changes in the dependency ratio among the poor, for example, were of little importance while this was not the case in the late 1970s.

---

[24] The decline in income inequality in Brazil fulfills the "Lorenz dominance" test and it is statistically significant. Barros et al., 2009.
[25] Barros et al., 2009.
[26] Ibid.
[27] Labor income includes wages and remunerations of the self-employed. Non-labor income includes incomes from property, own businesses and transfers. Transfers, in turn, can be private (remittances and gifts, for example) or public (pensions and conditional cash transfers, for example).

Figure A.1 | Evolution of the Gini Coefficient for the Brazilian Distribution of Persons According to their Family Per Capita Income

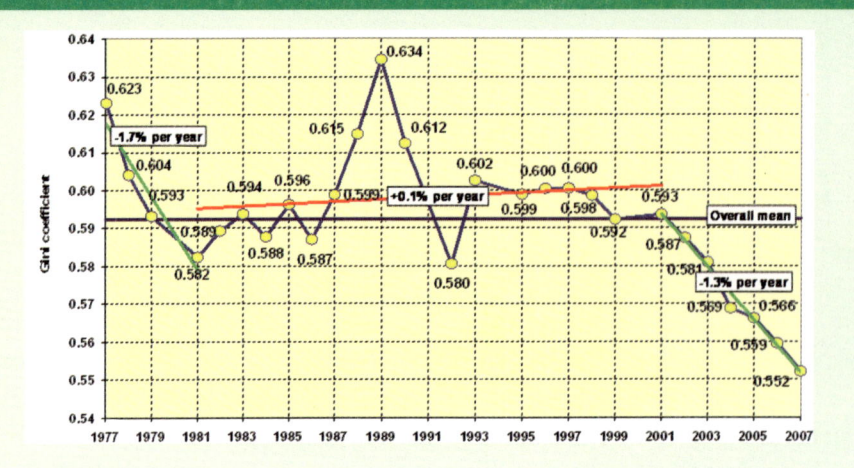

Gini coefficient values by year (1977–2007):
- 1977: 0.623
- 1979: 0.604
- 1981: 0.582
- 0.593
- 0.589
- 0.588
- 0.587
- 0.594
- 0.596
- 0.599
- 0.615
- 1989: 0.634
- 0.612
- 0.580
- 0.602
- 0.600
- 0.600
- 0.599
- 0.598
- 0.593
- 0.592
- 0.587
- 0.581
- 0.569
- 0.566
- 0.559
- 2007: 0.552

Trend annotations: -1.7% per year; +0.1% per year; -1.3% per year; Overall mean.

Source: Based on Pesquisa Nacional por Amostra de Domicílios (PNAD) 1977 to 2007.

Table A.1 | Poverty and Extreme Poverty in Brazil, 2001-2007

Indicators	2001	2007	Variation, 2001-2007
Poverty			
Headcount Ratio	39	28	-29
Poverty Gap	18	12	-34
Poverty Severity	11	7	-37
Extreme Poverty			
Headcount Ratio	17	10	-42
Poverty Gap	7	4	-40
Poverty Severity	5	3	-37

Source: Estimates based on Pesquisa Nacional por Amostra de Domicílios (PNAD), 2001-2007.

Notes:
1. The poverty gap and severity are expressed in multiples of the poverty line.
2. Estimates made using regional poverty lines. The national average poverty line is equal to R$175 per month, and national average extreme poverty line is equal to R$88 per month.

Table A.2 | Annual Growth Rate for Per Capita Income in Brazilia, by percentile, 2001-2007

Percentile	Growth rate (%)
First	7
Second	6.2
Third	5.5
Fourth	5.1
Fifth	4.8
Sixth	4.5
Seventh	3.8
Eighth	3.1
Nineth	2.3
Tenth	1.1

National (reference line)

Source: Based on Pesquisa Nacional por Amostra de Domicilios (PNAD) 1977 to 2007.

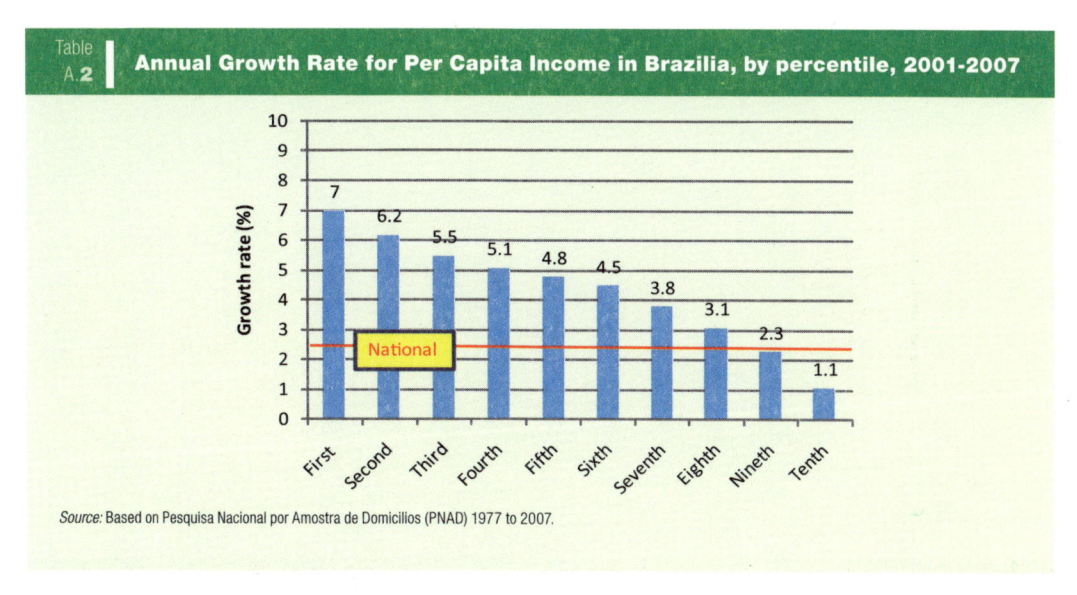

In the past, a rise in unemployment among the poor prevented the fall of inequality from being more pronounced. In the current episode, unemployment has not played a role. All in all, the decline in labor income inequality was primarily due to the reduction in wage inequality, and the reduction in wage inequality was associated to the reduction in education inequality (Figure A.3) due to the large expansion of access to education for the lower end of the distribution. Since 1995, labor earnings differentials by education level have declined at all levels. This reduction is much clearer after 2002, particularly for secondary and higher education.

Another factor that has contributed to the decline in labor earnings inequality is the reduction in special segmentation. In Figure A.4 it is shown that the labor earnings differential has been narrowing between metropolitan areas and small municipalities and metropolitan areas and medium-size municipalities. The question as to what factors explain this trend remains to be answered. Perhaps there has been a relatively higher expansion of some productive sectors in the Brazilian "hinterland" as opposed to the metropolitan areas thereby increasing the demand for labor and pushing up wages in the smaller and medium-sized cities compared to the past. The earnings gap between formal and informal workers, in contrast, did not fall but went up which means that this type of labor market segmentation played an unequalizing role during the period 1997-2007. Changes in discrimination (labor earnings are different between females and males, blacks and whites, etc., without differences in productivity) were not found to be significant in explaining the reduction in labor earnings inequality.

As mentioned above, the decline in non-labor income inequality is also very important in explaining the reduction in overall household income inequality. While the size of the contribution varies depending on the methodology, for consistency purposes here we show the results that use the same method as the one used for estimating the contribution of the change in labor income inequality.[28] The

---
28 See Barros et al., 2009.

Table A.3 | **Education and Inequality among Workers in Brazil, 1995-2007**

Source: Barros et al., 2009.

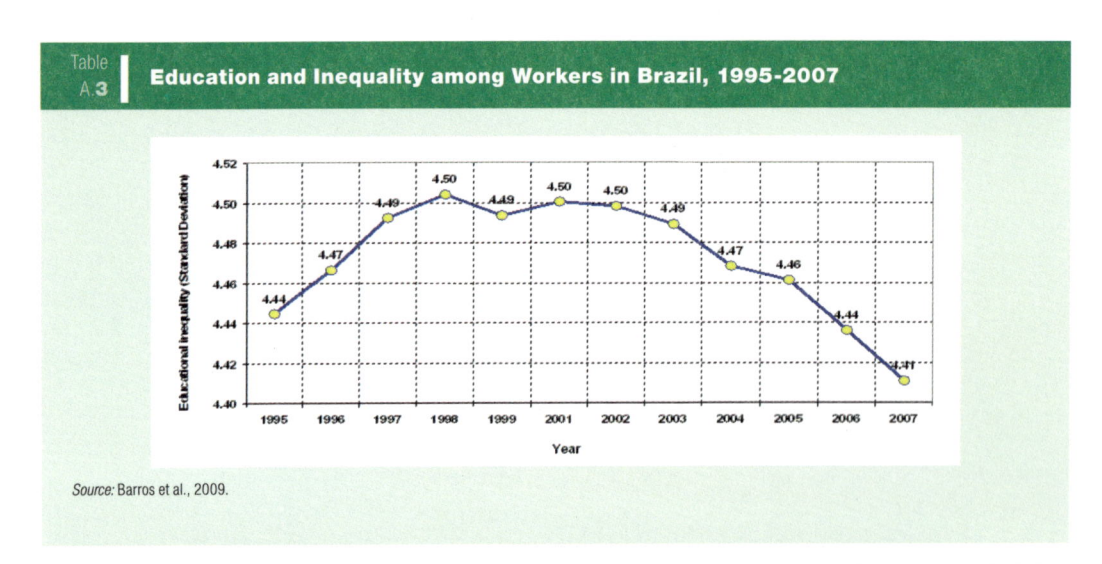

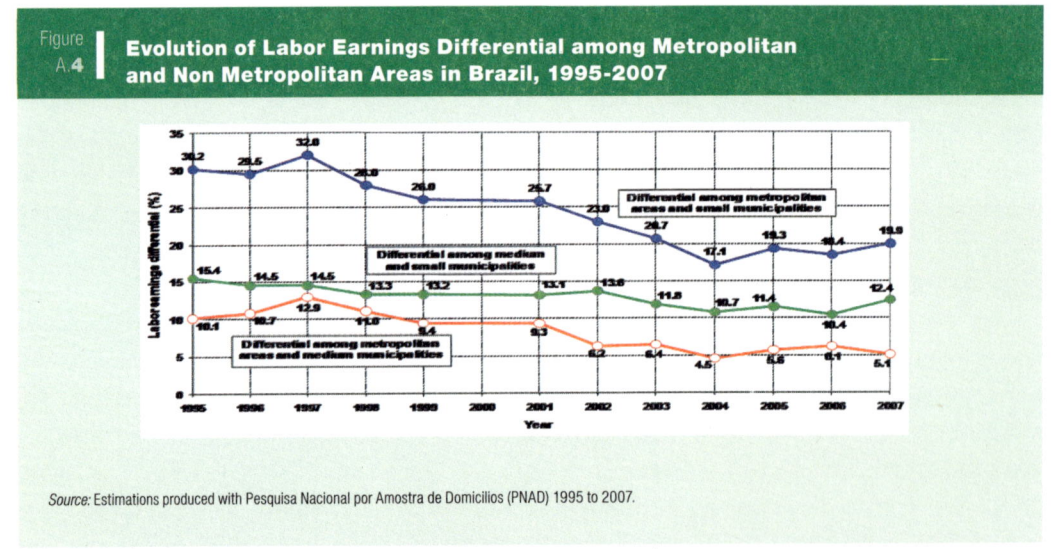

Figure A.4 | **Evolution of Labor Earnings Differential among Metropolitan and Non Metropolitan Areas in Brazil, 1995-2007**

Source: Estimations produced with Pesquisa Nacional por Amostra de Domicilios (PNAD) 1995 to 2007.

decomposition exercises attempt to isolate the contribution of each source to the overall change in inequality: assets (rents, interest and dividends), private transfers, and public transfers.

Public transfers account for over 80 percent of families' non-labor income[29] and the percentage of the population in families with at least one beneficiary increased by 10 percentage points since 2001. Impacts of changes in the distribution of income from assets and private transfers were limited. Most of the impact of non-labor income on the reduction of overall income inequality was due to changes in the distribution of public transfers which account for 49 percent of the total decline in non-labor income

---

29 Household surveys usually do not capture well households at the very top of the distribution whose income is likely to come from assets. This is true for all countries.

inequality. Although, both contributory and non-contributory transfers were important factors, the role of contributory transfers was predominant. In particular, changes in social security benefits explain almost 30 percent of the overall reduction in non-labor income inequality. The increasing coverage of non-contributory benefits, like BPC (Benefício de Prestação Continuada) and Bolsa Família—Brazil's signature conditional cash transfer program—were also important. Despite representing just a tiny fraction of total family income (0.5 percent), each of these non-contributory benefits explains about 10 percent of the overall decline in non-labor income inequality.

In sum, in the case of Brazil the rapid decline in income inequality observed since 2001 may be attributed to the reaping of the benefits of the expansion of education, the changes in spatial patterns of labor demand and supply, and the larger size and increased progressivity in some public transfers, both from social security and social assistance, but more importantly the former. However, the wage gap between formal and informal workers continued to increase and some government policies which tempered the progress achieved in inequality reduction. In particular, it seems that raising the minimum wage—which in effect raises the social security benefits which are tied to the minimum wage—is less effective in reducing inequality and extreme poverty than targeted programs such as Bolsa Familia.

Mexico

After a period of rising household income inequality from 1984 until the mid-1990s, Mexico's inequality has been falling. In particular, between 2000 and 2006, the Gini coefficient dropped from close to .53 to close to .49 or by 4 percentage points. This means a fall of 1.3 percent per year which is equal to the one observed in Brazil for the same time period (Figure A.5).

Extreme poverty[30] has also been consistently falling since the mid-1990s following the spike in poverty caused by the 1994-95 peso crisis (Figure A.6).[31] In particular, extreme poverty fell by 43 percent between 2000 and 2006. This is particularly remarkable given that during this period per capita GDP grew at a modest 2.5 percent or less per year. The latter emphasizes the role played by the reduction in inequality in explaining the reduction in poverty.

The growth incidence curve[32] for 2006/2000 plotted in Figure A.7 shows that the incomes of the poorest 40 percent grew faster than the mean of the growth rates for the entire distribution—the higher of the two horizontal lines in the Figure.[33] Thus, during this period Mexico experienced "pro-poor" growth. The next question is which factors explain this growth pattern: changes in demographics, changes in employment patterns, changes in wage inequality or changes in government transfers?

Recent decomposition exercises of the change in inequality between the period 2000 and 2006 find the following results. Demographic changes as measured by the proportion of adults were equalizing and so were the changes in the proportion of employed adults. This means that the dependency ratio and the number of working adults per household "improved" relatively more for the

---

30 The incidence of poverty is measured using the headcount ratio. In Mexico, extreme poverty is measured using the official "food poverty" line.
31 The 2005 figures should be taken with caution because survey may not be comparable to surveys in the rest of the years.
32 A "growth incidence curve" plots the changes in household per capita income (or expenditure) for each quantile of income (or expenditure), from poorest to richest households. Quantiles are usually percentiles or smaller.
33 The mean of the growth rates of the entire distribution was slightly above 2.5 percent.

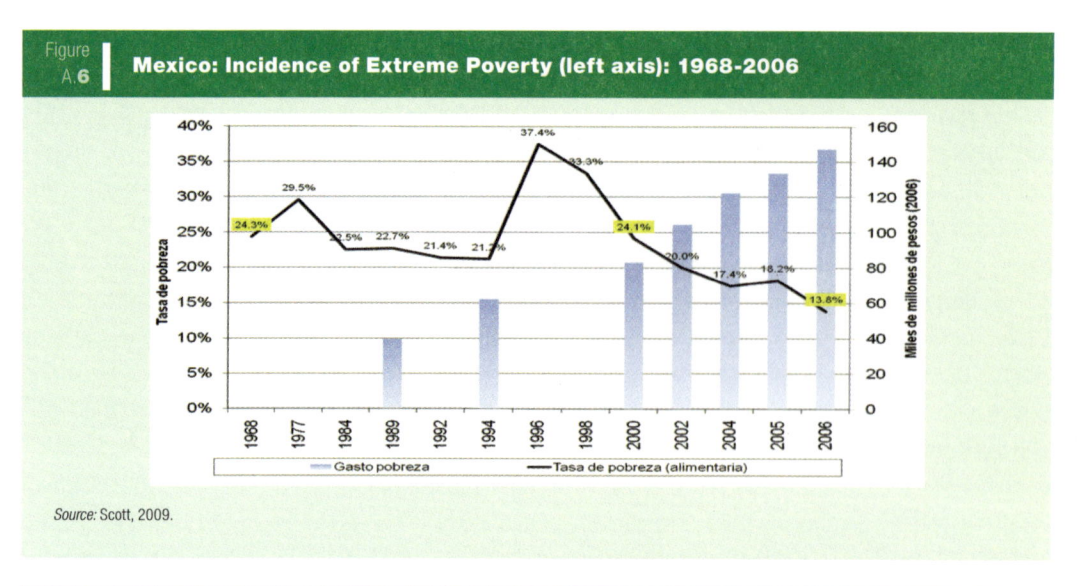

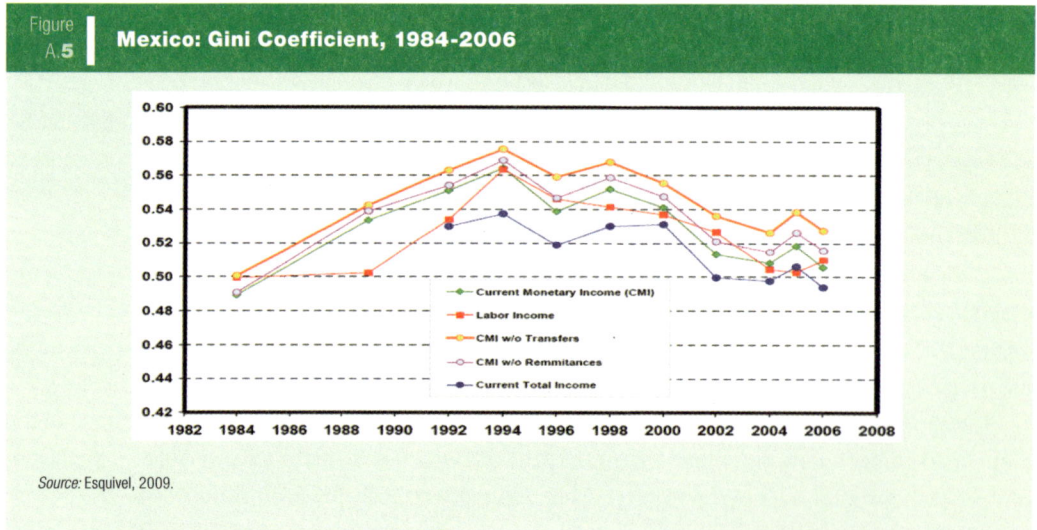

Figure A.6 | Mexico: Incidence of Extreme Poverty (left axis): 1968-2006

Source: Scott, 2009.

Figure A.5 | Mexico: Gini Coefficient, 1984-2006

Source: Esquivel, 2009.

poorer households than for the richer households. The inequality in the distribution of labor and non-labor income fell, thereby both contributing to the reduction in overall household income inequality. Labor income includes wages and remunerations of the self-employed. Non-labor income includes incomes from property, own businesses and transfers. Transfers, in turn, can be private (remittances and gifts, for example) or public (pensions and conditional cash transfers, for example).

The fall in inequality of labor income is by far the most important factor explaining the decline in overall household income inequality. Between 2000 and 2006, the Gini coefficient fell by 3.07 percentage points or by 5.8 percent. If the only thing that would have changed was the distribution of labor income and all the other factors remained the same in 2006 as they were in 2000, the Gini would have fallen by 3.19 percentage points—that is, by even more than the overall decline in inequality.[34]

The decline in labor income inequality reflects the fall in the skilled/unskilled workers wage gap. In Figure A.8 one can observe how the wage gap rose in the period following trade liberalization in the mid-1980s. This was one of the major drivers explaining the increase in overall income inequality between the mid-1980s and mid-1990s. Since the mid-1990s, however, this trend was reversed. Because it coincided with the implementation of the North American Free Trade Agreement (NAFTA) in 1994, there has been a lot of interest to determine to what extent this equalizing trend in relative wages was a product of NAFTA. So far, this question remains unanswered. With NAFTA there was an increase in demand for low-skilled workers for the "maquiladora" sector. However, during the same period there was also an increase in the share of workers with post-secondary education relative to those with less. The share of less-skilled workers (those with less than secondary education) went from 55 percent in 1989 to 32 percent in 2006.

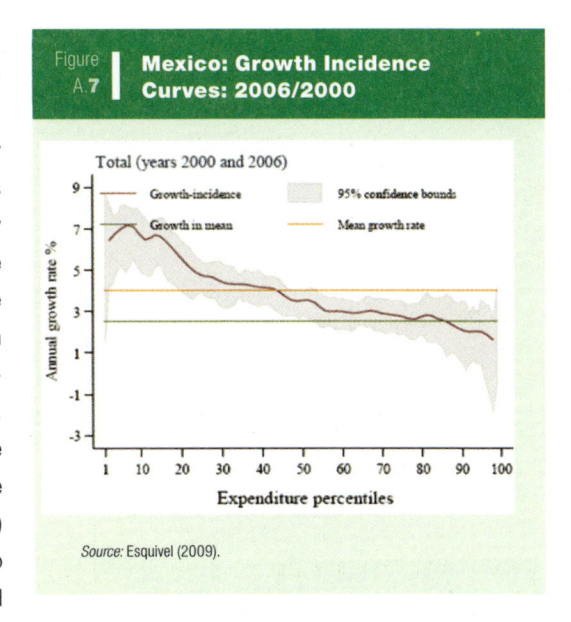

Figure A.7 | Mexico: Growth Incidence Curves: 2006/2000

Source: Esquivel (2009).

So, it seems that both demand (for example, increased employment in maquiladoras) and supply (changes in the relative abundance of low-skilled workers) factors may have played a role in reducing the wage gap between the skilled and the low-skilled. Figure A.9 shows how the wages of the less educated-less experienced—that is, the low-skilled—workers increased while the wages of the high-skilled workers fell slightly between 1996 and 2006. This is consistent with the shape of the growth-incidence curve and the large contribution to the decline in household income inequality stemming from the fall in labor income inequality.

In sum, the decline in household income inequality in Mexico appears to be determined by a relative (relative to workers with more skills, that is) increase in the demand for low-skilled workers and a relative fall in their supply The latter must be the product of the progress made in education as more and more cohorts stay in school for more years (something that is confirmed by the steady increase in years of schooling). On the demand side, part of the story could be NAFTA-related: a higher demand for low-skilled workers in the "maquiladoras" as production processes became increasingly more integrated across North America after NAFTA went into effect.

Other factors that may have contributed to a rise in demand for workers at the bottom of the

---

34 Alejo et al, 2009.

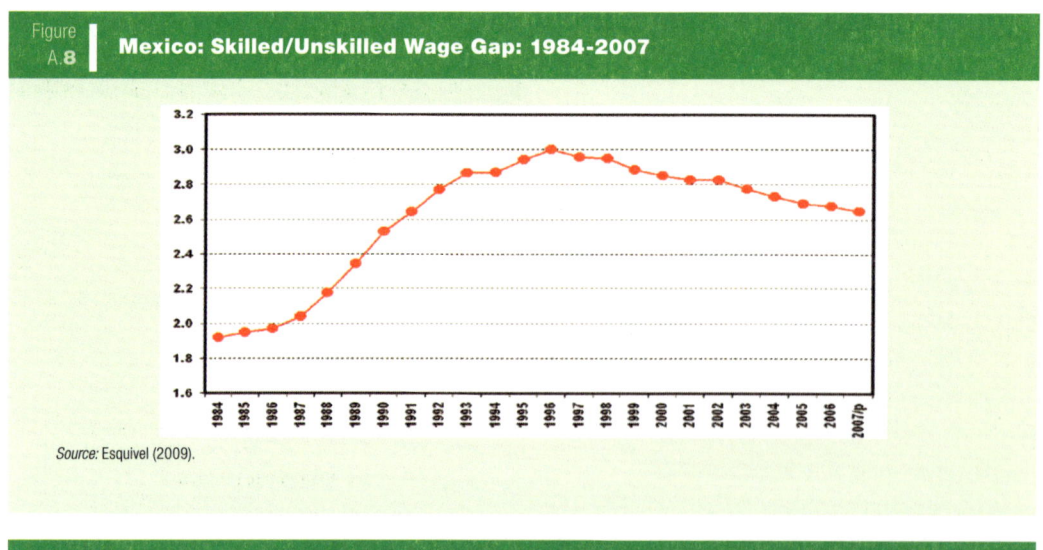

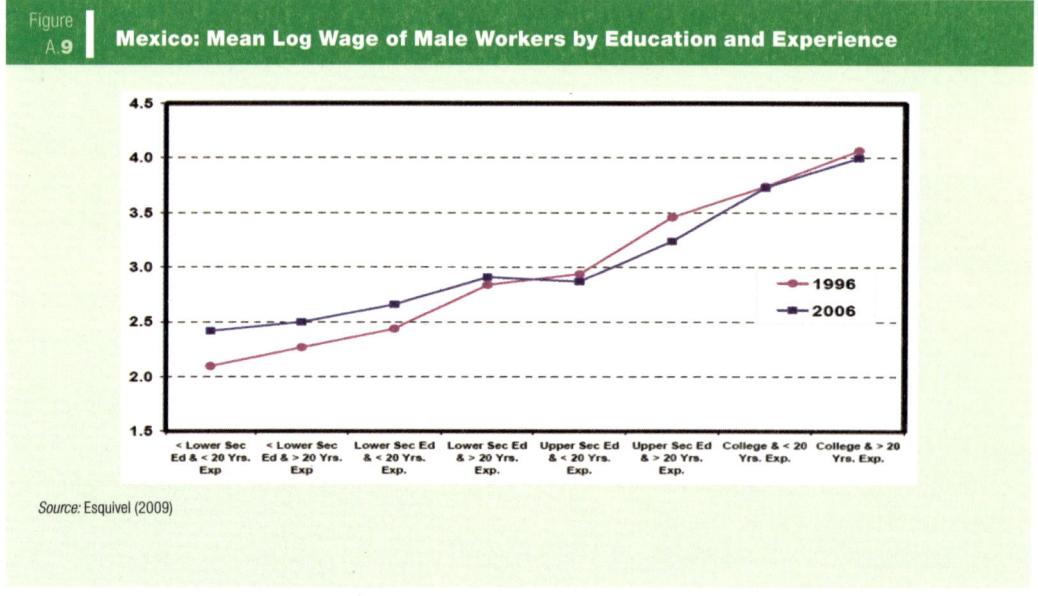

Figure A.8 | Mexico: Skilled/Unskilled Wage Gap: 1984-2007

Source: Esquivel (2009).

Figure A.9 | Mexico: Mean Log Wage of Male Workers by Education and Experience

Source: Esquivel (2009)

distribution might have been the increase in remittances and cash transfers from Progresa/Oportunidades, the Mexican government's signature anti-poverty program. However, the direct effect of remittances and cash transfers seem to affect the level but not necessarily the trend in income inequality since they all move more or less in tandem. What might be more important is the indirect effect: that is, the spillover effect that remittances and cash transfers have on employment in poor local economies. Households which receive remittances tend to use them to build, expand or refurbish their dwellings. This generates demand for construction workers in the local economy, who in turn generate demand for other goods and services, and so on. One can think of remittances and cash transfers as myriad "stimulus packages" benefiting poor communities.

Mexico, thus, seems to be a case of lackluster overall growth in GDP and total factor productivity because a large portion of the employment generation occurs at the low-productivity/low-wage end instead of in the high-wage/high-productivity sectors. However, even if the new employment opportunities are low-wage, the wages (or remunerations) they pay are higher than what this group of low-skilled workers used to receive before 2000. In this sense, Mexico's growth pattern is "pro-poor." Although the launching of the anti-poverty conditional cash transfer program Progresa/Oportunidades made public spending more progressive, the bulk of transfers (pensions, in particular) is not.[35] By some estimates, without Oportunidades the Gini coefficient would be around one percentage point higher[36], which is not insignificant. Nonetheless, public spending remains largely not pro-poor and in a number of cases it is plainly regressive. Thus Mexico's recent reductions in inequality, while important, remain limited because social policy still has serious shortcomings and inconsistencies. The good news is that this means that there are plenty of opportunities to further reduce poverty and inequality.

---

[35] Scott (2009).
[36] Ibid.

Chapter 5
How Can Education Help Latin America Develop?

Jeffrey M. Puryear and Tamara Ortega Goodspeed

"...schooling appears relevant for economic growth only insofar as it actually raises the knowledge that students gain..."

-Hanushek and Woessman, 2009

Most analysts agree that high quality education can make a significant contribution to a country's development. It boosts earnings and stimulates economic growth. It is a powerful tool for moving people out of poverty and improving the distribution of income. And it can foster democratic governance by creating an informed citizenry that can make good decisions. Unfortunately, most Latin American public schools—from pre-school to graduate school—provide low-quality education that fails to meet the needs of countries or students. Poor and minority students, who are principally those enrolled in public K-12 schools, are particularly ill-served.

To be sure, the region has made real progress. In virtually every country, governments have increased spending on education—building schools, adding teachers, raising salaries, and enrolling more children. These efforts have clearly expanded the quantity of education (in terms of the number of children attending school), but there is little evidence that they have improved the quality of education (measured by scores on achievement tests). This is regrettable. If education is to play its role in promoting growth, equity and democracy in Latin America, governments need to move beyond their historic emphasis on expanding enrollments, to an emphasis on expanding learning.

Governments have Invested in Access

Spending

Public spending on education has grown steadily in Latin America over the past two decades, both as a share of total public expenditure and as a percent of GNP.[1] On average, the region went from spending just under 4 percent of GNP in 1990 to nearly 5 percent today.[2] This is almost the same as the world average of 4.9 percent and higher than in other developing regions, although still below the 5.5

---
1 OECD (2009). p. 24
2 Regional average for 1990 from UNESCO, 2000, Table 12, p.118. Regional average for 2007 from UNESCO, 2010, Table 11, p.410

percent invested by countries in North America and Western Europe (Figure 1). Spending per primary pupil has also risen in most countries.[3] However, in part because there are more school-age children in Latin America than in high-income nations, spending per pupil remains significantly lower than in developed countries (Figure 2).

The problem is that these additional resources have not had a significant impact on education quality. The Latin American countries that participate in PISA (Program in International Student Achievement) all show performance that is below what would be predicted given their countries' expenditure per student.[4] A large share of the region's scarce resources are "lost" to inefficiencies such as high repetition rates or poor teaching, and few countries are spending enough to provide poor children with the additional attention most of them need. At the same time, wide variations in spending among countries almost certainly translate into differences in the quality and equity of education that children receive.

Enrollments

A greater share of children and youth attend school today than at any time in the region's history (Figure 3). Pre-school enrollments, which cover nearly two thirds of the eligible population in Latin America, are well above the world average (around 40 percent). In most countries, all but the poorest and most isolated children enroll in primary school, and most manage to graduate (Figure 4). Enrollments at the secondary and tertiary level have also expanded significantly. Tertiary enrollments nearly doubled from

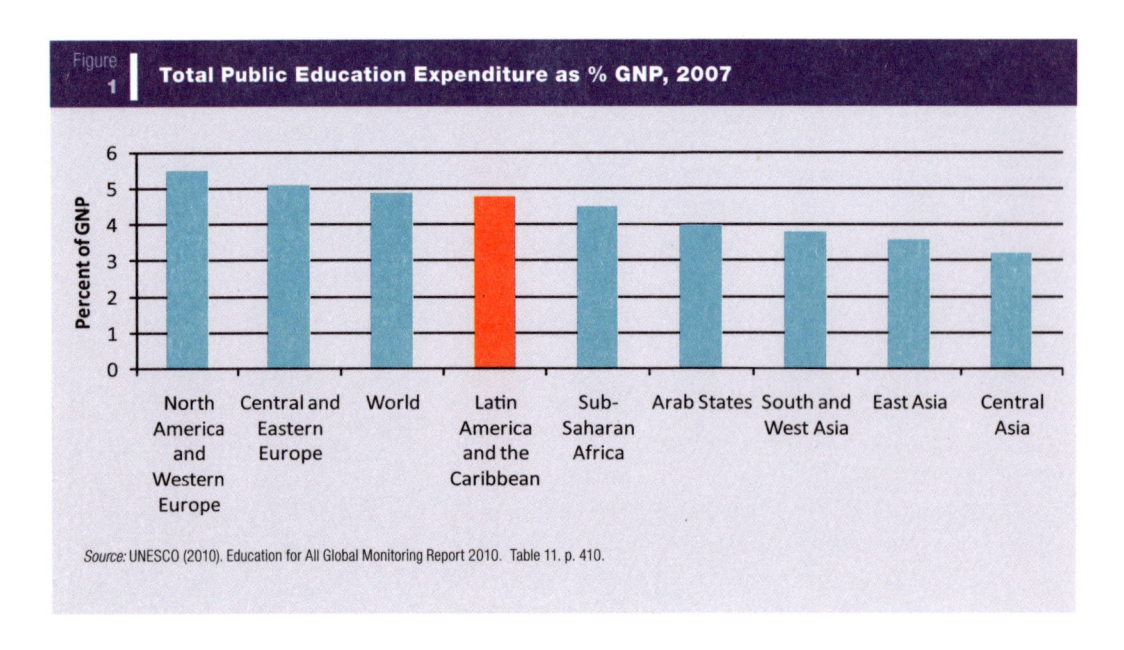

Figure 1 | Total Public Education Expenditure as % GNP, 2007

Source: UNESCO (2010). Education for All Global Monitoring Report 2010. Table 11. p. 410.

---

3   UNESCO (2008), Annex. Table 11 p. 364-371 and UNESCO (2007) Annex Table 11 p. Table 11 p. 314-321
4   PREAL Advisory Board (2005), Figure 13, p. 21

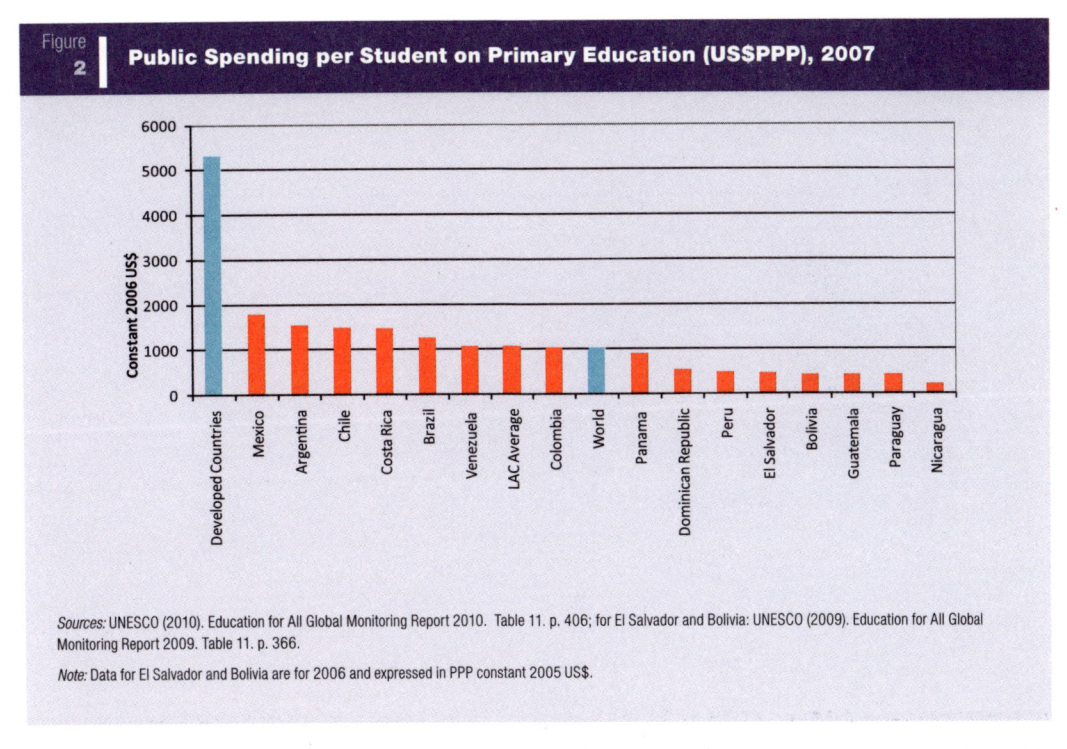

Figure 2 | Public Spending per Student on Primary Education (US$PPP), 2007

Sources: UNESCO (2010). Education for All Global Monitoring Report 2010. Table 11. p. 406; for El Salvador and Bolivia: UNESCO (2009). Education for All Global Monitoring Report 2009. Table 11. p. 366.

Note: Data for El Salvador and Bolivia are for 2006 and expressed in PPP constant 2005 US$.

16 percent in 1985 to 34 percent today.[5] By contrast, the world average for enrollment at this level is 26 percent and the average for East Asia and the Pacific is 22 percent.

Particularly in younger age groups, expanded access has included an ever greater number of poor children, reducing the gaps with their wealthier peers. Brazil, Honduras, Nicaragua, El Salvador, and Paraguay have made the greatest progress in closing the gap between rich and poor in primary school attendance (Figure 5).

Even so, coverage is far from universal. More than one in three preschool-aged children is out of school, depriving poor children in particular of the early instruction they need to set the stage for successful learning. While in high-income countries and in growing economies like Korea, Finland, and Ireland nearly nine of every ten youths enroll in secondary school, in Latin America, only around 70 percent of secondary-aged youths are enrolled.[6] Moreover, completion rates for secondary education in Latin America are unsatisfactory; in many countries, less than half of students graduate. The most competitive economies have much higher rates (Figure 6).

At the tertiary level, enrollments are still half the average for high-income countries and well below rates in more successful economies, like the United States and Korea.[7] Moreover, most Latin American university students do not complete their studies. Forty percent of Argentine university students drop

---

5   World Bank (2006b), Winkler (1990)
6   World Bank, Edstats Online Database, accessed June 2009
7   World Bank, Edstats Online Database, accessed June 2009

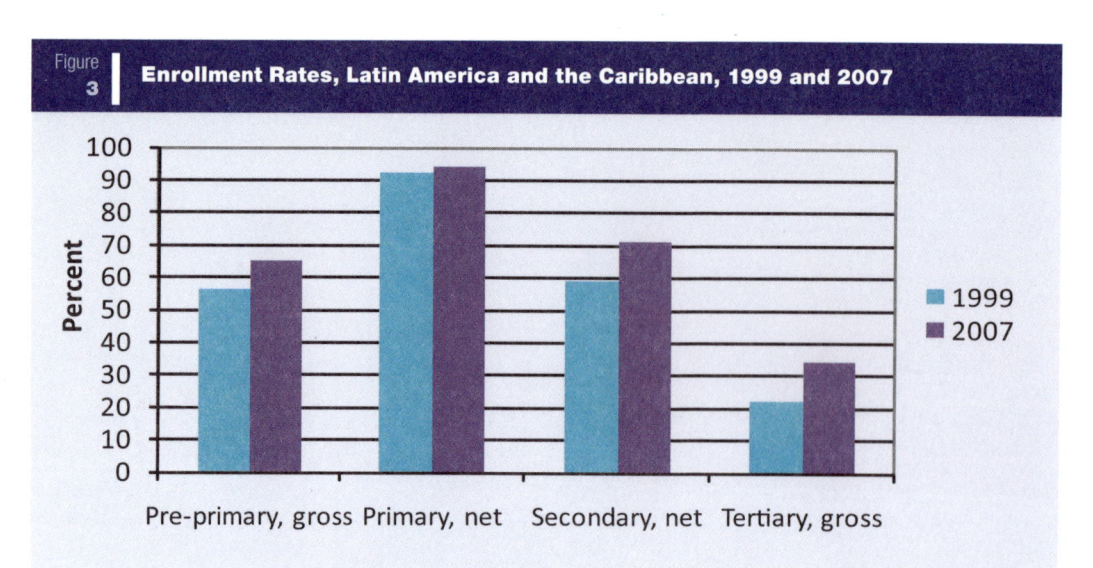

Figure 3 | Enrollment Rates, Latin America and the Caribbean, 1999 and 2007

Source: World Bank Edstats Online Database. Last accessed: February 2010. Pre-primary from UNESCO (2010). Education for All Global Monitoring Report 2010. Table 3B, p 330.

Figure 4 | Primary Completion (%), 2008

Source: World Bank Edstats Online Database. Last accessed: February 2010.

Notes: Completion rates were capped at 100%. However, because figures are calculated using all graduates (regardless of age) as a percentage of the population at typical age of graduation, rates over 100% are possible where graduates include over or under-age completers. All years within two of date listed unless otherwise noted. Brazil 2005.

Figure 5: Difference in Attendance between Richest and Poorest 20% 7 to 12-year olds, 1990-2006

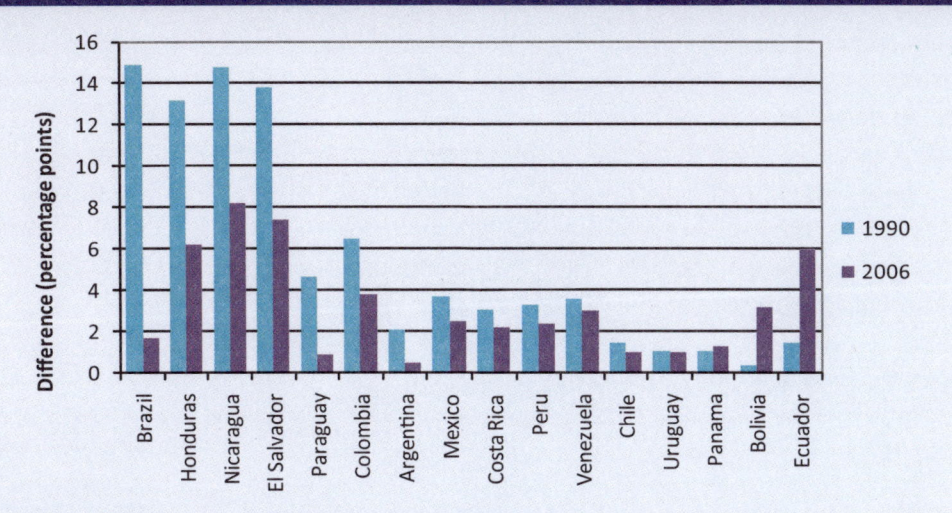

Source: ECLAC (2007). Social Panorama. Table 29, pp. 401-402. Data within two years of ate listed unless otherwise noted. Nicaragua 1993 and 2001. Paraguay 1994. Peru 1997 and 2003.

Note: Countries are ranked according to how much they have reduced the rich-poor attendance gaps, from those with the largest reductions on the left to those with the smallest reductions (or increases) on the right.

Figure 6: Secondary Graduation Rates, 2007

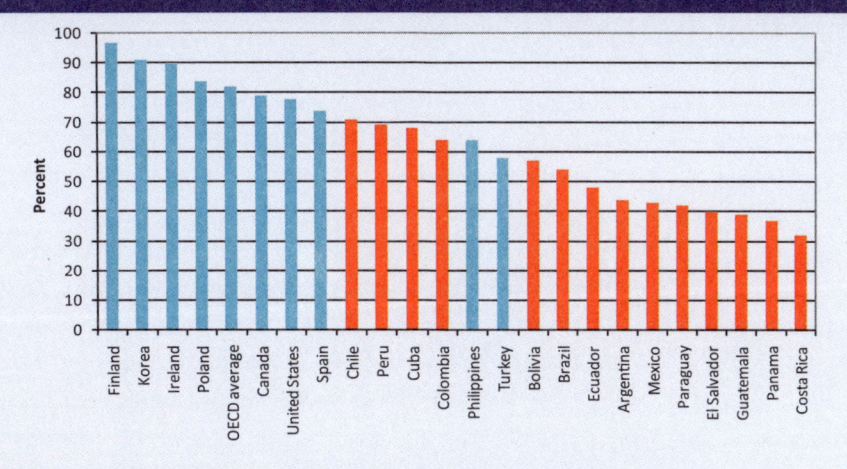

Source: OECD (2007-2009). Education at a Glance. Table A2.1. Data for the Philippines and all Latin American countries except Brazil, Chile, and Mexico from UNESCO (2009). Global Education Digest 2009. Table 7. pp. 124-127.

Note: All data within two years of date listed. Data for OECD countries and Chile show upper secondary graduates (all programs) as a percent of the population at a typical age of graduation. All other countries show graduates from ISCED3A programs only (Gross graduation rates at ISCED3B and ISCED3C in these countries either have no data or are listed as 5% or less).

out in the first year, and only a quarter of those admitted goes on to graduate. Only a third of those admitted in Chile and half of those admitted in Colombia graduate.[8] The situation is similar in Mexico, where only 30 percent of those that enter in any given year graduate.[9] This has serious implications for education finance. Taxpayers are supporting a small cadre of (largely middle-class) college students who seldom complete their degrees, with funds that might otherwise help large numbers of poor students who are failing to complete secondary school.

Latin America also produces a limited number of scientists and advanced degree recipients, which hinders the region's development. While OECD countries produce one new Ph.D. per 5,000 people, in Brazil the ratio is 1 per 70,000; in Chile, 1 per 140,000, and in Colombia 1 per 700,000.[10] Without more qualified advanced degree recipients, the ability of countries to use and generate knowledge, and to carry out research, is limited.

Serious Deficits in Quality and Equity
Unfortunately, increased spending and coverage have not been accompanied by increased learning. Latin America still has a long way to go to ensure that all children receive a quality education.

Quality
The quality of the education that most children receive is low and therefore contributes only modestly to increasing human capital. Latin America scores near the bottom on every global test of student achievement. In the OECD's most recent (2006) Program in International Student Achievement (PISA) exam, which evaluated the skills of 15-year-olds in math, reading, and science, all six Latin American countries (Argentina, Brazil, Chile, Colombia, Mexico and Uruguay) ranked firmly in the bottom third of the 57 participating countries (Tables A.1-A.3 in Appendix).

Over half of students in Argentina, Brazil, Colombia and Mexico, and around 40 percent of students in Chile and Uruguay, scored at or below the lowest level in science—which the OECD characterizes as not being able "to participate actively in life situations related to science and technology" (Figure 7). By contrast, less than 10 percent of students performed at this level in top-scoring countries like Finland. Scores in reading and math showed similar trends.[11]

Even relatively well-off Latin American students fail to excel by world standards. In five of six countries (Chile being the exception), the richest 20 percent of Latin American students failed to outperform the poorest 20 percent of European OECD students in all three subjects (reading, math and science).[12] In fact, few students from any background receive a high-quality education. In Mexico just 0.29 percent of students scored at the advanced level in the PISA mathematics exam (defined as capable "of advanced mathematical thinking and reasoning and can interpret complex information about real-world situations") compared with 18.2 percent of Korean students and 6.5 percent of U.S. students.

8 Holm-Nielsen, et. al., (2005), p.46
9 Oppenheimer (2005), p.318
10 Holm-Nielsen, et.al, (2005), p.41
11 OECD (2007). PISA 2006. Volume 2: Data. Tables 6.1a and 6.2a.
12 Vegas, E. and J. Petrow (2008). p. 29

Figure 7 | Students with Low Achievement in PISA Science Test, 2006

Source: OECD (2007). PISA 2006: Executive Summary. Table 1, p. 20.

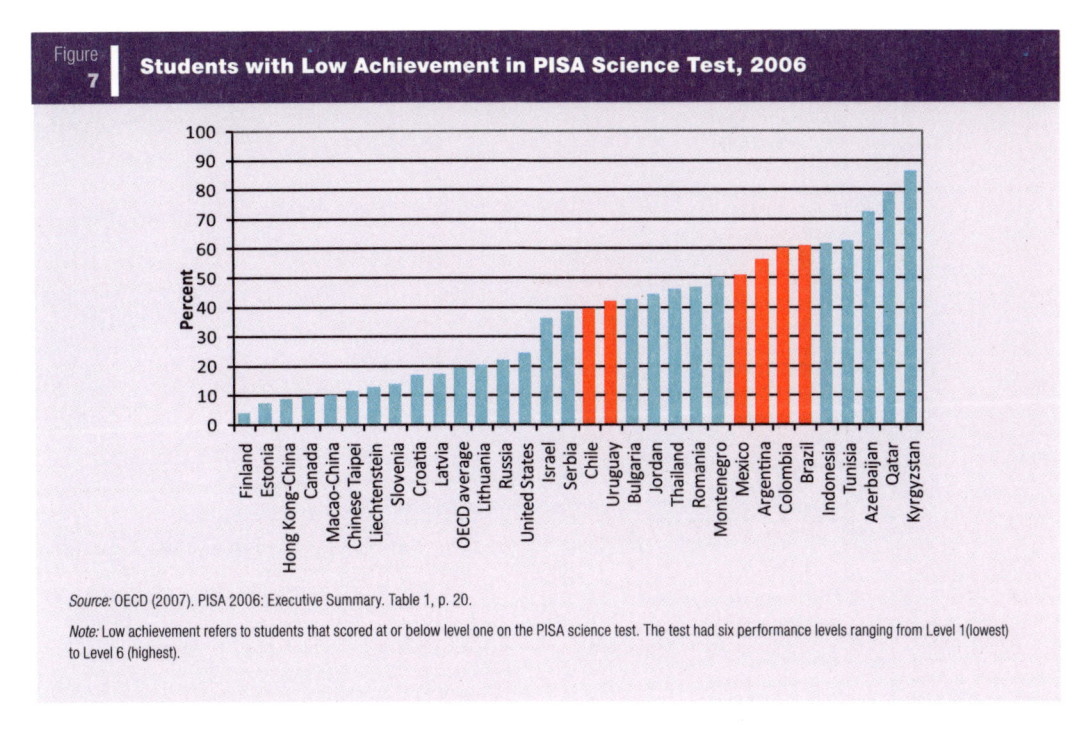

Note: Low achievement refers to students that scored at or below level one on the PISA science test. The test had six performance levels ranging from Level 1(lowest) to Level 6 (highest).

The results for reading and science were similar.[13]

Nor is poor performance limited to global exams. In a separate exam covering 16 Latin America countries and the Mexican state of Nuevo Leon—UNESCO's Second Regional Comparative and Explanatory Study (SERCE)—almost half the region's third-graders performed at or below the lowest level in math (Figure 8). Roughly the same proportion scored at the lowest level in science, and roughly a third scored at the bottom in reading.

Latin America's consistently low scores on international student achievement tests have major implications for the region's competitiveness in a global knowledge economy.

Quality also varies widely from country to country. A few (Costa Rica, Chile, Cuba, Mexico and Uruguay) do better. Others (the Dominican Republic, Ecuador, Guatemala, Nicaragua, Panama and Paraguay) do worse. The two outliers, however, are Cuba and the Dominican Republic. Cuba scores way above the rest of Latin America while the Dominican Republic scores way below. In third-grade reading, nearly half of Cuban students scored at the highest level, compared with one percent in the Dominican Republic. By contrast, nearly a third of students in the Dominican Republic scored below level one, compared with one percent in Cuba (Figure 9).

Cuba is the major exception to Latin America's pattern of education quality. Its students have by far the best overall performance in the SERCE reading, math and science exams. Roughly 50 percent scored at the highest level in each subject (compared to at most 35 percent in the other countries) and

---

13 Pritchett, L. and M. Viarengo (2009).

Figure 8 | Third Grade Students with Low Achievement in SERCE Math Test, 2006

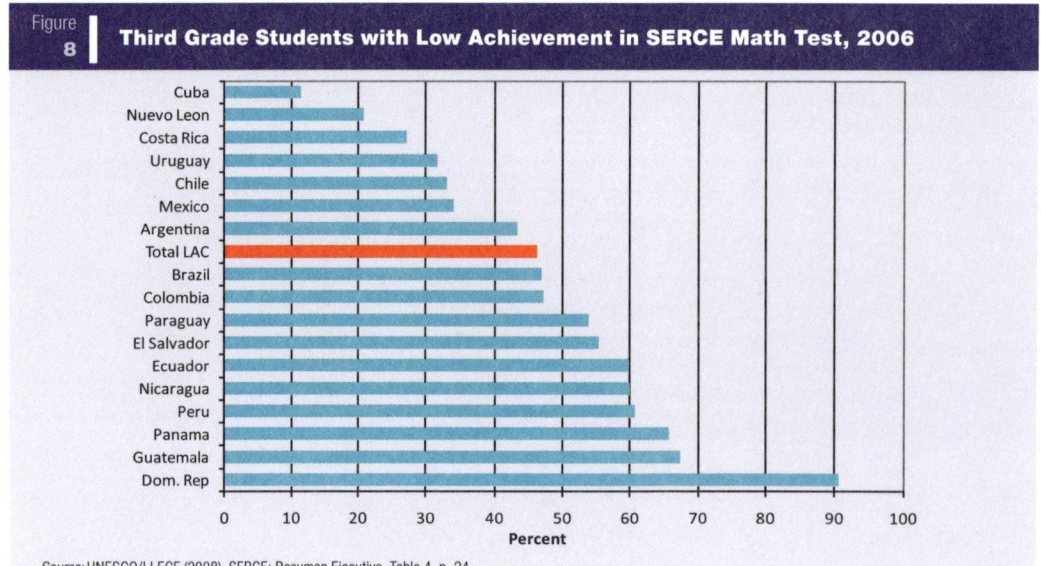

Country	Percent
Cuba	~10
Nuevo Leon	~20
Costa Rica	~27
Uruguay	~31
Chile	~33
Mexico	~34
Argentina	~42
Total LAC	~46
Brazil	~47
Colombia	~48
Paraguay	~53
El Salvador	~55
Ecuador	~59
Nicaragua	~60
Peru	~61
Panama	~65
Guatemala	~67
Dom. Rep	~91

Source: UNESCO/LLECE (2008). SERCE: Resumen Ejecutivo. Table 4, p. 24.

Note: (1) The graph shows third graders performing at or below Level 1. (2) SERCE included four performance levels, with Level 1 the lowest and Level 4 the highest. SERCE also kept track of students performing below Level 1. (3) Total LAC shows the figure for Latin America taken as a whole, with each country weighted by population.

(except for math) only 5 percent of them scored at or below the lowest level (compared to well over 10 percent for all but a few of the others).

At the tertiary level, hard data on quality is scarce. Accreditation systems are weak, are not widespread,[14] and have had limited impact.[15] Two of the region's largest public universities, the National Autonomous University (UNAM) in Mexico and the University of Buenos Aires in Argentina, have traditionally resisted participation in national accreditation systems or external evaluations.[16] Brazil is an interesting exception, having evaluated university graduates, under various systems, since 1995.

The limited evidence that exists suggests

Figure 9 | Third Grade Performance in SERCE Reading Test, 2006 (Cuba and Dominican Republic)

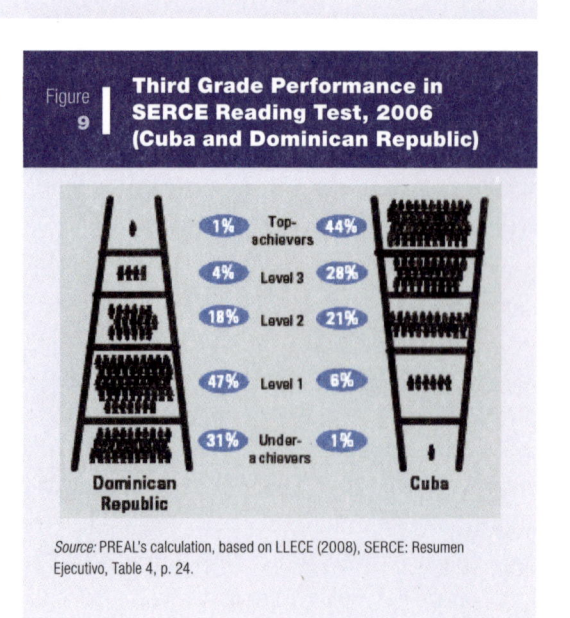

Dominican Republic	Level	Cuba
1%	Top-achievers	44%
4%	Level 3	28%
18%	Level 2	21%
47%	Level 1	6%
31%	Under-achievers	1%

Source: PREAL's calculation, based on LLECE (2008), SERCE: Resumen Ejecutivo, Table 4, p. 24.

---

14 According to a recent UNESCO/IESALC study, Argentina, Bolivia, Brazil, Chile, Colombia, Costa Rica, Ecuador, El Salvador, Mexico, Nicaragua, Paraguay, and Uruguay have established national accreditation organizations over the last decade (Fernández Lamarra, 2006). Brazil has a long-standing program to accredit graduate programs as well (Holm-Nielsen, et. al., 2005).
15 Fernández Lamarra, (2006). Most accreditation systems do not cover non-university tertiary education, especially distance and virtual programs.
16 Oppenheimer, (2005)

that the region's universities are not globally competitive. In a 2008 ranking of the world's 200 top universities,[17] no Latin American University ranked in the top 100, and only three (National Autonomous University of Mexico, University of Sao Paulo and University of Buenos Aires) were included at all—at ranks 150, 196 and 197. In a similar 2008 ranking of the world's top 500 universities conducted by the Shanghai Jiao Tong University,[18] no Latin American university ranked in the top 100, and only three (University of Sao Paulo in Brazil, Universidad de Buenos Aires and Universidad Nacional Autónoma in Mexico) ranked in the top 200. In total, only 10 Latin American universities made the top 500 (six of them from Brazil). By comparison, South Korea had eight universities in the top 500, China had eighteen (excluding Hong Kong and Taiwan), Taiwan had seven, Hong Kong had five and South Africa had three.

Science, Technology and English

Latin American schools do a poor job of providing the more specific skills necessary to be competitive. Even those who achieve basic competency in reading and math are unlikely to acquire the advanced math, science, technology and English skills that allow countries to innovate and attract foreign investment.

Science and Technology

The region's universities produce very few science or engineering graduates. The bulk of university graduates are in social science, law, or business. In most countries, less than a quarter receive science or engineering degrees. By contrast, nearly 35 percent of all university graduates from Hong Kong and Korea, and nearly 30 percent of all Finnish graduates are trained in science or engineering. In Latin America, only Mexico and Colombia have similar rates (Figure 10). Not surprisingly, when business executives in 133 countries were asked to rate the availability of scientists and engineers in their country, only three Latin American and Caribbean countries ranked in the top 50 (Chile, Costa Rica, and Trinidad and Tobago), and only two more scored above the mean (Brazil and Barbados).[19]

Latin America's scientific output is also low compared to other regions, both in terms of scientific and engineering articles and patents granted

Photo Credit: De Troya et al.

---

17 The 2008 Times Higher Education ranks the top 200 universities based primarily on peer review. Rankings are available at: www.thes.co.uk
18 Shanghai Jiao Tong University's ranking is based on a variety of factors including alumni and faculty receiving Nobel Prizes in physics, chemistry, medicine or economics (or Fields Medals in mathematics); number of highly cited researchers in life sciences, medicine, engineering, physical or social sciences; articles in major academic journals; and quality of education in relation to size. Rankings are available at: http://www.arwu.org/rank2008/EN2008.htm
19 Schwab, (2009)

Figure 10 | **Tertiary Graduates in Science and Engineering, 2007**

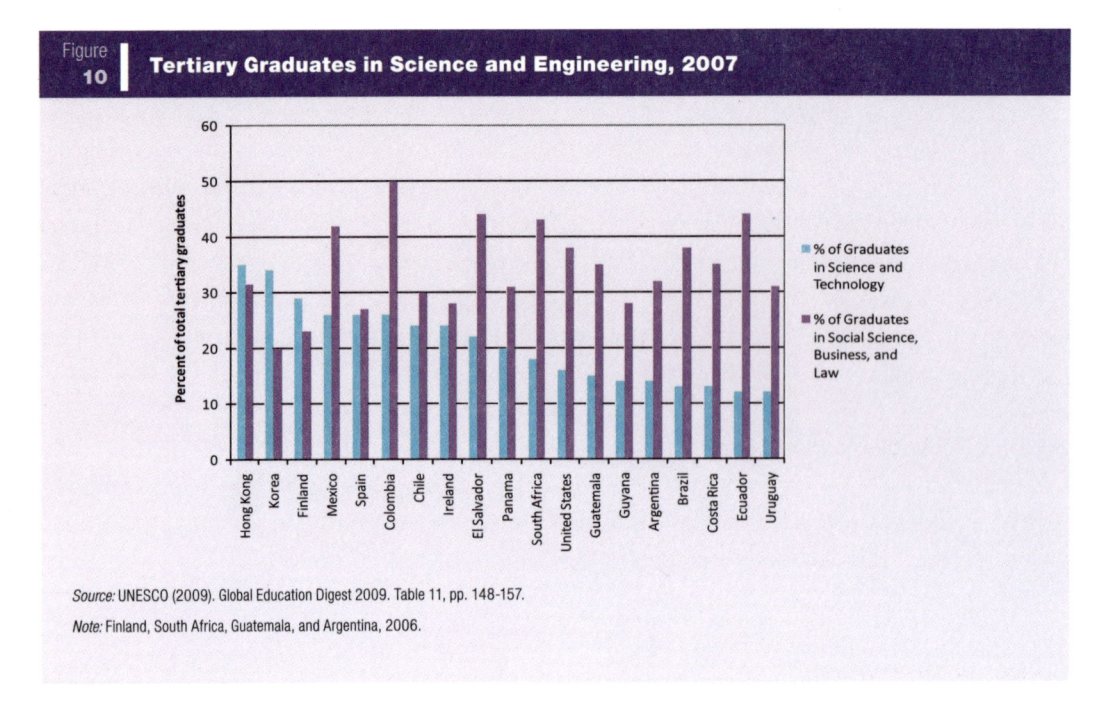

[Bar chart showing percent of total tertiary graduates by country, with two series: % of Graduates in Science and Technology, and % of Graduates in Social Science, Business, and Law. Countries listed: Hong Kong, Korea, Finland, Mexico, Spain, Colombia, Chile, Ireland, El Salvador, Panama, South Africa, United States, Guatemala, Guyana, Argentina, Brazil, Costa Rica, Ecuador, Uruguay.]

Source: UNESCO (2009). Global Education Digest 2009. Table 11, pp. 148-157.
Note: Finland, South Africa, Guatemala, and Argentina, 2006.

(Figures 11 and 12).

English-Language Skills

Few studies track how many people speak English in any given country or their level of proficiency. Existing evidence suggests, however, that Latin American governments give English relatively low priority, and less priority than East Asian competitors. Most Latin American English classes start in 7th grade with two hours of instruction per week. Meanwhile in Singapore, Thailand and Malaysia English instruction starts in 1st grade and in China and Korea it starts in 3rd. Chinese students meet four hours a week and Singaporean students meet for eight hours each week.[20] Studies in Chile suggest that only 2 percent of the population has achieved basic reading and speaking proficiency in English.[21]

Equity

Moreover, the region's school systems do little to reduce inequality. Poor children in Latin America tend to begin school later, repeat more grades, drop out sooner, and score lower on tests than their better-off peers, regardless of their gender, race, ethnicity, or area of residence.

The education gap between rich and poor appears to start early. Children from the richest fifth of the population benefit from better-educated parents, greater access to reading materials and higher levels of nutrition and healthcare, all essential to being ready to learn. Access to early childhood

---

20 Oppenheimer, (2005)
21 Ibid

HOW CAN EDUCATION HELP LATIN AMERICA DEVELOP? **175**

Figure 11 | Scientific and Engineering Article Output of Emerging and Developing Countries by Region, 1988-2001

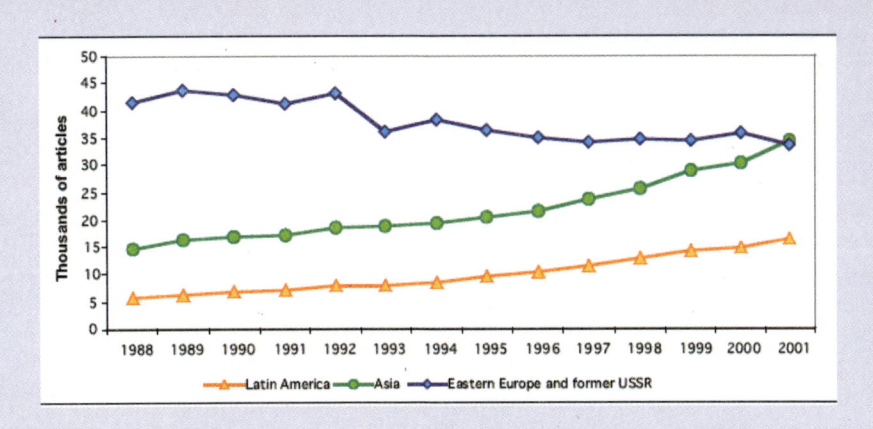

Source: IDB (2006). Graph B.3.2.b.

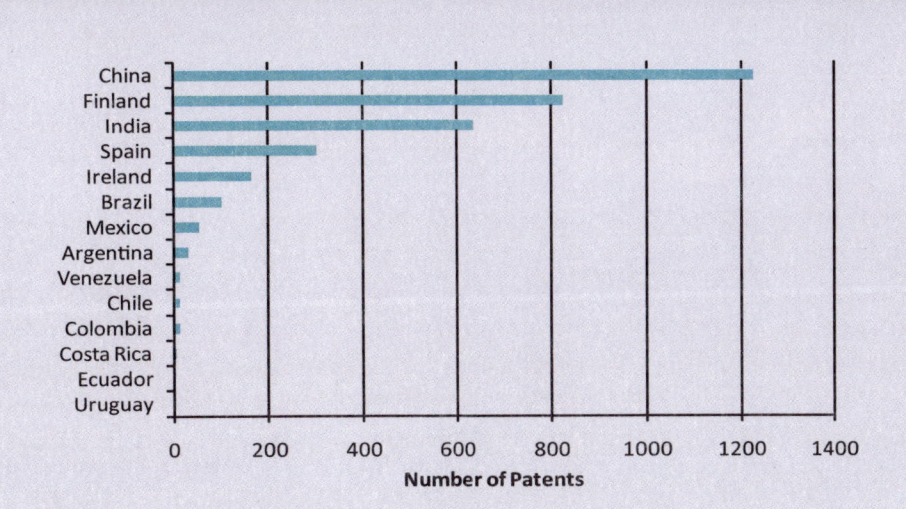

Figure 12 | Patents Granted by United States Patent and Trademark Office, 2008

Source: IDB (2010, forthcoming). *The Age of Productivity: Transforming Economies from the Bottom Up.*

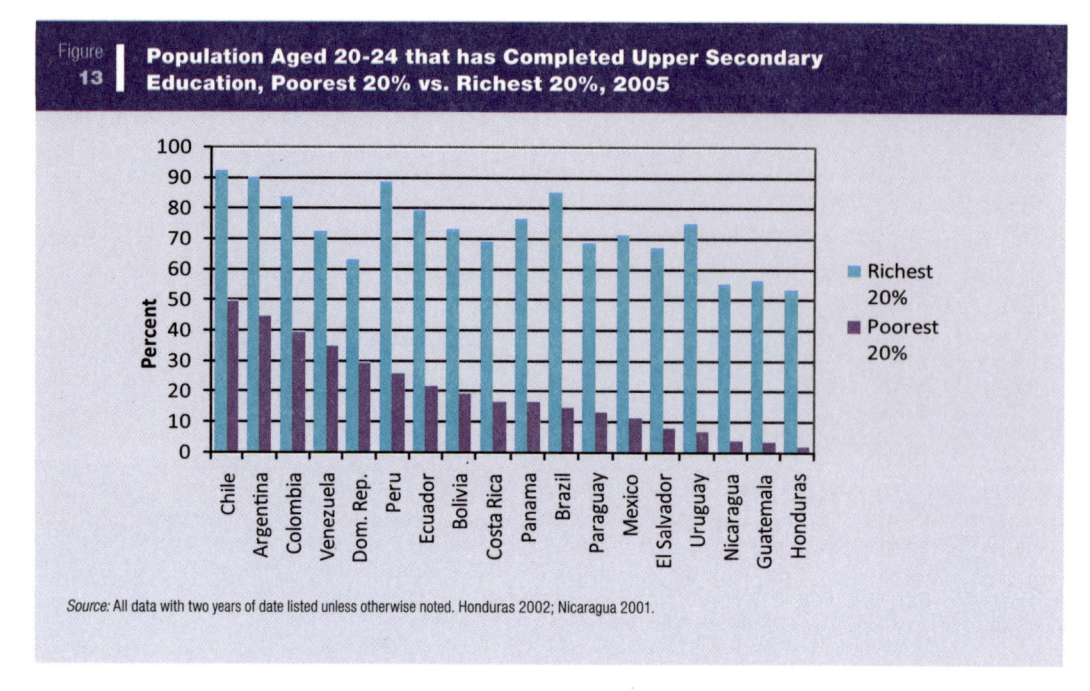

Figure 13 | Population Aged 20-24 that has Completed Upper Secondary Education, Poorest 20% vs. Richest 20%, 2005

Source: All data with two years of date listed unless otherwise noted. Honduras 2002; Nicaragua 2001.

education is highly unequal. Studies suggest that the poorest children are almost half as likely to enroll in pre-school as their richest peers.[22]

As children move through the system, the gap between rich and poor students grows. In the best of cases (Chile) the richest 20 percent of students are almost twice as likely to complete upper secondary education; in the worst of cases (Honduras) the richest 20 percent are at least ten times more likely to complete upper secondary (Figure 13).

Even when the poor remain in school, they perform well below their more advantaged peers. In the 2006 PISA exam, the poorest students from Argentina, Brazil, Chile, Mexico and Uruguay scored more than one achievement level below the wealthiest students (Figure 14).

The achievement gap between rich and poor students does not appear to be shrinking, at least for the few countries (Brazil, Mexico and Uruguay) for which data are available.[23]

Differences are often greater among disadvantaged racial and ethnic groups. Indigenous children are less likely to enroll in school and graduate than their peers (Tables 1 and 2). These gaps widen at the secondary level. Enrollment rates for indigenous youths are 40 percent of the national average in Mexico.[24] Indigenous children in Bolivia, Chile, Guatemala, Mexico, and Peru also perform significantly below their peers in reading and math[25]—in fact, Guatemala's language test score gaps are among the largest of any country in the Americas.[26]

---

22 Vegas, E. and L. Santibañez (2009).
23 OECD (2007). PISA – Vol. 2: Data. Table 4.11, p. 15.
24 Birdsall, N., A. De La Torre, R. Menezes (2008). p. 138
25 McEwan, P. J. (2004). 53(1): 157-90. See also Murillo, F. J. (2007). p. 8
26 McEwan, P. J. and M. Trowbridge (2007). P. 61-76

Table 1 | Percentage of 15 to 19-Year Olds who have Completed Primary Education, 2004

Country	Indigenous	Non-Indigenous
Bolivia	85	92
Brazil	91	93
Chile	97	99
Colombia	98	98
Costa Rica	88	93
Dom. Republic	42	69
Nicaragua	48	65
Panama	73	97
Paraguay	83	96
Peru	88	90

Source: UNESCO/PRELAC (2007). The State of Education in Latin America and the Caribbean. p. 226.

Table 2 | Percentage of 20 to 24-Year Olds who have Completed Secondary Education

Country	Lower Secondary Indigenous	Lower Secondary Non-Indigenous	Upper Secondary Indigenous	Upper Secondary Non-Indigenous
Bolivia	69	81	46	58
Brazil	66	71	41	49
Chile	87	95	60	75
Cuba	87	87	46	49
Ecuador	42	66	27	51
Guatemala	16	43	10	34
Nicaragua	18	37	7	27
Panama	28	74	12	56
Paraguay	43	76	26	58
Peru	68	72	58	62

Source: UNESCO/PRELAC (2007). The State of Education in Latin America and the Caribbean. pp. 227-228.
Note: All data within two years unless otherwise noted. Cuba 2002; Nicaragua and Peru 2001.

Similar disparities exist between Afro-descendant children and their white counterparts. In Brazil,

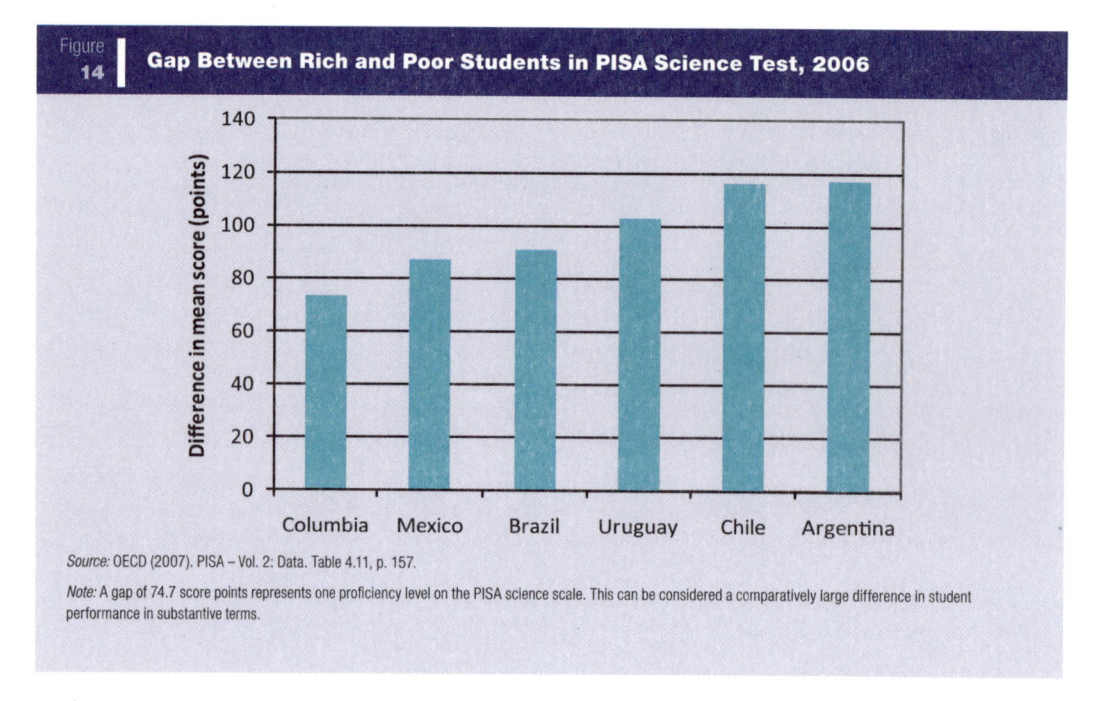

Figure 14: Gap Between Rich and Poor Students in PISA Science Test, 2006

Country	Difference in mean score (points)
Columbia	~73
Mexico	~87
Brazil	~90
Uruguay	~103
Chile	~115
Argentina	~116

Source: OECD (2007). PISA – Vol. 2: Data. Table 4.11, p. 157.

Note: A gap of 74.7 score points represents one proficiency level on the PISA science scale. This can be considered a comparatively large difference in student performance in substantive terms.

children identifying themselves as mixed or black are more prone to repeat and drop out than their white peers.[27] While both whites and non-whites are staying in school longer, the gap in years of schooling between whites and Afro-descendants has remained almost the same over the past decade.[28]

Latin America has, however, done a relatively good job of closing the gender gap in education. Girls are as likely, and in some countries more likely, to enroll in and complete their schooling as boys. On international exams, girls appear to do better than boys in reading, while boys appear to do better than girls in math, and only sometimes in science (Figures 15a and 15b). The big exception is indigenous girls, who remain at a disadvantage in virtually every country. In Guatemala, for example, only 55 percent of 7-year-old indigenous girls enroll in school, compared with 71 percent of indigenous boys and 74 percent of non-indigenous girls.[29]

The region's pronounced education inequalities are largely a reflection of the fact that Latin America is the most unequal region in the world. Five of the world's ten most unequal countries are in Latin America and one of them—Brazil—accounts for nearly one-third of the region's population.[30]

Education, of course, is widely agreed to be one of the most powerful tools for reducing inequality. But government spending on education, despite significant growth, is making only limited headway in reducing inequality. To be sure, public spending on primary and secondary education is for the most

---

27 Birdsall, N., A. De La Torre, R. Menezes (2008). p. 138
28 Paixão, M., L. M. Carvano (2008). p. 70
29 UNESCO (2009). p. 7. See more evidence on Guatemala in Hallman, K., S. Peracca (2007)
30 Puryear and Jewers (2009) (forthcoming)

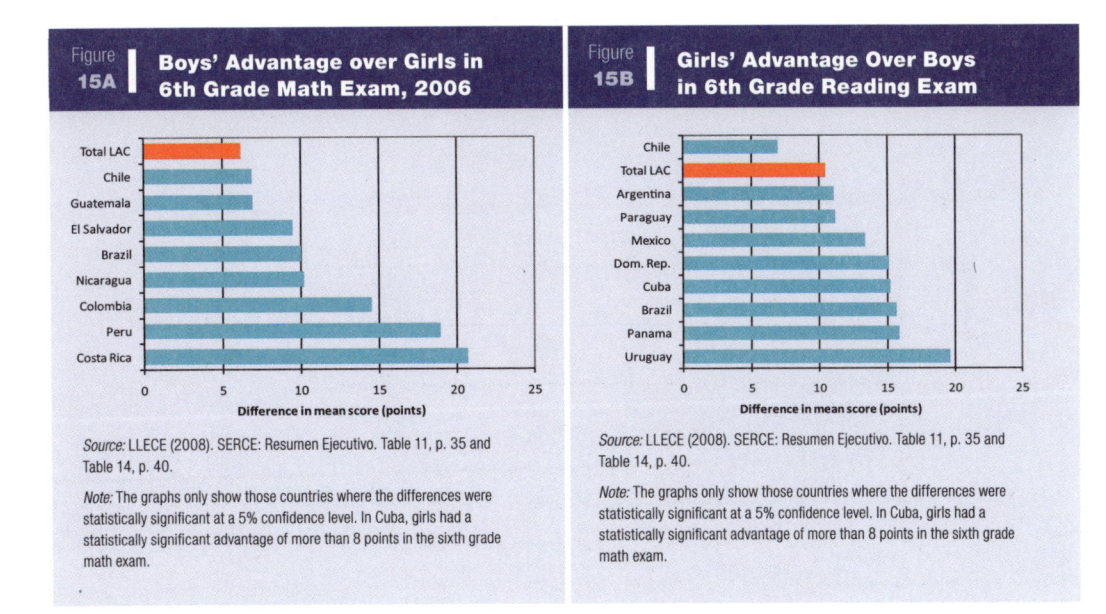

Figure 15A: Boys' Advantage over Girls in 6th Grade Math Exam, 2006

(Countries listed: Total LAC, Chile, Guatemala, El Salvador, Brazil, Nicaragua, Colombia, Peru, Costa Rica)

Difference in mean score (points)

Source: LLECE (2008). SERCE: Resumen Ejecutivo. Table 11, p. 35 and Table 14, p. 40.

Note: The graphs only show those countries where the differences were statistically significant at a 5% confidence level. In Cuba, girls had a statistically significant advantage of more than 8 points in the sixth grade math exam.

Figure 15B: Girls' Advantage Over Boys in 6th Grade Reading Exam

(Countries listed: Chile, Total LAC, Argentina, Paraguay, Mexico, Dom. Rep., Cuba, Brazil, Panama, Uruguay)

Difference in mean score (points)

Source: LLECE (2008). SERCE: Resumen Ejecutivo. Table 11, p. 35 and Table 14, p. 40.

Note: The graphs only show those countries where the differences were statistically significant at a 5% confidence level. In Cuba, girls had a statistically significant advantage of more than 8 points in the sixth grade math exam.

part pro-poor or at least neutral, since most middle- and upper-class families opt out of the public system, sending their children instead to private primary and secondary schools. But governments tend to overspend at the tertiary level so as to provide tuition-free higher education for all. Public spending per higher education student in Latin America is often five (or more) times public spending per primary school student in Latin America, compared with ratios of approximately 1:1 in countries like Spain or Canada. Since the vast majority of students from poor families never reach the tertiary level, the result is a massive subsidy to the middle- and upper- classes. More than half of the benefits of public spending on higher education go to the richest 20 percent of the population, while less than two percent of those benefits go to the poorest 20 percent (Figure 16).

That portion of government education spending that does reach the poor, largely through public primary and secondary schools, provides education whose quality is so low that it does not significantly increase their human capital nor equip them to compete with the graduates of the relatively better private primary and secondary schools.

What should Governments do?

The chief obstacles to improving the region's education systems are both technical and political, and serious

Photo Credit: CAF

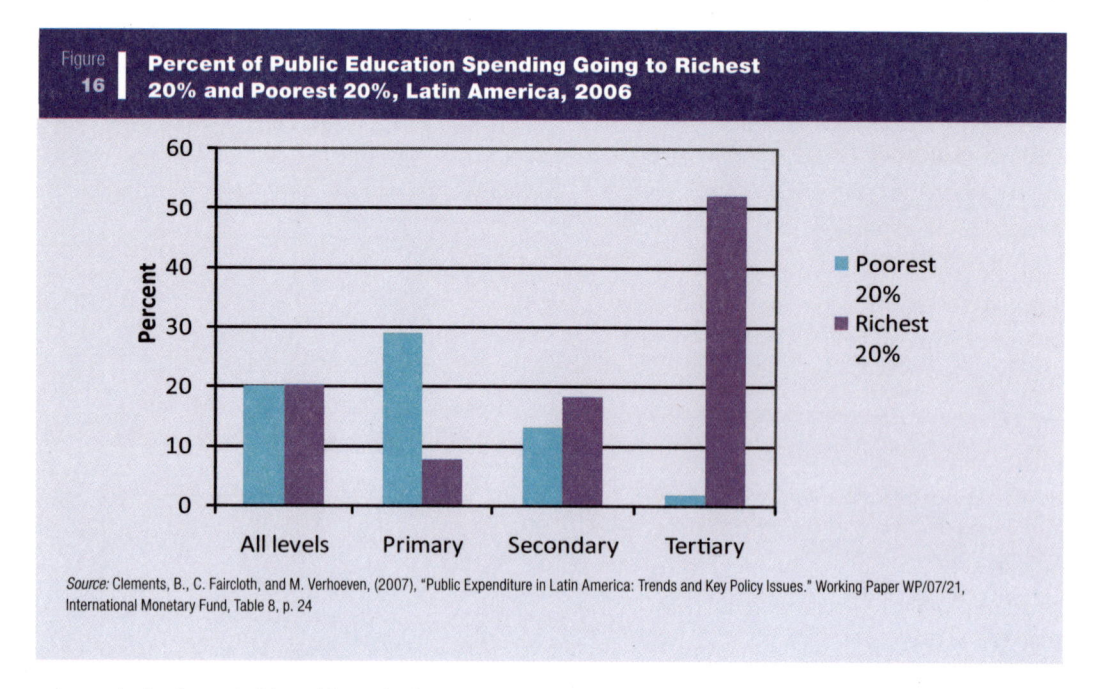

Figure 16: Percent of Public Education Spending Going to Richest 20% and Poorest 20%, Latin America, 2006

Source: Clements, B., C. Faircloth, and M. Verhoeven, (2007), "Public Expenditure in Latin America: Trends and Key Policy Issues." Working Paper WP/07/21, International Monetary Fund, Table 8, p. 24

reform strategies need to address both aspects.

On the technical side, most ministries of education are weak—even incompetent—and so have limited capacity to manage a large and diverse education system.[31] Teaching (at least in the public system) does not attract the best and brightest applicants—in part because training is inadequate, standards and prestige are low, incentives do not reward merit and management is poor. Thus even when good policies are adopted, education systems often lack the capacity to implement them.

Clearly, ministerial bureaucracies need to be re-engineered so as to strengthen their capacity to develop and implement policy. Emphasis should be on setting and enforcing standards, regularly assessing progress and promoting quality and equity. Governments should recognize that the direct provision of education services can be done effectively and equitably by either the public or private sector, and concentrate on establishing the accountability, incentives and oversight necessary to make that happen. And the teaching profession needs to be fundamentally re-thought so as to make teaching a high-status occupation that demands and rewards good performance.

On the political side, government leaders are understandably reluctant to anger powerful interest groups that benefit from the status quo—such as teachers' unions or university students—and can mobilize protests or shut down schools. Teachers' unions are particularly strong—often constituting the largest labor organization in the country and holding a near monopoly over public education. Their strikes can endanger a country's political stability.

Governments have little control over such groups, and seldom receive much political support

---

[31] IDB (2005), Chapter. 1

when they confront them. The clients of public schools—mostly poor families—have almost no power in the school system. They have little information on how schools are doing, few mechanisms for influencing education policy or practice, and no tradition of citizen activism. Those parents with real power to influence schools, primarily middle- and upper-class, send their children to private schools, helping them escape the failings of the public system. Consequently, they do not bring significant pressure to bear on governments (or on teachers unions) for improvement.

The result is a system that serves the interests of teachers relatively well (providing them with iron-clad job security regardless of performance) but neglects the interests of parents and students (providing them with third-rate education in under-funded and poorly managed public schools).

To redress this political imbalance, governments need to strengthen their position vis-à-vis at least some of the interest groups that have "captured" the public education system. How best to accomplish that is not entirely clear. On the one hand they need to reduce the inordinate power that interest groups, particularly teachers unions, wield. Doing so will be politically difficult. On the other, they need to develop a stronger, more effective demand for quality education—by parents and employers—that can provide political support for presidential reform efforts.

Specific Policy Measures

Governments should make learning the central objective of their education systems, and stress policies that promote learning, particularly among the poor. They should consider the following policies:

1. Provide all children with quality pre-school education. Governments should build on existing public and private providers, target the poor and reach children not only at age 5, but at ages 3 and 4 as well.
2. Establish world-class learning standards in reading, math and science for all grades. Standards should be clear, measurable and high. Teacher training, textbooks and student assessments should be keyed to them.
3. Develop robust and transparent evaluation systems that regularly assess the learning of all children in reading, math and science. Results should be used to inform teachers, parents, politicians and opinion leaders and to improve schools.
4. Tackle failure quickly, by identifying students who are falling behind, particularly in the early

grades, and providing them with intensive remedial instruction.
5. Recruit top graduates into teaching by setting high standards, making entry much more selective, and training intensively in classroom instruction.
6. Restructure teacher management, strengthening the power to hire and fire, keying pay to performance, assessing effectiveness and providing in-class support. Work intensively with teachers to make sure they become effective instructors, granting tenure only to the best and removing poor performers from the classroom.
7. Experiment with interventions that promote accountability through alternative models of service that set clear expectations, provide meaningful consequences for good and bad performance, and allow schools and communities to make key decisions about how best to make sure their students are learning. Examples include charter schools, vouchers, school-based management reforms and public-private partnerships.
8. Invest more funds in high-quality basic education. Resources should be adequate to provide every child with a first-rate education, and be conditioned on meeting minimum levels of quality and ensuring that the poor are properly served.
9. Make proficiency in English a fundamental goal of the education system. Governments should make a strong effort to provide the poor with basic writing and speaking skills in English, beginning in primary school.
10. Develop a stronger, more effective demand for quality education by: 1) providing parents with reliable, timely, and user-friendly information on how their schools are doing; 2) establishing mechanisms for parental participation in policy decisions; and 3) giving the poor real power, by permitting them to choose the school their children attend.
11. Condition funding for universities on meeting specific performance objectives. Emphasis should be placed on improving quality, strengthening science and technology, and promoting equity. Rather than channeling all public funds directly to universities, governments should experiment with providing some part of funding directly to students (principally from poor families) via scholarships they can use to attend any qualified university—public or private.
12. Require public universities to charge tuition to those who can afford to pay. Charges should be on a sliding scale, depending principally on socioeconomic background. Higher education should be fully free only for students from poor families.

Appendix

Table A.1 | PISA: Mean Score on the Math Test (points), 2000, 2003, and 2006

Country	2000	2003	2006	Country	2000	2003	2006
Finland	536	544	548	Spain	476	485	480
Hong Kong	560	550	547	Azerbaijan	..	..	476
Korea, Rep.	547	542	547	Russia	478	468	476
Netherlands	..	538	531	United States	493	483	474
Switzerland	529	527	530	Croatia	..	..	467
Canada	533	532	527	Portugal	454	466	466
Liechtenstein	514	536	525	Italy	457	466	462
Macao	..	527	525	Greece	447	445	459
Japan	557	534	523	Israel	433	..	442
New Zealand	537	523	522	Serbia	..	437	435
Australia	533	524	520	Uruguay	..	422	427
Belgium	520	529	520	Turkey	..	423	424
Estonia	..	..	515	Thailand	432	417	417
Denmark	514	514	513	Romania	..	..	415
Czech Republic	498	516	510	Bulgaria	430	..	413
Iceland	514	515	506	Chile	384	..	411
Austria	515	506	505	Mexico	387	385	406
Germany	490	503	504	Montenegro	..	..	399
Slovenia	..	..	504	Indonesia	367	360	391
Sweden	510	509	502	Jordan	..	..	384
Ireland	503	503	501	Argentina	388	..	381
France	517	511	496	Brazil	334	356	370
Poland	470	490	495	Colombia	..	..	370
United Kingdom	529	..	495	Tunisia	..	359	365
Slovak Republic	..	498	492	Qatar	..	..	318
Hungary	488	490	491	Kyrgyz Rep.	..	..	311
Luxembourg	446	493	490	Albania	381	..	..
Norway	499	495	490	Macedonia	381	..	..
Latvia	463	483	486	Peru	292	..	..
Lithuania	..	..	486				

Source: World Bank Edstats Online Database. Last accessed: November 20, 2008.

Note: The baseline for comparison of progress in math achievement over time was established in the PISA 2003 test, which focused on this subject. Therefore, PISA measures progress in math achievement according to countries' performance in the 2003 exam. According to this criterion, the countries that have seen a statistically significant increase in their math achievement scores are (from most to least improved): Indonesia, Mexico, Greece, and Brazil. By contrast, the countries that have seen a statistically significant decrease in their scores are (from most to least worsened): France, Canada, Japan, Liechtenstein, Iceland, Belgium, United States, Netherlands, Sweden, and Canada. Levels of statistical significance vary. To consult these levels, see OECD (2007). PISA – Vol. 1: Analysis. Figure 6.21, p. 319.

Table A.2 — PISA: Mean Score on the Reading Test (points), 2000, 2003, and 2006

Country	2000	2003	2006	Country	2000	2003	2006
Korea, Rep.	525	534	556	Lithuania	..	..	470
Finland	546	543	547	Italy	487	476	469
Hong Kong	525	510	536	Slovak Rep.	..	469	466
Canada	534	528	527	Spain	493	481	461
New Zealand	529	522	521	Greece	474	472	460
Ireland	527	515	517	Turkey	..	441	447
Australia	528	525	513	Chile	410	..	442
Liechtenstein	483	525	510	Russia	462	442	440
Poland	479	497	508	Israel	452	..	439
Netherlands	..	513	507	Thailand	431	420	417
Sweden	516	514	507	Uruguay	..	434	413
Belgium	507	507	501	Mexico	422	400	410
Estonia	..	..	501	Bulgaria	430	..	402
Switzerland	494	499	499	Jordan	..	..	401
Japan	522	498	498	Serbia	..	412	401
Germany	484	491	495	Romania	..	..	396
United Kingdom	523	..	495	Brazil	396	403	393
Denmark	497	492	494	Indonesia	371	382	393
Slovenia	..	..	494	Montenegro	..	..	392
Macao	..	498	492	Colombia	..	..	385
Austria	507	491	490	Tunisia	..	375	380
France	505	496	488	Argentina	418	..	374
Iceland	507	492	484	Azerbaijan	..	..	353
Norway	505	500	484	Qatar	..	..	312
Czech Republic	492	489	483	Kyrgyz Rep.	..	..	285
Hungary	480	482	482	Albania	349	..	..
Latvia	458	491	479	Macedonia	373	..	..
Luxembourg	441	479	479	Peru	327	..	..
Croatia	..	..	477	United States	504	495	..
Portugal	470	478	472				

Source: World Bank Edstats Online Database. Last accessed: November 20, 2008.

Note: (1) The baseline for comparison of progress in reading achievement over time was established in the PISA 2000 test, which focused on this subject. Therefore, PISA measures progress in reading achievement according to countries' performance in the 2000 exam. According to this criterion, the countries that have seen a statistically significant increase in their reading achievement scores are (from most to least improved): Chile, Korea, Poland, Liechtenstein, Indonesia, Latvia, and Hong Kong. By contrast, the countries that have seen a statistically significant decrease in their scores are (from most to least worsened): Argentina, Romania, Spain, Bulgaria, Japan, Iceland, Russia, Norway, Italy, France, Australia, Greece, Thailand, and Mexico. Levels of statistical significance vary. To consult these levels, see OECD (2007). PISA – Vol. 1: Analysis. Figure 6.9, p. 301.

Table A.3 — PISA: Mean Score on the Science Test (points), 2000, 2003, and 2006

Country	2000	2003	2006	Country	2000	2003	2006
Finland	538	548	563	Spain	491	487	488
Hong Kong	541	539	542	Norway	500	484	487
Canada	529	519	534	Luxembourg	443	483	486
Estonia	..	..	531	Russia	460	489	479
Japan	550	548	531	Italy	478	486	475
New Zealand	528	521	530	Portugal	459	468	474
Australia	528	525	527	Greece	461	481	473
Netherlands	..	524	525	Israel	434	..	454
Korea	552	538	522	Chile	415	..	438
Liechtenstein	476	525	522	Serbia	..	436	436
Slovenia	..	..	519	Bulgaria	448	..	434
Germany	487	502	516	Uruguay	..	438	428
United Kingdom	532	..	515	Turkey	..	434	424
Czech Republic	511	523	513	Jordan	..	..	422
Switzerland	496	513	512	Thailand	436	429	421
Austria	519	491	511	Romania	..	..	418
Macao	..	525	511	Montenegro	..	..	412
Belgium	496	509	510	Mexico	422	405	410
Ireland	513	505	508	Indonesia	393	395	393
Hungary	496	503	504	Argentina	396	..	391
Sweden	512	506	503	Brazil	375	390	390
Poland	483	498	498	Colombia	..	..	388
Denmark	481	475	496	Tunisia	..	385	386
France	500	511	495	Azerbaijan	..	..	382
Croatia	..	..	493	Qatar	..	..	349
Iceland	496	495	491	Kyrgyz Rep.	..	..	322
Latvia	460	489	490	Albania	376	..	..
United States	499	491	489	Macedonia	401	..	..
Lithuania	..	..	488	Peru	333	..	..
Slovak Republic	..	495	488				

Source: World Bank Edstats Online Database. Last accessed: November 20, 2008.

Note: The baseline for comparison of progress in science achievement over time was established in the PISA 2006 test, which focused on this subject. Therefore, PISA will measure progress in science achievement according to countries' performance in the 2006 exam. In the meantime, PISA measures progress in science achievement using "link items" (i.e., a subset of common items in the test), calculating the difference between PISA 2006 and PISA 2003 science scores. According to this criterion, the countries that have seen a statistically significant increase in their science achievement scores are (from most to least improved): Uruguay, Mexico, Greece, Brazil, and Tunisia. By contrast, the only country that has seen a statistically significant decrease in its scores is France. Linking errors vary. To consult these levels, see OECD (2007). PISA – Vol. 1: Analysis. Table A7.1, p. 369.

Chapter 6
Innovation and Technology Development for Economic Restructuring

Vinod K. Goel

In today's globalized world, a nation needs to transform its science, technology and innovation system to sustain growth trajectory, create more and better paying jobs, and enable all citizens to realize their aspirations.

Innovation[1] today is widely recognized as a major source of competitiveness and economic growth for all countries—advanced and emerging economies alike. Innovation has a critical role in creating jobs, generating incomes and in improving living standards of a society. Innovation can also be a powerful tool in broader social development including in moving people out of poverty and improving the distribution of income. The 21st Century will be the "century of innovation"; in the coming decades, knowledge and innovation will drive the comparative advantage of some countries, and a lack of it will lead to disappointing examples of failed economic performance for others. In the new global economy, a nation's wealth lies increasingly in its skilled people—not in its land or capital—who generate new knowledge and convert it into useful and value-added ideas, goods, services and processes. For economic growth, a nation cannot rely on investment and labor force expansion alone, but also must take account of the technology and innovation factor, which has a strong impact on productivity growth and competitiveness.

In an advancing nation, many sectors of the economy require workers with specialized knowledge who can create knowledge and use it as a productive tool. An educated workforce is a prerequisite for a vibrant technology and innovation system that serves as a major source of economic and social growth. Rising labor productivity accounted for at least half of per capita GDP growth in high-income countries during 1990-2000. Better educated workers are generally more productive and help to boost the productivity of co-workers. Larger stocks of human capital facilitate investments in physical capital and enhance the development and diffusion of new technologies, raising output per worker.[2]

---

1 Innovation here is defined broadly as the process of creation, acquisition, diffusion, absorption and use of knowledge which creates added value in the economy in the form of new or improved products (goods and services), processes or organizational models. Research & Development (R&D) includes creation of new knowledge, as well as capacity to be able to evaluate, acquire, adapt, and use existing technology particularly in the productive sector. Technology absorption also includes services related to metrology, standards, testing and quality, technology extension, and broader range of issues including the purchase of capital goods and skills. The innovation concept encompasses "technological" innovation, as well as "non-technological" forms of innovation such as "organization" innovations that include new approaches to management and marketing, supply and logistics, communications, etc.

2 Studies tracing the relationship between the stock of education and GDP find that a one-year increase in average educational attainment raises output per

Over the long-term, the main drivers of global economic growth include technological advance in rich countries and catch-up technology adoption in a group of fast-growing globalizers, which are shifting resources from low to higher productivity activities (such as Chile, South Korea, China and India). Typically, there are differences in productivity (total factor productivity, TFP) between countries and between formal enterprises in the same industry as well as between the formal sector and the informal sector, where most entrepreneurial activity takes place. Eradicating disparities in productivity growth in different sectors of the economy by creating a system that efficiently produces, disseminates and applies knowledge can unleash a major source of economic and social growth. Almost half of the differences in growth performances between Mexico and South Korea over 40 years are attributable to technology-related improvement in productivity.[3]

The governments have traditionally played an important role in the promotion of technology by directly supporting the development of technologies (e.g. space, defense, agriculture, health, etc.), or, more indirectly, by creating a climate favorable to innovation through various types of incentives or laws. In developing countries, the bulk of R&D activities are devoted to technology search, adaptation and development, rather than to basic, and even applied research. For developing countries, considerable economic and social benefits can be realized by tapping into globally available knowledge and technologies and adapting them to local conditions. Sources of foreign knowledge and technologies include FDI, trade activities (equipment and goods imports), education, multinational corporations, and skilled Diaspora.

Photo Credit: CAF

The innovation climate is largely determined by the overall, macroeconomic, business, and governance environment. Despite those conditions, proactive innovation policies remain very relevant since they can be an efficient policy tool for triggering change and improvement in the overall framework conditions. The drivers for innovation in the developed world were centered on getting more (performance and productivity) from less (physical, financial, human capital) for more (profit and value to the shareholder). But, the drivers in the developing world would be to get more (performance or productivity) from less (cost) for more and

---

capita 3–6 percentage points and the GDP growth rate about 1 percentage point. The cumulative impact of a 1 percentage point increase in the rate of growth soon exceeds the one-time increase in output (Dahlman, 2008).
3   World Bank, 2006, Korea as a Knowledge Economy, Evolutionary Process and Lessons Learned

more (people). In other words, innovation in the developing world will also need to focus on 'inclusive growth'.

Emerging nations today are increasingly pursuing policies that promote inclusive growth in order to improve social equity. Four billion people, a majority of the world population, form the bottom of the pyramid (BOP), living on less than two dollars per day. In this context, innovation not only has a critical role in enhancing competitiveness and economic growth, it is also important for promoting inclusive growth and social development—called "inclusive innovation". Inclusive innovation is a recent phenomenon where the innovation efforts are targeted directly at the BOP population, thus making the benefits of technology and innovation available to all citizens. This is done in many ways including (i) by encouraging the formal public R&D systems to create and adopt technologies that will address the problems of the BOP section of the society; and (ii) by supporting the development, commercialization and marketing of innovations conceived at the grass-roots. Thus, the promotion of "inclusive innovation" or "pro-poor innovation" is essential for improving the lives of poor people.[4]

Poor communities can be involved with innovation through: the organization of formal linkages and cooperative initiatives with the surrounding research, education or business sectors; and through the exploitation of the indigenous knowledge and entrepreneurial drive (grass-root and social entrepreneurs) generated and available in such communities. Many countries (e.g. India, China) are pursuing inclusive innovation with greater success and are developing products and services that benefit directly (and at affordable prices) the poor people. For example, India's National Innovation Foundation setup to promote inclusive innovation has catalogued some 70,000 grass-roots innovations and is working with technology and engineering institutions as well as with business community to convert many of these grass-roots innovations into viable products and services.

While in the 1970s and the early 1980s, TFP levels in many Latin American countries were quite good, the TFP levels have generally stagnated during the last three decades in most of the countries in the region. Furthermore, the level of technological sophistication of Latin American economies lags behind many of their competitors such as South Korea, Singapore, Malaysia as well as China and India. The education quality and enrolment in the region are also low, the R&D expenditures inadequate, and the activities of R&D system are narrow (Table 1). Like many other parts of the world, the challenge for countries in Latin America is to deploy their human and other resources effectively. The region can do this with a large increase in the amount and scope of investments in science, technology and innovation (STI) accompanied by notable improvements in the capacity and quality of education at all levels, especially the higher education. To implement this agenda, a change in the political commitment, mind-set and approach will be needed—including a redefinition of the roles

---

[4] Inclusive or harmonious development is recognized as an important goal for socio-economic development in most developing countries, particularly in India, China, Brazil and South Africa. Inclusion can take place by treating economically poor and disadvantaged people as consumers of public policy on assistance and aid for basic needs or as consumers of low-cost products made by large corporations or by the state or other enterprises. Inclusion can also take place by building the capacity of the poor to produce what they already know how to and do produce or to use their innovations and outstanding traditional knowledge either as is or by blending/bundling it with knowledge of others into products marketed by them or other enterprises. In addition, linkages with R&D institutions that can take such technologies/products and develop value added products for eventual diffusion through commercial or non-commercial channels can also help inclusion. Source: Gupta, Anil K. 2007.

Table 1: Key Science, Technology and Innovation Indicators, Selected Countries

Indicator	Brazil	China	India	Japan	Mexico	South Korea	United States
Gross secondary enrolment ratio, 2006 (%)	105.5	75.5	54.0	101.4	87.2	93.9	93.9
Gross tertiary enrolment ratio, 2006 (%)	25.5	21.6	11.8	57.3	26.1	91.03	81.8
Science enrolment ratio, 2006 (%)	8.4	n/a	14.3	2.9	13.1	8.6	8.9
Science and engineering enrolment ratio (%), 2006	15.9	n/a	20.3	19.5	31.1	37.5	15.6
Researchers in R&D, 2006	84,979	926,252	117,528	677,206	33,484	17,9812	1,334,628
Researchers in R&D, 2006 (per million People), 2006	462	715	119	5,300	331	3,723	4,628
Total expenditure on R&D, 2006 (% of GDP)	1.02	1.43	0.85	3.18	0.41	3.20	2.68
Manufacturing trade, 2005 (% of GDP)	14.9	53.5	17.1	18.2	46.6	32.7	16
University-industry R&D collaboration, 2007 (scale of 1, low, to 7, high)	3.4	4.1	3.5	4.9	3.2	5.1	5.6
Scientific and technical journal articles, 2005	9,895	41,604	14,622	55,471	3,902	16,396	205,320
Scientific and technical journal articles, 2005 (per million people)	52.9	31.9	13.4	434.1	37.8	339.5	692.5
Availability of venture capital, 2007 (scale of 1, low, to 7, high)	2.5	3.0	4.1	3.9	2.8	3.2	5.3
Patents granted by U.S. Patent and Trademark Office, 2002–06 average	135.2	448.2	316.4	35,469	96.4	4,233	94,217
Patents granted by U.S. Patent and Trademark Office, 2002–06 average (per million people)	0.75	0.35	0.3	278.0	0.95	88.4	324.1
High-technology exports as share of manufacturing exports, 2005 (%)	12.8	30.6	4.9	22.5	19.6	32.0	31.8

Source: Goel, Vinod K. & Mashelkar, R.A., 2009.

of the government and the private sector. With timely actions, and with an increase in the capacity and quality of technology development and innovation (and in the amount and scope of investments in it), and a shift in the government's role, Latin American countries can provide new meaning and legitimacy to the aspirations of their people, improve social equity, and enhance competitiveness and growth potential of their economies.

Key Recommendations for Upgrading Technology Development and Innovation

For upgrading the science, technology and innovation systems, Latin American countries need to increase significantly their investment in R&D—from the current 0.6 percent of GDP to about 2.0 percent. They should focus on the following key aspects. Of course, the specificity and level of upgrading would depend upon the capabilities and needs of a particular country.

1. *Regional Collaboration.* Enhance cooperation and collaboration between countries in the region (and outside the region) to leverage existing STI facilities and capabilities in countries with better STI systems (such as Argentina, Brazil, Chile, Mexico). This will help achieve easier, faster results and benefits for all countries and at a lower cost. Smaller countries which either do not have the capacity to build STI systems or lack adequate demand to use expansive STI systems should use STI facilities of larger countries.

2. *Educated and Skilled Workforce.* Increase investments in education to improve education at all levels. Improve the number (and quality) of the education and training institutions, including production of more science and engineering graduates, especially MS and PhDs, in order to increase the supply of skilled workforce with capabilities to generate, adapt and use knowledge and technology. Human capital is critical for tapping into domestic and global knowledge. Increasing enrolment of the rural and urban poor should advance the spread of new ideas, best practices, newer technologies, and the application of knowledge to low-productivity agriculture and industries. The region should consider establishing a few world class "Regional Universities" (with international collaboration) with modern governance, management and curricula, and which adopt a merit-based process for faculty and students intake. These Universities, which could be set up with help from international institutions (such as CAF) should help offer opportunities to students from all of the countries in the region.

3. *Inclusive Innovation.* Pursue frontier as well as "inclusive innovation" with the dual purposes of global competitiveness and inclusive growth to benefit all people. By encouraging research institutions and universities to also focus on the needs of poor people and by improving the ability of informal firms to absorb new technologies and knowledge, the costs of goods and services can be lowered and income-earning opportunities for poor people and rural populations can be created.

4. *Innovation Infrastructure.* Upgrade basic innovation infrastructure as appropriate, such as metrology, standards, testing, and quality (MSTQ) system, intellectual property rights (IPR) regime, training and skills upgrading, and incubators, to enhance innovation and technology commercialization and diffusion, and contribute to enterprise competitiveness and trade. Of

course, the level of such upgrading would depend upon the capabilities and needs of a particular country.
5. *R&D and Technology Absorption.* Provide public finance for basic research, applied research, technology diffusion and skills upgrading. There is a significant potential to increase productivity by diffusing knowledge produced at the local and regional academic and R&D institutions, and knowledge available globally.
6. *Centers of Excellence.* Create "Centers of Excellence" in certain countries (with regional mandates). These could include increased efforts in producing more economically relevant public goods, such as pre-competitive research, and socially relevant innovations, such as access to clean water, urban congestion, urban transport, clean energy technologies, renewable energy, traditional medicine, public health, and technologies for sustainable livelihoods.

The following sections present a summary of the status of the science, technology and innovation in the region.

The Status of the Science, Technology and Innovation in the Latin America Region
Total factor productivity (TFP) growth in Latin America is low compared with many parts of the world, particularly the United States and Europe as well as with some countries within the region (Figure 1). While many emerging economies (e.g. South Korea, Singapore) have made great strides (China, Malaysia and India are doing now) in improving TFP in their economies, TFP in most countries in Latin America has generally stagnated during the last 30 years (Figure 2). Moreover, there are large differences in productivity in between countries and between formal enterprises in the same industry as well as between the formal sector and the informal sector, where a significant part of region's entrepreneurial activity takes place.

The progress on the Human Development Index (HDI) also shows a similar pattern. As shown in Figure 3, while looking at the conditions in certain Latin American countries (Argentina, Brazil, Chile, Mexico), the progress achieved in HDI during 1980-2007 has been much lower than in some Asian countries such as China, Indonesia, India and Malaysia.[5]

Competitiveness and Knowledge Economy
According to the World Economic Forum (WEF)'s Global Competitiveness Report (2009-2010), the only country in Latin America, which features among the most competitive economies in the world, is Chile which ranked 30th in the Global Competitiveness Index (GCI). According to the same report, Brazil ranked 56th, Mexico 60th, Columbia 69th, Peru 78th, Argentina 85th and Venezuela 113th. In comparison, the GCI ranking for the United States was 2nd, Singapore 3rd, South Korea 19th, China 29th and India 49th. The leading country in the innovation factors in Latin America is Brazil (38th) followed by Chile (43rd) and Mexico 67th; South Korea, India and China ranked above Brazil, 16th, 28th and 29th, respectively. Russian Federation (73rd) is the lowest ranked country in the BRIC economies

---
5 UNDP Human Development Report, 2008.

Figure 1 | TFP, 2009 Relative Levels and Changes during 1980-2009
Latin America (red), Asia (blue), and OECD (green)

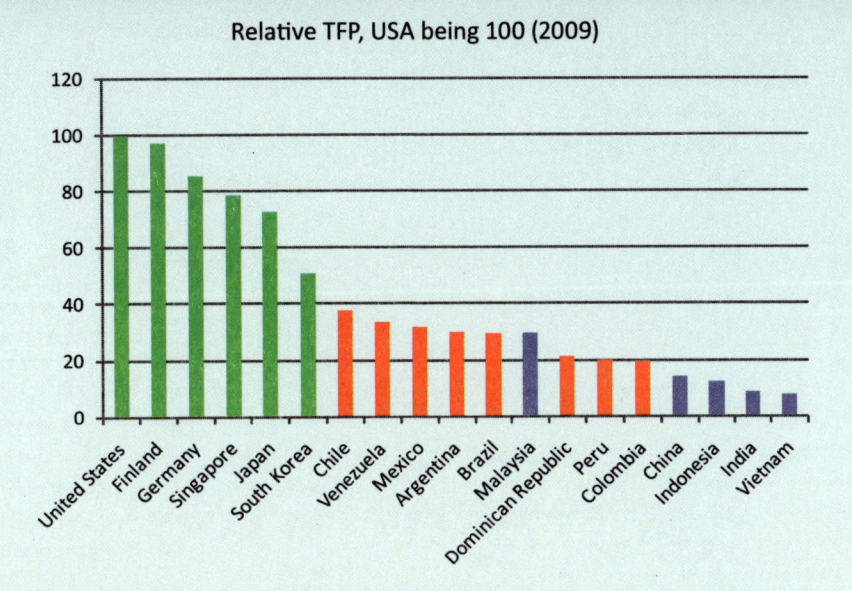

Relative TFP, USA being 100 (2009)

United States	100
Finland	97
Germany	86
Singapore	79
Japan	73
South Korea	51
Chile	38
Venezuela	34
Mexico	32
Argentina	31
Brazil	30
Malaysia	30
Dominican Republic	22
Peru	21
Colombia	21
China	15
Indonesia	14
India	10
Vietnam	9

TFP Change 1980-2009 (%)

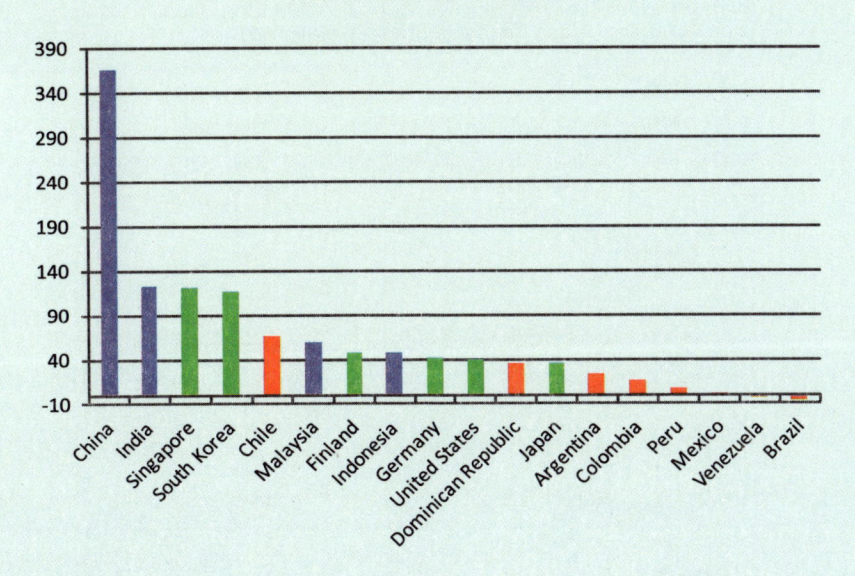

Order (highest to lowest): China (~365), India (~120), Singapore (~120), South Korea (~115), Chile (~65), Malaysia (~55), Finland (~50), Indonesia (~50), Germany (~42), United States (~42), Dominican Republic (~38), Japan (~38), Argentina (~25), Colombia (~20), Peru (~8), Mexico (~0), Venezuela (~0), Brazil (~-2).

Source: Estimates by Homi Kharas.

Figure 2 | **TFP—Latin American countries (red) vs. OECD & NICs (green), Developing Asia (blue), 1980-2007**

TFP 1980-2009 - Latin American & OECD Countries

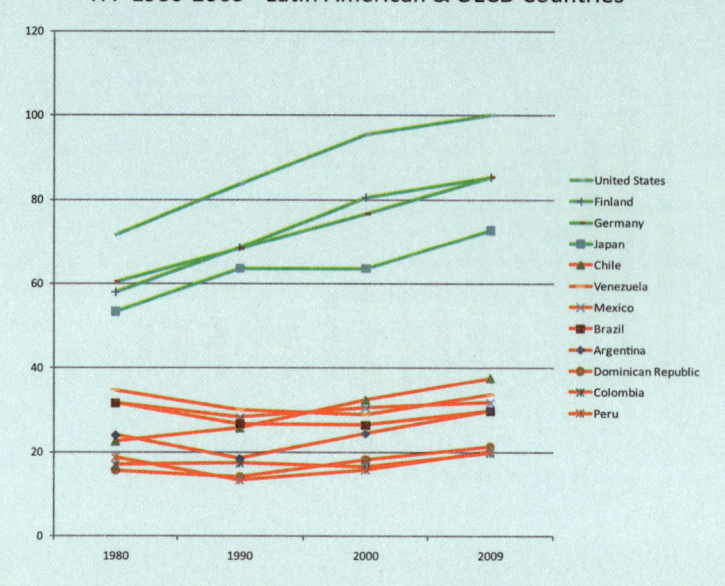

TFP 1980-2009 - Latin American & Asian Countries

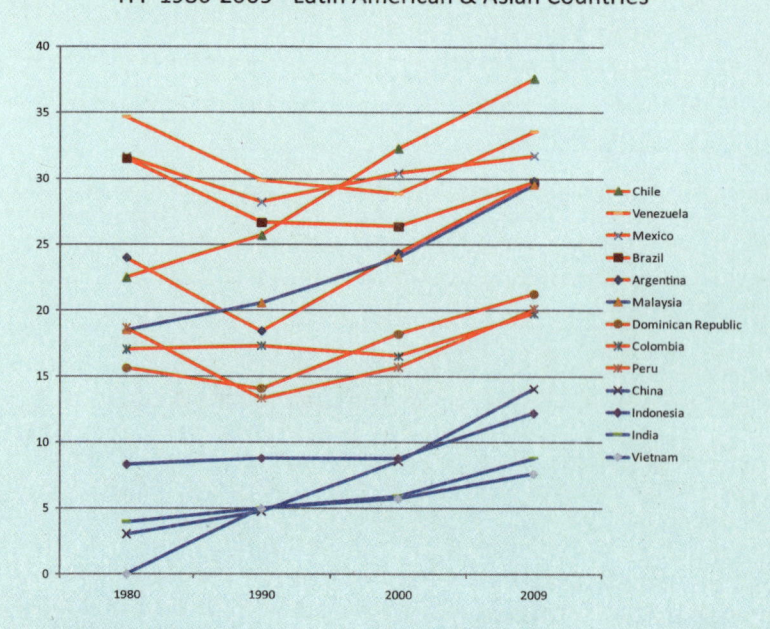

Source: Estimates by Homi Kharas.

Figure 2 cont. TFP—Latin American countries (red) vs. OECD & NICs (green), Developing Asia (blue), 1980-2007

TFP 1980-2009 - Latin American & NIC Countries

Chile, Venezuela, Mexico, Brazil, Argentina, Malaysia, Dominican Republic, Colombia, Peru, China, Indonesia, India, Vietnam

Source: Estimates by Homi Kharas.

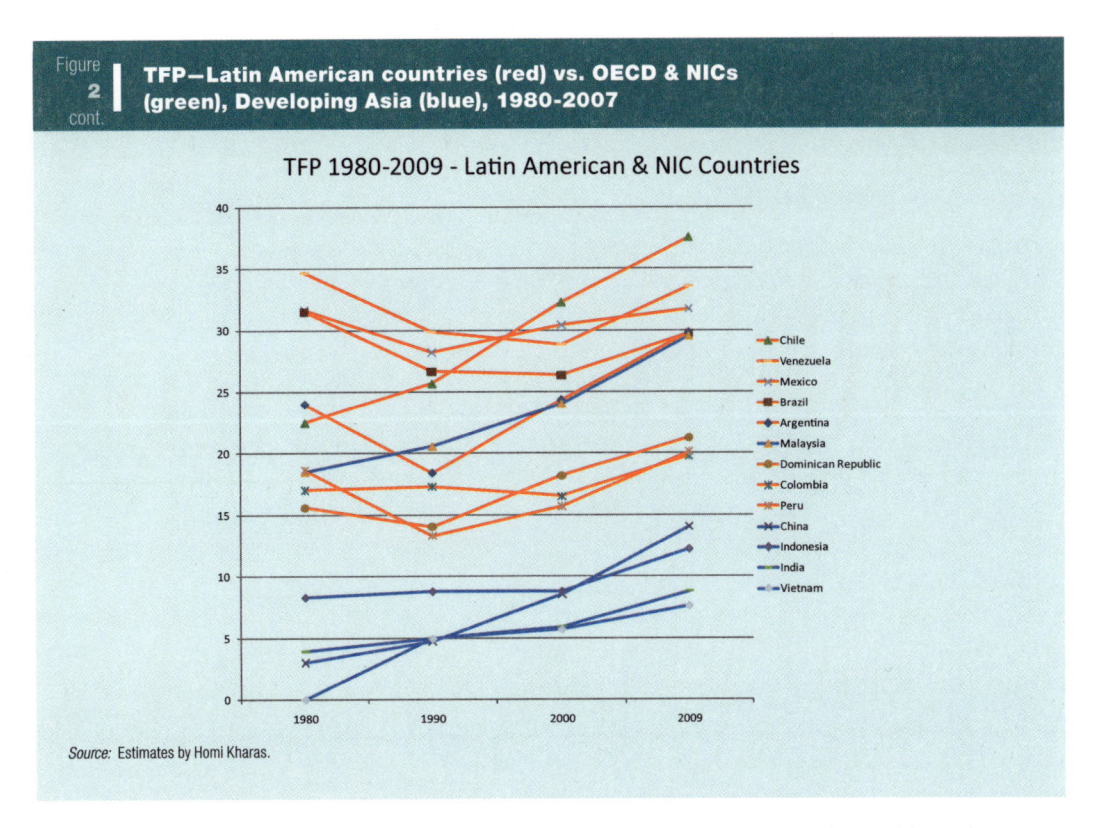

(Brazil, Russia, India and China). The scores of selected Latin American countries and few other economies in the world according to the Global Competitiveness Index are presented in Figure 4 and the Innovation Index in Figure 5.[6]

According to the World Bank's Knowledge Assessment Methodology (KAM) Knowledge Economy Index (KEI),[7] Latin America is lagging behind several regions in the world, such as East Asia and the Pacific, and Europe and Central Asia. Furthermore, Latin America has scores in all categories that are lower than the average of all countries (Table 2).

---

[6] Innovation factors sub-index is composed of business sophistication (networks and supporting industries–local supplier quantity and quality, and state of cluster development-, and sophistication of firms' operations and strategy–nature of competitive advantage, value chain breadth, control of international distribution, production process sophistication, extent of marketing, willingness to delegate authority and reliance on professional management) and innovation (capacity for innovation, quality of science research institutions, company spending on R&D, university-industry research collaboration, government procurement of advanced technology products, availability of scientists and engineers, utility patents and industrial property protection).

[7] The World Bank's Knowledge Assessment Methodology (KAM)'s Knowledge Economy Index (KEI), which is an aggregate index that represents the overall level of development of a country or region towards the Knowledge Economy, takes into account whether the environment is conducive for knowledge to be used effectively for economic development. The Knowledge Index (KI), which measures a country's ability to generate, adopt and diffuse knowledge, is an indication of overall potential of knowledge development in a given country. Innovation system (represented by the variables of Royalty and License Fees Payments and Receipts, Patent Applications Granted by the US Patent and Trademark Office, and Scientific and Technical Journal Articles) is one of the Knowledge Economy pillars used to calculate the KI and KEI index.

Figure 3 | **HDI—Levels and Changes, Selected Countries in Latin America (red), Asia (blue) and OECD (green)**

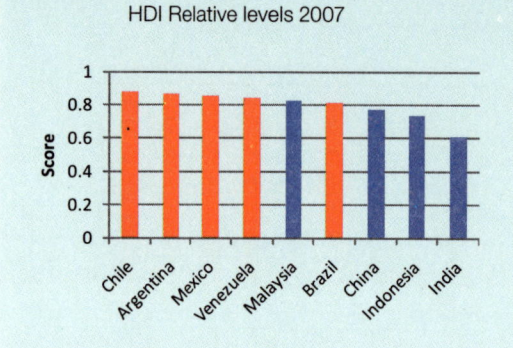

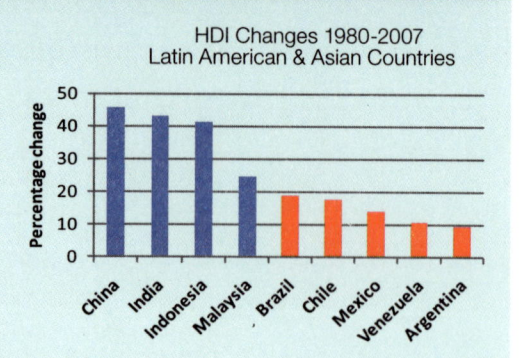

HDI Relative levels 2007: Chile, Argentina, Mexico, Venezuela, Malaysia, Brazil, China, Indonesia, India

HDI Changes 1980-2007, Latin American & Asian Countries: China, India, Indonesia, Malaysia, Brazil, Chile, Mexico, Venezuela, Argentina

Source: UNDP Human Development Report, 2009.

Figure 4 | **Global Competitive Index, 2009—Latin America (red), OECD and NICs (green), Asia (blue)**

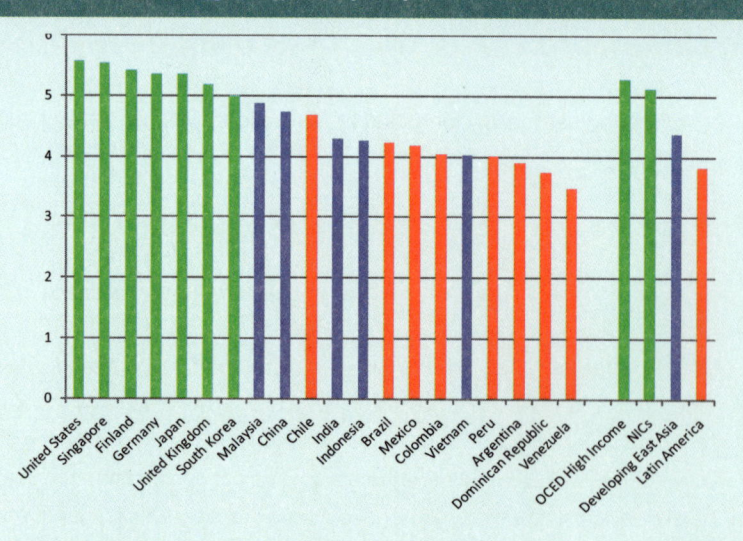

United States, Singapore, Finland, Germany, Japan, United Kingdom, South Korea, Malaysia, China, Chile, India, Indonesia, Brazil, Mexico, Colombia, Vietnam, Peru, Argentina, Dominican Republic, Venezuela, OECD High Income, NICs, Developing East Asia, Latin America

Source: World Global Competitiveness Report, 2009-2010.   Economic Forum,

Figure 5: GCI Innovation Index, 2009 LATAM (red), OECD and NICs (green), Asia (blue)

Source: World Economic Forum, *Global Competitiveness Report*, 2009-2010.

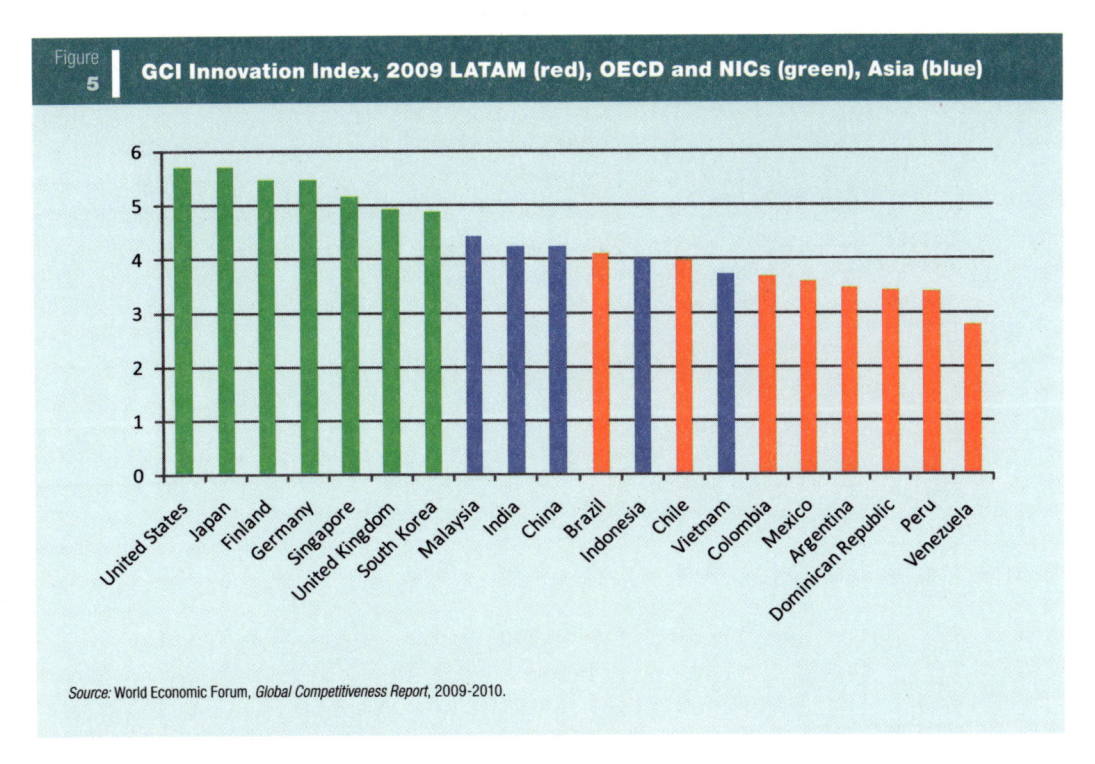

Educated and Skilled Workforce

Latin America needs education in innovation, and innovation in education.

As mentioned earlier, an educated workforce plays a critical role for improving productivity and economic growth. This is also important for improving social growth and equity. In general, Latin American schools do not do a good job of providing the specific skills necessary to be competitive in today's highly globalized world. Even those who achieve basic competency in reading and math are unlikely to acquire the advanced math, science, technology and English skills that allow countries to innovate and attract foreign investment.

Today, as stated in Chapter 5, a greater share of children and youth attend school than at any time in Latin America's history. Pre-school enrollments, which cover nearly two thirds of the eligible population in Latin America, are well above the world average (around 40 percent). In most countries, all but the poorest and most isolated children enroll in primary school, and most manage to graduate. Enrollments at the secondary and tertiary level have also expanded significantly and are larger than world average and other regions. However, increased spending and coverage have not been accompanied by increased learning. Latin America still has a long way to go to ensure that all children receive a quality education.

As shown in Figure 6, the quality of education in Latin American countries lags behind its major competitors in the world. At the tertiary level, enrollments are still half the average for high-income

Table 2. Knowledge Economy Index (KEI) for Selected Groups and Regions, 2009

Country	KEI recent	KEI 1995	Innovation recent	Innovation 1995	Education recent	Education 1995	ICT recent	ICT 1995
Latin America	**5.21**	**5.51**	**5.80**	**6.12**	**5.05**	**4.68**	**5.27**	**6.32**
Western Europe	8.76	8.95	9.27	9.21	8.29	8.66	8.78	9.25
G7	8.72	9.12	9.19	9.3	8.75	9.13	8.8	9.22
High Income	8.23	8.35	9.02	9.14	7.47	7.68	8.42	8.62
Europe and Central Asia	6.45	6.25	6.99	6.90	6.62	6.73	6.46	7.02
East Asia and the Pacific	6.41	6.96	8.49	8.90	5.00	5.50	6.64	7.76
All Countries	5.95	6.35	8.11	8.20	4.24	4.85	6.22	7.52
Upper Middle Income	5.66	5.90	6.03	6.36	5.63	5.59	5.89	6.73
Middle East and North Africa	5.47	5.84	7.57	7.49	3.75	4.13	5.71	7.00
Lower Middle Income	3.78	4.27	4.96	4.93	3.32	3.64	3.85	5.38
Africa	2.71	3.37	4.31	4.57	1.38	1.66	2.45	4.89
South Asia	2.58	3.06	3.29	3.04	1.92	2.15	2.45	4.28
Low Income	2.00	2.83	2.52	2.77	1.61	1.85	1.82	4.54

Source: World Bank, KAM, 2009

countries and well below rates in more successful economies, like the United States and South Korea (Figure 7).

The region's universities produce very few science or engineering graduates. In most countries, less than a quarter receive science or engineering degrees compared to nearly 40 percent of all South Korean university graduates, and nearly 30 percent of all Irish and Finnish graduates (Figure 8). In Latin America, only Mexico has similar rates. The region produces a limited number of scientists and advanced degree recipients, which hinders the region's development. While OECD countries produce

INNOVATION AND TECHNOLOGY DEVELOPMENT FOR ECONOMIC RESTRUCTURING 199

Figure 6. Quality of Education, 2008—Latin America (red), Asia (blue), OECD (green)

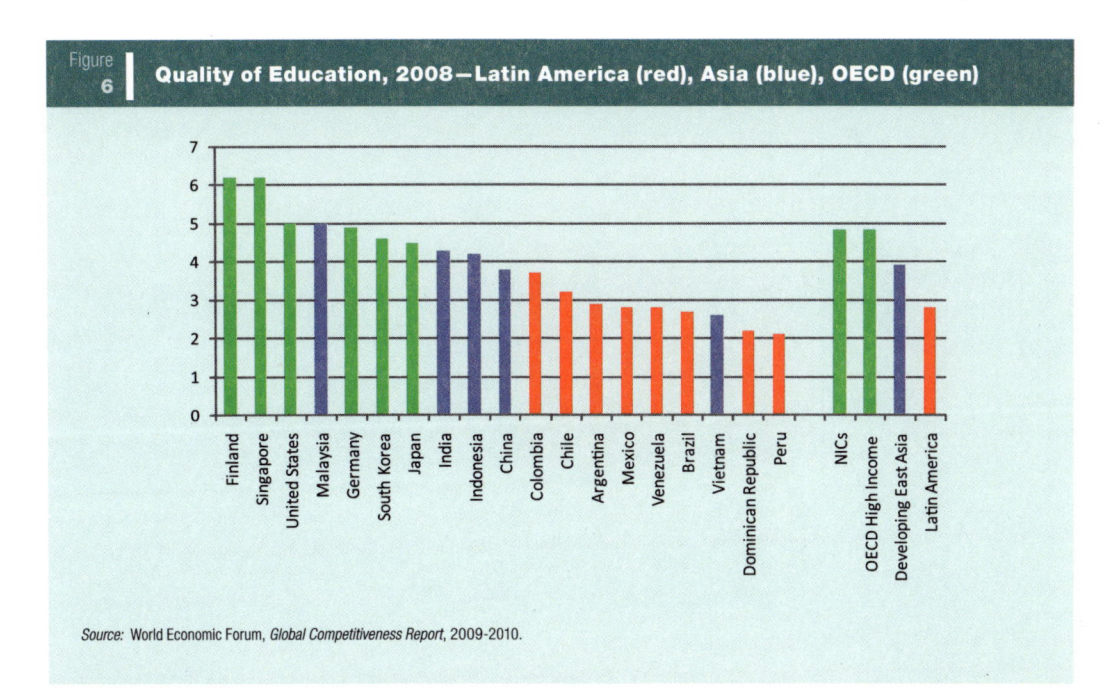

Source: World Economic Forum, *Global Competitiveness Report*, 2009-2010.

Figure 7. Tertiary Enrollment, 2008—Latin America (red), OECD and NICs (green), Asia (blue)

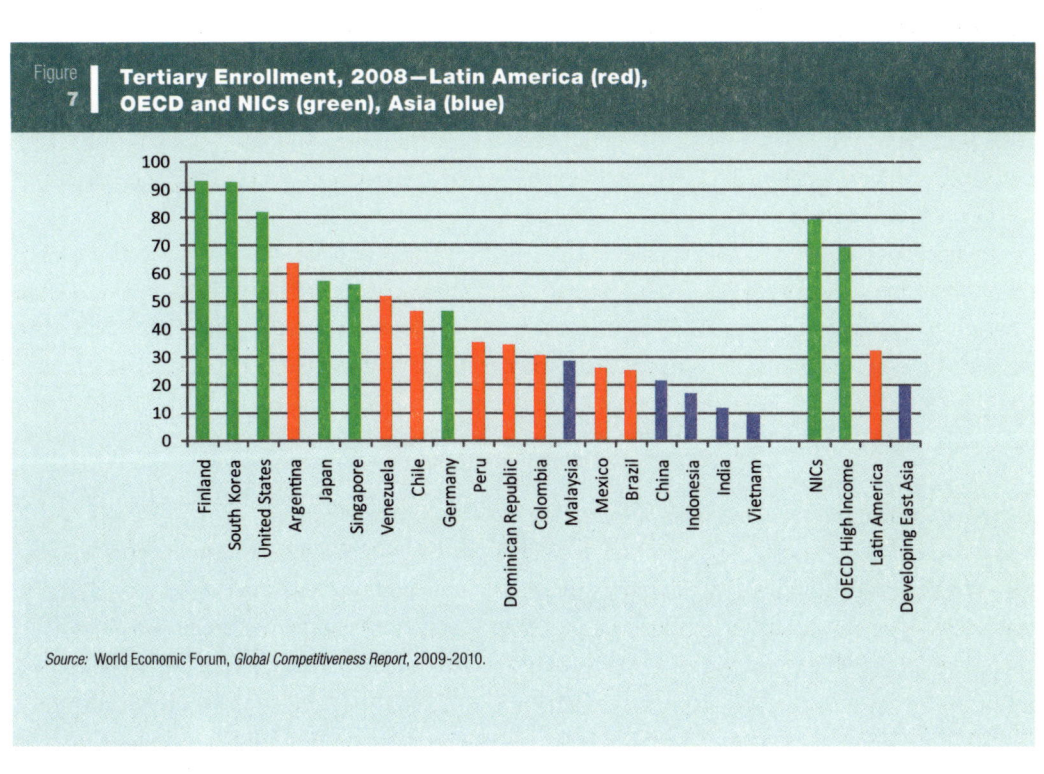

Source: World Economic Forum, *Global Competitiveness Report*, 2009-2010.

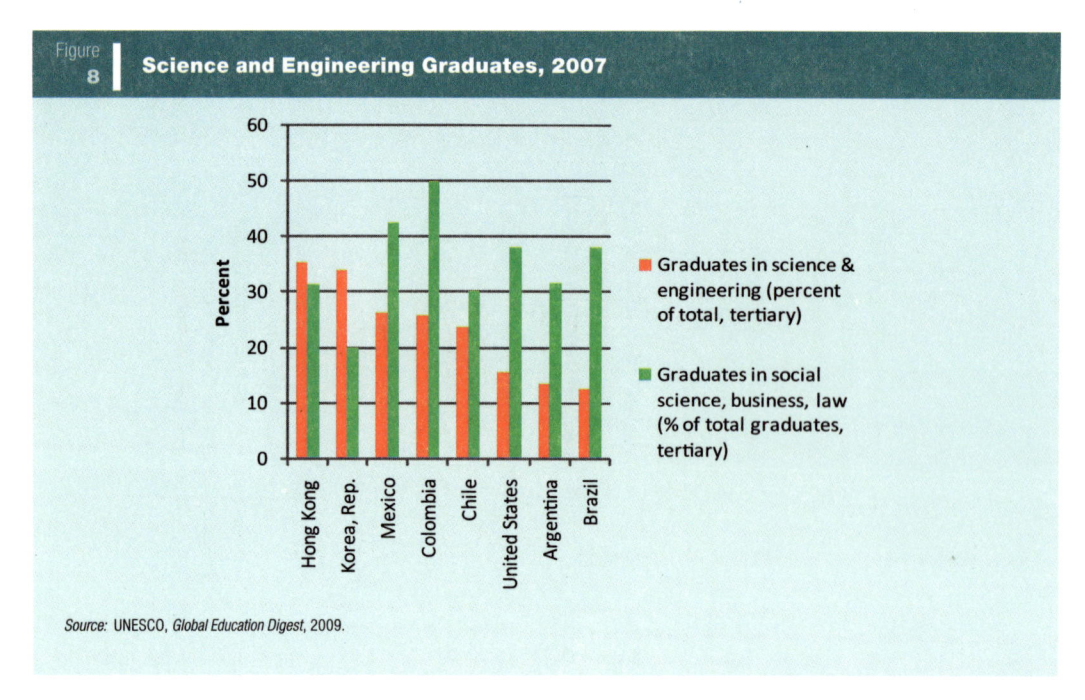

Figure 8. Science and Engineering Graduates, 2007

Bar chart showing percent of graduates in science & engineering (percent of total, tertiary) and graduates in social science, business, law (% of total graduates, tertiary) for Hong Kong, Korea Rep., Mexico, Colombia, Chile, United States, Argentina, and Brazil.

Source: UNESCO, *Global Education Digest*, 2009.

one new PhD per 5,000 people, in Brazil the ratio is 1 per 70,000; in Chile, 1 per 140,000; and in Colombia 1 per 700,000.[8] Brazil produces around 7,000 PhDs per year and scores the highest in domestically formed PhDs in the region (accounting for more than 70 percent of total Latin American PhDs according to RICYT's estimates). Without more qualified advanced degree recipients (especially, in science and engineering), the ability of countries to use and generate knowledge, and adapt and use technology is limited.

As mentioned earlier, education quality in Latin America is low, and the R&D expenditures are inadequate while the activities of R&D system are narrow and disconnected from market demands. Figure 9 depicts technology readiness of selected countries in Latin America in comparison to its major competitors- the index is 4.3 for Latin America in comparison to 6.2 for the OECD high income economies. The index for Chile is 5.2, Brazil 4.8, Mexico 4.0 and Argentina 3.9 in comparison to the United States 6.5, Singapore 6.2, South Korea 5.8 and India 5.2.

Inclusive Innovation: Practical Solutions for the Bottom of the Pyramid

Four billion people—almost 60 percent of the world population—form the base of the economic pyramid—the so called "Bottom of the Pyramid" (BOP) with an income of less than two dollars a day. In many Latin American countries, a significant part of their population live in rural areas and depend on agriculture for their livelihood. Stuck in the poverty zone, they lack access to even basic necessities

---

8 Jeffrey M. Puryear and Tamara Ortega Goodspeed, 2009.

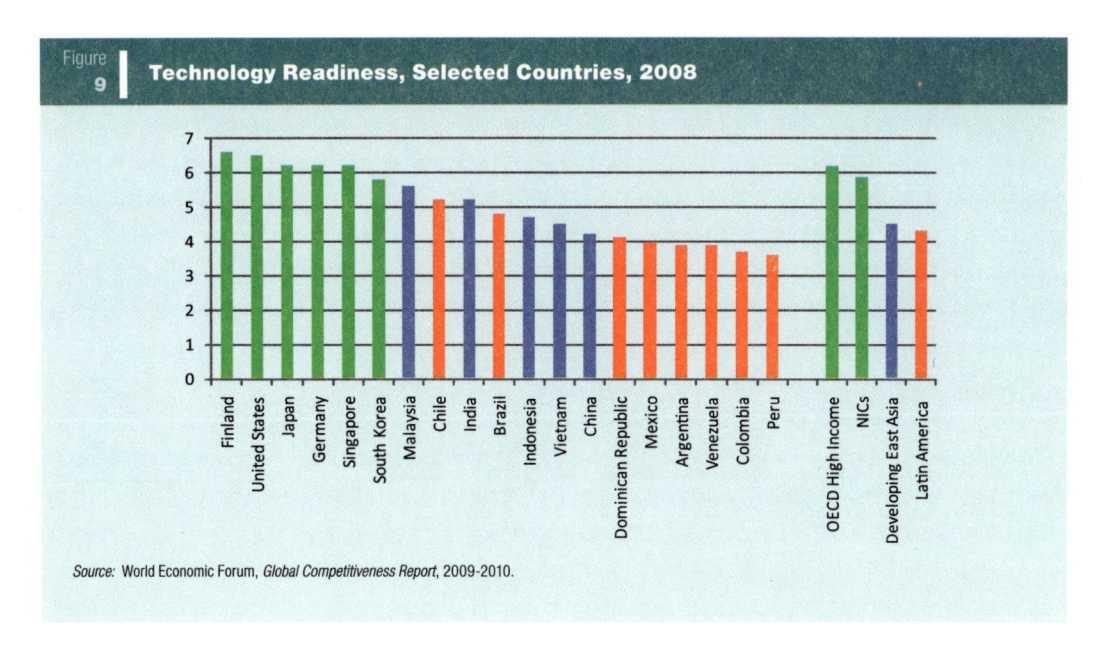

Figure 9 | Technology Readiness, Selected Countries, 2008

[Bar chart showing technology readiness scores (0-7 scale) for: Finland, United States, Japan, Germany, Singapore, South Korea, Malaysia, Chile, India, Brazil, Indonesia, Vietnam, China, Dominican Republic, Mexico, Argentina, Venezuela, Colombia, Peru, OECD High Income, NICs, Developing East Asia, Latin America]

Source: World Economic Forum, *Global Competitiveness Report*, 2009-2010.

of life, such as water and sanitation services, housing, quality education, basic health care, electricity, telephones, roads, and modern financial services. Moreover, they lack access to reliable markets to sell their goods and services, compounded by similarly restrained access as consumers: poorer people are often limited to goods and services that are more expensive and of lower quality—if they are available at all. Yet this group of 4 billion has substantial purchasing power: the BOP constitutes a US$5 trillion global consumer market. Addressing the unmet needs of the BOP segment is therefore not only just an essential element in raising welfare, productivity and income, but also a plausibly sustainable one and important to enhance their contribution to economic activity. Nations and the development community alike need to use creative thinking and all available tools and instruments of public policy and finance to help realize such sustainable provision of basic goods and services to the BOP population.

One such tool which has a great potential is the use of science, technology and innovation (STI) to uplift and empower the BOP, especially the rural society. Innovation-led inclusive growth can "include" hundreds of millions of resource poor people excluded from access to the essential necessities of life. Technologies produced through inclusive innovation need to be "high performance" and "ultra-low cost", and universally applicable and sustainable production.

"Inclusive innovation" or "pro-poor innovation" refers to the knowledge creation, acquisition and absorption efforts targeted directly at meeting the needs of the BOP population, thus making the benefits of science, technology and innovation available to all citizens, especially the disadvantaged. Put differently, inclusive innovation is about harnessing sophisticated science and engineering know-how to addressing the mundane problems faced by billions of people at the BOP. The power behind the concept is perhaps best illustrated through examples of its potential, and examples of boundary-breaking propositions of what can be achieved (Box 1).

All this may seem impossible. Such innovations have already been made possible in many parts of the world—from rural India to MIT in the US. These developments, however, have been episodic, many times made possible by individual initiatives. A central goal for Inclusive Innovation, then, is to deploy our understanding of STI to institutionalize and scale up the innovations done in 'laboratories of life'— achievements that have remained isolated in scope, number and impact and have failed to operate on a large scale due to lack of public funding as well as ineffective innovation chain that links the invention to potential BOP users scattered around the world.

Specifically, Inclusive Innovation can serve these ends by (i) improving access to the most fundamental basic services, (ii) facilitating the diffusion and absorption of knowledge to expand the set of beneficiaries of new and existing BOP innovations, and (iii) providing opportunities for grass-roots innovators to participate in the gains their ideas bring to the economy. The key realization is that private and public sector initiatives can create a self-sustainable system that expands the market for extremely low-cost and quality products, increases the volume of inclusive innovations, focuses resources and attention on this market segment, and makes the provision of public services cheaper and more efficient, and thus more enjoyable by more people. What currently appears far from cost-effective for the private sector—and feats that seem impossible for the public sector given fiscal constraints—need not always be. Applying current technology and know-how to targeted ends—and producing more of it for the precise purpose of lifting up the poor—has already served (millions) across the globe. While Inclusive Innovation would focus on addressing the needs of BOP people, it can also be useful for non-poor people in poor countries as well as people in wealthy countries.

Perhaps the most powerful justification for Inclusive Innovation lies in its already demonstrated results. Recognizing its tremendous potential, many countries (Brazil, China, India, and South Africa) are already pursuing inclusive innovation with increasing success: they are developing quality and affordable products and services that directly benefit the BOP. For example, India's National Innovation Foundation set up to promote inclusive innovation has catalogued some 70,000 grass-roots innovations and is working with technology and engineering institutions as well as with business community to convert many of these grass-roots innovation into viable products and services. That many of these examples appear isolated and serve only a small number of people is no reason to doubt the capabilities of an Inclusive Innovation Agenda. Rather, it explains just how powerful such an agenda can be: Inclusive Innovation agenda would increase the frequency of pro-poor ideas, and facilitate scale-up, diffusion, and absorption of pro-poor technology—removing constraints that limit the impact and scope of such innovations.

Given that many countries do not possess sophisticated STI capabilities, pursuit of the Inclusive Innovation agenda would require forming partnerships with global, regional and national organizations both STI bodies and development finance institutions. This approach will: (i) bring together an unrivalled developmental, financial and STI resource base with significant influence and potential high impact; (ii) provide a potentially powerful approach to leveraging STI resources for the benefit of the

> **Box 1 — Examples of Inclusive Innovation Potential**
>
> **Quality of Life Improvements**
> 1. Access to affordable technology—computers, mobile phones, internet.
> 2. Access to education—access to information, remote access to class room and laboratory facilities, distance learning, online training, access to virtual libraries, books and journals, collaboration with other institutions in the country and abroad to expand education access fast and at lower cost.
> 3. Access to financial services—financial inclusion, online banking, bill payment, delivery of micro-finance services, ATM machines, insurance and investments products.
> 4. Access to health services—ultra low cost diagnostics, therapeutics and vaccines, patient information, access to doctors, information about disease, child and maternity care, etc.
> 5. Farmer services—information on crop patterns and prices, markets conditions, weather forecasts, use of fertilizers and pesticides, crop and livestock insurance.
> 6. Town management—smart towns, access to internet and education services, crime and transport management, and reduction in pollution.
> 7. Use of radio and television broadcasts (sometimes via satellites) for education, agriculture, entertainment, providing information on laws, emergencies and disasters, etc.
> 8. Climate change—energy efficiency, use of renewable energy, use of solar lamps and solar cooking stoves, grid less electricity supply.
> 9. Emergency and disaster management—forecasting tsunami, hurricanes, floods, storms; evacuation plans; and delivery of emergency assistance to victims.
> 10. Access to government—information about policies, laws, rules and regulations, access to land, property and birth records, targeting of public services, etc.
> 11.
>
> **To How Many of These Questions Can Innovation Answer Yes?**
> - Can we make a Hepatitis-B vaccine costing $20 per dose available at 40 times less?
> - Can we make a psoriasis treatment costing $20,000 available at 200 times less?
> - Can we make a comfortable, safe and fuel efficient car available, not at $20,000, but at ten times less?
> - Can we make an artificial foot costing $10,000 made available at 300 times less?
> - Can we make a high quality cataract eye surgery made available, not at $3,000 but at 100 times less
> - Can we make a prostate treatment drug costing $10,000 available today at a price that is 60 times less?
>
> **Above are not just dreams—they have been done already—but on a limited scale.**
>
> *Source:* Vinod K.Goel, 2010

BOP and alleviating poverty, and in meeting the MDGs; and (ii) expedite rolling out of this important agenda at a lower cost. Examples of such partners may include the international financial institutions, donors, the Global Research Alliance (GRA), national and regional S&T and academic institutions, business angel networks, patient capital providers, philanthropic foundations, business community and NGOs.

One of the key Partners could be the Global Research Alliance, a network of nine of the world's most prestigious knowledge-intensive technology and innovation organizations,[9] with a goal of creating "A Global Knowledge Pool for Global Good." The GRA has a capacity to undertake projects with a magnitude and complexity that transcend the capabilities of any single organization. The GRA includes organizations of the Northern and Southern hemisphere, with more than 50,000 scientists and engineers. The Alliance partners perform basic and applied research, technology transfer and commercialization and specialize in the implementation of innovative commercially and socially viable solutions. The GRA has within its ranks highly innovative members who amongst other breakthroughs have developed: the MP3 player, the Xerox copying technology; carbon fiber composite wings for light combat aircraft, space satellite, drought resistant millet, mesh networking for rural internet provision, the world's first 'flu drug, low cost HIV and tuberculosis drugs, an open-source drug discovery platform, etc.

The National Innovation System

The National Innovation System (NIS) of a nation consists of the institutions, laws, regulations and procedures that affect how knowledge is acquired, created, disseminated and applied in the economy. The National Innovation System in Latin America varies across countries. For example, countries such as Argentina, Brazil, Chile and Mexico have a comprehensive and well developed system, while the NIS in countries such as Colombia, Peru, El Salvador and Venezuela is not comprehensive. The Governments from time to time have been taking steps for promoting science, technology and innovation. But most countries lack a coherent STI policy and related tools to implement such a policy, and the actual results on the ground, remain well below desired levels. Although there are exceptions, generally, the public sector dominates in most aspects of STI activities, R&D institutions (RDIs) are not up-to-date, innovation support institutions are mostly ineffective, use of technology and innovation by industry (especially SMEs) is low, and the workforce lacks the requisite skills to generate and use technology. Also, the STI policies in the region have not paid enough attention to the structural transformation of the Public R&D Institutes. The collaboration between innovation actors is either ineffective or weak.

The region is at a cross-road where it needs to upgrade its technology and innovation capabilities in order to improve the competitiveness of its economy, which is necessary for sustainable and inclusive growth, and to move up the value chain ladder in a highly competitive and globalized world. This is all the more critical at a time when the region is looking to advance as a knowledge-based economy that will position the region well for economic expansion and integration into the global economy. The region has a considerable potential for TFP growth and significant catch-up potential in technology for economic growth as well as for improving the lives of all its citizens. In their development strategies, the Governments need to accord a high priority to building an appropriate modern

---

9   These include Battelle Memorial Institute (USA), Commonwealth Scientific and Industrial Research Organisation (CSIRO Australia), Council of Scientific and Industrial Research (CSIR, India), Council for Scientific and Industrial Research (CSIR, South Africa), Danish Technological Institute (DTI, Denmark), Fraunhofer-Gesellschaft (Germany), Netherlands Organization for Applied Scientific Research (TNO), SIRIM Berhard (Malaysia), and Technical Research Centre (VTT Finland).

science, technology and innovation system that is comprehensive, of high quality, and responsive to the demands of their respective economies and society at large. It must be noted that not every country is the same. Therefore, what a STI system should look like, and how (including when and what) this should be achieved will depend upon each country's specific economic and industrial conditions, as well as its needs, capabilities and resources (human, financial and institutional).

Technological Specialization

The technological specialization index (TSI) that measures the degree of technological specialization of a country's exports, proxies the technological dynamism of different countries (and regions) with respect to world trends; TSI is calculated as the share of knowledge intensive sectors in total manufacturing value added. While Asian economies have experienced an increase in the value of the TSI since 1985, Latin America has experienced only a slight increment (Table 3). Furthermore, excluding Mexico, the pattern of the TSI in Latin American countries is almost a flat curve.

In Latin America, the share of technology-intensive sectors, on average, is below 30 percent of the total value added of the domestic manufacturing industry; while in frontier and emerging economies, those sectors contribute to generate more than 60 percent of total manufacturing value added, as it is the case of the United States and South Korea. On average, during the eighties and the nineties, Latin American countries have experienced a process of erosion of production capacities and technological capabilities, coupled with less entrepreneurial efforts in R&D and increased imports of capital goods

Table 3 | Technological Specialization Index: Selected Countries, 1970-2007

Country	1970	1980	1990	1997	2003	2007
Argentina	22.7	24.9	14.1	17.4	13.0	17.2
Brazil	22.0	32.3	27.8	33.7	33.2	39.6
Chile	16.6	11.0	10.2	12.4	11.3	11.6
Colombia	11.3	11.3	10.4	12.4	11.2	12.3
Mexico	20.2	26.9	26.3	30.5	33.0	41.3
Venezuela	9.0	14.2	9.4	13.5	10.3	12.9

Source: Cimoli et al., 2009.

for modernization. In more recent years, between 2003 and 2007, there has been a slight revival of those sectors, which started to regain weight in the regional industry.

However, Latin America stays behind the technological frontier both in terms of technological specialization and productivity growth. In many Latin American countries (such as Argentina, Chile and Colombia), the increasing share of natural resources has not been accompanied with a process of generalized technological upgrading. Brazil and Mexico are, to some extent, exceptions since the industrial structure has been transformed in favor of the engineering sectors; however, this has failed to produce a significant impact on aggregate productivity. The combination of a traditional macroeconomic management with a lack of real coordination in policies fostering industrial development and structural change contributes to explain the general stickiness in aggregate productivity growth in Brazil. Mexico, on the other hand, followed a different strategy, pushing for increasing openness coupled with policies to support the integration of the local manufacturing industry to global production networks.

R&D Expenditure and R&D Capacity

Generally, for emerging economies, research and development (R&D) should be both a high value-added sector and an engine of increased productivity across other industries and of improved quality of life. While world expenditure on R&D follows a rising trend, the US, Japan, Germany, France and the United Kingdom represent around 66 percent of total investment in R&D. Latin America is still a marginal player accounting for less than 2 percent of world R&D expenditure. There is a persistent gap in R&D expenditure as percent of GDP between Latin America and the rest of the world. With the exception of Brazil, the gross expenditure on R&D (GERD) as a percentage of GDP in Latin American countries is below 1 percent. The average R&D intensity in the region was 0.6 percent in 2006 as opposed to the 2.7 percent in the USA, 3.0 percent in Japan, 2.3 percent in OECD and 1.8 percent in the EU-27. Brazil, Chile and Argentina are the three Latin American countries which have the highest share of GERD in GDP in the region (Figure 10).

Total R&D expenditures for those Latin American countries for which data are available increased from around US$15 billion in 1997 (PPP) to US$34 billion (PPP) in 2007. This figure is less than 10 percent of the R&D investment of the USA (US$368 billion) in 2007 and certainly a much lower ratio to GDP. Brazil is the only country with a notable R&D investment which is comparable to that of Canada and Spain (Figure 13). Four countries account for 88 percent of all R&D expenditures in the region (Brazil 60 percent, Mexico 16 percent, Argentina 8 percent, and Chile 4 percent).

The number of total researchers (Full Time Equivalent, FTE) in Latin America is significantly lower than in the advanced economies and catching-up countries like China and India. Brazil, the best performing country in the region in this indicator, has the lowest number of total FTE R&D personnel among the BRIC economies: The total number of FTE researchers in Brazil is 84,979 while it is 466,253 in Russia, 115,936 in India and 1,223,756 in China. The rate of increase in China has been dramatic (123 percent) in ten years during 1996-2006. The only Latin American country that experi-

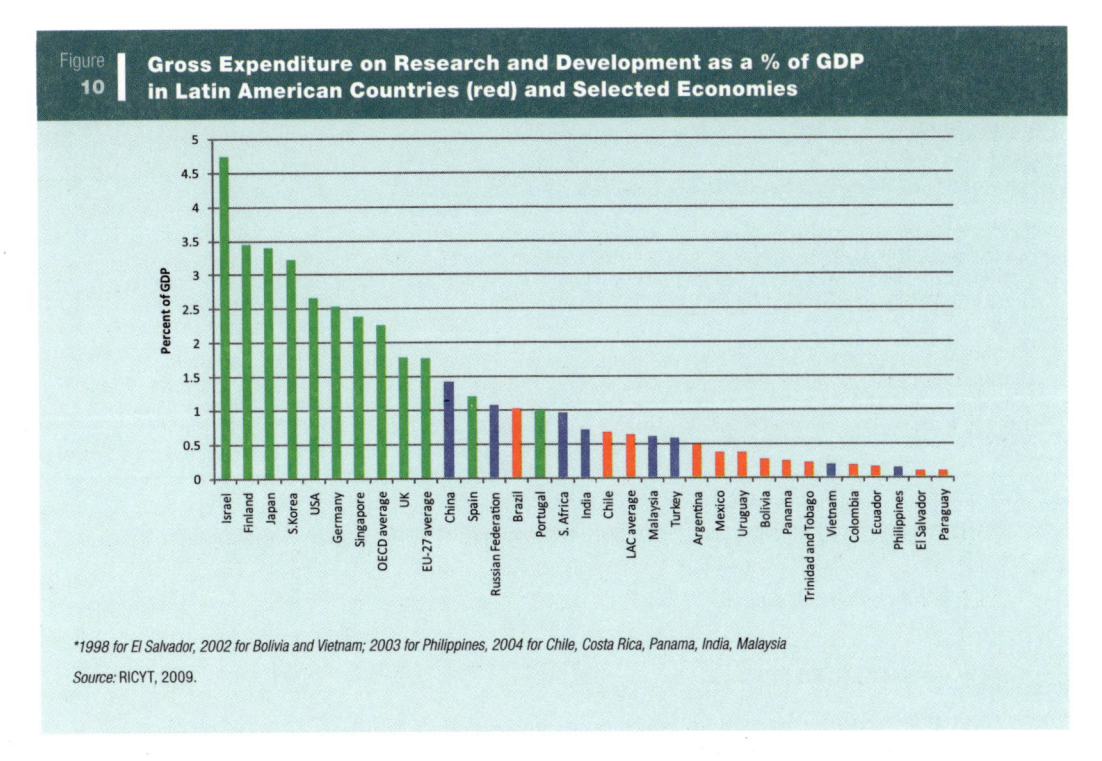

Figure 10 | Gross Expenditure on Research and Development as a % of GDP in Latin American Countries (red) and Selected Economies

*1998 for El Salvador, 2002 for Bolivia and Vietnam; 2003 for Philippines, 2004 for Chile, Costa Rica, Panama, India, Malaysia

Source: RICYT, 2009.

enced a similar progress in this indicator has been Mexico, which achieved an increase of 143 percent over the same period.

In Latin America, R&D spending is not homogeneously spread among regional countries (Figure 11). More proactive countries in terms of R&D spending are Brazil, Mexico, Argentina and Chile, which as a whole account for almost 88 percent of the regional spending. The business sector is the smaller actor in R&D performance in Latin America, accounting for 40 percent of total expenditure, even though it augmented its share from the 20 percent of the 1980s. Almost 70 percent of R&D spending is carried out by enterprises in OECD countries including USA, Japan, South Korea, Singapore and China. Furthermore, deep heterogeneity emerges within regional countries. In Argentina, Brazil, Mexico, Paraguay and Uruguay, enterprises carry out more than 30 percent of total R&D spending, while in Ecuador and Colombia, the participation of the private sector in R&D execution is the lowest. Divergences in terms of efforts and type of R&D activities carried out mirror the asymmetry in specialization patterns between the region and more advanced economies. Box 2 provides a snapshot of BRIC economies.

As mentioned earlier, in most cases, the R&D expenditures in the region are inadequate and the activities of R&D system are narrow and disconnected from market demands. Some Latin American countries have created significant capacity in R&D but they have not been able to build virtuous links among relevant social actors involved in knowledge production and use. Today, in most nations of the region, knowledge created in the R&D laboratories tends to stay in the lab, remaining to the confines

> **Box 2 | Innovation in BRIC Countries**
>
> The BRIC economies (Brazil, Russia, India and China) form a diverse group of countries that are the world's largest developing and transition economies. The last 10 to 15 years have been characterized by a substantially higher economic growth at the world level driven by the emerging BRIC economies, and accompanied with an expansion of world trade and capital movements.
>
> Looking at the current growth trends, the three fastest growing economies in the world over the five-year period 2004-2008 are China (10.8 percent), India (8.5 percent) and Russia (7 percent). The growth in Brazil (4.7 percent) over this five-year period has not quite reached these figures. The average economic growth rate of BRICs in this period was about 7.8 percent, far above that of the world.
>
> | | Brazil | Russia | India | China |
> | --- | --- | --- | --- | --- |
> | GDP (2008, current US$ billion) | 1,575 | 1,680 | 1,160 | 4,327 |
> | GDP per capita (2008 PPP) | 9,500 | 14,700 | 2,721 | 5,515 |
> | Merchandise exports (% of world total) | 1.14 | 2.52 | 1.00 | 8.02 |
> | Service exports (% of world total) | 0.65 | 1.11 | 2.71 | 3.30 |
> | Population (million, 2008) | 192 | 142 | 1,140 | 1,325 |
> | Gini Coefficient (2007) | 55.0 | 43.7 | 36.8 | 41.5 |
> | R&D spending (2006, nominal US$ billion) | 11.1 | 10.65 | 7.3 | 37.7 |
> | R&D spending (2006, % of GDP) | 1.02 | 1.07 | 0.79 | 1.42 |
> | S&T articles (2005) | 9,895 | 14,424 | 14,622 | 41,604 |
>
> Source: Dahlman, Carl, 2008 and World Bank - *World Development Indicators* database

Figure 11: Expenditure on R&D (US$ billion PPP), 2007*

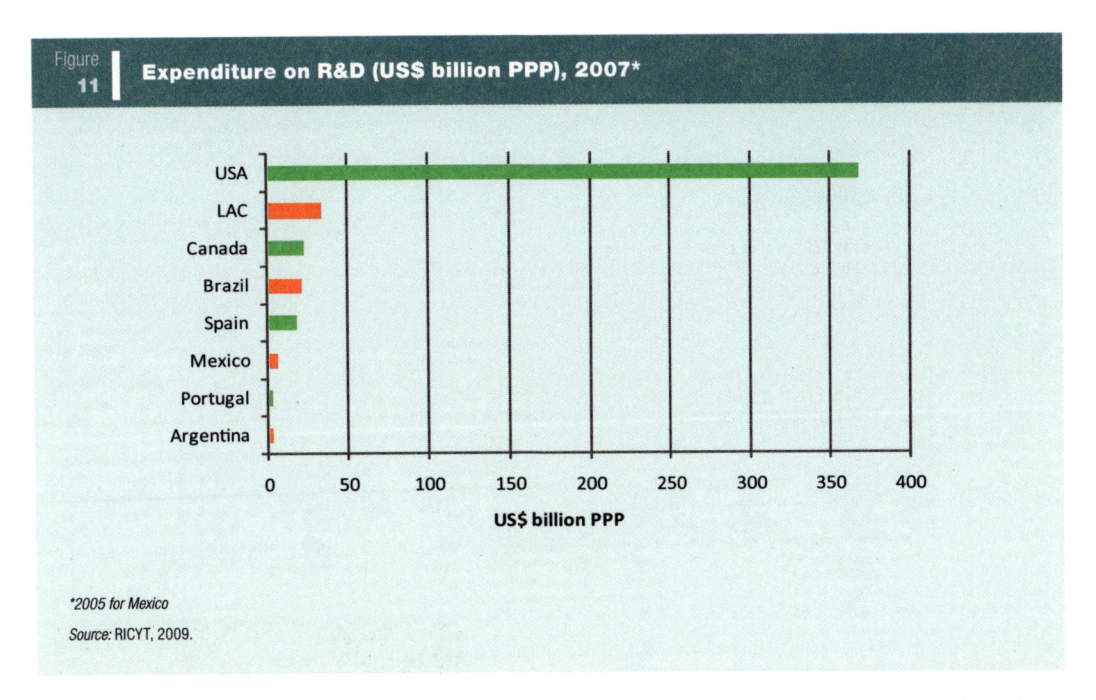

Country	US$ billion PPP
USA	~370
LAC	~30
Canada	~22
Brazil	~20
Spain	~18
Mexico	~5
Portugal	~3
Argentina	~2

*2005 for Mexico
Source: RICYT, 2009.

of research papers rather than converted into licenses, patents, products, processes and services. Further, most nations are not taking full advantage of the global knowledge that is becoming increasingly abundant and cheaper. There are problems at both the supply and demand side. On the supply side, universities and public RDIs which together perform almost 70 percent of R&D, have not created mechanisms to identify/market user needs of their economies; instead they focus mostly on the publishable mainstream science. At the same time, there has not been much demand for local R&D from the industry. Government initiatives to address this imbalance have not been too successful. With appropriate reforms, Latin American countries can convert their aspiring populations into knowledge workers, build an environment conducive to innovation, and tap into this source of long-term economic and social growth.

Agenda for the Transformation of Technology Development and Innovation

For their people, Latin American countries need to transform a narrow conduit into a veritable pipeline of opportunity, starting with basic education and moving on to higher and vocational education and creating high-paying jobs. They need to increase the supply of trained and highly educated workers to improve competitiveness and growth trajectory, create more and better quality jobs and enable all people to realize their aspirations. They should strive to create conducive macro-economic and business environment, and invest in technology development and innovation, where enterprises in all sectors of their economy achieve domestic (and international as appropriate) benchmark levels of productivity. They must ensure that education and job opportunities are available to all citizens and that the benefits of progress reach rich and poor, rural and urban alike. At the same time, the region should advance its strategic pursuits, including energy efficiency and clean energy provision beyond hydroelectricity, low-cost healthcare, and other applications such as agriculture, space and defense.

Governments in many countries are devoting increased attention to bolstering business innovation capabilities. This interest reflects growing recognition of both the importance of technology and innovation in driving economic growth and the dominant role of the business sector in that process. In developed economies, business not only outspends the public sector on R&D (by a factor of two in OECD countries), but is the main source of the new products, processes and services that innovation brings to the market place. Designing effective incentives and support systems for private sector innovation is a challenging task. While many of the standard policy instruments—government grants, tax incentives, loans, partnerships and the like—are well-known and widely used, their effectiveness depends on their specific design and degree of adaptation to local (national) needs. In addition, policy makers must consider the overall mix of policies used to stimulate innovation. They must determine, for example, how best to balance broad-based horizontal policies against targeted measures that support specific sets of firms, technologies or industry sectors.

It must be recognized that not every country is the same and each has different economic, industrial, educational, social and cultural conditions. Therefore, what a STI system should look like in a given country, and how this should be built will depend upon each country's specific economic, industrial and social conditions, as well as the needs of its economy and society and its human, financial and institutional capabilities. Furthermore, not every country needs, or even more importantly, can afford to build a sophisticated STI infrastructure due to its economic conditions and capabilities. Therefore, nations need to be pragmatic while designing STI policies, institutions and programs. They must give high priority to cooperation and collaboration with other countries in the region (and internationally) before embarking on this endeavor by themselves. This will be a highly sensible, effective and efficient approach to follow, taking advantage of already existing facilities and capabilities in countries with better STI systems.

In this context, for the purposes of designing strategies for the upgrading of their STI systems, we classify Latin American countries into three groups from the technology and innovation point of view (not on political or economic aspects). In designing a pragmatic innovation policy agenda adapted to local conditions in a particular country, it is important, inter alia, to consider: (i) implementation of innovation programs and policies, taking due account of strengths and capabilities of countries at different development

Photo Credit: CAF

Table 4: Innovation Strategies for Selected Country Clusters

Clusters (selected countries)	Technological Capabilities and Demand Level	Suggested Innovation Strategy
I. Argentina, Brazil, Chile, Colombia, Mexico	High STI capabilities High Needs	Development of frontier technologies Increase value added of natural resources Technology commercialization
II. Dominican Republic, El Salvador, Panama, Peru, Uruguay, Costa Rica	Medium STI capabilities Good Needs	Adaptation of technologies available worldwide Upgrading NIS over time
III. Bolivia, Ecuador, Venezuela, Honduras, Paraguay	Low STI capabilities Medium Needs	Adoption of technologies and expertise Collaboration with other countries

Source: Author's own estimates, 2009.

levels; (ii) evaluation of innovation systems and policy actions, and related methods; and (iii) a long term agenda for innovation policies and programs to tackle global challenges to be faced in the 21st century. An appropriate and efficient intervention at the macro level should focus on those sectors or sites and groups of people who have the most likelihood of successful development in view of their competences, comparative advantages, networking, etc.

- Group I would include countries such as Argentina, Brazil, Chile, Colombia and Mexico. These are innovation leaders in the region today with comprehensive NIS capabilities as well as high demands for the use of technology and innovation in their economies.
- Group II would include countries such as El Salvador, Panama, Peru and Uruguay. They possess a medium level of NIS capabilities but have good needs for the use of technology and innovation in their economies.
- Group II would comprise countries such as Bolivia, Ecuador, Venezuela, Honduras and Paraguay. These are characterized by weak NIS capabilities as well as medium needs for the use of technology and innovation.

As presented in Table 4, different STI strategies can be considered depending on the scientific and technological level of a country and the technological needs of its economy and business climate. The objective in all cases is to promote a successful "self discovery process" by appropriate combinations of public and private players, taking the best advantage of the situation they are facing with its constraints and opportunities.

Group I countries, such as Argentina, Brazil, Chile, Colombia and Mexico, should pursue frontier as well as inclusive innovation to benefit their entire people. They need to have an integrated science, technology and innovation system that is driven by excellence to improve their place in the global technology ladder, as several East Asian countries (such as Japan, South Korea and Singapore) have done in the past 50 years and as China and India are doing today. They need a technology and innovation system that is driven by the private sector, is highly productive, globally competitive, and capable of meeting the needs of their globalizing economy, uplifting the productivity of the formal and informal sector, as well as satisfying the aspirations of all their citizens. This will require an increase in R&D expenditure from 0.6 percent to 2 percent of GDP in the long run-- to be invested by both the public sector and the private sector-- pursuing frontier, strategic and inclusive innovation, enhancing commercializable R&D, and creating a foundation to diffuse and encourage the absorption of existing and newly created technologies.

Group II countries, such as Dominican Republic, El Salvador, Panama, Peru, Uruguay and a few others, should also pursue a similar strategy. Initially, they should focus on the adoption and absorption of globally available technologies throughout their economies. At the same time, they need to take steps to develop over time an integrated science, technology and innovation system. This will require an increase in R&D investments to around 1.0-1.5 percent of GDP in the long run.

Group III countries, such as Bolivia, Ecuador, Venezuela, Honduras, Paraguay and others, should pursue technology absorption and inclusive innovation to benefit their people. This will require an increase in investments to much less than 1.0 percent of GDP in the long run.

As mentioned earlier, all countries need to improve the quality of education at all levels (especially, at the tertiary education) and to increase the supply of highly educated and skilled workforce, including an increase of science and engineering graduates.

Possible Agenda for Reform and Transformation

To translate the above ambitious technology and innovation agenda into concrete actions will require a major shift in the roles of the government and the private sector including FDI. The governments should normally play a facilitating role with smart regulations, proper oversight, and financing, as well as through enhancing private sector participation with proper policies, tax and other incentives, and by leveraging international knowledge and financial resources. Governments should focus their energy and resources on public goods where social returns are highest. A large presence of the private sector and FDI is necessary to ensure expansion, high quality output and relevance where public sector initiatives have been inefficient, insufficient and unreliable and have affected both quantity and quality outputs. The region has much to learn from the "islands of excellence", countries that are innovating- (e.g., Chile, Brazil, Mexico, China, India, and South Korea) and from the U.S. system, which has the most creative, productive and market-relevant STI system that excels globally.

To pursue the above agenda for the upgrading of their science, technology and innovation system, the Latin American countries could benefit from some of the following. Countries will have to be pragmatic and selective in choosing relevant initiatives that best suit their economic, social and cultural conditions, and requirements.

1. *Enabling Environment.* Improve political stability, macro-economic conditions, and business environment (including trade, competition, education and skills, land and labor markets, exit and entry conditions, access to finance, ICT infrastructure, etc.). These are necessary elements for promoting technology development, use and innovation in any economy. **Applicable to All countries.**
2. *Regional Cooperation.* Enhance cooperation and collaboration between countries in the region (and outside the region) to leverage existing STI facilities and capabilities in countries with better STI systems (such as Argentina, Brazil, Chile, Mexico). This will help achieve easier, faster results and benefits for all countries and at a lower cost. Smaller countries which either do not have the capacity to build STI systems or lack adequate demand to use expansive STI systems should use STI facilities of larger countries. **Applicable to All countries.**
3. *Educated and Skilled Workforce.* Increase investments in education to improve education at all levels. Improve the number (and quality) of the education and training institutions, including production of more science and engineering graduates, especially MS and PhDs, in order to increase the supply of skilled workforce with capabilities to generate, adapt and use knowledge and technology. Human capital is critical for tapping into domestic and global knowledge. Increasing enrolment of the rural and urban poor should advance the spread of new ideas, best practices, newer technologies and the application of knowledge to low-productivity agriculture and industries. **Applicable to All countries.**
4. *Regional Universities.* Establish few world class "Regional Universities" (with international collaboration) with modern governance, management and curricula, and with a merit-based process of faculty and students intake. These Universities, which could be setup with help from international institutions (such as CAF), should help offer opportunities to students from all the countries in the region. **Applicable to Group I countries.**
5. *Inclusive Innovation.* Pursue frontier as well as "inclusive innovation" with the dual purposes of global competitiveness and inclusive growth to benefit all people. By encouraging research institutions and universities to also focus on the needs of poor people and by improving the ability of informal firms to absorb new technologies and knowledge, the costs of goods and services can be lowered income-earning opportunities can be created for poor people and rural population. **Applicable to All countries.**
6. *Centers of Excellence.* Create "Centers of Excellence" in certain countries (with regional mandates). These could include increased efforts in producing more economically-relevant public goods, such as pre-competitive research, and socially-relevant innovations, such as access to clean water, urban congestion, urban transport, clean energy technologies, renew-

able energy, traditional medicine, public health, and technologies for sustainable livelihoods. **Applicable to Group I Countries.**

7. *Research & Development.* Provide public finance for basic research and also support applied research and technology dispersion, since R&D has both public good and private good elements. Such support should be result-based and provided competitively. The government should provide incentives (such as R&D tax credits, matching grants, loan guarantees, technology rewards and training support) to the public and private sector for applied research, technology development, use and dispersion. There is a significant potential to increase productivity by diffusing knowledge produced at the local and regional academic and R&D institutions. This requires appropriate technological commercialization infrastructure, including IP protection, technology transfer units at universities and R&D institutes, science and technology parks, incubators, early stage finance and venture capital. For example, the United States government provides 20-25 per cent of funds for early-stage technology development through programs such as the Small Business Innovation Research program and the Advanced Technology Program, a stage in the innovation cycle that private investors often find too risky. Such programs help to develop synergies among universities, R&D labs and industry. **Applicable to Group I and II Countries.**

8. *Public Research Institutions.* Review the performance of public R&D institutions, and pursue appropriate actions to right size them—including exit, privatization and transfer to universities, as well as closing some. The remaining ones should be operated like commercial corporations with increased cross-institutional (and regional) synergies. They should earn revenues and be subject to transparent management and accountability with a strong focus on commercialization of R&D and meeting of market needs. After their restructuring, the RDIs should position themselves to focus strongly on key areas of national importance—technology diffusion, inclusive innovation, and the development of cutting edge technologies such as climate change related technologies. The public R&D networks must play a strong role in these areas as the private sector is not likely to invest in such technologies at least during the next decade. **Applicable to Group I and II countries.**

9. *Innovation infrastructure.* Upgrade basic innovation MSTQ and IPR infrastructure. Latin American countries need modern intellectual property and metrology, standards, testing, and quality (MSTQ) systems to enhance innovation and technology diffusion and contribute to enterprise competitiveness, innovation and trade. A modern intellectual property regime is critical for promoting innovation and facilitating technology commercialization. At the same time, nations must protect their knowledge dissemination interests at the lowest possible costs, especially in areas of public concern such as health, and defend their interests in new technologies not yet fully regulated by international agreements. The government, recipients of funds, the inventor, and the public benefit from the protection and commercialization of intellectual property in the legislative framework introduced recently (similar to the U.S. Bayh-Dole Act of 1980) for incentivizing innovators and commercializing public funded R&D. While

some Latin American countries have a fairly well developed MSTQ system, it is dominated by the public sector, and coverage, quality and use of services are low. **Applicable mostly to Group I and II countries.**

10. *Innovation Eco-system.* Develop an innovation eco-system that facilitates rather than restricts intellectual property policies; venture capital financing, whose tolerance of risk taking, failure and ambiguity is built into its policy framework; attractive and appropriate rewards and incentive systems; positive tax credits that facilitate research and innovation; and science and technology parks and incubation centers. Some selective countries in Latin America need to set up science and technology parks with world-class infrastructure through private partnerships in large metropolitan cities with clusters of higher education and R&D institutions, along the lines of similar zones in China (China has more than 100 science and technology parks). The region can also benefit by establishing export promotion zones, where universities, national laboratories and industry are encouraged to set up R&D facilities and start-ups in promising high-technology areas in manufacturing and services. In addition, programs should promote the establishment of technology incubators in major universities to support scientists in starting commercial activities based on indigenous technologies developed at their institutions. **Applicable mostly to Group I & II countries.**

11. *Agricultural R&D.* Increase investments in agricultural R&D and technology absorption to improve productivity, reduce dependence of population on agriculture, and improve the lives of rural people. This will require increased R&D, technology extension, training, better access to markets, and developing agro-business enterprises. Agriculture will continue to play a significant role in most Latin American countries. In most countries, a significant portion of population is employed and still depends on agriculture for their livelihood. **Applicable to almost all countries—R&D for Group I and II countries.**

12. *Domestic and Global Knowledge.* Provide incentives to businesses to harness domestic and global knowledge. Creating new knowledge, while necessary, is costly and risky and requires scientific talent and other infrastructure. Economies that are still behind the technological frontier get larger gains in productivity and improvements in welfare from adopting existing knowledge than from doing R&D to push back the technological frontier. The main means of tapping into rapidly expanding global knowledge are trade, FDI, technology licensing, copying and reverse engineering, foreign education and training, stronger regional and foreign collaboration, access to Diaspora, and foreign technical information in print and on the Internet. **Applicable to All countries.**

13. *Research and Education Networks.* Establish, on a public-private basis, Regional Research and Education Networks—high-speed region-wide dedicated links to expand opportunities, tap global knowledge and improve access to information and technology for Latin American citizens. This will act as a tool for expanding education opportunities and as an anchor of a productive innovation system. While it would be very difficult (and expensive) to rapidly scale up the domestic education outputs that are required by many countries, a regional research

and education network could tap into global knowledge and improve access to information for all citizens. Using high-speed dedicated links (of 10 gigabits per second), the network should establish its own information and communication technology system within the country/region and with the world's foremost national research and education networks. The network infrastructure linking colleges, universities, R&D labs, libraries and other resources could significantly benefit educators, researchers and students across a wide range of disciplines. Many colleges and universities do not have adequate lab and library facilities, while many other institutions in some countries and abroad have excellent teaching and research facilities that could be available through distance learning programs to institutions that lack such tools. With its own high-speed links, the region can also join in the international collaboration on new standards and new global network infrastructure technologies and applications. **Applicable mostly to Group I and II countries.**

Chapter 7
Infrastructure Needs for a Resurgent Latin America

Harpaul Alberto Kohli and Phillip Basil

Introduction[1]

Central to Latin America's long-term economic prospects and social well-being is increased investment in infrastructure. Various studies carried out by multilateral institutions such as Corporación Andina de Fomento (CAF) and the World Bank, as well as many national authorities have repeatedly emphasized the critical role of quality infrastructure services in enhancing economic productivity and competition, and in accelerating social inclusion. Additionally, it is widely acknowledged that physical connectivity is essential for facilitating regional trade and cooperation between Latin American economies. In short, infrastructure development is critical to all three major pillars of the strategy proposed in this book: enhancing social inclusion, increasing economic productivity, and promoting greater openness and regional cooperation.

Yet, it is widely acknowledged that, as a result of inadequate investment during the past three decades, most Latin American economies now lag behind fast-growing East Asian economies in the quality of infrastructure services. A major report released by CAF in 2009[2] provides an excellent analysis of the current state of play of infrastructure in its member countries, the reasons for it, and, importantly, the necessary remedial measures—policy, strategy, and institutional reforms. A brief summary of these measures is given in Chapter 1 of the CAF report. Accordingly, this chapter does not cover these aspects.

Photo Credit: CAF

---

1 This chapter is based on a more detailed forthcoming paper (Kohli and Basil 2011). The authors extend thanks to Drew Arnold and Mark Williams for invaluable research help, and to Anil Sood, Claudio Loser, and Harinder Kohli for their valuable advice and suggestions.
2 Corporación Andina de Fomento 2009

The CAF report also recommends a sharp increase in investments in infrastructure. However, there is no recent systematic estimate of the desirable investment levels by sector and country. This chapter is an attempt to fill this gap. For a detailed explanation of the estimates presented here and the methodology, readers are referred to the study[3] being published in the January 2011 issue of the Global Journal of Emerging Market Economies.

Infrastructure Requirements During 2011-2040

Chapter 5 presents order-of-magnitude estimates of infrastructure investment requirements for 21 Latin American countries, during the period 2011-2040, to support the convergence economic growth scenario presented in Chapter 1. The countries covered are Argentina, Belize, Bolivia, Brazil, Chile, Colombia, Costa Rica, Dominican Republic, Ecuador, El Salvador, Guatemala, Guyana, Honduras, Mexico, Nicaragua, Panama, Paraguay, Peru, Suriname, Uruguay and Venezuela. The study also estimates investment needs under the lower growth business-as-usual scenario in order to understand the sensitivity of investment requirements to the economic growth rate.

The estimates cover the following major infrastructure sectors and subsectors: Energy (Power); Telecommunications (Fixed Broadband, Landlines, and Mobile Phones); Transport (Airports, Ports, Railways, and Paved Roads); and Water and Sanitation. The investment requirements include both new capacity and maintenance of existing infrastructure.

The analysis, based on a proprietary structural equation model that includes four simultaneous equations,[4] confirms that the region's long-term infrastructure requirements remain substantial despite the recent global economic slowdown. Under the convergence scenario for the Latin American economies, these needs would be over US$13 trillion (2009 prices), with about US$9.6 trillion for new capacity and US$3.4 trillion for maintenance (Table 1, Figure 1). Under the business-as-usual scenario, the 21 Latin American countries covered in this study would need to invest US$7.8 trillion during the next thirty years (2011–2040). This comprises about US$5.1 trillion for new capacity and about US$2.7

Table 1 | Total Investment Needs (2011-2040)

	Business-as-Usual Scenario		Convergence Scenario	
	bn $	% of GDP	bn $	% of GDP
New Capacity	5,089	2.5	9,612	3.0
Maintenance	2,705	1.3	3,397	1.1
Total	7,794	3.8	13,008	4.0

Source: Kohli and Basil 2011

---

3   Kohli and Basil 2011
4   Ibid.

Figure 1 **Total Investment Requirement Costs: 2011-2040**

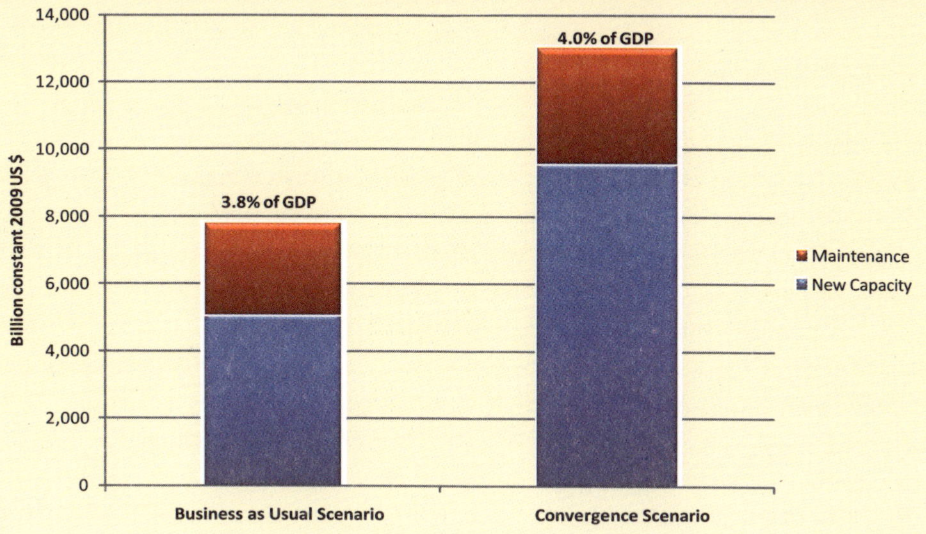
14,000
12,000
10,000
8,000
6,000
4,000
2,000
0
Billion constant 2009 US $
3.8% of GDP
4.0% of GDP
Business as Usual Scenario
Convergence Scenario
Maintenance
New Capacity

Source: Kohli and Basil 2011

Figure 2 **Total Investment over Time (billion $ and % GDP)**

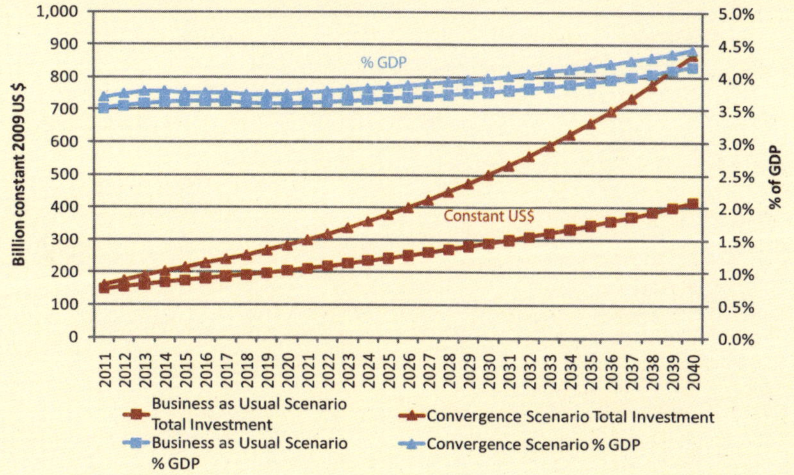
1,000
900
800
700
600
500
400
300
200
100
0
Billion constant 2009 US $
5.0%
4.5%
4.0%
3.5%
3.0%
2.5%
2.0%
1.5%
1.0%
0.5%
0.0%
% of GDP
% GDP
Constant US$
2011 2012 2013 2014 2015 2016 2017 2018 2019 2020 2021 2022 2023 2024 2025 2026 2027 2028 2029 2030 2031 2032 2033 2034 2035 2036 2037 2038 2039 2040
Business as Usual Scenario Total Investment
Convergence Scenario Total Investment
Business as Usual Scenario % GDP
Convergence Scenario % GDP

Source: Kohli and Basil 2011

trillion for maintenance. The investment requirements under the convergence scenario are over two-thirds higher than under the business-as-usual scenario. In fact, by 2040, the convergence scenario's yearly investment needs would be over double those of the business-as-usual scenario (Figure 2).

Investments as Percent of GDP

Although the aggregate requirements are staggering, as a percentage of GDP (Figure 3) these needs are significantly lower than those for other countries, particularly in Asia. Latin America needs to invest between 3.8 percent and 4.0 percent of GDP into infrastructure in the next 30 years (Figure 1). Although, for the most part, these requirements are roughly double the current investment levels, they are significantly lower than Asia's estimated investment needs of between 6.0 percent and 6.5 percent of GDP over the next decade.[5] Latin America's comparatively lower infrastructure requirements as a share of GDP reflect several factors: first, its slower growth generates less new-capacity demand, which in turn lowers subsequent maintenance costs. Also, the share-of-GDP denominator is proportionally larger because Latin America enjoys a level of income well over three times higher: in 2009, per capita income was US$7,187 for the 21 Latin America countries in this study and just US$2,200 in developing Asia.

Further, there is a longer history of middle-income-level capacity for infrastructure investment: at 2009 prices, per-capita income in 1950 for 14 of the 21 Latin American countries for which data is available was over US$2,400 per person, but was just a ninth, at US$253, for the developing Asian

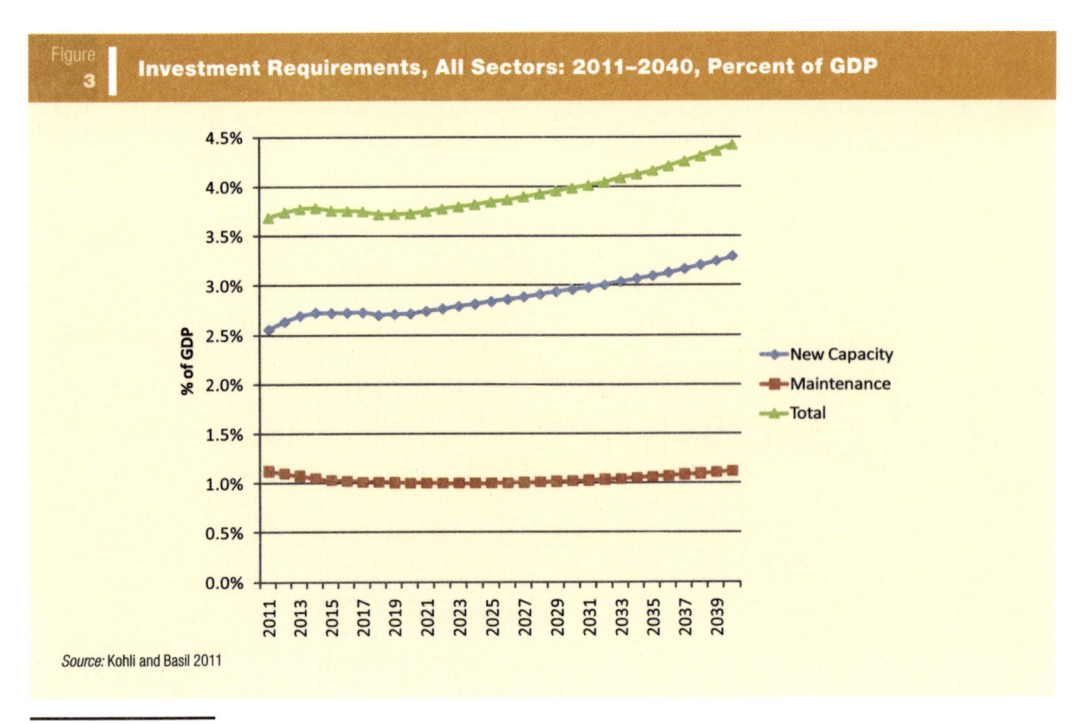

Figure 3 | Investment Requirements, All Sectors: 2011–2040, Percent of GDP

Source: Kohli and Basil 2011

---

[5] Centennial Group International for ADB 2010

countries with data available. Therefore, in the past sixty years, Latin America has been more able to build up an existing stock of water, roads, and rail, which helps to meet current needs. Asia's comparatively lower pre-existing stock has required higher investment rates to catch up to the present.

One example appears in comparing the ratios of what electricity capacity was in place sixty years ago to today's economic activity. For the developing Asian countries for which there is data, the aggregate ratio of electricity capacity in 1950 to GDP in 2009 is 1,576 W/US$, but is a quarter higher, at 1,940 W/US$, for the 17 of this study's 21 Latin American countries for which there is data. This head start makes a practical difference now, if US experience can be extrapolated: 91 percent of power plants built by 1949 lasted at least sixty years. Its 21st century economic activity relies heavily on what was in place by 1950: nearly 20 percent of its 2008 power plants had been built by then.[6] Assuming this also holds for such other long-lived sectors as roads, rail, and water, what Latin America did sixty years ago has given it a head start in meeting today's economic needs, and so less investment has been needed since. However, this effect remains smaller than the impact of the region's slower growth rates.

The remainder of this chapter discusses estimated investment requirements by sector and by country. To simplify the discussion, it is limited to the needs under the convergence scenario.

Investment Requirements by Sector

Amongst the sectors, power requires the largest share (US$9 trillion, or 2.9 percent of GDP) (Figures

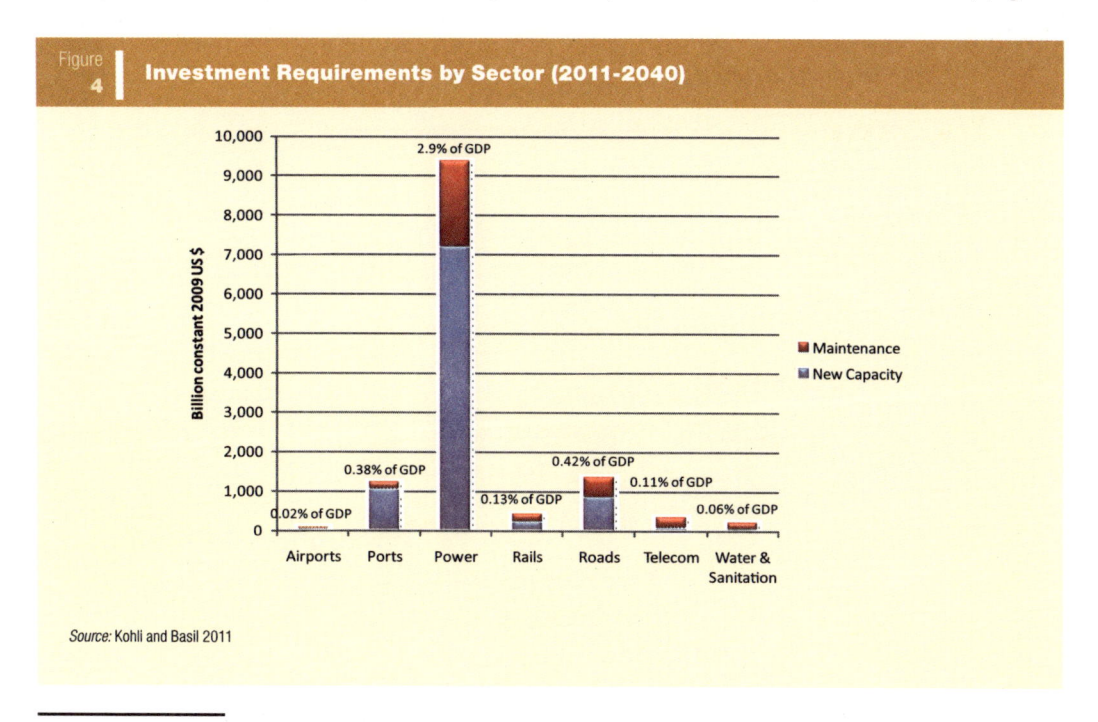

Figure 4 | Investment Requirements by Sector (2011-2040)

Source: Kohli and Basil 2011

---

6 Kohli and Basil 2011. That 2,598 of the US's 13,359 plants in operation in 2008 were built by 1950 yields about 20%.

Figure 5 | Aggregated Needs by Sector as Percent of GDP

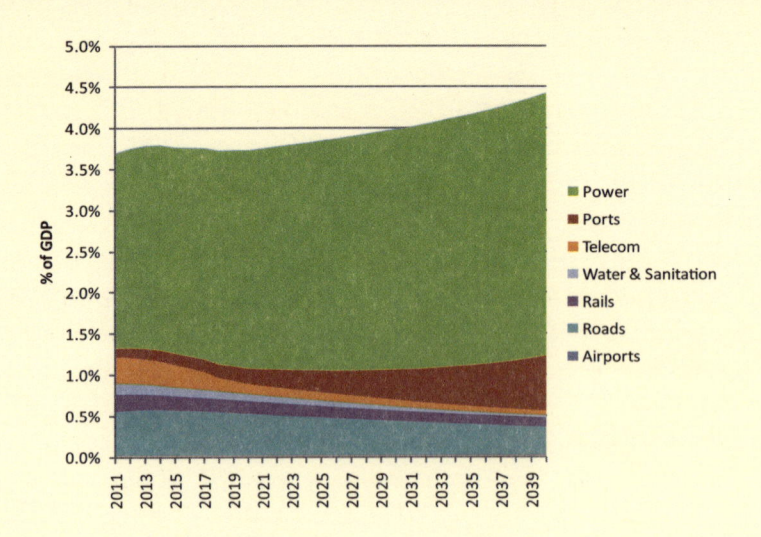

Table 2 | Total Investment Requirements by Sector (2011-2040) (bn US$, 2009 Prices)

	New Capacity	Maintenance	Total Investment	% of Total
Airports	58	16	74	0.6%
Broadband	15	19	34	0.3%
Landlines	14	59	73	0.6%
Mobiles	67	166	233	1.8%
Ports	1,071	159	1,230	9.5%
Power	7,211	2,157	9,368	72.0%
Rails	239	193	432	3.3%
Roads	886	482	1,368	10.5%
Sanitation	37	91	127	0.98%
Water	15	55	70	0.5%
Total	9,612	3,397	13,008	

Source: Kohli and Basil 2011

4 and 5, Table 2). Second to power are roads, with US$1.4 trillion, or 0.4 percent of GDP. The third-largest needs exist in ports: US$1.2 trillion, or 0.4 percent of GDP, almost all new capacity (87 percent of the costs), due to the importance of international trade to both domestic producers and increasingly wealthier consumers.

Requirements by Countries

Table 3 gives the country breakdown of the above investment requirements. Given that they are by far the two largest economies in the region, it is not surprising that between them Brazil and Mexico account for almost 55 percent of total requirements. The next two largest investment needs are in Colombia and Argentina, the former due to its higher economic growth and the latter because it is the third-largest economy of Latin America. These four countries are joined by Peru, Chile, and Venezuela to constitute the top seven economies, accounting for as much as 88 percent of total regional needs.

Table 4 shows the investment requirements of Latin America's major countries as a percent of national GDP, aggregated over the entire 30-year timeframe. The range of percentages generally

Table 3 | Total Investment Requirements by Country, 2011-2040 (bn US$, 2009 Prices)

Country	New Capacity	Maintenance	Total	% Total
Brazil	3,369	1,131	4,500	34.6%
Mexico	1,870	713	2,583	19.9%
Argentina	711	353	1,063	8.2%
Chile	557	188	745	5.7%
Venezuela	456	219	675	5.2%
Colombia	925	237	1,162	8.9%
Dominican Republic	198	69	267	2.1%
Peru	663	151	813	6.3%
Costa Rica	105	37	142	1.1%
Ecuador	75	45	120	0.9%
Other Countries	683	254	938	7.2%
Total	9,612	3,397	13,008	100.0%

Source: Kohli and Basil 2011

reflects the level of development and economic sectoral mix.

Brazil and Mexico again stand out, this time because their requirements are low relative to the absolute size of their economies, just 3.1 percent and 3.4 percent of GDP respectively. As described above, their economic activity over the course of the twentieth century allowed them to build up a stock of infrastructure—electrical plants, roads, rail, water, and sanitation—that is long-lived. Therefore, what already exists is better able to serve their needs. Already 95 percent of Mexico's and 91 percent of Brazil's populations enjoy improved water. So despite Brazil's recent 9 percent annualized GDP growth rate, no other countries have investment needs as a share of GDP as low as these two.

The countries with the highest needs as a share of GDP are the Dominican Republic, Chile, and Costa Rica. Their high needs are characterized by different realities: all

Photo Credit: Aaron Szyf

Table 4 | Investments as Percentage of GDP 2011-2040, Base Case

	Total GDP (bn 2008 US$)	New Capacity	Maintenance	Total Investment
Brazil	143,150	2.4	0.8	3.1
Mexico	76,835	2.4	0.9	3.4
Argentina	18,586	3.8	1.9	5.7
Chile	12,279	4.5	1.5	6.1
Venezuela	16,570	2.8	1.3	4.1
Colombia	21,640	4.3	1.1	5.4
Dominican Republic	3,489	5.7	2.0	7.7
Peru	15,031	4.4	1.0	5.4
Costa Rica	2,079	5.1	1.8	6.8
Ecuador	3,145	2.4	1.4	3.8
Other Countries	10,401	6.6	2.4	9.0
Total (Base Case)	323,205	3.0	1.1	4.0

Source: Kohli and Basil 2011

are forecast to enjoy healthy growth of 4–5 percent after 2020, but the Dominican Republic has historically been poorer and so must build much new capacity to catch up, which is why its needs are even higher than the historically more prosperous Chile and Costa Rica.

Cautionary Notes

Two important caveats must be kept in mind while using these estimates. First, these estimates describe what is required to meet these countries' needs and avoid constraining economic growth. They do not predict what may actually be spent. And second, these top-down order-of-magnitude projections derived from econometrically determined relationships merely serve as a reference points for broad inter-country comparisons and so cannot substitute for detailed "bottom up" sector- and country-specific estimates that take into account individual infrastructure projects and such actual conditions as local unit costs and implementation capacities.

Photo Credit: CAF

Annex

Table A1 demonstrates that sharp divides exist between countries. But even within countries, certain areas, particularly rural, suffer from access to telecom, paved roads, water, and sanitation that is far poorer than that enjoyed not only in developed countries but even in urban areas of the same countries. This stems, in part, from the fact that, per capita, it is much more expensive to extend infrastructure services to the rural poor than to the urban poor, leading to a "coverage gap" even after the efficient market gap is eliminated. New capacity for mobile telephony, for example, may cost as little as US$45 per new subscriber in developed areas but as much as US$120 in rural areas. And with water, sanitation, and other sectors requiring groundwork for which connectivity costs are roughly proportional to the distance from existing networks, the urban-rural servicing cost discrepancy may be even more pronounced. Such intra-country infrastructure-access inequalities exist not only between rural and urban areas but also within individual cities: in 2008, 45 percent of Nicaragua's urban population lived in slums.[1] In these conditions, the poor suffer from much lower rates of access to electricity, telecom, water, and sanitation than residents of other parts of their city.

---

[1] Corporación Andina de Fomento 2009

Table A.1 Current State of Infrastructure in Latin American Countries

	Air transport, passengers carried, per capita (passengers per 1000 ppl)	Container port traffic per capita (TEU/1000 ppl)	Electric power consumption (kWh per capita)	Electricity installed Capacity per capita (Watts/person)	Mobile cellular subscriptions per 100 inhabitants	Fixed telephone lines per 100 inhabitants	Fixed broadband subscriptions per 100 inhabitants	Improved sanitation facilities (% of population with access)	Improved water source (% of population with access)	Rail lines per Area (total route-km per 000 sq km)	Roads paved, per area (km/1000 km2)
Argentina	154	50	2.7	734	129	24	8.8	91	96	13	25
Belize	1590			249	53	10	2.6	47	91	0	21
Bolivia	177		0.5	156	72	8	2.9	43	86	3	4
Brazil	306	36	2.2	526	90	21	7.5	77	91	4	11
Chile	477	186	3.3	950	97	21	9.8	94	95	8	22
Colombia	274	43	1.0	296	92	16	4.6	78	93	2	15
Costa Rica	227	222	1.9	470	43	33	6.0	96	98	8	183
Dominican Republic	1	110	1.4	558	86	10	3.9	79	95	36	129
Ecuador	217	51	0.8	335	100	15	1.8	84	95	3	23
El Salvador	372		0.9	224	123	18	2.4	86	84	27	96
Guatemala	47	67	0.6	158	123	10	0.8	84	96	8	45
Guyana	63			423	37	17	0.3	81	93	0.9	3
Honduras	113	80	0.7	217	103	11	0	66	84	6	25
Mexico	173	29	2.0	521	76	18	9.1	81	95	14	71
Nicaragua	12		0.4	159	56	4	0.8	48	79	2	18
Panama	617	1509	1.6	435	164	16	5.8	74	92	5	54
Paraguay	75		1.0	1316	88	6	2.2	70	77	1	7
Peru	214	48	1.0	245	85	10	2.8	72	84	2	9
Suriname	640			759	147	16	1.6	82	92	2	7
Uruguay	171	91	2.2	666	113	28	7.3	100	100	17	44
Venezuela	205	47	3.1	808	98	24	6.5	68	83	0.4	37

Sources: Canning World Infrastructure Stock Database, Centennial Database, Goldson Airport (Belize), International Telecommunications Union, US Energy Information Administration, World Development Indicators, and World Population Prospects. Telecom data for 2009. Other data for most recent year.

Chapter 8
Greater Openness: Regional Cooperation and Trade

Harinder S. Kohli, Claudio M. Loser, and Anil Sood

Major Trends in Latin American Trade in the Context of the World Economy[1]

Over the last thirty years, trade and capital flows to and from emerging market economies have increased at a very rapid pace. Without question, their economic and trade growth have constituted the most dynamic aspect of international cooperation and globalization in recent years. After a period of relative decline, in part associated with soft commodity prices, emerging markets have regained their share in world output. This has been particularly the case after the Great Recession of 2008-09 hit advanced economies very hard. Emerging markets in Asia and Latin America were generally hit less hard and recovered faster. The recovery has reflected strong world demand and improved terms of trade, which resulted in a boost for domestic activity.

Table 1 provides a view of the growth of export volumes for different regions. From the table, it is clear that trade—or more specifically exports—grew at the fastest rate in the newly industrialized Asian countries, as well as developing Asia, and particularly China and South East Asia. Over the period, the volume of world exports has grown at an average rate of 5.3 percent, almost double the rate of growth of world output (3.2 percent), reflecting the increasing interaction among various countries.[2]

Photo Credit: CAF

Within these parameters, Latin America made considerable progress in opening and integrating

---

1 This section draws extensively on the paper Cross-Border Trade and Investment among Emerging Economies: Lessons from differing experiences in Africa, Asia and Latin America, prepared by Claudio M. Loser for the Emerging Market Forum of Hanoi, Vietnam (June 2008).
2 The numbers presented here are based on the statistics included in the Data Base of the World Economic Outlook. During the same period manufacturing export prices have increased at an average rate of 2.0%, while commodity prices (excluding fuels) grew at a rate of less than 1% a year. Over a more recent period (1992-09) manufactures grew by an average of 1.6% a year while commodities grew by 4.7% (including fuel) and 2.2%, excluding fuel.

Table 1 — World Export Volume (2000=100)

	1980	1990	2000	2009	Average Annual % Growth
World	31.6	49.8	100	140.2	5.3
Advanced economies	30.7	51.2	100	127	5.1
Newly Industrialized Asian Economies	13.1	36.5	100	182.5	9.8
Emerging and developing Economies	33.6	44.7	100	180	5.8
Of which: Asia	15.8	29.2	100	237.6	10.1
Latin America	26.5	42.4	100	142.9	6.0
Memorandum: World GDP	53.5	73.6	100	135.2	3.2

Source: WEO Database, April 2010; Centennial Database, and own estimates.

into the world economy, possibly the most noticeable structural advance achieved in the last two decades. In the region, there has been a high correlation between the ratio of exports to GDP and trade liberalization. Figure 1 presents the indicator of trade restrictiveness developed by the IMF, and shows the effect of trade liberalization on trade on the basis of actual prices and of constant relative prices.

The impact of liberalization has been significant—albeit with a lag—and Latin America's increasing openness to world trade has resulted in considerable gains relative to its situation 25-30 years ago. The ratio of trade to GDP in actual prices increased dramatically between 1984 and 2009, from around 18 percent to 47 percent. However, as shown in Figure 2, even as Latin America has opened up considerably, it remains behind world and OECD averages (64 percent and 52 percent respectively). It is frequently noted that trade numbers are biased because there is an inverse correlation between the ratio of trade to GDP and population size. On that basis, as illustrated in Figure 3, Latin America shows a somewhat higher ratio than without corrections, but actually performs worse in relative terms.

Its population-adjusted ratio of trade to GDP of under 60 percent compares with close to 160 percent for the NICs, over 100 percent for China and developing Asia and around 80 percent for India; Latin America falls behind virtually behind every major region of the world.[3]

The story of Latin American exports is similar. The efforts of the previous decade had a significant

---

[3] The chart shows both the raw index of trade (the ratio of exports plus imports to GDP) and also corrected to offset the effect of the size of countries, based on population. The population neutral series corrects on the basis of a simple regression of trade to population.

GREATER OPENNESS: REGIONAL COOPERATION AND TRADE 231

Figure 1. Latin American Trade Restrictiveness and Trade Share to GDP

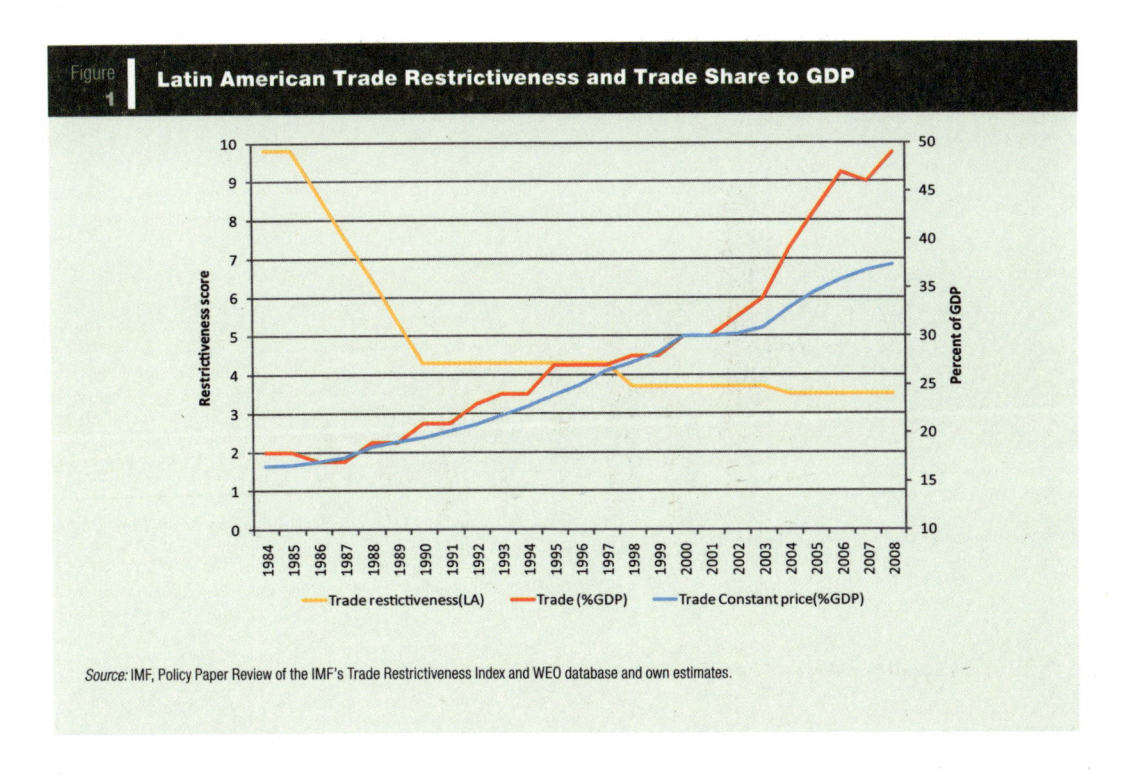

Source: IMF, Policy Paper Review of the IMF's Trade Restrictiveness Index and WEO database and own estimates.

Figure 2. Trade to GDP Ratios

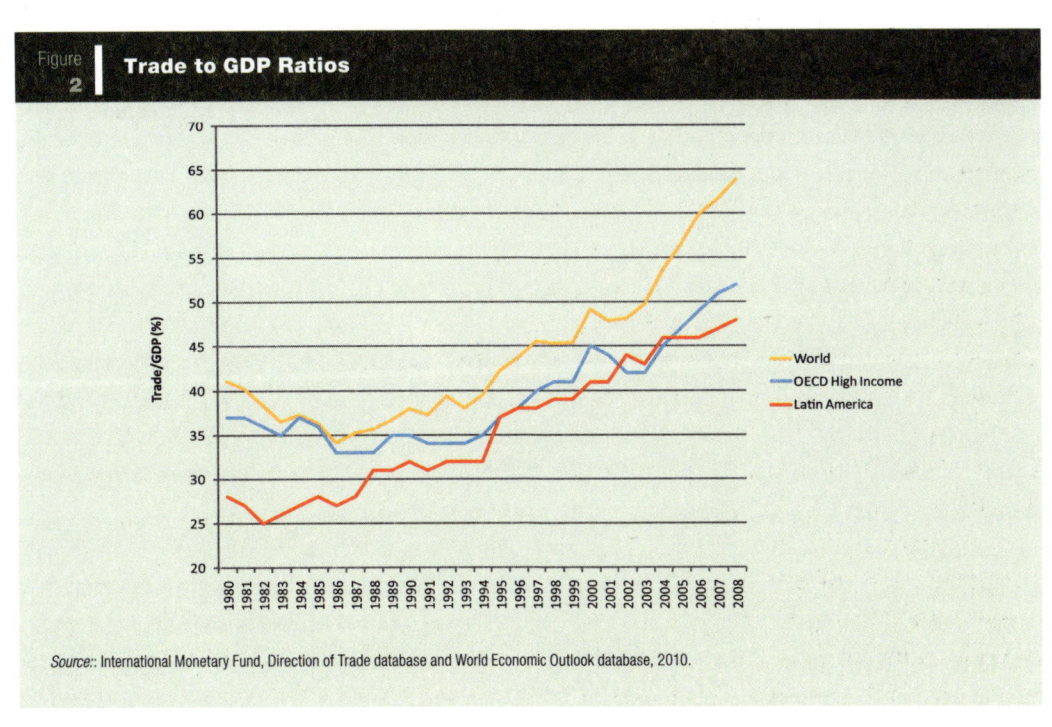

Source: International Monetary Fund, Direction of Trade database and World Economic Outlook database, 2010.

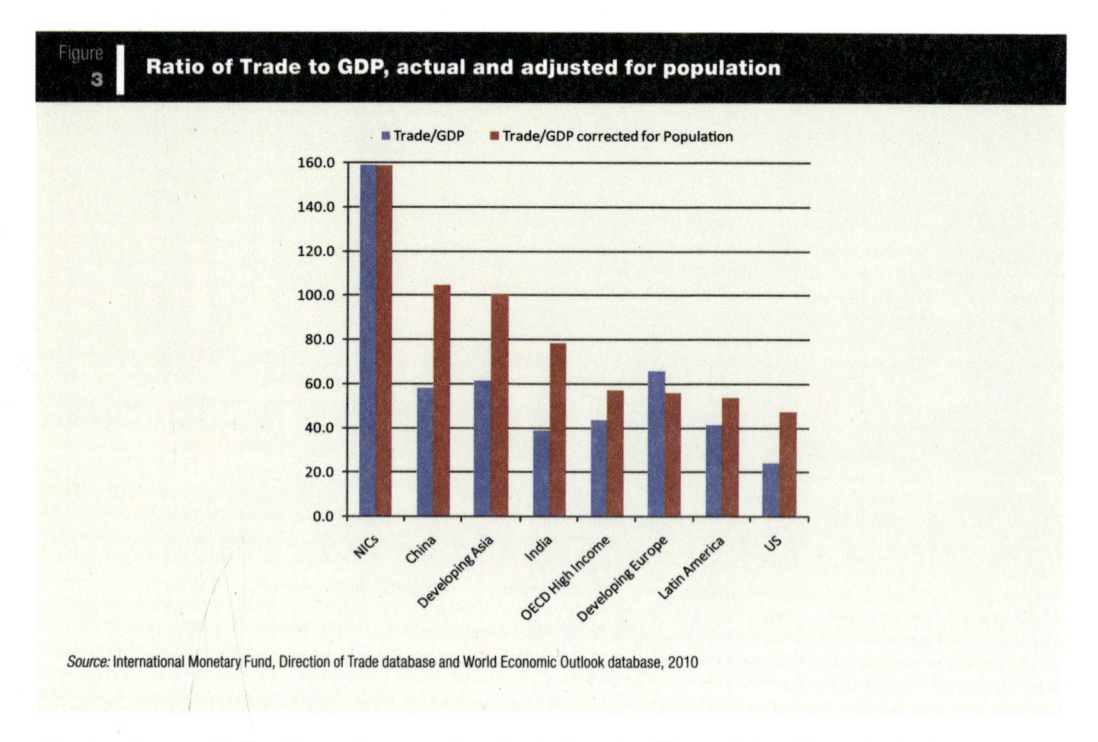

Figure 3 | Ratio of Trade to GDP, actual and adjusted for population

[Bar chart showing Trade/GDP and Trade/GDP corrected for Population for: NICs, China, Developing Asia, India, OECD High Income, Developing Europe, Latin America, US]

Source: International Monetary Fund, Direction of Trade database and World Economic Outlook database, 2010

effect on the growth in volume of exports from Latin America (Figure 4), but the region's share of world exports has been falling behind that of the most dynamic countries in Asia. As commodity prices declined in the 1980s and 1990s, the share of Africa and Latin America in total trade tended to decline, notwithstanding the increased openness of the regions. Over the last few years, improving commodity prices may have distorted the outcome in the opposite direction. But while Latin America maintained its share of world exports of around 5 percent, the NICs have more than doubled their share, and developing Asia's share has more than tripled, from under 5 percent to over 16 percent. Worldwide, the rapid growth of exports has resulted in a steady increase in the ratio of exports to GDP, as seen in Figure 4, which shows the advances in the ratio of exports to GDP at constant prices terms, with a common base in 1979. That Figure shows a strong performance for Latin America as the data are adjusted to eliminate the effect of lower commodity prices (the bulk of Latin American exports) during the period 1980-1995 and the subsequent rise. Thus, through higher volumes, and most recent higher commodity prices, the region has recovered its share in world trade, both regarding exports and imports (Table 2). However, adjusted to eliminate the effect of terms of trade, the share of the region declined.

The pace of growth in exports has not been even, either over time or across countries in the region. Mexico's exports grew strongly in the 1980s when it moved toward assembly exports (maquiladoras), while the rest of the region suffered from weak terms of trade. Mexico's exports grew at an extremely fast pace in the 1990s as it acceded to NAFTA. Thereafter, it slowed down as the economy lost dynamism and its competitive edge against China was eroded. The rest of the region, including

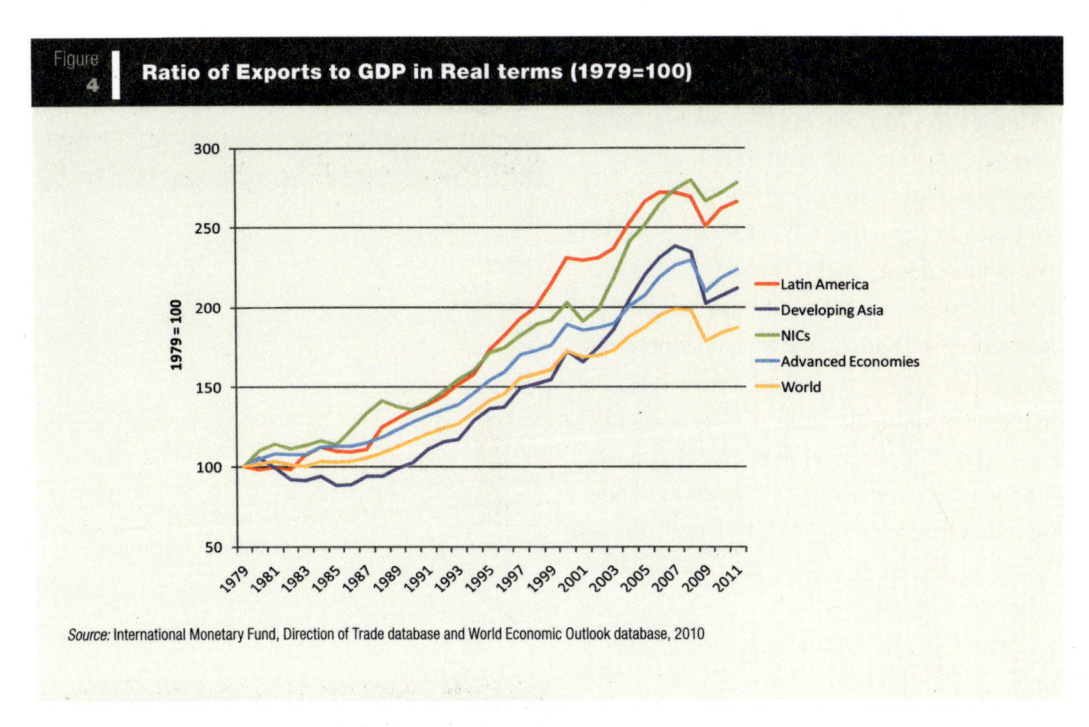

Figure 4: Ratio of Exports to GDP in Real terms (1979=100)

Source: International Monetary Fund, Direction of Trade database and World Economic Outlook database, 2010

Brazil, grew at a fast pace in the last decade on account of higher volumes of trade and also, more importantly, as a reflection of the sharp increase in commodity prices (Table 3).

Intra-Regional Trade and Regional Cooperation

Intra-Regional Trade

Trade relations with the developed world remain at the center of interest for most of the emerging economies, but the fast-growing flows among them have broken the traditional exchange mold. Initially, in the form of new markets for traditional exports, the structure of trade has evolved into more complex exchanges, as technological processes have allowed for increased competitiveness. Moreover, trade has become more specialized, as manufacturers have been able to separate industrial processes and have diversified geographically at a speed and complexity that has far exceeded the speed of the actions by governments in seeking to conclude formal integration agreements.

Trade integration has been a major objective among different emerging regions. These efforts were further enhanced by the stellar progress of the EU over the last half a century. The EU track record, even with its faults, has brought about the admiration of the developing world, particularly as the EU has made continuous moves to expand its membership and integrate the region. Asia has been able to integrate effectively without a complex institutional framework equivalent to that of the EU. Rather, the process has occurred in response to the liberalization efforts of many of its members, particularly China and India. However, this has not been the case in Latin America, notwithstanding official efforts that have extended for well over a century.

Trade flows reflect the process of regional cooperation and integration within each developing area and with other emerging economies. An increase in trade flows can be attributed to increased formal integration within the various areas, better use of comparative advantage in relation to the advanced economies, and also greater complementarity among developing countries. These seem to be the most important aspects of the growth in trade among countries in Asia, and particularly in connection to the initial influence of Japan, the emergence of the Newly Industrialized Countries, and more recently, the overwhelming presence of China.

Table 4 shows the changes in intra-regional trade in different regions. It includes information for developing countries as well as data that cover trade with the major developed countries in each area—Japan and the NICs in Asia, and the US and Canada in the Americas. All areas, with the exception of Latin America, have shown a significant increase in intra-regional trade. The degree of regional integration in Asia is particularly impressive at every level, explaining two thirds of total trade for the region, and about half for the emerging economies including China.[4] This level of integration is almost equivalent to that of the European Union. It may even soon surpass the intra-regional trade share within the EU. The Asian economies, advanced and emerging alike, are much more open, with a higher ratio of trade to GDP than the EU, not to speak of Africa and the American Continent.[5]

In the Americas, the degree of regional trade including the North American countries has increased, but after reaching 40 percent, it declined and remains at about one third of total trade. However, after some years of growth, intra-Latin American trade, at some 20 percent of the total, is at about the same

Table 2 | Share of World Exports

	1980	1990	2000	2009
Advanced Economies	72.6	80.6	74.3	62.8
NICs	3.1	6.0	8.0	7.5
Developing Asia	4.7	5.5	9.5	16.3
Latin America	5.6	3.8	5.7	5.8
Latin America (const. terms of trade) 1/	5.0	3.6	6.5	5.3

1/Adjusted for changes in relative prices of commodities relative to Manufactured Goods.

Source: International Monetary Fund, Direction of Trade database, 2010.

Table 3 | Export Growth (Annual Percentage Average)

	1981-1989	1990-1999	2000-2009
Latin America	0.7	11.8	9.4
Brazil	2.0	7.1	12.4
Mexico	5.1	20.6	5.8

Source: International Monetary Fund, Direction of Trade database, 2010.

---

4   Even excluding China from these trade statistics for Developing Asia, the degree of integration in the region is very high- about 40% of total trade, as opposed to 47%, including China.
5   The numbers for the Americas are somewhat distorted by the size and nature of the US economy, which in itself is a major trading area. Nonetheless, the Americas are more closed than any of the other major regions.

Table 4: Intra-regional Trade 1980-2007 (in percent of total trade for the region unless specified)

Region	1980	1990	2000	2007	Trade/GDP (%, 2007)
Developing Africa	5.0	7.6	9.5	9.5	58.3
Developing Asia	24.1	33.9	41.6	47.3	105.9
Developing and Advanced East Asia 1/	36.5	48.3	60.0	65.3	72.5
Memo: Developing Asia intraregional trade and with Advanced Asia 1/	55.8	67.7	74.3	74.8	
Latin America and Caribbean	21.0	16.4	18.6	21.2	42.8
Americas 2/	18.0	29.9	39.3	36.0	20.4
Memo: Latin America intraregional trade with US and Canada 2/	56.0	58.1	71.6	62.1	
European Union	61.6	67.1	67.3	67.2	63.7

1/Includes Developing Asia, Japan and NICs (Hong Kong, Taiwan, S. Korea, and Singapore).
2/Americas Includes , Latin America, Caribbean, Canada and the US.
Source: International Monetary Fund, Direction of Trade database and World Economic Outlook database, 2010.

level as in 1980. This suggests that there has been only limited success in developing a process of integration in new activities in spite of the major efforts to establish trade agreements within the region, including trade blocks like Mercosur, the Andean Group, and the Central American Common Market, which have sought to provide the opportunity to integrate these economies.

Even though the trade agreements have lagged rather than preceded the flows of trade in today's dynamic world, their role is far from trivial. There is a need to complete global trade agreements to help eliminate the burden of protectionist policies both on consumers in importing countries and producers in the (mostly) poorer producing countries. Beyond these efforts, regional agreements can provide a stable institutional environment within which trade flows can take place, and be protected from discretionary policy actions by opportunistic national authorities in advanced, emerging, and poorer countries alike.

The question remains as to why integration has not been correlated to these agreements, particularly regional agreements. Although the underlying natural resource (Africa and Latin America) and labor (Asia) endowments explain part of the differential pattern, the causes run deeper. Much higher levels of savings and investment in Asia explains the region's dynamism. Furthermore, in the last decade, the institutional business and investment climate has been much more favorable in Asia, thus helping to generate the growth momentum that can be observed today.

Enhancing Regional Cooperation

There are three basic reasons for which the Latin America region should seriously consider significantly enhancing intra-regional trade, including through improved regional cooperation: i) to permit the economies to specialize, an important strategy to escape the middle income trap; ii) to overcome the reality that most Latin America economies are small by global standards and thus do not have domestic markets large enough to permit the economies of scale needed by firms to be globally competitive; and iii) to allow local firms to take advantage of their superior knowledge and understanding of the needs of customers in the neighboring countries compared to the competitors from other continents.

1. Need for Economies to Specialize

The Growth Commission led by Nobel laureate Michael Spence found that a major characteristic of the economies that have successfully avoided the middle income trap and made an effective transition from middle income status to becoming high income economies was their ability to become specialized in economic activities. They managed to develop a competitive advantage in the global marketplace by proactively building unique skill sets and creating economies of scale. Specialization and economies of scale, in turn, allowed the economies to enhance productivity and competitiveness. Such specialization involves investments in activities with greater value-added by shifting resources—labor and capital—from labor intensive activities, whose viability is dependent on low wages (and hence lower per capita income), into economic activities that have higher innovation and technology content, allowing greater returns to both capital and labor; the resulting higher wage levels raise people's living standards and boost the country's per capital income.

Photo Credit: CAF

A closer look at higher income countries (developed and NICs) reveals that, except for a few large economies, most high wage economies have achieved at least some degree of specialization in the global marketplace. While this is by no means an exhaustive list, some of the examples are: Korea in electronics, shipbuilding and automobiles; Japan in highly specialized machine tools, automobiles, innovation in and design of consumer and industrial electronics; the US in information technology, innovation in and design of electronics, commercial airplanes, and military equipment etc.; France in nuclear power plants, fashion industry and international tourism; the UK in financial and other services; Singapore in financial services, tourism, shipping and airline, biotechnology etc., and so on. By now, China has become the manufacturing hub for the globe and India has become the world leader in IT services and is seeking to do the same in pharmaceuticals. Until now, the key global role of much of Latin America has mainly been in supplying commodities and fuels to the rest of the world. Only Brazil and Mexico have managed worldwide reputation in selected manufacturing activities.

Given the earlier conclusion that many—though by no means all—Latin American economies have been mired in the middle income trap, it appears logical that an important step in Latin American countries' ability to escape this trap would be their success in moving towards such specialization on a global scale so as to raise their productivity. This, in turn, will allow local firms to gain higher profitability while investing in activities that would allow them to simultaneously pay higher wages to their employees with requisite skills.

However, to successfully achieve such specialization, firms need ready access to markets that are large enough to yield economies of scale at the national or regional level before they can compete in the global marketplace. Unfortunately, doing so at the national level in Latin America is not possible except in a handful of countries, such as Brazil and Mexico. This issue is discussed below.

2. Small Size of Most Latin American Economies

Tables 5 and 6 show the world's 15 largest economies in 2009. They compare the size of Latin American economies with other major economies in the world, in terms of both PPP and market exchange rates. Only two Latin American countries rank amongst the top 15 economies in the world: Brazil at number 9 and Mexico at number 11 in PPP terms, and at numbers 8 and 14 respectively, in terms of market exchange rates.

So what is the basic conclusion from this information? While most Latin American economies belong to the upper middle-income group, they are relatively small in absolute size—with the exception of Brazil and Mexico.

A similar conclusion is apparent when looking at the world's largest emerging markets economies shown in Tables 7 and 8. In 2009, again only Brazil and Mexico made the list of the top 10 emerging markets economies. On the other hand, the list includes as many as five countries in Asia (China, India, Korea, Indonesia and Taiwan). Only 9 years earlier, in 2000, three Latin American economies were on this list, with Brazil at number 2, Mexico at number 3 and Argentina at number 7. In other words, while Asian countries continued to climb the global economic ladder during the 1990s, Latin American economies fell behind in relative terms (except Brazil). Only two economies—Brazil and Mexico—had more than 1 percent of global GDP. And, in PPP terms their combined GDP was slightly less than that of India and less than half of China.

The basic conclusion of the above discussion is very simple: individually Latin American economies—with the exception of Brazil and Mexico—are small by global standards and therefore local firms operating exclusively in their home country markets would find it extremely difficult to

Table 5: GDP (PPP) Top in World 2009

	PPP Current US$	% World
United States	14,256	20.42
China	8,765	12.56
Japan	4,159	5.96
India	3,526	5.05
Germany	2,806	4.02
United Kingdom	2,139	3.06
Russia	2,110	3.02
France	2,108	3.02
Brazil	2,013	2.88
Italy	1,740	2.49
Mexico	1,466	2.10
Korea	1,364	1.95
Spain	1,361	1.95
Canada	1,281	1.84
Indonesia	962	1.38
World	**69,809**	

Source: International Monetary Fund, World Economic Outlook, 2010

Table 6: GDP (MER) Top in World 2009

	GDP Current US$	% World
United States	14,256	24.61
Japan	5,068	8.75
China	4,909	8.47
Germany	3,353	5.79
France	2,676	4.62
United Kingdom	2,184	3.77
Italy	2,118	3.66
Brazil	1,574	2.72
Spain	1,464	2.53
Canada	1,336	2.13
India	1,236	2.13
Russia	1,229	2.12
Australia	997	1.72
Mexico	875	1.51
Korea	833	1.44
World	**59,937**	

Source: International Monetary Fund, World Economic Outlook, 2010

achieve economies of scale, and thus face a significant challenge in becoming globally competitive and creating high paying jobs. Closer regional cooperation in the hemisphere that facilitates much greater regional trade and investment flows that significantly expand the "home" markets can go a long way in helping the region aspire to create global players.

3. Unexploited Potential within the Region
As discussed above, trade between the Latin American economies, at 21 percent in 2009, is less than a third of the European Union (65 percent) or developing and advanced Asia taken together (67 percent), and less than half of developing Asia (47 percent).

This outcome is partly due to the past focus of both the region's governments and private business on the US and European markets. But, it also appears to be a natural outcome of the government policies that have created barriers against trade and investment flows to neighboring countries over the years. Ironically, these barriers remained in place despite numerous regional and sub-regional agreements and treaties that were formally adopted during the last fifty years at the level of the heads of states, but were not implemented in practice. In addition, physical transport and logistics facilities between neighboring countries have also been a constraint.

Yet, from a business perspective, there appears to be significant unexploited potential for greater trade and investment flows within the region, provided the current barriers are removed. The economies—except in the Caribbean—are linked by a contiguous land mass, a common heritage and history, similar cultures and the same language (except for Brazil and the Caribbean). It should be natural for the consumers within the region to prefer similar (though not necessarily the same) products, and companies should have a competitive advantage in forging business relations with their regional counterparts and in marketing to the consumers in other parts of the region.

The resulting increase in intra-regional trade and investment flows—combined with greater focus on Asia (discussed below)—would not only create newer, faster growing market opportunities, but also help diversify the region's export markets and thus further reduce the current heavy reliance on exports to the US and Europe. While this process appears to be already underway, its pace can and should be significantly accelerated.

Diversification of Trade

Diversifying Markets

Table 7 shows the share of, and average annual growth in Latin America's trade with different regions of the world and with major countries during the past 30 years. It reveals some interesting and perhaps a few under-appreciated trends:

- The US share in trade rose from 33 percent in 1980 to a high of 53 percent in 2000 and has fallen back by 15 percent. Over the past 10 years, the slowest growth of trade was with the US (2.2 percent), the region's traditional and largest trading partner.
- The share of trade with Canada at 2.5 percent in 2009 is at about the same level as in 1980.
- The European Union lost significant share particularly between 1990 (24 percent) and 2000 (12.8 percent).
- Trade with India and developing Asia as a whole is also growing more quickly than trade with any other region, albeit from a very small base; the share of developing Asia reached 11 percent in 2009 from 1.3 percent in 1980.
- The sharpest growth in the last decade is with China (26 percent per annum) and India (22 percent per annum) as the Latin American countries sought to become a major beneficiary of their thirst for commodities with which the region is richly endowed.

Figures 5-8 show the breakdown of Latin America's exports at a somewhat more disaggregated level, separating out Brazil, Mexico and Venezuela. The general trend is a decline in the trade volume with the European Union and Japan, mainly accounted for by changes in the trade pattern for Brazil and Mexico. The other major change is the sharp jump in trade with developing Asia, mainly on account of China with most countries except for Mexico. The US trade participation is overwhelming in the case of Mexico but it has declined for others.

The figures show the very sharp increase of Brazil's exports to Asia. It is worth noting that last year,

Table 7 — Average Growth in Trade in past 10 years (2000-2009)

Exports	1980	1990	2000	2009	Average Annual Growth Rate (2000-2009)	Average Annual Growth Rate (1980-2009)
Canada	2.5	1.7	1.8	2.4	9.9	6.5
China	0.5	0.6	1.5	8.2	26.1	16.8
India	0.2	0.2	0.3	1.1	22.1	13.1
Dev Asia (w/o China, India)	0.6	0.9	1.6	1.7	7.1	10.6
European Union	22.5	24.0	12.8	13.3	7.1	4.8
Central & Eastern Europe	1.1	0.8	0.4	0.8	13.9	5.4
Africa	2.1	1.3	1.0	1.9	13.9	6.3
Japan	5.2	5.7	3.1	3.5	7.8	5.2
United States	33.3	38.6	52.8	34.8	2.4	6.8
Western Hemisphere	20.6	17.0	17.3	22.0	9.3	6.9
Rest of World	11.3	9.1	7.4	10.5	10.5	6.4

Source: International Monetary Fund, Direction of Trade, 2010

China became Brazil's largest trading partner, surpassing the United States.

Specifically, the increase in exports to developing Asia, particularly when Mexico is excluded, was mainly based on raw materials, including fuels, agricultural commodities, and metals, and in particular iron ore and copper to China, offsetting equivalent declines in exports to the EU. In contrast, the exports to the US from Mexico and the increased trade within the region has consisted to a large extent of manufactured goods, and to a lesser extent of fuels, with the exception of Venezuela, which has continued to export oil.[6]

This sharp rise in the region's trade with developing Asia overall—and with China and India in particular—has a number of advantages: it is helping the region to diversify its trade; it is strengthening economic ties with the fastest growing region of the world; it is reducing the region's dependence on the mature and slower growing markets in North America and Europe; and, through higher growth of exports, it is helping to boost the overall economic growth of Latin America.

Some global economic models—including the model used in this study—anticipate that Asia would continue to enjoy the fastest economic growth in the world and, as a result, Asia may account for as much as 50 percent of global GDP by 2050. Whether this scenario is realized or not and, if so when, is not important but the overall trends are. Accordingly, increasing its focus on Asia should be

---

[6] Global Journal of Emerging Market Economies-Vol. 1, Issue 1, January 2009- Claudio M. Loser- Cross Border Trade and Investment among Emerging Economies: Lessons from Differing Experiences in Africa, Asia and Latin America.

GREATER OPENNESS: REGIONAL COOPERATION AND TRADE   **241**

Figure 5. Destination of Exports: Latin America

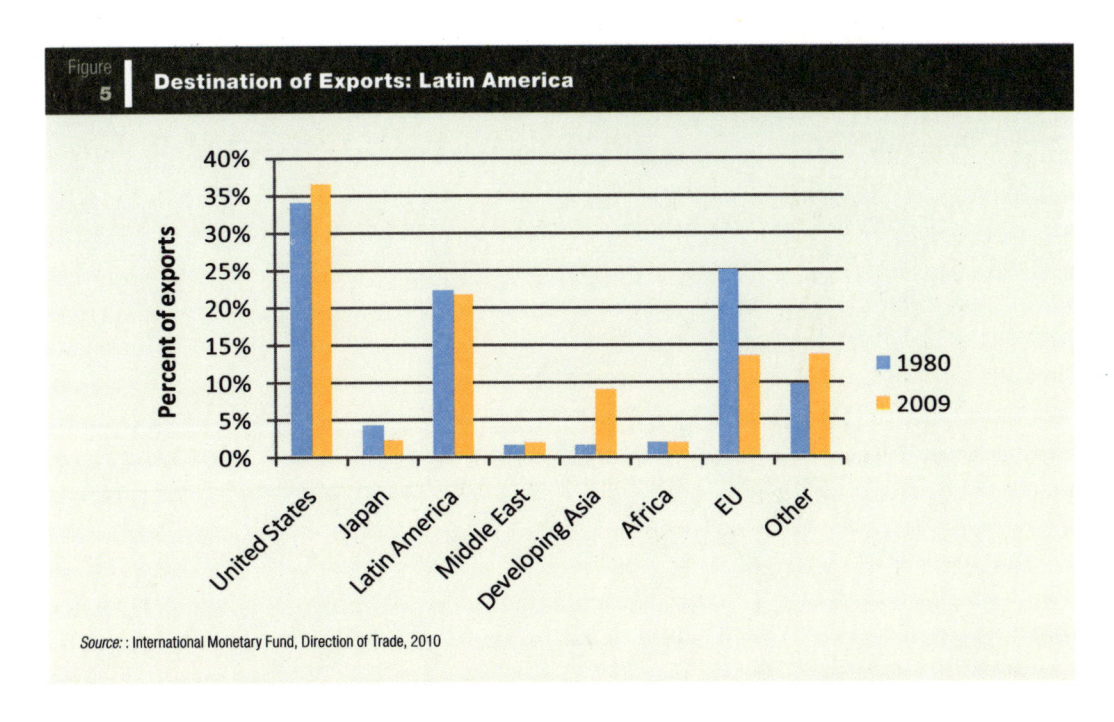

Destination	1980	2009
United States	34%	37%
Japan	4.5%	2.5%
Latin America	22.5%	22%
Middle East	2%	2%
Developing Asia	2%	9%
Africa	2%	2%
EU	25.5%	14%
Other	10%	14%

Source: International Monetary Fund, Direction of Trade, 2010

Figure 6. Destination of Exports: Latin America without Mexico, Brazil, Venezuela

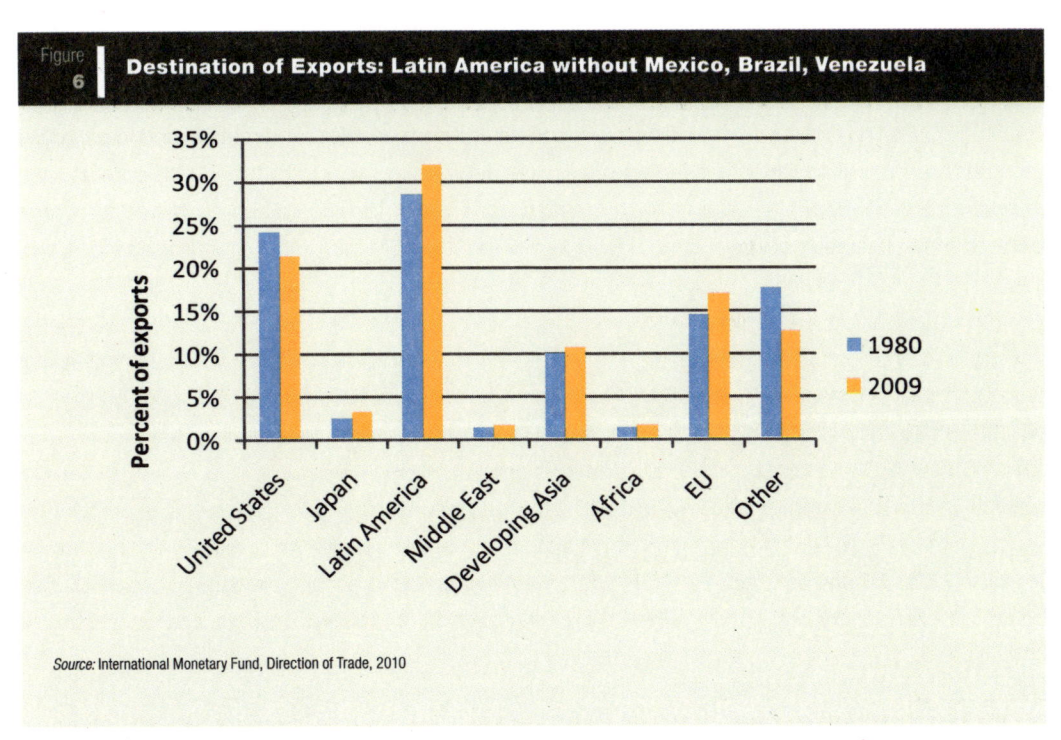

Destination	1980	2009
United States	24%	21.5%
Japan	2.5%	3.5%
Latin America	29%	32%
Middle East	1.5%	2%
Developing Asia	10%	11%
Africa	1.5%	2%
EU	15%	17%
Other	18%	13%

Source: International Monetary Fund, Direction of Trade, 2010

Figure 7. Destination of Exports: Mexico

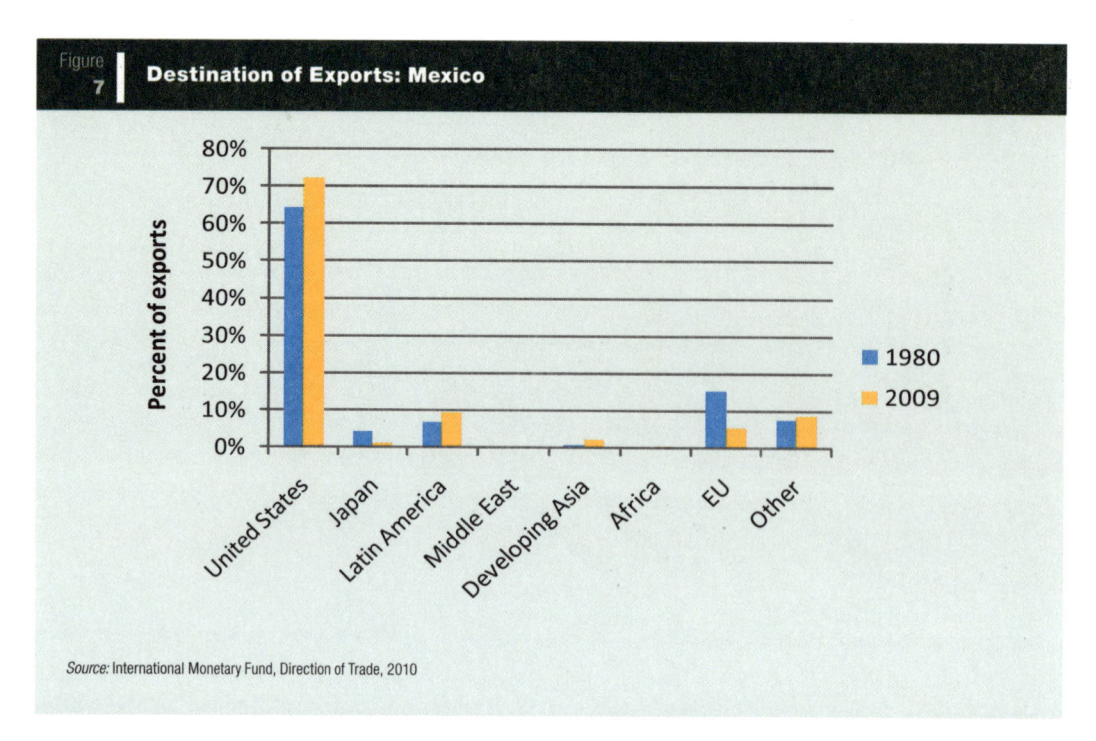

Source: International Monetary Fund, Direction of Trade, 2010

Figure 8. Destination of Exports: Brazil

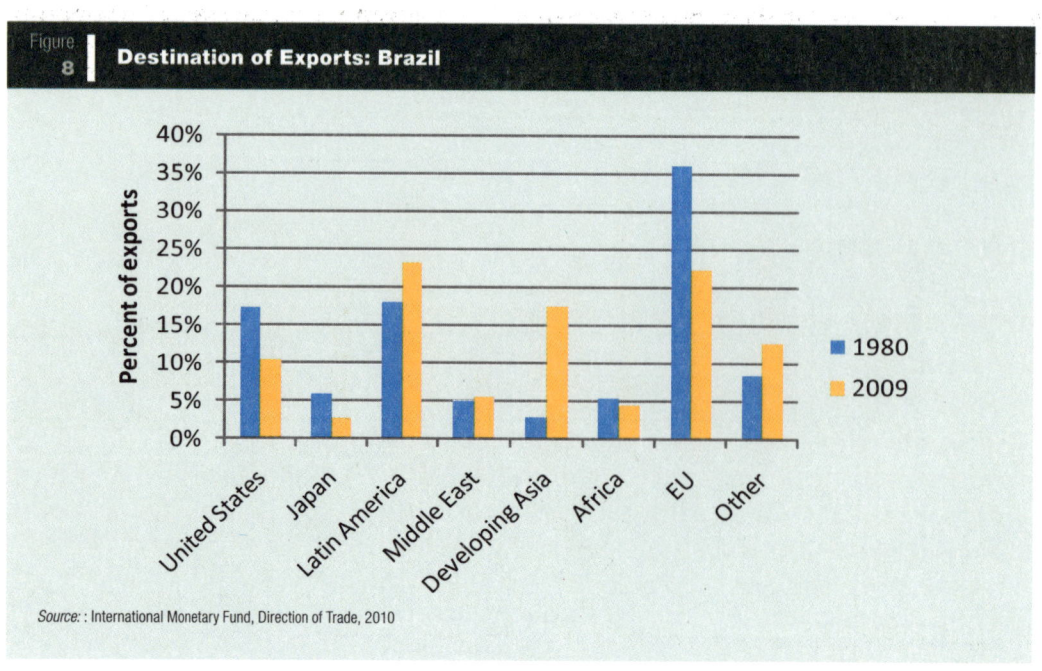

Source: International Monetary Fund, Direction of Trade, 2010

an integral part of Latin America's long-term growth strategy.

Diversifying into higher value-added Products

The composition of exports of different groups of countries in Latin America provides an insight into where the region stands with respect to the world and into the changes that have taken place in recent years. In summary terms, Latin American exports are dominated by primary commodities and fuels, but with some exports of manufactured goods both to advanced and emerging economies. Also, the composition of exports has been considerably less dynamic than the destination of exports. Mexico is by far the country with the highest level of manufacturing exports, while Brazil has increased its share of commodity exports, mainly on account of agricultural and some mining products. Venezuelan exports are overwhelmingly oil, while for the rest of the countries in the region, commodities of all types dominate export activities (Figures 9 and 10).

Most of the countries in the region, excluding Mexico and to some extent Brazil, remain heavily dependent on commodities (Figures 13-16). The share of primary commodities and fuels in regional exports has fluctuated around 50 percent and stands today at 56 percent. If Brazil, Mexico and Venezuela are excluded, the proportion rises to 75 percent in 2009 (Figures 11 and 12).

In terms of other commodities, volumes have increased significantly, reflecting the potential for the region, and in the case of agriculture, significant technological progress. Still, the region remains highly vulnerable to changes in terms of trade.

The figures suggest that when adjusted for changes in relative prices, most of the region, with the exception of Brazil, shows an upward trend in the participation of manufactures in total exports. In fact, when Brazil, Mexico and Venezuela are excluded, the remainder of the region shows significant progress—albeit from a small base—with the proportion of manufactured goods rising from 16 percent to over 25 percent of total exports.

Figure 17 shows that even though manufactured goods have been gaining ground in total Latin American exports, when compared to mature (US or Japan) or dynamic economies (like China and the NICs), the region's exports are heavily concentrated in raw materials or their manufactures. The

Photo Credit: CAF

Figure 9. Composition of Exports: Latin America

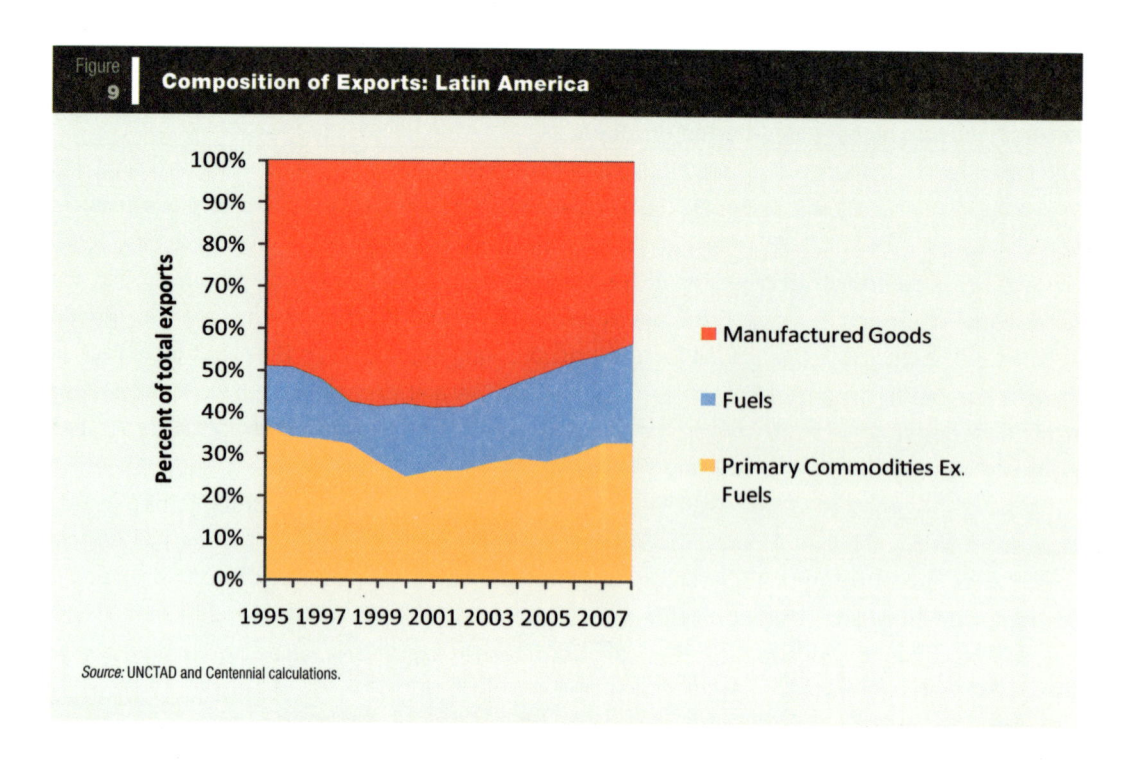

Source: UNCTAD and Centennial calculations.

Figure 10. Composition of Exports: Latin America (constant real prices)

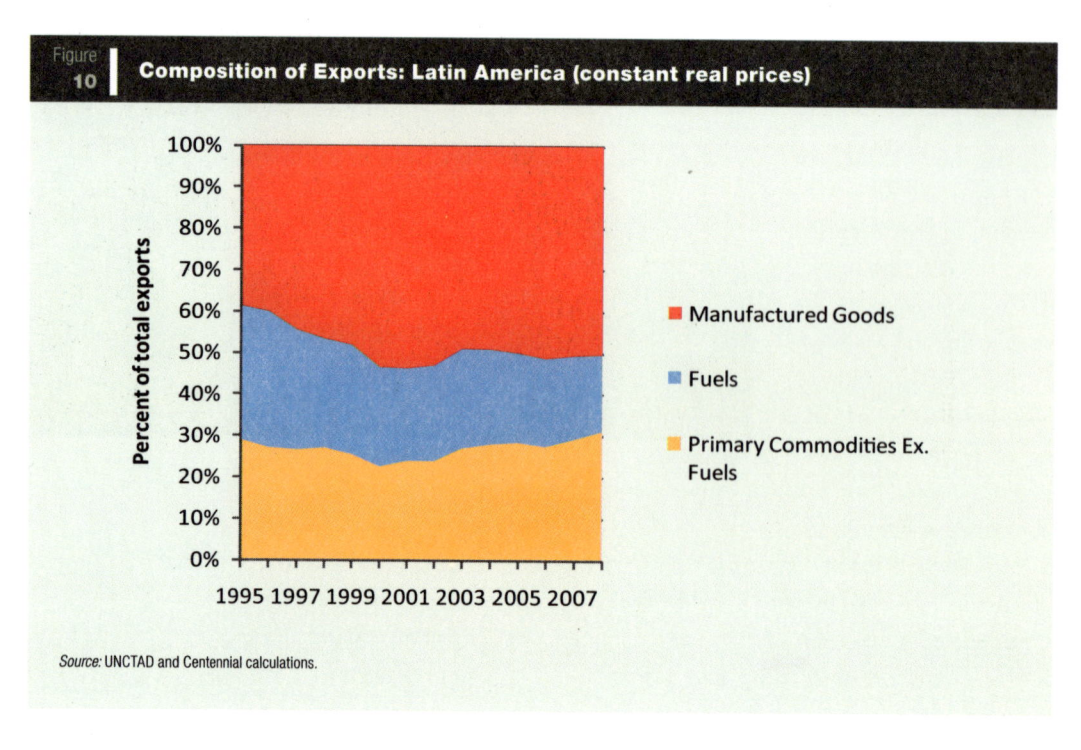

Source: UNCTAD and Centennial calculations.

GREATER OPENNESS: REGIONAL COOPERATION AND TRADE **245**

Figure 11 | Composition of Exports: Latin America excl. Mexico, Brazil, Venezuela

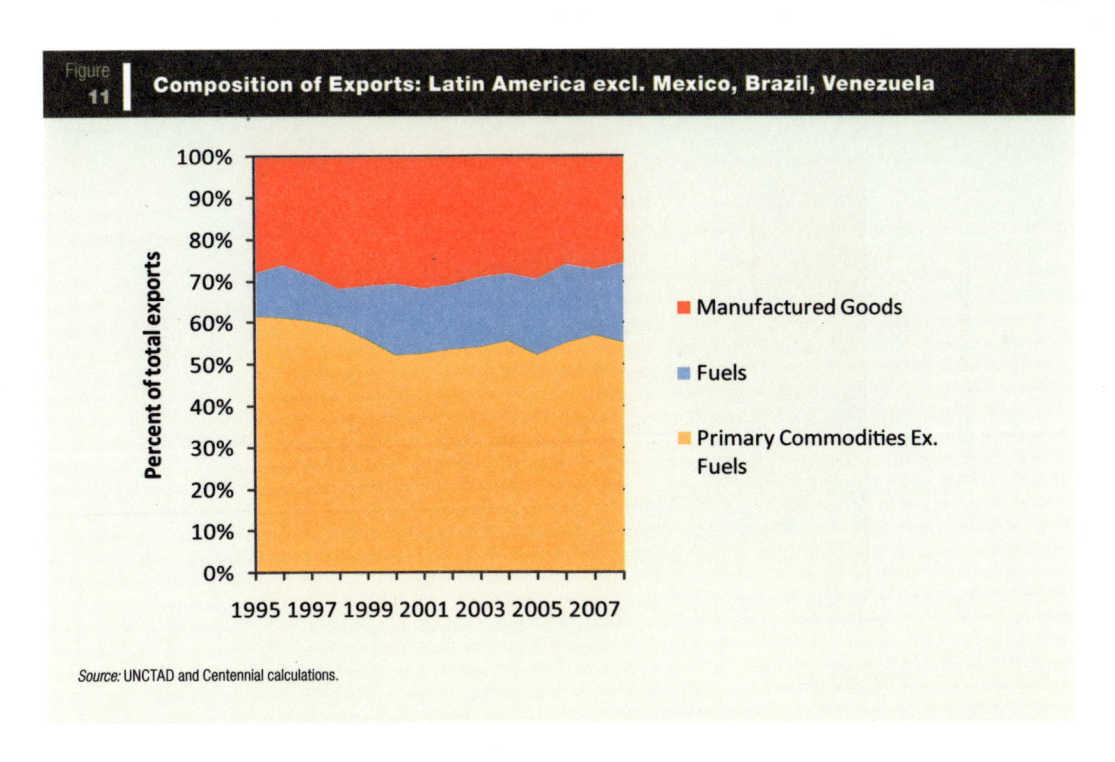

- Manufactured Goods
- Fuels
- Primary Commodities Ex. Fuels

Source: UNCTAD and Centennial calculations.

Figure 12 | Composition of Exports: Latin America excl. Mexico, Brazil, Venezuela (constant real prices)

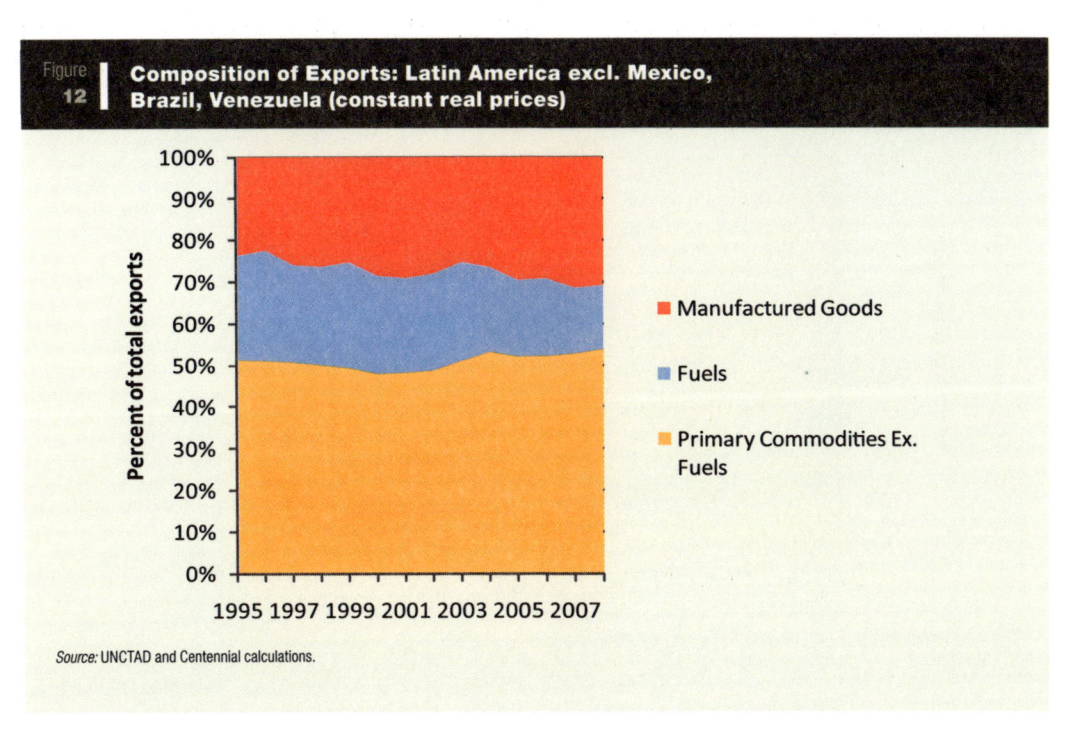

- Manufactured Goods
- Fuels
- Primary Commodities Ex. Fuels

Source: UNCTAD and Centennial calculations.

Figure 13. Composition of Exports: Mexico

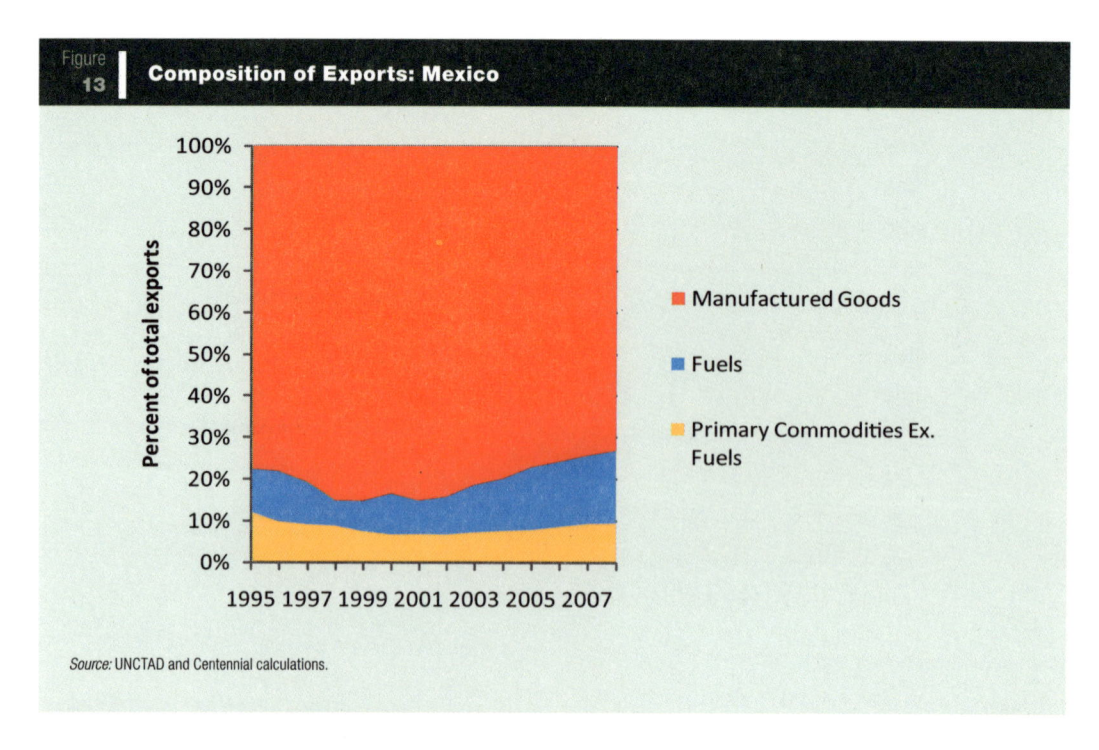

Source: UNCTAD and Centennial calculations.

Figure 14. Composition of Exports: Mexico (constant real prices)

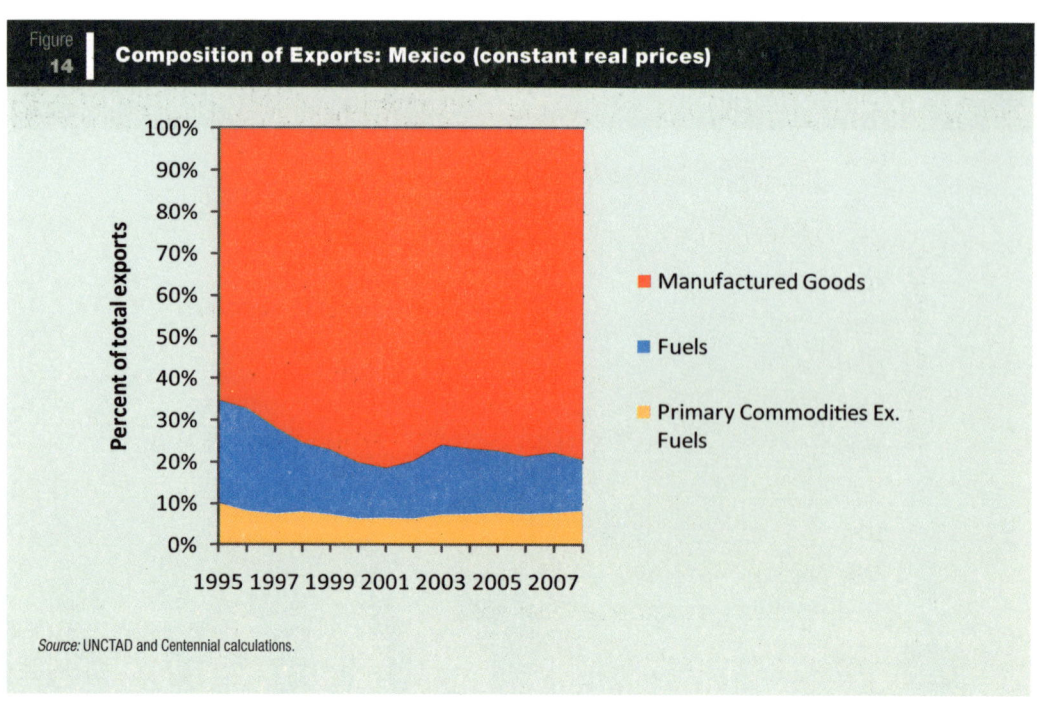

Source: UNCTAD and Centennial calculations.

GREATER OPENNESS: REGIONAL COOPERATION AND TRADE **247**

Figure 15 | Composition of Exports: Brazil

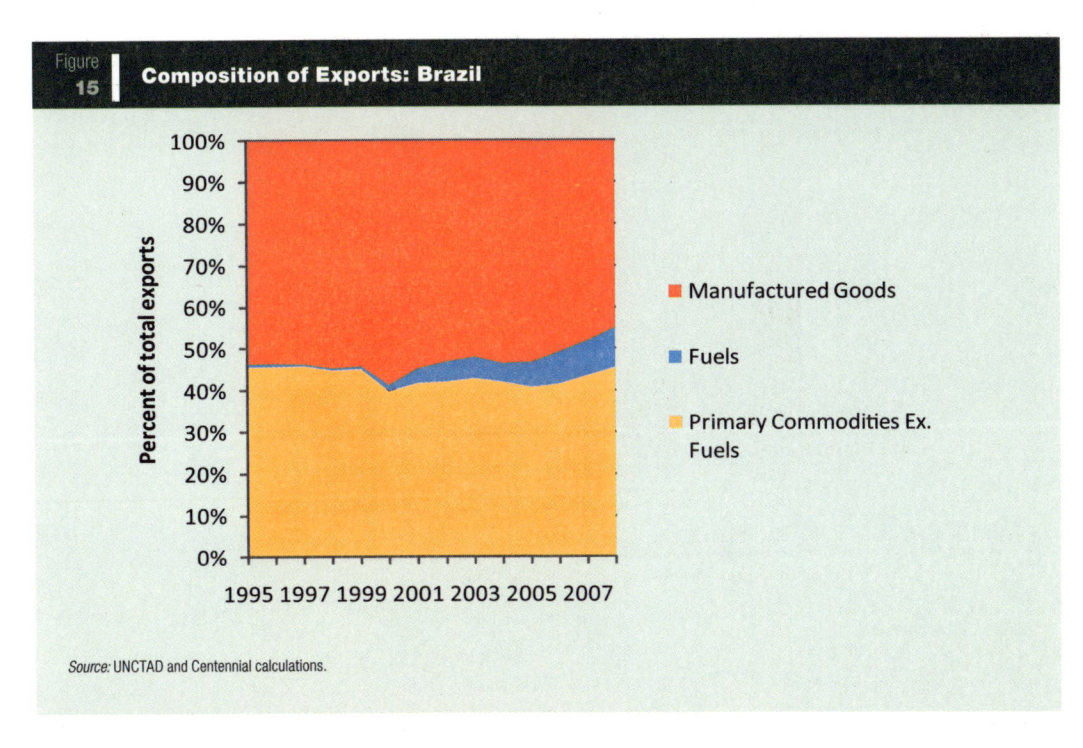

Source: UNCTAD and Centennial calculations.

Figure 16 | Composition of Exports: Brazil (constant real prices)

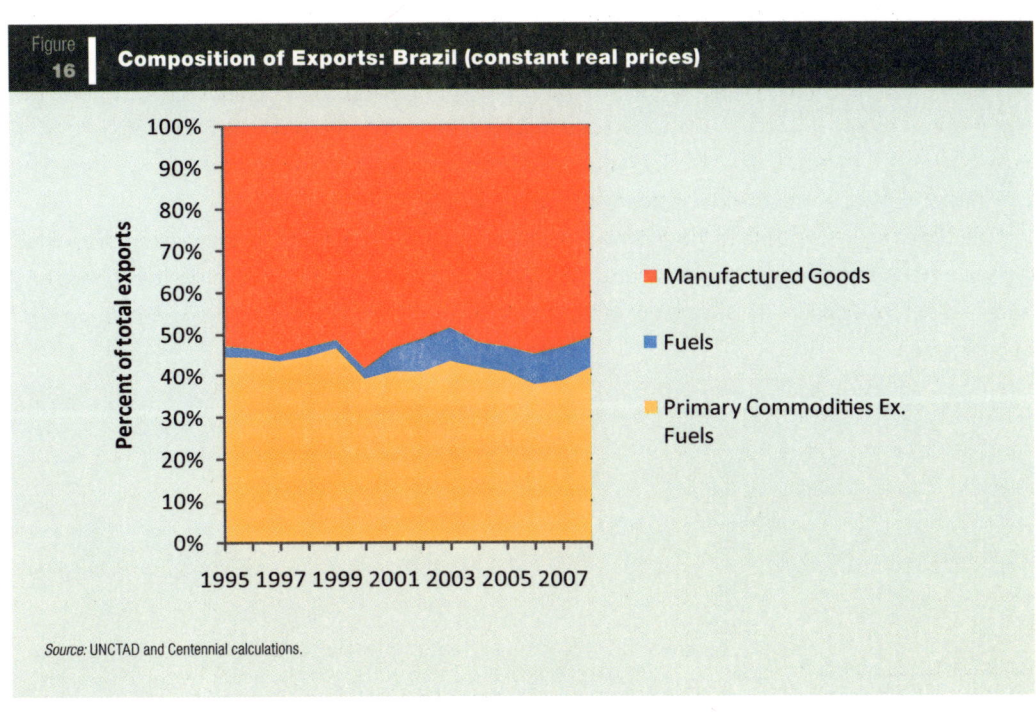

Source: UNCTAD and Centennial calculations.

Figure 17 | Export Composition

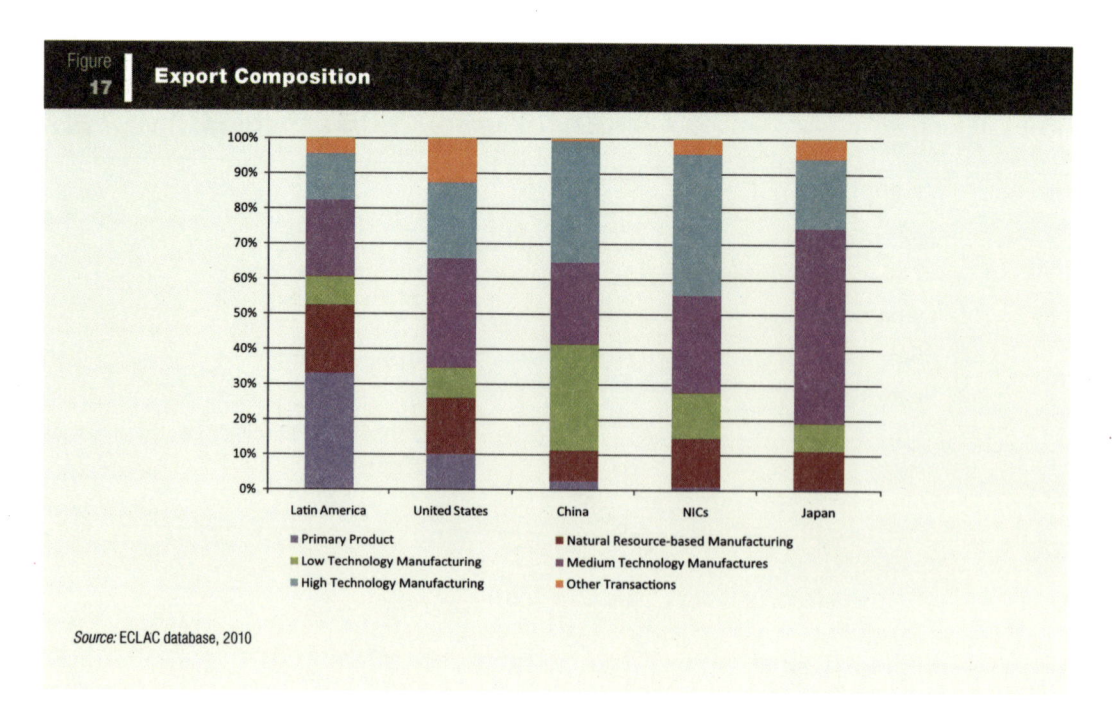

- Primary Product
- Natural Resource-based Manufacturing
- Low Technology Manufacturing
- Medium Technology Manufactures
- High Technology Manufacturing
- Other Transactions

Source: ECLAC database, 2010

region's manufacturing exports are mostly concentrated at the low and medium technology end. The proportion of high technology goods within manufacturing exports for the region as a whole is under 8 percent compared to 30 percent for China and 25 percent for East Asia and the Pacific (Figure 17). Expectedly, there is a wide variance in this proportion across the region, with Mexico and Brazil in the lead (Figures 18 and 19). When these two countries are excluded, the proportion falls below that of India (5 percent).[7] In fact, Latin America has lagged behind all major regions for the last two decades, even as performance worldwide has been uneven (Figure 20).

The above analysis points to the potential for Latin America to make significant gains by increasing the value-added of its output and exports and, within manufacturing, to move up the technology ladder—a critical measure for getting out of the middle income trap and making progress toward high income status.

---

[7] Figures 17 and 18-19 have different sources, with somewhat different definitions of High Tech exports. Thus, the export composition table, with a broader definition of high tech exports shows higher percventagespercentages, even though the rankings are not affected by these changes.

GREATER OPENNESS: REGIONAL COOPERATION AND TRADE   **249**

Figure 18 | High Technology Exports as Percent of Manufacturing Exports

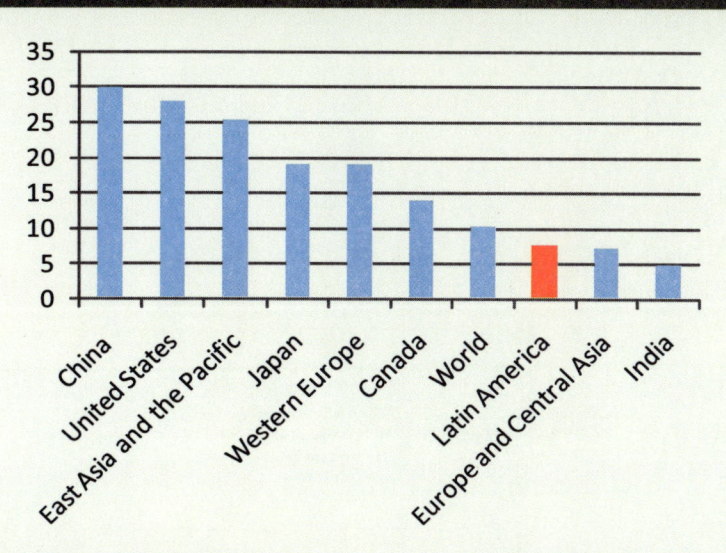

Country/Region	%
China	30
United States	28
East Asia and the Pacific	25
Japan	19
Western Europe	19
Canada	14
World	10
Latin America	7.5
Europe and Central Asia	7
India	5

Note: High Technology exports are products with high R&D intensity, such as aerospace, computers, pharma, scientific instruments, and electrical machinery.
Source: World Bank, KAM database, 2010

Figure 19 | High Technology Exports as Percent of Manufacturing Exports (Latin America)

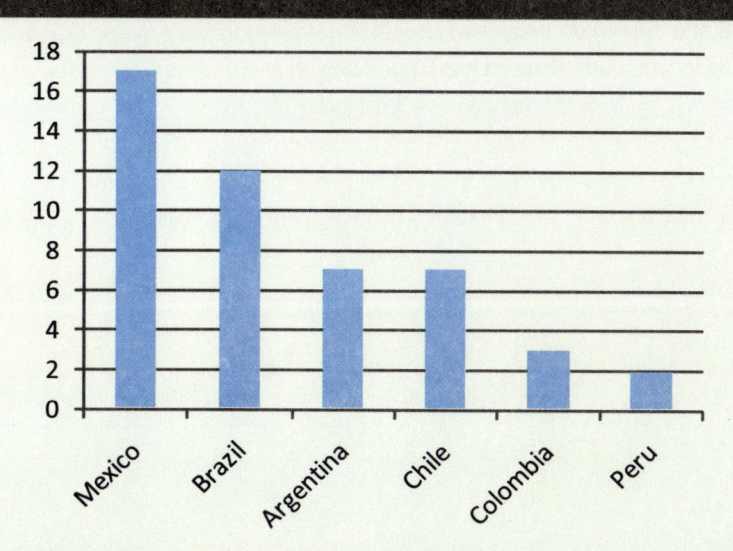

Country	%
Mexico	17
Brazil	12
Argentina	7
Chile	7
Colombia	3
Peru	2

Note: High Technology exports are products with high R&D intensity, such as aerospace, computers, pharma, scientific instruments, and electrical machinery.
Source: World Bank, KAM database, 2010

Figure 20: High Tech Exports (as % of total exports)

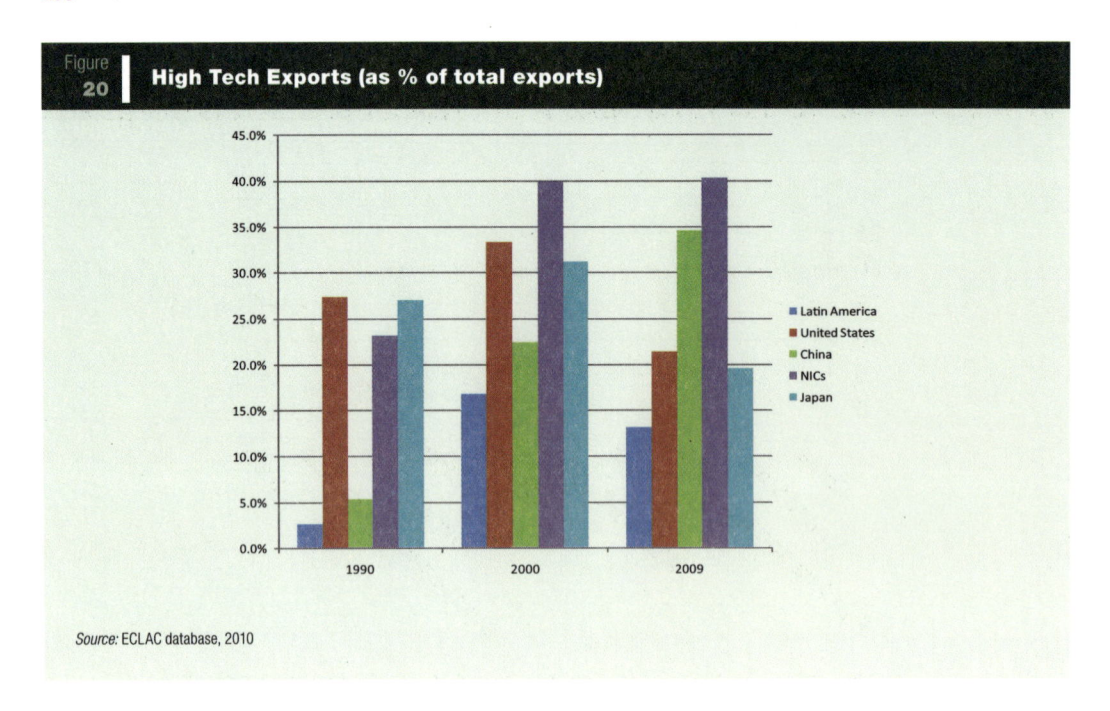

Source: ECLAC database, 2010

Chapter 9
Democratic Governance and Political Sustainability: Towards a Prosperous Latin America

Michael Shifter

For Latin America to pursue a path towards significantly enhanced prosperity in coming years, it will be crucial to build more effective democratic governance throughout the region. Ample empirical evidence has shown that such a political development is essential for the wider social and economic policies outlined in this book. To that end, governance should not be regarded as a separate realm. Rather, it is a cross-cutting concern with substantial bearing on the long-term successes of crucial goals, like promoting higher quality education or fostering greater innovation and increased competitiveness.

Although improving the quality of democratic governance is a formidable challenge, Latin America starts with a number of assets and advantages. Fortunately, elections are now commonplace, the "only game in town" throughout the region. Viewed from a long-term historical perspective, the last several decades have been highly positive in this regard, as a strong constituency and consensus has developed around the conviction that elections can provide the chief mechanism and most widely-accepted basis of legitimacy for selecting political leaders. The prevalence of elections does not mean, however, that they should be taken for granted. Their increasing use is in part the product of a salutary reaction in a number of countries to military regimes that not only committed human rights abuses, but also ultimately failed to construct sustainable and effective social and economic models. In contrast to other areas of the world—and in contrast to other periods in Latin America's history—reliable polling consistently reveals that most of the region's citizens prefer democracy to any other political model (Table 1, Figure 1), even as they are not fully satisfied.

To be sure—as Robert Dahl pointed out in his classic work *Polyarchy*[1]—though elections are essential for democracy, they are far from sufficient. Also critical are adherence to the rule of law, including a free and independent press, and a system of checks and balances, marked by a separation of powers, that effectively constrains executive authority. Vigorous citizen participation and full inclusion of all social groups are also indispensable features of a well-functioning democracy.

In these respects, as well as in the development of vital democratic institutions like political parties and the judiciary, Latin America's performance over recent years has been far more disappointing. The notion that somehow elections would necessarily be accompanied by improvements in other areas of democratic strengthening was proved mistaken, as was the theory that economic stabilization would be followed in the region by the adoption and implementation of second-generation institutional

---

1   Dahl, Robert A. Polyarchy: Participation and Opposition. New Haven: Yale University Press, 1972.

Table 1 | Support for Democracy

	Support for democracy		
	2007	2009	Variation
Paraguay	33	45	12
Venezuela	67	85	18
Colombia	47	49	2
El Salvador	38	68	30
Dominican Republic	64	67	3
Honduras	38	53	15
Chile	46	59	13
Brazil	43	55	12
Uruguay	75	81	6
Guatemala	32	41	9
Bolivia	67	71	4
Peru	47	52	5
Nicaragua	61	55	-6
Argentina	63	64	1
Mexico	48	42	-6
Panama	62	64	2
Ecuador	65	43	-22
Costa Rica	83	74	-9
Latin America	54	59	5

Source: Latinobarometro 2007-2009.

reforms. Progression in both economic policy and in political institutional development calls for sustained effort, discipline, and a long-term focus.

The latest volume of a study[2] launched in 1994 that tracks changes in effective democratic governance by examining a variety of countries and key, cross-cutting themes, found that overall the region lost some ground on this score since the first years of the 21st century. Electoral practices essentially remain intact, the study reported, but political parties in general have become less coherent and effective across the region, and the justice systems remain woefully inadequate. Major problems and risks to democratic governance—including rampant crime and citizen insecurity (much of it linked to the drug trade)—along with significant levels of corruption, are also more acute in a number of countries (Figure 2). The problem is less the absence of democracy than the relatively low quality of democracy

---

[2] Domínguez, Jorge I. and Shifter, Michael. Constructing Democratic Governance in Latin America. Baltimore: Johns Hopkins University Press, 2008.

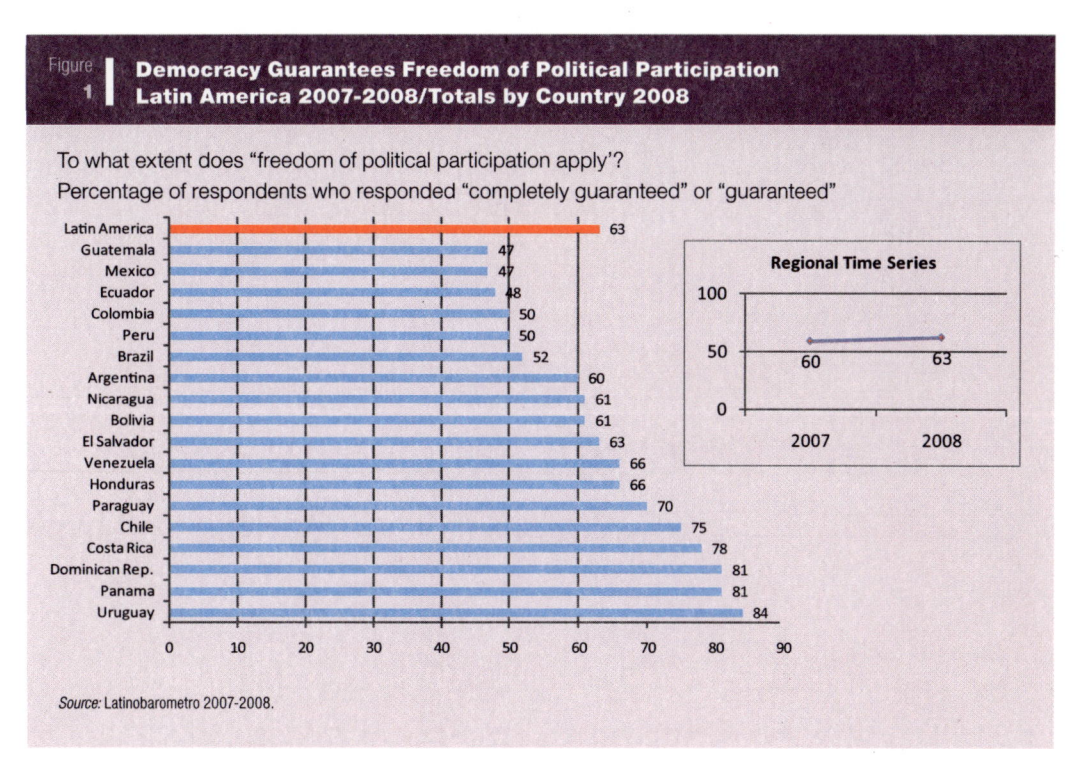

Figure 1. Democracy Guarantees Freedom of Political Participation
Latin America 2007-2008/Totals by Country 2008

To what extent does "freedom of political participation apply'?
Percentage of respondents who responded "completely guaranteed" or "guaranteed"

Country	%
Latin America	63
Guatemala	47
Mexico	47
Ecuador	48
Colombia	50
Peru	50
Brazil	52
Argentina	60
Nicaragua	61
Bolivia	61
El Salvador	63
Venezuela	66
Honduras	66
Paraguay	70
Chile	75
Costa Rica	78
Dominican Rep.	81
Panama	81
Uruguay	84

Regional Time Series: 2007: 60; 2008: 63

Source: Latinobarometro 2007-2008.

in much of the region.

The tasks of overcoming such obstacles are monumental and require a long-term, sharply-focused strategy, but unless such tendencies are reversed, the region's path to prosperity and stability will be considerably hampered. The bias towards formulas that emphasize effective democratic governance is not a matter of ideological preference. Rather, it reflects what experience in the region has worked best and has taught us. That, ultimately, is the standard against which any recommendation or idea should be measured.

Political Parties: Better than the Alternatives

The disenchantment with political parties is not peculiar to Latin America. Indeed, the decline and discrediting of political parties for failing to deliver and satisfy citizen demands is a global phenomenon. The reasons for the phenomenon are varied, including the explosion of new media and information technologies and the resultant increase in demands and expectations of the citizenry. Many parties which emerged during less globalized, technologically sophisticated and connected periods, have been struggling to cope with new pressures and thus adapt to challenging circumstances. Some have been able to reinvent themselves and perform effective roles. Others, however, have essentially imploded, leaving the political field open to individuals and forces that fill the vacuum, with no structures available to aggregate interests and mediate and channel demands. As a result, political representation has suffered (Figures 3 and 4).

Figure 2 | Most Important Problem: Crime and Unemployment
Latin America 1995-2008

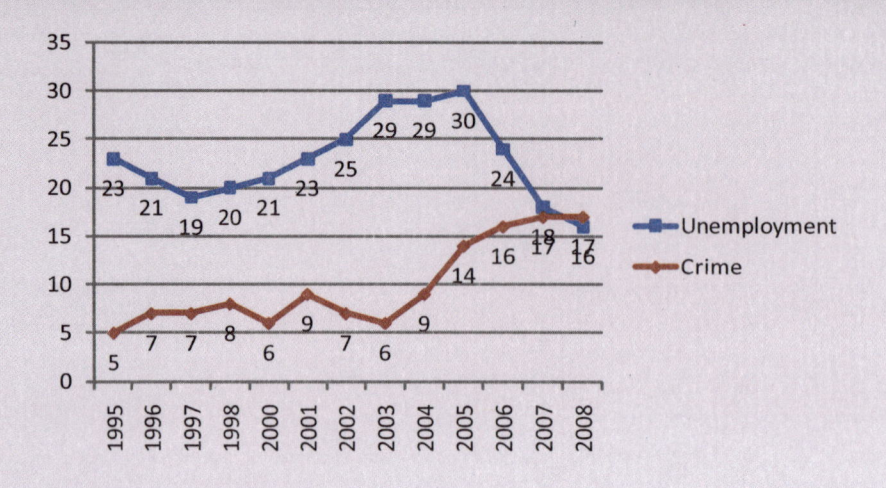

Unemployment (blue): 1995: 23, 1996: 21, 1997: 19, 1998: 20, 2000: 21, 2001: 23, 2002: 25, 2003: 29, 2004: 29, 2005: 30, 2006: 24, 2007: 18, 2008: 16

Crime (red): 1995: 5, 1996: 7, 1997: 7, 1998: 8, 2000: 6, 2001: 9, 2002: 7, 2003: 6, 2004: 9, 2005: 14, 2006: 16, 2007: 19, 2008: 17

Source: Latinobarometro 2008

Figure 3 | Evaluation of the Political Parties
Latin America 2006-2008/Totals by Country 2008

Is the work of the political parties "very good, good, bad, very bad or do you have insufficient information to reply"?

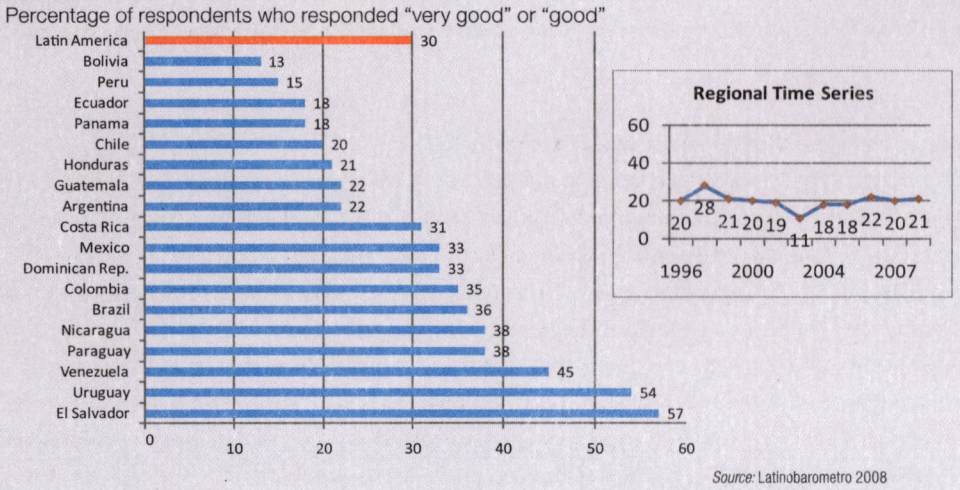

Percentage of respondents who responded "very good" or "good"

Country	%
Latin America	30
Bolivia	13
Peru	15
Ecuador	18
Panama	18
Chile	20
Honduras	21
Guatemala	22
Argentina	22
Costa Rica	31
Mexico	33
Dominican Rep.	33
Colombia	35
Brazil	36
Nicaragua	38
Paraguay	38
Venezuela	45
Uruguay	54
El Salvador	57

Regional Time Series
1996: 20, 1997: 28, 1998: 21, 2000: 20, 2001: 19, 2002: 11, 2004: 18, 2005: 18, 2006: 22, 2007: 20, 2008: 21

Source: Latinobarometro 2008

Figure 4 | Trust in Political Parties
Latin America 1996-2008/Totals by Country 2008

How much confidence do you have in political parties: a lot, some, little or no confidence?
Percentage of respondents who responded "a lot" or "some"

Country	%
Latin America	21
Peru	11
Bolivia	12
Argentina	14
Ecuador	15
Panama	16
Chile	16
Mexico	17
Honduras	20
Costa Rica	20
Colombia	20
Brazil	20
Guatemala	23
Paraguay	23
Nicaragua	24
Dominican Rep.	27
Venezuela	32
Uruguay	36
El Salvador	39

Regional Time Series

Year	Value
1996	20
	28
	21
	20
	19
	11
	18
	18
	22
	20
2007	21

Source: Latinobarometro 2008

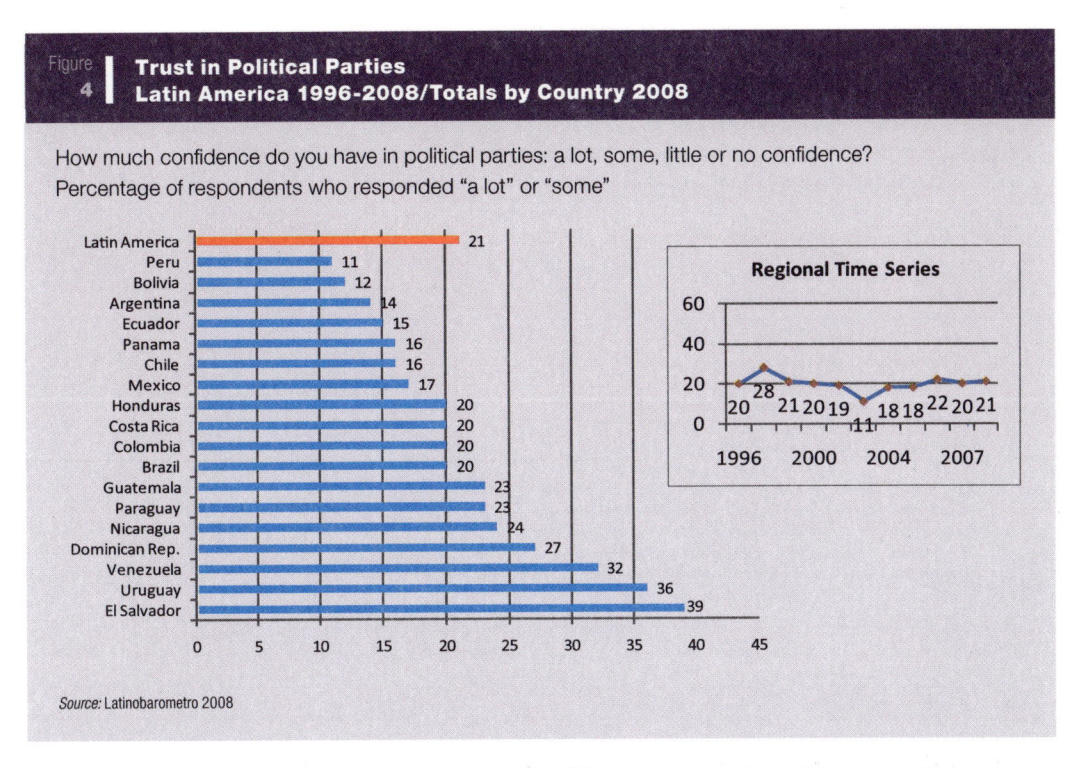

In Latin America, this phenomenon is evident to different degrees. It has taken place in a variety of situations, regardless of ideological orientation. The main precursor of the regional pattern was in Peru, with the surprise election of the consummate outsider, Alberto Fujimori, in 1990. Fujimori's support was a reaction to the bankrupt political class that had failed to resolve Peru's fundamental problems of hyperinflation and uncontrolled political violence in the late 1980s. Fujimori was able to resolve these twin problems, which were important accomplishments that helped improve both security and the economy.

But the undeniable short-term gains were put at risk by Fujimori's quest to remain in power, the erosion of the rule of law and institutional constraints, and the continued failure of political parties to renew themselves and pose a coherent alternative. Nearly two decades later, despite registering one of the best economic performances in Latin America, Peru remains politically uncertain and unpredictable (Figure 5 and 6). Political parties have failed to modernize and become effective, stable vehicles for political representation. If Peru is to pursue a more solid course of sustained development, the country will, among other challenges, need to construct more institutionalized political structures. Otherwise, it will face serious limitations.

Similar phenomena can also be discerned in the cases of Venezuela (1998), Bolivia (2005) and Ecuador (2006). The political parties failed to deliver adequately, resulting in their dissolution and the rise of popular leaders who represented an indictment of the old political order. Such cases also witnessed the mobilization and increased participation of social groups that had previously been marginal

MICHAEL SHIFTER

Figure 5 | Trust in Government
Latin America 1996-2008/Totals by Country 2008

How much confidence do you have in government: a lot, some, little or no confidence?
Percentage of respondents who responded "a lot" or "some"

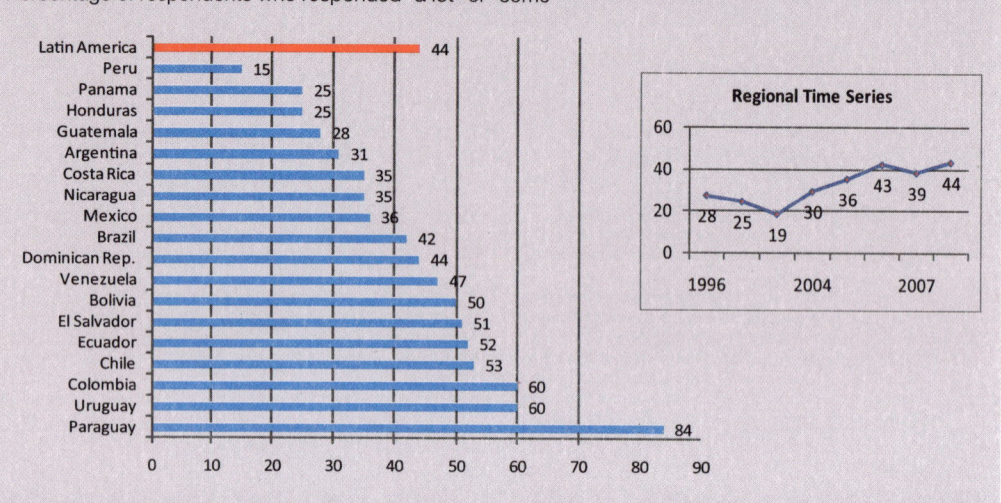

Country	%
Latin America	44
Peru	15
Panama	25
Honduras	25
Guatemala	28
Argentina	31
Costa Rica	35
Nicaragua	35
Mexico	36
Brazil	42
Dominican Rep.	44
Venezuela	47
Bolivia	50
El Salvador	51
Ecuador	52
Chile	53
Colombia	60
Uruguay	60
Paraguay	84

Regional Time Series

Year	Value
1996	28
	25
	19
2004	30
	36
	43
2007	39
	44

Source: Latinobarometro 1996-2008

Figure 6 | Democracy in My Country Works Better than in the Rest of Latin America 2008

Do you think that democracy in your country works better, worse or equal to the rest of Latin America?
Percentage of respondents who responded "better"

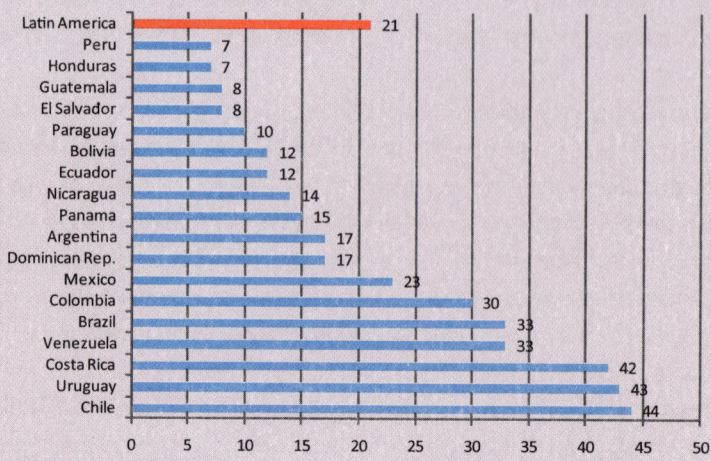

Country	%
Latin America	21
Peru	7
Honduras	7
Guatemala	8
El Salvador	8
Paraguay	10
Bolivia	12
Ecuador	12
Nicaragua	14
Panama	15
Argentina	17
Dominican Rep.	17
Mexico	23
Colombia	30
Brazil	33
Venezuela	33
Costa Rica	42
Uruguay	43
Chile	44

Source: Latinobarometro 2008

to, or excluded from, political life, including the indigenous community and afro-descendants.

This introduction of new political actors is surely a measure of democratic progress. But the opportunity for marginalized groups to affect change in the political sphere will only persist over the long term if national institutions are devised that can effectively express and represent the interests and demands of such groups outside of elections. It is noteworthy that heightened demands on the political system—and the emergence of "people power" in these societies—coincided with the period of strong and impressive economic growth in Latin America (2003-2008).

But there have been few signs of a corresponding robustness in political institutionalization, not only among these newly incorporated groups but among the traditional political parties that confront challenges of renovation and reform. The political models and systems that have emerged reflect deep changes in the society, and some temporary adjustments are in order. Over the longer term, however, it will be essential to develop political parties that will not only improve the quality of democracy but also make governance more predictable and effective. Greater certainty and consistency in governmental performance will eventually build higher levels of trust among average citizens.

As Latin America looks toward the next several decades, its focus will need to be on strengthening a variety of institutions, including political parties. To be sure, in some countries there has recently been alternation, which is a healthy ingredient for political competition. In 2000, Mexico ended a long-stretch of single party rule, as did Paraguay in 2008, and El Salvador in 2009. The same took place in Chile in December 2009. These examples also provoke a related issue which has received scant attention: the role of Latin America's opposition parties in demonstrating the importance of coalition building and substantive disagreement. Again, the tendency for such parties to criticize and denounce, without coming up with viable alternative policy ideas, is a global feature, but such behavior especially impedes Latin America's pursuit of a successful long-term strategy since it can encourage attempts to limit citizen access to opposing points of view.

In some countries with traditionally strong political parties, such as Chile and Colombia, the party system has become attenuated, but is far from imploding. On the other hand, Brazil's democratic governance has improved in recent years in part because a highly fragmented and fractured political party system has become more cohesive since the 1990s. In this case, overall steady performance and political development are mutually reinforcing. Continuity and predictability are best insured when political parties function effectively.

The reform agenda is a formidable one. It includes developing better mechanisms of representation between elites and the party followers; clearer and more modern rules on campaign financing; programmatic orientations that go beyond just being electoral vehicles and instead focus on generating new ideas and policies; and greater openness in selecting new leaders and stronger mechanisms of transparency and accountability for the parties' business. Solidifying such steps is critical for Latin America's long-term prosperity and success, especially given that political party development has not kept up with the profound transformations in the social fabric in many of the region's countries.

Institutions vs. Leadership: A False Choice

The weakening of political parties in recent years has resulted in the emergence of strong leaders who seem to display an appetite for remaining in power. Despite claims to the contrary, this is not a question of ideology; those leaders who have sought to cling to power reflect different ideological tendencies. In addition, it is a mistake to argue that for long-term success it is important to have strong institutions and weak leaders, or vice versa. The institutions/leadership relationship, so central to effective democratic governance, is not zero-sum. Rather, it is possible—indeed essential—to have institutions that are efficient, modern and open and leaders that exhibit these same characteristics. Striking the right balance—making them mutually reinforcing—is the most effective formula to overcome Latin America's barriers to sustained success and dynamism.

Moreover, there is no single, correct prescription for what has become increasingly commonplace throughout the region: consecutive presidential reelection. Today in Latin America, the countries that do not allow such consecutive reelection are the exception, not the rule. There are sensible arguments in favor and against the idea, and each country presents its own particular circumstances and challenges, with some needing to confront emergencies and others embarked on a self-described "revolutionary" path.

What is important, however, is that the rules of the democratic game be fully respected and adhered to, and that presidents do not ride roughshod over institutions to impose their will. When reelection reforms are carried out within a constitutional framework, in accordance with accepted procedures, there is no transgression involved. In this regard, the process through which to implement change is fundamental. There is a notable contrast, for example, between the way reelection changes were carried out in Brazil in the 1990s and today in Nicaragua, where adherence to basic rules of democratic procedure have been problematic.

To achieve political leadership that is salutary and competitive, and that can best contribute to long-term successful development, it is important to provide incentives for constant renewal and the incorporation of younger leaders from diverse backgrounds. This is a serious problem in a number of Latin American countries, where institutional rigidities and societal realities such as discrimination and exclusion stifle sufficient opportunities for upward mobility in political parties and movements.

A number of political scientists have studied the extent to which the same political figures remain on the scene for many years, without giving room to others with political aspirations.[3] That the same well-known figures continue to dominate politics for many years is an indicator of the weak mechanisms for political training. It also can become troublingly self-perpetuating, as such figures sometimes refuse to yield their positions to others, and manipulate the rules to keep out prospective leaders. Such practices contribute to political disillusionment and cynicism. If Latin America is going to pursue the thoroughgoing reforms necessary—and to compete effectively in the global economy—its leadership profile will have to undergo important changes.

In addition, the leadership style most suitable for the challenges facing Latin America over the long

---

[3] See for example Presidents Without Parties: The Politics of Economic Reform in Argentina and Venezuela in the 1990s by Javier Corrales (Pennsylvania State University Press, 2002).

term is one of consultation, dialogue and consensus-building. The alternative, a more arbitrary mode of decision-making, may have certain advantages in the short-term, but over an extended period it simply does not work in such a complicated globalized economy and society. In some of the Latin American countries with a dominant single leader, either of the left or the right, ministers have little autonomy to make critical decisions in their respective areas. Over time, this undermines morale and weakens any incentives to pursue the highest levels of public service. Decision-making needs to be shared and delegated, yet animated by a clear vision and focused agenda for progress.

In contrast, countries such as Chile (over the past two decades) and Brazil (most notably, since the mid-1990s) have been characterized by a political style that involves a great deal of negotiation and give-and-take. This has resulted in gradual, but considerable, success. For some, the progress may be frustratingly slow, but over the longer term such a model tends to work best and to minimize risks and uncertainties. Seen from a broader historical perspective, it is particularly striking that as Brazil faces a critical election in 2010, few analysts expect any significant departure from the country's current, reasonably successful, economic and political course.

Photo Credit: Uri Rosenheck

In fact, incremental reforms, moving in a positive direction, appear to be far more enduring and effective than attempts at major constitutional overhauls that promise to "refound" the nation. That is one of the main conclusions reached by Jorge Dominguez in *Constructing Democratic Governance*,[4] based on systematic case studies of some eight Latin American countries. Pursuing wildly ambitious, grandiose changes may be politically convenient and tempting, but it risks setting up the electorate for disappointment, since in practical terms it is often hard to fulfill the expectations raised.

Far more effective, Dominguez suggests, are piecemeal reforms and laws that seek to address a specific question and are carefully targeted and well thought out. In Latin America, limited political capital tends to be spent on rewriting constitutions or aiming for sweeping changes when more

---

[4] Domínguez, Jorge I. "Three Decades Since the Start of the Democratic Transitions" from Constructing Democratic Governance in Latin America. Baltimore: Johns Hopkins Press, 2008.

particular reforms would have greater feasibility and would not take away the oxygen from a political system that is already overwhelmed.

In Latin America, it is important to have leaders that are able to blend, as Albert Hirschman noted nearly four decades ago, both charisma and skills.[5] Each is important, and both sometimes enter into tension with one another. For Hirschman, skill had to do with the ability to perceive opportunities for change and not to keep too high a standard about what constitutes acceptable reform. He notes that in the periods of greatest reform, such as Colombia during the 1960s, political leaders demonstrated this skill and subsequently helped produce important changes.

The current challenge is to find leaders who are able to acknowledge relatively modest achievements and turn them to their political advantage. In Latin America, all too frequently there is pressure on a single, narrow issue that bears little relation to what is politically feasible and practical. The test of political leaders, in Latin America and elsewhere, is to be able to deal with such pressure and have the ability and skill to point to signs of progress.

Rule of Law: Critical Agenda for Reform

The judicial sector is another critical institution for effective democratic governance that has had a disappointing performance in recent years. At least since the early 1960s there have been major efforts, often backed by bilateral aid agencies and more recently by multilateral banks, to improve the quality and independence of the judiciary. Though no reliable, systematic evaluation has been carried out, the results appear to be mixed according to credible and independent human rights groups such as Freedom House and Human Rights Watch-Americas that closely track judicial performance.

There have surely been some notable advances. Many of the highest levels of Latin American judiciaries, including the Supreme Courts, enjoy a considerable degree of autonomy and have been able to make meaningful decisions with important consequences. For example, a May 2006 Constitutional Court decision in Colombia allowed for abortion (which had previously been criminalized without exception) to save the life of the mother or in cases of incest or rape. The decision was notable in this conservative country, and was based in part on international law. Another relevant example is Guatemala's Constitutional court, which has recently delivered critical decisions related to judicial reform in that country. In addition, there have been new institutions developed in many countries, such as ombudsman offices, that bolster the judicial system and can be effective in administrative and human rights matters.

In a number of countries, moreover, there has been a shift to the accusatory system, which has contributed greater openness and accountability in most court proceedings. It is also worth underlining the role of the independent Inter-American Human Rights Commission (and the Inter-American Human Rights Court), an arm of the Organization of American States that has developed an important body of regional jurisprudence on an array of issues. The efficacy of the Commission has not gone unnoticed in a region where other judicial actors are lacking; the IAHRC has been asked to handle a

---

5 Hirschman, Albert O. "Underdevelopment, Obstacles to Perception of Change, and Leadership," from A Bias for Hope: Essays on Development and Latin America. New Haven: Yale University Press, 1971. pp. 328-341.

huge number of cases in recent years. Through its useful thematic reports, it has also illuminated key human rights problems and challenges in the Americas, including discrimination against women and indigenous groups, and also the state of the region's prison system.

At the same time, however, longstanding problems of corruption, excessive red tape, and politicization persist in the judicial system in many countries. Pre-trial detentions of those accused of crimes continue to be unacceptably long, and impunity is more the rule than the exception, as credible groups like Human Rights Watch-Americas often emphasize. Public opinion surveys show a disturbingly low level of trust in the justice system (along with political parties) (Figure 7).

Even countries like Brazil that seem to be on a sound path towards greater prosperity are significantly handicapped because of a justice system (including prisons) that fails to meet modern, acceptable standards. Unresolved problems in judicial performance will pose major bottlenecks to the region's progress and prospects over the next several decades. A lack of judicial openness, professionalism, and minimal effectiveness will, for example, substantially discourage the investment in key economic sectors that is essential for long-term growth and enhanced competitiveness.

Moreover, governments throughout the region need to seriously confront the greatest risk and problem for effective democratic governance: spreading criminality. If the government fails to deliver basic security and is unable to protect its citizens from physical violence and assault on a significant scale, it will have a hard time marshalling the requisite confidence and focusing on tasks associated

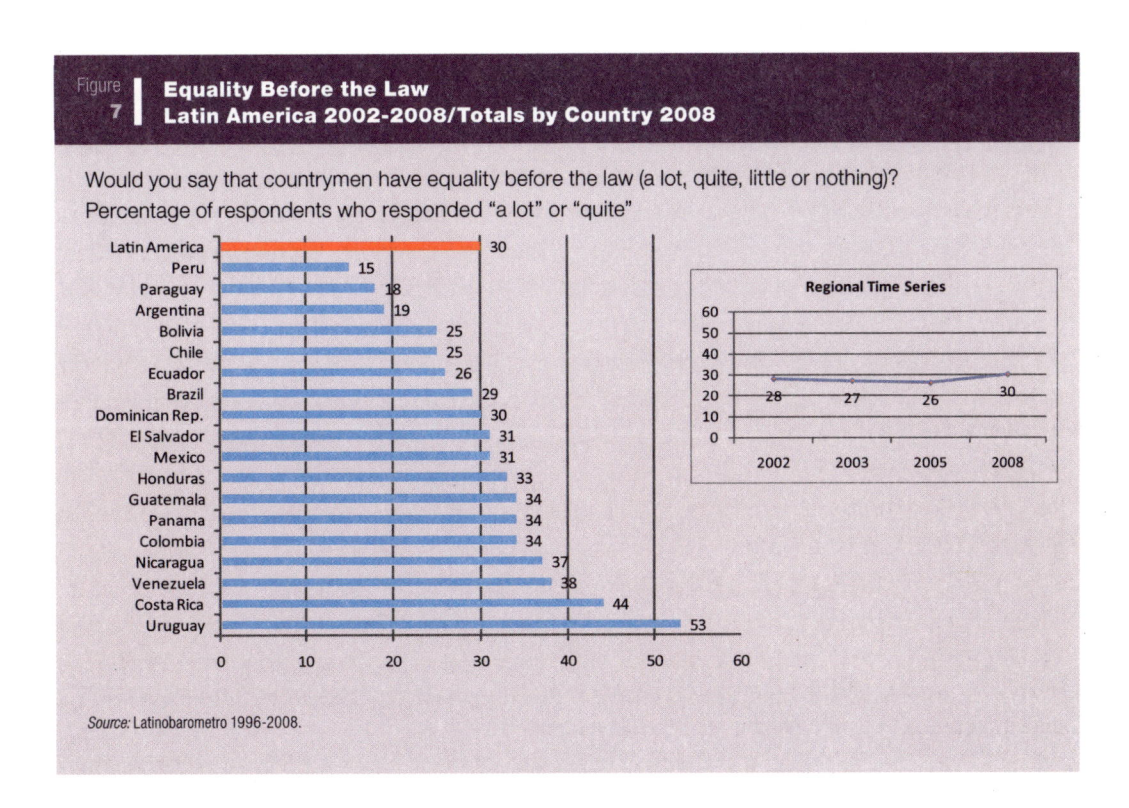

Figure 7

Equality Before the Law
Latin America 2002-2008/Totals by Country 2008

Would you say that countrymen have equality before the law (a lot, quite, little or nothing)?
Percentage of respondents who responded "a lot" or "quite"

Country	%
Latin America	30
Peru	15
Paraguay	18
Argentina	19
Bolivia	25
Chile	25
Ecuador	26
Brazil	29
Dominican Rep.	30
El Salvador	31
Mexico	31
Honduras	33
Guatemala	34
Panama	34
Colombia	34
Nicaragua	37
Venezuela	38
Costa Rica	44
Uruguay	53

Regional Time Series

Year	2002	2003	2005	2008
	28	27	26	30

Source: Latinobarometro 1996-2008.

with economic dynamism and growth. This is a problem that requires a far more energetic approach than in the past, as violence becomes ever more present throughout Central America, terrorist groups like the Shining Path regroup as drug traffickers in Peru, and drug cartels wreak sustained chaos in Mexico. It is true that a certain degree of criminality is found in even the most prosperous countries, but in Latin America the current levels are both unsustainable and far exceed those in other regions.

Aside from the serious flaws in many justice systems, and the urgent need for reform, there is an equally compelling case to be made for major governmental action on police reform. This has been a relatively neglected area of public policy, but the gap between the gravity of the problem (which, experts claim, shows no sign of abating in coming years) and the capacity of police forces to respond adequately, is growing. Rampant crime and insecurity will continue to limit growth and prosperity in a number of Latin American countries, including Brazil and, of course, Mexico. Corruption and lack of professionalism besets police forces throughout the region, and any long-term strategy for significant progress will have to tackle this problem seriously. Otherwise, the potential for huge strides forward will be jeopardized.

Civil Service Reform: Getting the Best Talent for a New Agenda
The likelihood of Latin American governments pursuing systematic reforms in the variety of necessary areas depends, in great measure, on engaging and trusting the right citizens to design and carry them out. It also hinges on having public officials serve continuously, for an extended period of time without constant interruption and turnover, without which any serious reform remains preemptively problematic. The region needs a significant push with the aim of assuring to the greatest extent possible the highest quality personnel remain active and supported in their roles, so that policy can be implemented and tweaked with a level of continuity.

For the most part, however, there has been a high dose of politicization in civil service bureaucracy, which too frequently stalls or impedes well-intentioned reform efforts. The turnover of top cabinet officials in Latin America has been particularly striking. According to the Inter-American Development Bank, between 1990 and 2000 "almost a quarter (22 percent) of all ministers in a sample of 12 Latin American countries remained in the same portfolio for less than six months," while 75 percent remained for less than two years. Notable exceptions have been Uruguay and Chile; the latter has had only one finance minister during each of the four successive governments of the Concertacion. Though Chile's relatively sound performance, both on economic and governance issues, can be explained by a number of variables, continuity at the finance and other ministries is a major positive factor and might offer some lessons and guidance for other countries.

The region would also benefit from a civil service reform that ensures that competent, capable persons hold key positions. One reason why Latin America's macroeconomic performance has improved in recent years, for example, is because many of the region's finance ministers and their teams have been of high caliber, with technical expertise. They have practiced fiscal discipline and, in many countries, have been effectively shielded from political pressures.

This is not, however, a trend that has been extended to the various other ministries in which reforms and sound policies are equally essential for significant advances. Rather, in many cases, those in charge have been appointed for their political function more than their substantive, technical competence. Selection on the basis of merit—and corresponding pay for the best talent— is fundamental for ensuring a high level of competence of those responsible for presiding over the region's most needed reforms. Otherwise, there will be continued mediocrity and frustration in the very areas that have for too long been neglected but that are most critical for long-term prosperity. Civil services need to be substantially retooled, aimed at greater professionalization and better technical expertise, to meet the challenges of globalized economies.

Decentralization: In Pursuit of Democracy and Efficiency

Latin America presents a highly varied landscape in terms of the balance between national and regional and local centers of power. Centralization has, in a number of countries, been an Achilles heel that has stood in the way of broad-based, equitable development. It is not uncommon for capital cities to have disproportionate political power and economic resources, creating highly skewed development with significant disparities, as well as contributing to social discontent and resentment between urban centers and provinces. For Latin America's long-term prosperity, it is critical to overcome the vast differences and move towards a greater equilibrium.

In fact, to Latin America's credit, the region has made significant strides in recent years in promoting decentralized governance and greater local control. State and municipal officials are now often elected directly instead of appointed. There have been important movements and tendencies in some countries towards greater local autonomy, both in terms of local political prerogatives and management of finances. But there are no hard and fast rules when it comes to the precise division of powers at the national and local levels. The principle of local control is important—for example, in education reform efforts—and should be applied to promote local democracy to increase participation and inclusion, but also to improve efficiency. Some of the region's initiatives on participatory budgets, for example, have been highly promising. The challenge, as always, is to combine maximum democratic input with workable, practical systems of governance.

At the same time, however, reformers need to be sensitive to the nature of power at the local level in a number of countries, which causes some concern about reversing positive trends. Traditional forms of patronage and clientelism are common outside of major cities, so it is important to avoid public policies that end up reinforcing such patterns and further concentrating power in the hands of a select few. The risks of unintended consequences in this policy sphere need to be borne in mind if a serious, long-term strategy aimed at sustained growth is going to be attempted. It will be crucial to look carefully at the circumstances, and local political structure, of each situation, and only after doing so seeking to further decentralized control and greater autonomy where it makes sense.

Forging New Partnerships: Government/Private Sector/Civil Society

If Latin America is to experience significantly enhanced growth and development in the coming decades it will be critical to build a partnership—in effect, a governance model—that involves a lean, efficient government, a socially conscious, responsible, and modern private sector, and a vibrant and pragmatic civil society. In Latin America, where such a combination exists, as in Chile and Brazil, the results have been highly favorable. In other countries there is a relationship marked by mutual suspicion and, sometimes, even antagonism. Such a negative dynamic poses a major obstacle for sustained progress on a variety of fronts.

It is hard to say what the precise balance should be between these three sectors; this will vary from country to country, and from issue to issue. But a formula that recognizes that each of the sectors has a vital part to play in the region's development is an important step forward. Still in Latin America, one of these sectors is vilified by another, and one is regarded as necessarily negative, and another as altogether positive (there are, for example, still such sterile discussions between civil society figures and those representing the private sector or even government). The relationship among the three is, moreover, seen as a zero-sum game, rather than a win-win situation.

Like the political leadership style that emphasizes consultation and dialogue, this kind of partnership may require a great deal of time and effort to construct. It is tempting for each to go its own way, and easier too (perhaps this explains the polarization that has often marked the past decades). But while such a practice might lead to short-term advantages and favorable positioning, it also risks missing an important opportunity to construct a style and model of governance that can be highly democratic and efficacious, and can eventually yield long-term growth and prosperity in Latin America.

To make such partnerships effective will require fundamental internal reforms and improvements in each of the three sectors. In a number of key Latin American countries the private sector continues to lag in fulfilling its fiscal responsibilities, without which it is virtually impossible to manage reasonably efficient government services. Higher levels of corporate social responsibility remains a fundamental challenge, including deeper engagement in questions of education reform, and a stronger commitment to philanthropic undertakings, still incipient at best in most countries of the region. Such a transformation in the private sector needs to be complemented by more thoroughgoing public sector reform, which has stalled in too many countries, in a variety of critical areas.

Photo Credit: CAF

Finally, though Latin America is endowed with a relatively rich tradition of civil society organizations, many of the groups in that sector are ill-equipped to meet challenges that could make the region more prosperous and equitable. In too many of these organizations there is a great degree of bureaucratization and often politicization. It is crucial to put more emphasis on professional, not political, criteria in guiding day-to-day operations.

It is similarly essential for such organizations to overcome insularity, make more systematic connections, and develop better working relationships with the private sector and the government. Many civil society organizations make a vital contribution in providing services, proposing viable policy alternatives, or holding government and private sector groups to account. Still, there is a crucial need and great opportunity to improve internal governance structures and thereby increase legitimacy and credibility in the eyes of the wider society.

Recommendations:
- Build on sound electoral institutions in most countries and focus on improving responsiveness and coherence of political parties, which have low levels of public confidence;
- Encourage a more constructive role for opposition parties, based on alternative policy options and ideas for reform, to enhance competitiveness of the political system;
- Develop incentives for promoting renewal and modernization of political leaders, with an emphasis on the younger generation. Current structures have become ossified in many countries;
- Pursue constitutional changes to support greater flexibility and accountability in the political system, but do so in an incremental way, not through abrupt overhauls. Any move to alter term-limit laws should be carried out in full accordance with accepted, democratic rules;
- Give priority attention to improving the effectiveness and independence of judicial systems, which is essential to strengthen the rule of law and reduce currently high levels of impunity;
- Undertake a significant, sustained effort to reform and professionalize police forces, absolutely critical to address spreading criminality in the region, the chief risk to effective democratic governance;
- Discourage high turnover in key ministries, to enable greater policy continuity and coherence. Retool the civil service by extending standards of competence and considerations of merit from finance ministries in many countries to other key agencies also vital for national, effective governance;
- Advance towards greater decentralization and local control in economic and political decision-making, without resorting to clientelism and traditional forms of patronage (that tend to breed corruption);
- Forge more effective partnerships among civil society organizations, the private sector, and government entities through collaborative efforts on specific policy areas and undertake internal reforms and modernization in each of the sectors.

References

Chapter 1

Ferreira, Francisco H. G. and Martin Ravallion. 2008. "Global Poverty and Inequality: A Review of the Evidence." Policy Research Working Paper 4623. Washington, DC: The World Bank, Development Research Group Poverty Team (May).

Gasparini, Leonardo, Guillermo Cruces, Leopoldo Tornarolli and Mariana Marchioni. 2009. "A Turning Point? Recent Developments on Inequality in Latin America and the Caribbean." Working Paper no. 81 (February). CEDLAS.

Intenational Emergy Agency (IEA). 2007.

Kohli, Harpaul Alberto and Phillip Basil. 2011. "Requirements for Infrastructure Investment in Latin American Under Alternate Growth Scenarios: 2011–2040." Global Journal of Emerging Market Economies, 3(1).

Latino-barómetro 2009.

Maddison, A. 2004. *The World Economy*, a Millennial perspective.

Intenational Emergy Agency (IEA) 2007.

International Monetary Fund. 2010. *Direction of Trade database*.

International Monetary Fund. 2010. *Non-feul Commodity Price Index*, 2010.

International Monetary Fund. 2010. *World Economic Outlook,* Washington DC, and various issues.

Scandizzo, Stefanio and Pablo Sanguinetti. 2009. *Infrastructure in Latin America: achieving high impact management.* CAF's annual Reporte De Economía y Desarrollo.

UNESCO. 2010. *Education for All Global Monitoring Report: Reaching the Marginalized.* Paris, France: UNESCO.

-- **2009.** *Global Education Digest*. Paris, France: UNESCO.

World Bank. 2009. *Edstats online database*.

World Bank. 2009, *KEI and KI Indexes*, KAM**.**

World Bank. 2010. *World Development Indicators*, and various issues

World Economic Forum. 2009. *Global Competitive Index* 2008-2009.

Chapter 2

Blanchard, Olivier, and John Simon. 2001. *The Long and Large Decline in U.S. Output Volatility,* Brookings Papers on Economic Activity, 1, pp. 135-64.

Council of Economic Advisers. February 28, 2009. *Economic Projections and the Budget Outlook*, available at: www.whitehouse.gov/administration/eop/cea

OECD. 2010. *Global Development Outlook* (forthcoming).

Spence, A. Michael (chair). 2008. *The Growth Report*, The Commission on Growth and Development.

H. Kharas et al. 2008. "Chilean Growth through East Asian Eyes," Working Paper No. 31, Commission on Growth and Development.

H. Kharas. 2008. *The Emerging Middle Class in Developing Countries*, background paper.

H. Kharas et al. 2010 (forthcoming). *The Four Speed World*, (forthcoming), The Brookings Institution.

H. Kharas, 2009. *The Promise: Makings of a Determined Marathoner*, Asian Development Bank.

Nomura International. 2009.

Paul Collier. 2007. *The Bottom Billion*, New York: Oxford UP.

Phillippe Aghion and Peter Howitt. 2006. "Appropriate Growth Policy," Schumpeter Lecture, Journal of the European Economic Association, Papers and Proceedings on why Europe converged with the US after WWII, but more recently has faced slower tfp growth.

Pritchett, Lant. 1997. "Divergence, Big Time," Journal of Economic Perspectives, American Economic Association, vol. 11(3), pages 3-17, Summer.

IGill and H. Kharas. 2007. *An East Asian Renaissance, were the first economists to develop this concept of the middle income trap.*

International Monetary Fund. 2009. *World Economic Outlook.*

World Bank. 2009. *World Development Indicators.*

Surjit S. Bhalla. 2010 (forthcoming). "*Devaluing Your Way to Prosperity*", Peterson Institute.

Surjit Bhalla. October 2008. "*Indian Economic Growth*, 1950-2008", available at: http://oxusresearch.com/downloads/CE140309.pdf.

United States Council of Economic Advisors. February 28, 2009. *Economic Projections and the Budget Outlook.*

Chapter 3

Boorman, Jack. 2008. Global Imbalances, Oil revenues and Capital Flows to Emerging market Countries, in Kohli H., *Growth and Development in Emerging Market economies* .Sage. New Delhi.

CEPAL. 2007. *Balance Preliminar de las economías de América Latina y el Caribe.*

CEPAL. 2007. *Anuario Estadístico de América latina y el Caribe.*

CEPAL. 2007. *Panorama Social de América Latina.*

REFERENCES

Chandy, L; Gertz, G; Linn, J. 2009. *Tracking the Global Economic Recovery: Insights on the IMF New World Economic Outlook*, Wolfensohn Center for Development at Brookings.

Corporación Andina de Fomento. 2004. "Reflexiones sobre como retomar el Crecimiento,"- Caracas, Reporte de Economía y Desarrollo.

Corporación Andina de Fomento. 2005. "América Latina en el comercio global," - Caracas, Reporte de Economía y Desarrollo.

Corporación Andina de Fomento. 2006. "Camino a la Transformación Productiva en América Latina," - Caracas, Reporte de Economía y Desarrollo.

Corporación Andina de Fomento. 2007-2008. "Oportunidades en América Latina: Hacia una Mejor política social,"- Caracas, Reporte de Economía y Desarrollo.

Institute of International Finance. January 2009. *Capital Flows to Emerging Economies.*

Emerging Market Forum, *Financial Development and Stability Index, supplement of de Emerging markets*

Institute of International Finance. June 2009. "Capital Flows to Emerging Market Economies",

International Monetary Fund. 2010. *Direction of Trade, database*

International Monetary Fund. April 2010. *International Financial Statistics*, IMF.org website.

International Monetary Fund. April 2010. *Regional Economic Outlook*: Western Hemisphere.

International Monetary Fund, *World Economic Outlook,* Washington DC, various issues.

International Monetary Fund,. 2002-2009. *Global Financial Stability Report*, Washington DC.

Loser, Claudio. 2008. "Financial Markets in Latin America", Claudio Loser, in "*Growth and Development in Emerging Market Economies*", Harinder Kohli, Ed. Sage Publications.

Loser, Claudio. October 2008. "Latin America: Into the Unknown" in Emerging Markets, *Where the Chips fall. How today's global markets will impact emerging market economies*, Washington.

Loser, Claudio. 2008. *Cross-Border Trade and Investment among Emerging Economies: Lessons from differing experiences in Africa, Asia and Latin America*, Emerging Market Forum.

Loser, Claudio. 2008. *The Prospects for Latin America: Risks and Opportunities with a Historical Perspective* (Rev. June 2008, Emerging Market Forum.

Loser, Claudio. October 2008-January 2009. *By the Numbers in Latin American Advisor.*

Loser, Claudio, "América Latina y el Caribe en la coyuntura económica internacional ¿Ilusión perdida o Nuevo Realismo?" Anual Report of Instituto Elcano (Madrid)

Loser, Claudio. January 2008. "The International Finance Institutions and Latin America: A return to the cycle." Center for Hemispheric Policy, Miami.

OANDA Corporation, FX History

UN World Tourism Organization. April 2009. *World Tourism Barometer* – Interim Update

UNCTAD. 2006, 2007, 2008. *World Investment Report*,

World Federation of Exchanges, database

Chapter 4

Alejo, Javier, Marcelo Bergolo, Fedora Carbajal, and Guillermo Cruces. 2009. "Cambios en la desigualdad del ingreso en América Latina. Contribución de sus principales determinantes. (1995-2006). Informe Final." Background paper prepared for the UNDP project Markets, the State and the Dynamics of Inequality in Latin America co-ordinated by Luis Felipe Lopez-Calva and Nora Lustig. (http://undp.economiccluster-lac.org/).

Altimir, Oscar. 2008. "Distribución del ingreso e incidencia de la pobreza a lo largo del ajuste" Revista de la CEPAL No. 96 (December).

Atal, Juan Pablo, Hugo Ñopo and Natalia Winder. 2009. "Gender and ethnic wage gaps in Latin America and the Caribbean. An extensive review of the literature and contemporary estimates for the region." Washington, DC: Inter-American Development Bank (June).

Atkinson, Anthony B., and Thomas Piketty, eds. 2007. Top Incomes over the Twentieth Century: A Contrast Between European and English Speaking Countries. Oxford: Oxford University Press.

___. 2010. Top Incomes over the Twentieth Century vol. II: A Global View. Oxford: Oxford University Press

Barros, Ricardo Paes de, Mirela de Carvalho, Samuel Franco, and Rosane Mendonça. 2010 (forthcoming). "Markets, the State and the Dynamics of Inequality: Brazil's case study." In Declining Inequality in Latin America: A Decade of Progress? (forthcoming), edited by Luis Felipe López Calva and Nora Lustig, chapter 5. Washington DC: Brookings Institution.

Barros, Ricardo, Francisco H. G. Ferreira, José R. Molinas Vega, and Jaime Saavedra Chanduvi. 2009. Measuring Inequality of Opportunities in Latin America and the Caribbean. Washington, DC: World Bank.

Chen, Shaohua, and Martin Ravallion. 2008. "The Developing World Is Poorer Than We Thought, But No Less Successful in the Fight against Poverty." Policy Research Working Paper 4703. Washington, DC: The World Bank.

De Ferranti, David, Guillermo Perry, Francisco H. G. Ferreira, and Michael Walton, eds. 2004. Inequality in Latin America and the Caribbean. Breaking with History? Washington, DC: World Bank.

Eberhard, Juan and Eduardo Engel. 2008. "Decreasing Wage Inequality in Chile." Background paper prepared for the UNDP Project Markets, the State and the Dynamics of Inequality: How to Advance Inclusive Growth, co-ordinated by Luis Felipe Lopez-Calva and Nora Lustig. (http://undp.economiccluster-lac.org/).

ECLAC. 2007. *Social Panorama of Latin America*. Santiago, Chile.

Esquivel, Gerardo. 2009. "The Dynamics of Income Inequality in Mexico since NAFTA." Background paper prepared for the UNDP project Markets, the State and the Dynamics of Inequality: How to Advance Inclusive Growth, co-ordinated by Luis Felipe Lopez- Calva and Nora Lustig. (http://undp.economiccluster-lac.org/).

Esquivel, Gerardo, Nora Lustig, and John Scott. forthcoming. "A Decade of Falling Inequality in Mexico: Market Forces or State Action?" In Declining Inequality in Latin America: A Decade of Progress? (forthcoming), edited by Luis Felipe López Calva and Nora Lustig, chapter 6. Brookings Institution.

Ferreira, Francisco H. G. and Martin Ravallion. 2008. "Global Poverty and Inequality: A Review of the Evidence." Policy Research Working Paper 4623. Washington, DC: The World Bank, Development Research Group Poverty Team (May).

Ferreira, Francisco H. G., Phillipe G. Leite and Julie A. Litchfield. 2007. "The Rise and Fall of Brazilian Inequality: 1981-2004." Macroeconomic Dynamics (June): 1-32.

Fiszbein and Psacharopoulos. 1995. "Income Inequality Trends in Latin America in the 1980s." in Coping with Austerity: Poverty and Inequality in Latin America edited by Nora Lustig, 71-100. Washington DC: Brookings Institution.

Gasparini, Leonardo, and Guillermo Cruces. 2010 (forthcoming). "A Distribution in Motion: The Case of Argentina." In Declining Inequality in Latin America: A Decade of Progress? edited by Luis Felipe López Calva and Nora Lustig, chapter 4. Washington, DC: Brookings Institution.

Gasparini, Leonardo, Guillermo Cruces, Leopoldo Tornarolli and Mariana Marchioni. 2009. "A Turning Point? Recent Developments on Inequality in Latin America and the Caribbean." Working Paper no. 81 (February). CEDLAS.

Gray Molina, George, and Ernesto Yañez. 2009. "The Dynamics of Inequality in the Best and Worst Times, Bolivia 1997-2007." Discussion paper prepared for the UNDP Project Markets, the State and the Dynamics of Inequality: How to Advance Inclusive Growth, co-ordinated by Luis Felipe Lopez-Calva and Nora Lustig. (http://undp.economiccluster-lac.org/).

Jaramillo, Miguel, and Jaime Saavedra. 2010 (forthcoming). "Inequality in Post-Structural Reform Peru: The Role of Market and Policy Forces." In Declining Inequality in Latin America: A Decade of Progress? (forthcoming), edited by Luis Felipe López-Calva and Nora Lustig, chapter 7. Washington, DC: Brookings Institution. (http://undp.economiccluster-lac.org/).

Levy, Santiago, and Michael Walton, eds. 2009. *No Growth without Equity? Inequality, Interests and Competition in Mexico.* Palgrave Macmilland and the World Bank

Londoño and Szekely. 2000. "Persistent Poverty and Excess Inequality: Latin America, 1970-1995" Journal of Applied Economics (May) no. 1: 93-134.

Lopez, J.Humberto and Guillermo Perry. 2007. "Inequality in Latin America: Determinants and Consequences." World Bank Conference: Paradigma y Opciones de Desarrollo en Latin America (June).

López-Calva, Luis F. and Nora Lustig. Declining Inequality in Latin America: A Decade of Progress?. Washington, DC: Brookings Institution, forthcoming.

Loser, Claudio. 2007. "Data on Latin America's Rich Highlights Region's Inequality." The Latin American Advisor, May 23. Washington, DC: Inter-American Dialogue.

Lustig, Nora. 1995. (Editor) Coping with Austerity: Poverty and Inequality in Latin America. Washington, DC: Brookings Institution.

___. 2000. "Crises and the Poor: Socially Responsible Macroeconomics." Economía, The Journal of the Latin American and Caribbean Economic Association 1 (Fall) no. 1: 1-45. Washington DC: Brookings Institution Press.

___. 2008. "Thought for food: The Challenges of Coping with Soaring Food Prices." Working Paper no. 155. Washington, DC: Center for Global Development.

___. 2009. "Protecting Latin America's Poor during Economic Crises. Lessons from the Past" Policy Brief No. 3. Washington, DC: Inter-American Dialogue.

Morley, Samuel. 1995. "Structural Adjustment and Determinants of Poverty in Latin America" in Coping with Austerity:Poverty and Inequality in Latin America edited by Nora Lustig, 42-70. Washington DC: The Brookings Institution.

Piketty, Thomas, and Emmanuel Saez. 2006. "The Evolution of Top Incomes: A Historical and International Perspective." American Economic Review, Papers and Proceedings 96, no. 2: 200-205.

Psacharopoulos, George, et al. 1992. "Poverty and Income Distribution in Latin America: The Story of the 1980s." Latin America and the Caribbean Technical Department Regional Studies Program Report 27. Washington DC: World Bank.

Puryear, Jeff, and Tamara Goodspeed. 2009. "How can Education Help Latin America Develop?" Inter-American Dialogue. Washington, DC.

Scott, John. 2009. "Gasto Público y Desarrollo Humano en México: Análisis de Incidencia y Equidad." Working Paper for Informe de Desarrollo Humano de México 2008/2009. México: PNUD.

SEDLAC (Socio-Economic Database for Latin America and the Caribbean), CEDLAS y Banco Mundial. La Plata, Argentina y Washington DC.

http://www.depeco.econo.unlp.edu.ar/cedlas/sedlac/.

World Bank. 1994. "Poverty Alleviation and Social Investment Funds: The Latin American Experience." LA2HR. Washington, DC (May).

Chapter 5

Birdsall, N., A. De La Torre, R. Menezes. 2008. "Fair Growth: Economic Policies for Latin America's Poor and Middle-Income Majority" Washington, DC: Center for Global Development and Inter-American Dialogue.

Clements, B., C. Faircloth, and M. Verhoeven. 2007. "Public Expenditure in Latin America: Trends and Key Policy Issues". Working Paper WP/07/21, International Monetary Fund. Washington, D.C.

ECLAC. 2007. *Social Panorama*, Santiago, Chile: ECLAC.

Fernández Lamarra, N. 2006. "La evaluación y la acreditación de la calidad: Situación, tendencias y perspectivas." In UNESCO/IESALC (Instituto Internacional para la Educación Superior en América Latina y el Caribe). 2006. *Informe sobre la educación superior en América Latina y el Caribe 2000-2005*. Caracas.

Hallman, K., S. Peracca. 2007. "Indigenous Girls in Guatemala: Poverty and Location." In Lewis, M. E., M. E. Lockheed (eds.) *Exclusion, Gender and Education: Case Studies from the Developing World*. Washington, DC: Center for Global Development.

Hanushek, Eric and Ludweg Woessmann. 2009. *Schooling, Cognitive Skills and the Latin American Growth Puzzle*. Working paper 15066. National Bureau of Economic Research. Cambridge, MA.

Holm-Nielsen, L., K. Thorn, J. Brunner, and J. Balán. 2005. "Regional and International Challenges to Higher Education in Latin America." In De Wit, H., I. Jaramillo, J. Gacel-Ávila, and J. Knight, eds. 2005. *Higher Education in Latin America and the Caribbean: The International Dimension*. Washington, DC: World Bank.

Inter-American Development Bank. 2010 (forthcoming). *The Age of Productivity: Transforming Economies from the Bottom Up*. Washington, D.C.: Inter-American Development Bank.

-- 2006. *Education, Science and Technology in Latin America and the Caribbean: A Statistical Compendium of Indicators*. Washington, D.C.: Inter-American Development Bank.

-- 2005. The Politics of Policies, Economic and Social Progress in Latin America, 2006 report. Washington, D.C.: Inter-American Development Bank and Harvard University (David Rockefeller Center for Latin American Studies).

LLECE, SERCE. 2008. *Resumen Ejecutivo.* Santiago, Chile: LLECE

McEwan, P. J. and M. Trowbridge. 2007. *The Achievement of Indigenous Students in Guatemalan Primary Schools. International Journal of Educational Development.*

Murillo, F. J. 2007. "Resultados de aprendizaje en América Latina a partir de las evaluaciones nacionales." Background paper prepared for UNESCO's *2008 Education for All Global Monitoring Report.* Santiago: UNESCO/OREALC.

OECD 2009. *Latin American Economic Outlook.* Overview, p. 24. Paris, France: OECD.

-- 2007-2009. *Education at a Glance,* Paris France: OECD.

-- 2007 (PISA) 2006 Executive Summary, Paris France: OECD.

Oppenheimer, A. 2005. *Cuentos Chinos: El engaño de Washington, la mentira populista y la esperanza de America Latina.* Buenos Aires, Argentina: Editorial Sudamericana.

Paixão, M., L. M. Carvano. 2008. *Relatório Annual das Desigualdades Raciais no Brasil;* 2007-2008. Rio de Janeiro: Garamond.

PREAL Advisory Board. 2006. *Quantity without Quality: A Report Card on Education in Latin* America. Washington, DC.

Pritchett, L. and M. Viarengo. 2009. "Producing Superstars for the Economic Mundial: The Mexican Predicament with Quality of Education." *Program on Education Policy and Governance Working Paper Series.* Cambridge, MA: Harvard Kennedy School.

Puryear, J. and Mariellen Malloy Jewers. 2009. *Social Policy Brief No.1: How Poor and Unequal is Latin America and the Caribbean?* Washington, D.C: Inter-American Dialogue.

Puryear, J., T. Ortega Goodspeed, and A. Ganimian. 2009. *Improving Education's Contribution to Development in Latin America.* Miami, FL: Center for Hemispheric Policy, University of Miami.

Puryear, J. and T. Ortega Goodspeed. 2008. "Building Human Capital: Is Latin American Education Competitive?" In *Can Latin America Compete? Confronting the Challenges of Globalization,* Jerry Haar and John Price, eds. New York: Palgrave Macmillan.

Schwab,K. 2009. *Global Competitiveness Report 2009-2010.* New York, NY: World Economic Forum.

Shanghai Jiao Tong University ranking. 2008. Available at http://www.arwu.org/rank2008/EN2008.htm.

Times Higher Education. 2008. Available at http://www.thes.co.uk.

UNESCO. 2010. *Education for All Global Monitoring Report: Reaching the Marginalized.* Paris, France: UNESCO.

-- **2009.** *Global Education Digest.* Paris, France: UNESCO.

-- **2008.** *Global Education Digest.* Paris, France: UNESCO.

-- **2008.** *Education for All Global Monitoring Report: Education for All by 2015: Will We Make It?* Paris, France: UNESCO.

-- **2007.** *Education for All Global Monitoring Report: Strong Foundations.* Paris, France: UNESCO.

--**2000.** *World Education Report: The Right to Education: Towards Education for All Throughout Life.* Paris, France: UNESCO.

UNESCO/PRELAC. 2007. "The State of Education in Latin America and the Caribbean". Paris, France: UNESCO.

Vegas, E. and J. Petrow. 2008. *Raising Student Learning in Latin America: The Challenge for the 21st Century.* Washington, DC: The World Bank.

Vegas, E. and L. Santibañez. 2009 (forthcoming). "The Promise of Early Childhood Development in Latin America and the Caribbean." Washington, DC: The World Bank.

Winkler, Donald R. 1990. Higher Education in Latin America: Issues of Efficiency and Equity. *World Bank Discussion Papers 77.* Washington, DC: World Bank.

World Bank. 2008. *World Development Indicators.* Washington, D.C: World Bank.

-- **2006.** *World Development Indicators.* Washington, D.C.: World Bank.

Chapter 6

Anlló G. & Suárez D. 2008, *Innovation: Something More Than R&D: Latin American Evidence from Innovation Surveys: Building Competitive Business Strategies.*

Agarwal, S. K. ed. 2008. *Towards Improving Governance.* New Delhi: Academic Foundation.

Brazilian Ministry of Science and Technology, 2006, *Science, Technology and Innovation for National Development Action Plan, 2007-2010.*

Bound K. 2008, *Brazil the Natural Knowledge Economy.*

Chhokar, Jagdeep S. 2008. "Criminals in Elections." *The Tribune,* November 23.

Dahlman, Carl. 2008, *Innovation Strategies of the BRICKS: Brazil, Russia, India, China, and South Korea.* Paper presented at the joint OECD-World Bank Conference on Innovation and Sustainable Growth in a Globalized World, Paris, November, 2008.

The Economist. 2008. *Battling the Babu Raj.* March 6.

Goel, Vinod K. & Mashelkar, R.A. 2009. *India 2039, Climbing the Global Technological Ladder- Improving Higher Education, Technological Development and Innovation.* Paper prepared for the Emerging Markets Forum–the Centennial Group.

Government of India, Department of Administrative Reforms and Public Grievances, Ministry of Personnel, Public Grievances and Pensions. 2008. *Splendour in the Grass: Innovations in Administration.* New Delhi: Penguin Enterprise.

Gupta, Anil. 2007. *Towards an inclusive innovation model for sustainable development.* Paper presented at the Global Business Policy Council of A.T. Kearney, Dubai Retreat, December, 2007.

Inter-American Development Bank. 2006. *Education, Science and Technology in Latin America and the Caribbean, A Statistical Compendium of Indicators.*

Jeff Puryear and Tamara Ortega Goodspeed. 2009. *Inter-American Dialogue, How can Education Help Latin America Develop?* Paper prepared for the Centennial Group.

Juan Carlos Del Bello. 2007. *Governance of Public Research Institutes in Latin America and the Caribbean,* Paper prepared for the I Hemispheric Meeting of the Science, Technology and Innovation, Network, April 2007, Inter American Development Bank.

Kharas, Homi. 2009. *Latin America: A Forgotten Region,* Paper Prepared for Centennial Group; The Brookings Institution.

Lasagabaster Esperanza. 2008. Chile, *Towards a Cohesive and Well Governed National Innovation System,* The World Bank Report.

LAVCA. 2009. *Scorecard, The Private Equity and Venture Capital Environment in Latin America.*

Mario Cimoli, Joao Carlos Ferraz, Annalisa Primi. 2009. *Science, Technology and Innovation Policies in Global Open Economies: Reflections from Latin America and the Caribbean*, Paper published in Globalization, Competitiveness & Governability, Georgetown University Journal 2009.V3.N1.02.

Mashelkar, R.A. 2009. *Leveraging High Technology to Drive Innovation & Competitiveness & Building the Sri Lanka Knowledge Economy*, Paper presented at World Bank Conference on High Tech in Colombo, Sri Lanka, September

Network on Science and Technology Indicators (RICYT). 2009.

OECD. 2009. *Main Science and Technology Indicators.*

OECD. 2009. *Territorial Reviews: Chile.*

PRO INNO EUROPE, Halme & Grutzmann. 2009. *Emerging Economies (BRIC Countries) and Innovation, INNO-Views* Policy Workshop Background Paper, European Commission.

Rodriguez, Alberto & Dahlman, Carl. 2008. Knowledge and Innovation for Competitiveness in Brazil, The World Bank Publication

Sud, Inder. 2009. *Urbanization and Public Services: Creating Functioning Cities for Sustaining Growth.* India 2039 Policy Paper 3. Washington, D.C.: Centennial Group.

Supreme Court of India. 2008. *Court News.* July–September. [http://www.supremecourtofindia.nic.in/court%20news%20July_Sept2008.pdf]

Transparency International India. 2005. *India Corruption Study 2005.* New Delhi: Transparency International India.

———. 2008. *India Corruption Study 2007.* New Delhi: Transparency International India.

UNDP. 2008. *Human Development Report.*

UNESCO. 2009. *Institute for Statistics.*

UNESCO. 2009. *Global Education Digest.*

USPTO Statistics. 2009.

WEF. 2009-2010. *The Global Competitiveness Report.*

WEF. 2008–2009. *The Global Competitiveness Report.*WIPO Statistics Database. 2009.

World Bank. 2006. *Korea as a Knowledge Economy, Evolutionary Process and Lessons Learned*, Book Published by the World Bank, Washington DC.

World Bank KAM. 2009. *Knowledge Economy Database* http://info.worldbank.org/etools/kam2/KAM_page5.asp

World Bank Institute. 2009. *Innovation Policy: A Guide for Developing Countries, Draft Book to be Published by the World Bank,* Washington DC.

Chapter 7

Centennial Group International for ADB. 2010. "Infrastructure Investment Requirements of Developing Asia: 2010–2020."

Corporación Andina de Fomento. 2009. Caminos para el futuro. Gestió de la infrastructura en América Latina. Caracas: Corporación Andina de Fomento.

Kohli, Harpaul Alberto and Phillip Basil. 2011. "Requirements for Infrastructure Investment in Latin American Under Alternate Growth Scenarios: 2011–2040." Global Journal of Emerging Market Economies, 3(1).

Chapter 8

Asian Development Bank. 2008. *Emerging Asian Regionalism*.

Centennial-Group data base

Corporacion Andina de Fomento. 2005. *Latin America in the Global Economy: Advancing market Access*, RED.

Inter-American Development Bank. 2002. *Más allá de las Fronteras. El Nuevo regionalismo en América Latina*.

International Monetary Fund. 2010. *World Economic Outlook*.

International Monetary Fund. 2010. *World Economic Outlook database*.

International Monetary Fund. 2010. *Balance of payments Statistics*.

International Monetary Fund. 2010. *Directions of Trade*.

International Monetary Fund. 2010. *International Financial Statistics*.

Kohli, Harinder. 2008. *Growth and Development in Emerging Market Economies* Sage, New Delhi,

Loser, Claudio M. 2009. *Cross Border Trade and Investment among Emerging Economies: Lessons from Differing Experiences in Africa, Asia and Latin America*. Global Journal of Emerging Market Economies-Vol. 1, Issue 1, January.

Loser, C. and Guerguil, M. 2005. *Trade and Trade reform in Latin America and the Caribbean in the 1990s*. Journal of Applied Economics, Vol. II, No. 1 (May 1999); IMF, Policy paper Review of the IMF's Trade Restrictiveness Index , February 14.

World Bank. 2010. *Doing Business*.

World Bank. 2010. *World Development Indicators*.

World Trade Organization. 2010. web based database.

Chapter 9

Dahl, Robert A. 1972. *Polyarchy: Participation and Opposition.* New Haven: Yale University Press.

Domínguez, Jorge I. and Shifter, Michael. 2008. *Constructing Democratic Governance in Latin America.* Baltimore: Johns Hopkins University Press.

Domínguez, Jorge I. 2008. "Three Decades Since the Start of the Democratic Transitions" from *Constructing Democratic Governance in Latin America.* Baltimore: Johns Hopkins Press.

Hirschman, Albert O. 1971. "Underdevelopment, Obstacles to Perception of Change, and Leadership," from *A Bias for Hope: Essays on Development and Latin America.* New Haven: Yale University Press, pp. 328-341.

Corrales, Javier. 2002. *Presidents Without Parties: The Politics of Economic Reform in Argentina and Venezuela in the 1990s.* Pennsylvania State University Press.

Photo Credits

Ahunt. Photograph. Wikimedia Commons. 31 Dec. 2005. Web. 5 Aug. 2010. <http://commons.wikimedia.org/wiki/File:Embraer175-01.jpg>. Public domain.

Corporación Andina De Fomento. Photograph.

De Troya, Eneas, and Olga Cadena. Photograph. Wikimedia Commons. 6 July 2008. Web. 5 Aug. 2010. <http://commons.wikimedia.org/wiki/File:UNAM_Ciudad_Universitaria.jpg>. Creative Commons Attribution 2.0 Generic: http://creativecommons.org/licenses/by/2.0/deed.en

Photograph. Wikimedia Commons. 13 May 2008. Web. 5 Aug. 2010. <http://commons.wikimedia.org/wiki/File:UNMSM_CasonadeSanMarcos_1920.png>. Public doman.

Rosenheck, Uri. Photograph. Wikimedia Commons. 8 Jan. 2008. Web. 5 Aug. 2010. <http://commons.wikimedia.org/wiki/File:Brazilian_Congress_and_Chamber_of_Deputies_2.JPG>. GNU Free Documentation License: <http://commons.wikimedia.org/wiki/Commons:GNU_Free_Documentation_License>

Szyf, Aaron. Photograph.

Index

Afro-descendant children
    disparities between white people and, 51, 178
Amazonia
    defence against threat, of climate change, 1
Andean Group, 62, 235
attendance rate in Latin America schools, 169

Basel II capital framework, 135–36
Bolsa Familia program, 149
Bottom of the Pyramid (BoP), 189, 200
    constitutes $5 trillion global consumer market, 201
Brazil, declining of income inequality factors, 155
    dependence on commodities, 244, 246–47
    during 1980, 72
    economy of, 38
    education and inequality among workers, 158
    FTE researchers in, 206
    Gini coefficient, 155
    growth pattern of, 155
    higher minimum wages in, 150
    per capita GDP, 73
    poverty and extreme poverty in, 156
    stock market during recession, 116
    technology level of, 77
Brazil, Russia, India and China (BRIC) countries
    economy of, 34
    innovation in, 208
Business-as-usual (BAU) scenario
    Latin America under, 87–88
    results of, 84–86
    scenario, 80–84

Central American Common Market, 235
Century of innovation, 21st century as, 187

Chile, innovation commission, 90–91
    policy-making process in, 90
    rank in global competitiveness index (GCI), 192
civil service need for reform, in Latin America, 262–63
Cobb-Douglas function, 80
Commercial banks, in Latin America impact of great recession on, 120–22
Commission on Growth and Development, 33
commodity prices, evolution of, 113
    vs. Latin America share in world GDP, 25
convergence vision by Latin America countries, 89–91
Corporacion Andina de Fomento (CAF), role in Latin America, 16–18
    advocacy of ambitious vision, 16
    enhancement of productivity, 17–18
    fostering competition, regional cooperation and inclusive society, 17
    openness, 18
    report in 2009, 217–18
credit markets, impact of great recession on, 116–19
crime rate, in Latin America, 254
cross border flow and impact of great recession, 120–22
current account, Latin America, deterioration of, 123

debt management facility by World Bank, 134
debt problem, Dubai, of, 101
decentralization governance, of, 263
democracy, Latin America, in, 66
    freedom of political participation, guaranteeing, 253
    hurdles towards, 252
    measures for improvement of, 265
    support for, 252

disenchantment with political parties, in Latin America, 253
disposable income, Europe and Latin America, of, 143

Ease of Doing Business (2010), 30–31
East Asia vs. Latin America, 39
equal distribution of income, 7
economic crisis, impact on Latin American economies, 22, 86–87
education quality (2008), Latin America, of, 31
education system, of Latin America deficits in quality and equity of, 141–42
    measures to overcome obstacles in, 181–82
    objectives of, 52–53
    obstacles in, 51–52
    political, 180
    public spending on, 165
    rich and poor people, 180
    technical, 180
electoral practices, Latin America, in, 252
emigrants declining rate during recession, 114
employment rate estimation by ECLAC and ILO, in Latin American countries, 115
english-language skills among Latin America people, 174
    at tertiary level, 197
enrollment, in Latin America, 166–70
    at tertiary level, 199
environmental degradation Latin America, in, 21
Euro-zone crisis, 102
exports, Latin America, in composition, 244–45, 229
    declining, 232
    growth of, 232, 234
    volume, 230
    world share in, 232, 234

financial market(s) impact on great recession on, 116–19
financial wealth estimation of build up and destruction of wealth (2002–09) gain and loss, to financial assets, 127–28
    reasons for loss, of financial assets, 129
    total financial assets, 127
Flexible Credit Line (FCL), 134
focus of political leaders, 7

movement from low to middle income group, 7
    total factor productivity (TFP), achievement of, 7
foreign direct investment (FDI) impact of great recession, 119–20
    Latin America, in, 24
    role in transformation and reform, in science and technology, 212–16
Four Speed World, categories of, 82–83
Full Time Equivalent (FTE) researchers in Latin America, 206

G-7, 109
G-8, 109, 133
G-20, 109, 130–36
gender gap, in education, closing of, 51
Gini coefficient, 44, 26, 26, 141, 143–47, 155–63, 208
    evolution of, 47
Global Competitiveness Report (2009–2010), report on Latin America, 192
global economic growth, main drivers for, 188
global economy, Latin America share in, 34
Global Research Alliance (GRA), 204
governance system, of Latin America, need for improvement in, 65–70
government trust of people, in Latin America, 256
Great Moderation, 71
Great Recession, 3, 90, 101
    conditions in Latin America and Asian countries prior to, 102–4
    declining of gross domestic product, of Latin America countries during, 105
    foreign direct investment, impact on (see foreign direct investment, impact of great recession on)
    impact on economic activities, 110–14
    lessons from, 135
    low rate of saving, in United States, 104
    origin of boom in global economy, in 2007, 104
    recovery of growth, in Latin America after, 123–25
    regulation of financial sector, 137
    transmission of, 110
gross domestic product (GDP) growth projections
    after great recession, 105
    historical trends about, 72
    Latin America, of, 21
    per capita in 2009, 32
    projections methodology, 92–100

share of world, 4
sources for growth of, 75–77
Growth Commission, 30, 45, 62, 90, 236

heterodox model, 11
high technology exports, Latin America, in, 65, 190, 215, 248–50
human capital, 11, 13, 30, 40, 43, 47, 50, 138, 147–49, 170, 179, 187–88, 191, 213
   tertiary education, 53–54
Human Development Index (HDI) progress, in Latin America, 192, 196

inclusive innovation, 181, 200–03, 212–14
   goal of, 202
   meaning of, 189, 201
   potential of, 203
   success of, 202
income distribution, 7, 22, 26, 39, 43, 68, 80, 98–99
   state action impact, 148
income inequality, Latin America, in, 47–48, 141–47
   Brazil and Mexico, in, 155–63
   impact of, 141
   reasons for, 142
income levels, 2–3, 5–6, 21–22, 26, 30, 33, 37, 39, 42, 71, 75, 78–84, 86, 89–90, 95–99
inflation rate, Latin American countries, in, 2–3, 7, 25, 68, 103–04, 108
   during 1990s, 103
   during 2007–2008, 106
   Brazil, in, 33, 38, 78
   Hyperinflation, Peru, in, 103, 255
infrastructure, in Latin America current status of, 227
   East Asia, in, 39
   innovation infrastructure, 57, 191, 214
   need for investment in, 43, 77, 91, 217–26
   pro-poor, 151
   quality of, 30–31
   requirement during 2011–2040, 218–19
   rural, 41
   technological, 210, 214–15
   upgrading and integrating, 47–60
innovation, 47, 54–57, 62, 187–216, 257
   economic activities, in, 236
   incentives for, 48, 79

Latin America needs education in, 197
   poor communities involvement in, 189
   strategies, 211–12
Innovation Commission, Chile, 90
institutions, in Latin America vs. leadership (see Leadership vs. institutions, in Latin America)
Inter-American Development Bank, 132–34, 148, 262
Inter-American Human Rights Commission, 260
International Monetary Fund (IMF), 134–36
   contraction of world trade volumes, during great recession, 110
   forecast on Latin America economy, by 2010–14, 72
intra-Latin American trade, 62, 234
intra-regional trade, Latin America, in, 14, 45–46, 61–62, 64, 233–36, 239
   between various countries (1980–2007), 235
   East Asia, in, 7

judicial sector, Latin America, of, 260–62

Knowledge Economy Index (KEI), 55, 195, 198

labor force, 24–25, 35, 42, 83, 149, 152
   growth of, 75, 80, 87,
labor intensive sector, cost advantages in, 5
Latin America
   achievement after independence, 1
   Andina de Fomento (CAF) role in (see Corporacion Andina de Fomento [CAF], role in Latin America)
   business-as-usual scenario, 35, 87–89
   convergence/revival scenario and payoff, of, 35–38, 89, 218–21
   economic and political developments of, 2–3
   economic history, characteristic of, 11
   elements for strategy development of human capital, 50–54
   emphasis on ideology and ideological policies, 30
   enhancement of productivity and competitiveness, in economy, 12–13, 42–44
   focus on improve governance system, 14–15
   fostering of technology, for development and innovation, 54–57
   GDP in 1980, 2
   improvement in governance and institutions, 65–70
   lesson from Asian success, 11

long term performance of economic and political
   natural advantages of, 1–2
   policies, comparison with East Asia, 3–4
   production rate, of scientists, 170
   promotion of competition and openness to economies, of neighboring countries, 13–14, 44–46
   promotion of equity and inclusion, 47–50
   regional cooperation and trade, advancement of, 61–65
   revival scenario, of economy, 89
   share in world economy, 22–23
   strategic framework for convergence, 38
   strategy for building prosperous, 40
   to achieve inclusive society, 12, 41–42
   upgrading and integrating infrastructure, 57–60
   vs. East Asia (see East Asia vs. Latin America)
   2040, in, 8–9, 34–37, 59–60, 88–89
leadership vs. institutions, in Latin America, 258–60
left-behind continent, 32
Lehman Brothers closing of, 107
liberalization impact on Latin America trade, 230
liquidity crisis during great recession, 107–10
low income traps, 81
low-skilled workers scarcity of, 150

market liberalization, 48, 153
Mercosur trade block, 62, 235
Mexico, declining of income inequality, 159, 161
   dependence on commodities, 245, 246, 248
   economy of, during 1980, 72
   extreme poverty rate in, 159, 160
   Gini coefficient, 160
   household income inequality, decline in, 161
   quality of education in, 170
   single party rule, end of, 257
   wage gap between skilled and unskilled workers, 162
middle class, importance in fuelling of growth, 6, 42
middle income countries, 5–6, 33, 42, 78–81
middle income trap, Latin America, in, 4–7, 32–33, 39, 63, 78–80, 237
   avoided the, 46, 62
   Brazil and Mexico, 83
   escaping/getting out of the, 9, 14, 46, 65, 236, 248
   meaning of, 5

monetary policy of Latin America, after great recession, 126

National Autonomous University (UNAM), Mexico, 53, 172
National Innovation Foundation, India, 189, 202
National Innovation System (NIS)
   Latin America performance in, 56, 204–5
Newly Industrialized Countries (NICs), 4, 6–7, 21, 24, 27, 33, 39, 43, 61, 65, 103, 110, 230
Nikkei Index, Japan
   impact of recession on, 116
non-convergers classification into low and middle income groups, 82
North American Free Trade Agreement (NAFTA), 161
   Mexico's accession in 1990s, 232

Pan American highway, 1
partnership, significance among government, private sector and civil society, 263–65
people power, emergence of, 257
per capita income, Latin America, of, 2, 23–24
physical connectivity, importance for trade and cooperation between Latin American economies, 217
political parties
   evolution of, 254
   trust in, 255
ports sector requirement of investment, in Latin America, 221
poverty declining rate, in Latin America, 2, 25, 26, 144, 148
power sector requirement of investment, in Latin America, 221
pre-school enrollments, in Latin America, 166
primary education, public spending on, 167
   rate in Latin America, 177
Program for International Student Assessment (PISA), 170, 183–85
   gap between rich and poor students, 176–78
   participation of Latin America countries in, 51, 166
   students low achievement, in science test, 171
Progresa/Oportunidades program, 149, 151, 162–63
pro-poor innovation (see inclusive innovation)

quality education, Latin America, in, 170–73, 199

real exchange rate (RER), 95–98
  convergence process of, 98
regional cooperation and trade, Latin America, in, 229
  Asia, in, 234
  intra-regional trade and regional cooperation, Latin America, 234–35, 61–64
  need for advancement of diversification of trade, 64–65
  size of Latin economies, 237–38
  specilization of economies, need for, 236–37
  un-exploitation potential, within region, 238–39
remittances
  impact of decline in economic activities, 114–15
  workers, 115
Research and Development (R&D), Latin America
  activities in, 206
  spending on, 207
roads sector requirement of investment, in Latin America, 221

science graduates
  Latin America, in, 173
science, technology and innovation (STI), 189, 190
  need to increase investment, in research and development, 191–92
  promotion in Latin America countries, 56–57
  status of, 192
scientists
  availability in Latin America, 54, 55, 170, 173, 198
  vs. East Asia, 7, 39
secondary graduation rates in Latin America schools, 169, 176, 177
Second Regional Comparative and Explanatory (SERCE) study, by UNESCO, 171
standard reform-oriented model, 11
stimulus packages for emerging economies, during great recession, 130–31
stock market changes during great recession, 118

Mexico, impact of recession on, 116

Technological Specialization Index (TSI)
  calculation of, 205
technology-intensive sectors share, in Latin America, 205
tertiary graduates, science and engineering, in, 174
total factor productivity (TFP), of Latin America, 27–30, 193–95
  level in 1980s, 189
  reasons for poor performance of low level, of competition, 29–30
  quality of education, 30
tourism
  impact of recession, 115
trade, in Latin America
  diversification of,
    through higher value-added products, 243
    through markets, 239–43
  restrictiveness of, 231
  share to gross domestic product, 231
  trends of, 229
Troubled Asset Relief Program (TARP) program, 109

unemployment rate in, Latin America, 254
  rate in, United States after great recession, 101
University of Buenos Aires, Argentina, 53, 172

Venezuela, economy of
  by 2010–2014, 72–73

World Economic Forum (WEF)'s report on Latin America, 192
world trade
  Latin America, in, 24
  increment in capital flows, 27
  share in gross domestic product, 37

About the Editors and Contributors

Editors

Harinder S. Kohli is the Founding Director and Chief Executive of the Emerging Markets Forum as well as President and CEO of Centennial Group International. He is also the Editor of the Global Journal of Emerging Market Economies, and serves as Vice Chairman of the institution-wide Advisory Group of the Asian Institute of Technology. Prior to starting his current ventures, he served for some 25 years in various senior managerial and staff positions at the World Bank. He has published five other books, and written and spoken extensively on issues related to emerging market economies. He is currently working on the long-term economic and social prospects of the Asia-Pacific region.

Claudio M. Loser is CEO and President of Centennial Latin America, and is Advisor for the Emerging Markets Forum. Loser is also a Senior Fellow at the Inter-American Dialogue. Since 2005 he has been an adjunct professor of Economics (Latin American Economic Development) at George Washington University, and lectures at the Foreign Service Institute of the US Department of State. For thirty years and until November 2002, Loser was a staff member of the International Monetary Fund. During the last eight years of his tenure he was Director of the Western Hemisphere Department at the IMF. He graduated from the University of Cuyo in Argentina and received his MA and PhD from the University of Chicago. Loser has published extensively, including the book Enemigos together with the Argentine journalist Ernesto Tenenbaum, where they discuss the relations of the IMF and Argentina in the 1990s.

Anil Sood is a Principal of Centennial Group International. Earlier, in his 30 year career at the World Bank, Anil Sood occupied many senior positions including Vice President, Strategy and Resource Manager, and Special Advisor to the Managing Directors. He has since advised the chief executives and senior management of a number of development organizations including the African Development Bank, the International Monetary Fund, the World Bank, the Islamic Development Bank, the United Nations Development Program, and the United Nations Economic Commission of Africa on matters of strategy and development effectiveness. He co-edited the book India 2039: An Affluent Society in One Generation, published in January 2010.

Contributors

Phillip Basil is a native of the Washington, D.C. area. He received his B.A. in Mathematical Economic Analysis from Rice University. After spending time in research at the Federal Reserve, he received his M.S. in Financial Mathematics from the University of Chicago. He is currently living and working in D.C. in the fields of business development and economic research.

Vinod K. Goel, a former World Bank official, is head of the Global Knowledge and Innovation Practice at Centennial Group International, and consultant for the World Bank and other international organizations. He is a leading expert on private sector issues and is well known in the international community for his pioneering work on higher education, technology and innovation, which includes a number of books that he published on the subject. He advises on enterprise reform, public sector management, competitiveness, small and medium enterprise development, rural and micro-finance, venture capital, and resource planning and management. He has a Ph.D. and MBA from Cornell University, USA, and Masters of Technology from National Dairy Research Institute, India.

Tamara Ortega Goodspeed is a Senior Associate in the education program at the Inter-American Dialogue where she manages the report card program for the Partnership for Educational Revitalization in the Americas (PREAL). She holds a Master's in Public Affairs with a focus on international development from Princeton University and an undergraduate degree in political science from Yale University. Prior to working with PREAL, she served as a Peace Corps volunteer, teaching English in Equatorial Guinea, and as a family educator for a local literacy project in Nebraska.

Homi Kharas is a Senior Fellow at the Wolfensohn Center for Development at the Brookings Institution in Washington D.C. Kharas is also a member of the Working Group for the Commission on Growth and Development chaired by Michael Spence, a non-resident Fellow of the OECD's Development Center, a member of the National Economic Advisory Council to the Prime Minister of Malaysia, and a senior Associate of Centennial Group International. His research interests are now focused on global trends, Asian growth and development, and international aid for the poorest countries.

Harpaul Alberto Kohli is the manager of information analytics at Centennial Group International. He graduated with honors in mathematics and philosophy from Harvard University, where he also served as co-president of both the Society of Physics Students and the Math Club and was elected a class vice president for life by his classmates. He later earned an MBA from Georgetown University, focusing on both psychology and financial markets and public policy, and is a Microsoft Certified Technology Specialist. Prior to joining Centennial, he served as a teacher in prisons in both Ecuador and Massachusetts, a researcher at UBS and in both houses of the US Congress, a field staffer for the 2004 American general election, and a press staffer for Wesley Clark's Presidential primary campaign.

Nora Lustig is the Samuel Z. Stone Professor of Latin American Economics at Tulane University and a nonresident fellow at the Center for Global Development. Her research focuses on inequality, poverty, social policy and development economics. A sample of her publications includes: Declining Inequality in Latin America. A Decade of Progress?; Thought for Food: the Challenges of Coping with Soaring Food Prices; The Microeconomics of Income Distribution Dynamics; Shielding the Poor: Social Protection in the Developing World; Mexico: The Remaking of an Economy (received Choice's Outstanding Academic Book award). Lustig was co-director of the World Development Report 2000/1, Attacking Poverty, founding member and President of LACEA (Latin American and Caribbean Economic Association), and chair of the Mexican Commission on Macroeconomics and Health. She is currently a member of the editorial board of Feminist Economics, the Journal of Economic Inequality and Latin American Research Review; and a member of the board of directors of the Institute of Development Studies and the Global Development Network. She received her doctorate in Economics from the University of California, Berkeley.

Jeffrey M. Puryear is Vice President for social policy at the Inter-American Dialogue, and directs its Partnership for Educational Revitalization in the Americas (PREAL). He previously served as head of the Ford Foundation's regional office for the Andes and the Southern Cone, and as head of its Caribbean program. He has been a research scholar at New York University and at Stanford University. He received his Ph.D. in Comparative Education from the University of Chicago. Puryear has authored various articles on inter-American affairs. His book on intellectuals and democracy in Chile was published by the Johns Hopkins University Press.

Michael Shifter is President of the Inter-American Dialogue, a Washington-based policy forum on Western Hemisphere affairs. He previously served as the Dialogue's Vice President for policy, and directed the group's Andean and democratic governance programs. Since 1993, he has been an adjunct professor of Latin American politics at Georgetown University's School of Foreign Service. Shifter directed the Latin American and Caribbean program at the National Endowment for Democracy and the Ford Foundation's Democracy Program in the Andean region and the Southern Cone, where he was based in Lima, Peru, and then Santiago, Chile.